W9-ADL-509

THE ROLLING STONES CHRONICLE

FEATURES PH[illegible] ROM
THE STEEL WHEE[illegible]

THE FIRST THIRTY YEARS

MASSIMO BONANNO

THE ROLLING STONES CHRONICLE

THE FIRST THIRTY YEARS

MASSIMO BONANNO

An Owl Book

Henry Holt and Company
New York

I would like to dedicate this book to Joseph Sciarrone

Published in the United States by
Henry Holt and Company, Inc., 115 West 18th Street,
New York, New York 10011.

Library of Congress Cataloging-in-Publication Data
Bonanno, Massimo.
The Rolling Stones chronicle: the first thirty years/Massimo
Bonanno.—1st American ed.
p. cm.
ISBN 0-8050-1301-6 (An Owl Book: pbk.)
1. Rolling Stones—Chronology. 2. Rock groups—England—
Biography. I. Title.
ML421.R64B65 1990 89-28547
CIP
MN

Henry Holt books are available at special discounts
for bulk purchases for sales promotions, premiums,
fund-raising, or educational use. Special editions
or book excerpts can also be created to specification.

For details contact:
Special Sales Director
Henry Holt and Company, Inc.
115 West 18th Street
New York, New York 10011

First American Edition

Printed in the United States of America

10 9 8 7 6 5 4 3 2 1

Acknowledgments

It is often an impossible task to thank all the people who have helped to create a book. This is especially true of *The Rolling Stones Chronicle*. Many people have lent their voices here, but we must first make a friendly salute to the Rolling Stones without whom . . .

When Massimo Bonanno first brought us his manuscript it took us some time to realise that he truly intended us to publish a chronicle of everything that each of the Rolling Stones has ever done from 1960 to the present day. An endless task which had to be pared down. To enable us to create such a definitive work, a team is necessary. For their help editorially, we would like to thank Nicky Adamson for editing, weeding and rewriting, along with Pepsi Denning for transcribing, annotating and integrating millions of facts and dates and Helen Williams who put in endless labour, thought and consideration. Frank Rogers and Stuart Holt of St George's admirably handled the typesetting and our daily headaches. Trevor Myhill, Nigel Trapmore, Alan Keen and George Prior for their continued help and support.

We would also like to thank the following individuals, record companies, picture agencies, newspapers and magazines who contributed to the gathering of photographs and visual material for the book: ABKCO Records Inc; A&M Records; Mark Anderson, Retna; Brian Aris, Camera Press; Atlantic Records; David Bailey, Camera Press; Tom Beach; Cecil Beaton, Camera Press; John Bellissimo, Retna; David Thompson; Judy Burstein, Topix Photos; Larry Busacca, Retna; CBS Records; Camera Press; Mike Charity, Camera Press; the *Chicago Daily News; Circus* (Circus Enterprises Corporation); Corgi Books in association with Beat Publications; Ito Cornelson, Camera Press; Fin Costello; André Csillig; the *Daily Express;* the *Daily Mirror;* the *Daily Star;* Alan Davidson; Decca Records; Bernard Docherty, Laister Dickson; EMI Records; Robert Ellis; *L'Espresso;* the *Evening News;* the *Evening Standard; Fab* Magazine; Tony Gale, Pictorial Press; Gary Gershoff, Retna; Bob Gruen, Topix Photos; Heilemann, Camera Press; Gary Herman; *Hit Parader* (Charlton Publications); Dezo Hoffman; Hollis, Retna; Hulton Deutsch Collection; Steve Kagan, Photo Reserve; Robin Kaplan, Retna; London Features International; London Records; London Weekend Television; Gered Mankowitz; *Melody Maker*; The Music Library; Musidor BV; the National Film Archive; *New Musical Express;* the *News Of The World*; Terry O'Neill, Camera Press; Norman Parkinson, Camera Press; Pictorial Press; *Playgirl;* Barry Plummer; Promotone BV; Chuck Pulin, Topix Photos; Michael Putland, Retna; *Queen* Magazine; RBO; *Reader; Record Mirror;* David Redfern Photography; Denise Richardson; the *Richmond And Twickenham Times;* Ripple Records; *Rock; Rock And Folk; Rolling Stone;* Rolling Stones Records; Dimo Safari, Rolling Stones Records; Silhouette Records; Kate Simon, Topix Photos; *Der Spiegel*; Stone Promotions Ltd; *The Sun;* Syndication International; Robert Thomas, Retna; *Time; The Times;* Topix Photos; the *Toronto Star*; the *Toronto Sun*; United Artists; Warner Bros. Records Ltd; Wide World Photos; Valerie Wilmer, The Music Library.

A special thanks to Michael Putland of Retna, Tony Gale of Pictorial Press and Bernard Docherty of Laister Dickson for photographs and the front cover picture by Dimo Safari.

It has not been possible in all cases to trace the copyright sources, and the publishers would be glad to hear from any such unacknowledged copyright holders.

The Publishers

I would like to thank the following magazines and newspapers who have been of enormous help during my research:

In the UK: *New Musical Express, Melody Maker, Record Mirror, Sounds, Disc, Music Scene, Music Week,* the *Daily Mirror,* the *Daily Express, The Sun,* the *Daily Star,* the *Daily Telegraph, The Times, The Observer,* the *Daily Mail,* the *News of the World,* the *Daily Sketch,* the *Daily Worker,* the *Evening Standard,* the *Evening News, Men Only, TV Guide* and *Q Magazine.*

In the USA: *Rolling Stone, Cream, Hit Parader, Circus, Billboard, Cashbox, Record World, Performance Magazine, Playboy, Playgirl, Oui,* the *New York Times,* the *New York Daily News, Soho News, Village Voice,* the *Chicago Daily News,* the *Chicago Tribune, Chicago Triad Guide,* the *Los Angeles Times, USA Today, Musicians International* and the *International Herald Tribune.*

In Canada: *The Toronto Sun* and *Montreal Gazette.*

In France: *Rock and Folk, Best, Rock and Roll, Rock and Stock, Pop Superhebdo, Extra, Paris Match, L'Express, Le Figaro, Ici Paris* and *Nice Matin.*

I have averaged all chart placings from those published in *New Musical Express, Melody Maker, Cash Box, Billboard* and *Music Week.*

Compiling this book would have been considerably harder without the previously published work of the following authors and editors: Mandy Aftel (Death Of A Rolling Stone: The Brian Jones Story); Roy Carr (The Rolling Stones: An Illustrated Record); David Dalton (The Rolling Stones: The First Twenty Years); Chet Flippo (On The Road With The Rolling Stones); and Robert Palmer (The Rolling Stones).

Special thanks are due to Musicland Studios in Munich and the Mountain Recording Studios in Montreux. Judi Seimour of the *Toronto Sun*, Wendy Blume in New York, *Beggars Banquet* magazine and its editor, Bill German, and to the following: Peter Bergsma, Jenni Royer, Nancy Winters, Renata Hunnekens, Judi Caines, and Ian Dawson.

I am indebted to Georgio Sogni for his help, and for lending his material. And a special thanks to Andy and Debbie Wilkinson and Brad Blank.

I would also like to thank the following people for their kind hospitality and friendship throughout my years of research on this book: Betsy Livingood and family, Mr Philip and Baba, Rosie and Joseph Sciarrone, Edda Rizzotti, Alberto Rizzotti, Nanette Steele, Preben, Martin, Robin and Mona, Anna and Donatella.

My thanks to Roberto Zucconi, Tino and Gero for their continued support.

To my publishers, Sandra Wake and Terry Porter, for their insight and suggestions and their help visually and to Helen Williams for her inexhaustable patience and for helping them pull it all together. Most of all they will not forget the immortal line 'I have a very important Taiwanese picture disc of "Paint It Black" which I think should go in'.

Massimo Bonanno

MICK JAGGER (Michael Philip Jagger)
Born 26 July 1943 in Dartford, Kent.
Vocal, harp, guitar, piano, synthesiser
'I'll be keeping it up until my body starts to fall apart and that's a long time off. The Rolling Stones might not last for ever but we'll be going until sometime this side of ever.'

BRIAN JONES (Lewis Brian Hopkin Jones)
Born 28 February 1942 in Cheltenham, Gloucestershire.
Died 3 July 1969 in Hartfield, Sussex.
Guitar, bottleneck guitar, slide guitar, harp, autoharp, keyboards, mellotron, saxophone, flute, sitar, dulcimer, harpsichord, koto, clarinet, xylophone, marimbas, percussion, vocals.
'The government? One always finishes up with the lesser of two evils. Really I'm an anarchist.'

KEITH RICHARDS (Keith Richards)
Born 18 December 1943 in Dartford, Kent.
Guitar, bottleneck guitar, slide guitar, bass, piano, vocals.
'It took the cops a full half hour to wake me up. It's pretty frightening waking up with cops all around your bed.'

CHARLIE WATTS (Charles Robert Watts)
Born 2 June 1941 in Islington, London.
Drums, percussion.
'Regretfully, I never took acid and I wish I'd taken it to know about it. I think I was the only rock star never to wear a pair of beads.'

BILL WYMAN (William Perks)
Born 24 October 1936 in Lewisham, London.
Bass guitar, guitar, harp, autoharp, keyboards, synthesiser, vocals.
'Over the years, Mick Jagger and Keith Richards have written so many excellent songs... they know precisely what they're doing... the kind of things I write may not be the right kind of songs for the Stones.'

MICK TAYLOR (Michael Taylor)
Born 17 January 1948 in Welwyn Garden City, Hertfordshire.
Guitar, slide guitar, bottleneck guitar, bass, piano, vocals.
'I just assume I was the best guitarist available at the time.'

RONNIE WOOD (Ronald Wood)
Born 1 June 1947 in Hillingdon, Middlesex.
Guitar, bottleneck guitar, slide guitar, bass, harp, dobro, saxophone, vocals.
'We'll stay on stage for a long time, that's where we feel alive the most. I never want just to make records.'

Mick Jagger

Brian Jones

Charlie Watts

Mick Taylor replaced Brian Jones in 1969.

Keith Richards

Bill Wyman

Ronnie Wood replaced Mick Taylor in 1975.

NINETEEN 60·61

IN THE BEGINNING

SOUTH-EAST LONDON SUBURBS
Mick Jagger and Keith Richards, both aged eighteen, meet on a train. They had known each other as children. Mick is an undergraduate at the London School of Economics in Central London, Keith is a student at Sidcup Art School, on the Kent/London borders. He had previously been at Dartford Technical School, but was expelled.

Mick and Keith discover their common interest in Rhythm'n'Blues as Mick is carrying some interesting albums which he bought direct from Chess Records in Chicago. Mick Jagger and Keith Richards have a mutual friend, Dick Taylor, who plays guitar in a group with Mick called Little Boy Blue and the Blue Boys, which also includes Bob Beckwith and Allen Etherington.

Keith Richards, whose chief influence is Chuck Berry, joins the band. They rehearse at Jagger's home, but move to Keith Richards' when neighbours complain about the noise. Later they move on to Dick Taylor's in Bexleyheath, Kent, for the same reason.

CHELTENHAM, GLOUCESTERSHIRE
Having left school at the age of seventeen, Brian Jones devotes his time to music and girls. He is already the father of two illegitimate children, and will later father six others from different women. He is keen on jazz and blues (Muddy Waters, obscure Chicago blues, T-Bone Walker, Elmore James), and meets Alexis Korner, legendary father of British blues, at a concert in Cheltenham. The two become friends, and Korner invites Brian to visit him in London. Brian Jones has already had various jobs but is depressed and bored, so before going to London, he travels to Scandinavia where he earns some money playing guitar and harmonica, then hitch-hikes around Europe. When he returns to Cheltenham he plays alto sax in a band called the Ramrods.
Soon he and his girlfriend, Pat Andrews, mother of his second child, move to London. They rent a small flat in Edith Road, West Kensington; Brian Jones gets work in a department store. He wants to form his own band, so he places an advertisement in *Jazz News*. Pianist Ian Stewart replies and through him Brian Jones meets up with singer Andy Wren and guitarist Geoff Bradford.

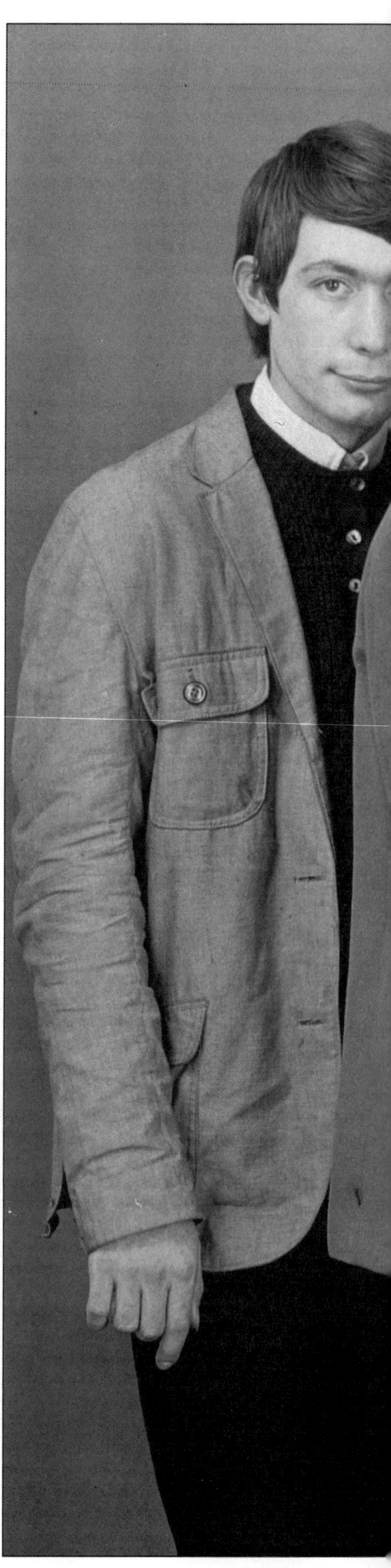

NINETEEN 62

LONDON
R&B was a minority interest in England during the early sixties, but one of the few places where the real thing was regularly played live was in the Ealing Jazz Club, at Ealing Broadway in West London.

MARCH 17
Alexis Korner's Blues Incorporated start a regular Saturday night gig at the Ealing Jazz Club. The band features Alexis Korner on electric guitar, Charlie Watts on drums, Cyril Davies on harmonica, Andy Hoogenboom on bass (replaced two weeks later at the Marquee by Jack Bruce), Dave Stevens on piano and Dick Heckstall Smith on tenor sax.

APRIL 7
Mick Jagger, Keith Richards and Dick Taylor meet Brian Jones at the Ealing Jazz Club, where Brian plays guitar with singer P. P. Bond (Paul Jones, later with Manfred Mann). They play Muddy Waters and Elmore James numbers. Brian Jones is so obsessed with the music of Elmore James that he calls himself Elmo Lewis. Keith Richards will say afterwards: 'As I saw Brian Jones playing I said, ''What the fuck? Playing bar slide guitar!'' We get into Brian Jones after he finishes ''Dust My Blues''. He's really fantastic and a gas... He's been doin' the same as we'd been doin'... thinkin' he was the only cat in the world who was doin' it.' At the time, Brian Jones, Ian Stewart, Geoff Bradford and P. P. Bond are playing together as a band. Brian invites Keith Richards to listen to them play in various Soho pubs, where Keith meets Ian Stewart for the first time. Keith says of Ian: 'He blew my mind too, when he started to play. I never heard a white piano like that before. Real Albert Ammons stuff.'

APRIL/MAY
Before the end of April, Mick Jagger, Keith Richards, Dick Taylor and two members of Blues Incorporated, Charlie Watts and Cyril Davies, play at the Ealing Jazz Club, where they perform a version of Chuck Berry's 'Around And Around'. It is received with polite applause but nothing more.
A week later, Mick Jagger sends Alexis Korner a tape of Little Boy Blue and the Blue Boys playing 'Around And Around', 'La Bamba', 'Reelin' And Rockin'', 'Bright Lights Big City'. (Original band members Allen Etherington and Bob Beckwith are no longer with the band.)
At this stage Keith Richards, Mick Jagger and Dick Taylor are trying to turn Brian Jones on to Chuck Berry and Jimmy Reed material as they want him to join their band. It isn't long before he does join the line-up which now features Mick Jagger on vocals, Brian Jones on guitar and harmonica, Keith Richards on guitar, Dick Taylor on bass, Ian Stewart on piano and Geoff Bradford on guitar, plus a succession of drummers, mainly introduced by Ian Stewart.
Bradford leaves the band after a while because he is not interested in rock'n'roll. Around this time Mick Jagger also joins Blues

Incorporated as vocalist alongside Cyril Davies. Mick's repertoire includes 'Bad Boy', 'Ride 'Em On Down', 'I've Got My Mojo Working' and 'Don't Stay Out All Night'. The band plays every Thursday night at the Marquee Club, then situated in Oxford Street, plus other dates here and there, but Mondays and Wednesdays are free so the future Rolling Stones rehearse at the Bricklayer's Arms in Broadwick Street, Soho. Later they move to the Wetherby Arms, at the working class end of King's Road, Chelsea, which is not far from the grubby flat that Brian, Mick and Keith have rented at 106 Edith Grove. Keith Richards says: 'Downstairs was livin' four old whores from Liverpool. Isn't it a coincidence? Real old boots they were.'

MAY
In an attempt to get work, the boys become members of the National Jazz Federation. But the jazz circuit is hard to break into and the music mainly traditional. Club owners and promoters are not keen to book musicians who play different styles of music. Says Mick Jagger: 'They, we were sure, simply wanted to keep the old scene as long as they could.'

JUNE
The boys continue to rehearse. Mick Jagger is still studying at LSE, but Brian Jones quits his job and breaks up with Pat Andrews, who returns to her parents in Cheltenham. Brian says later: 'I got a few jobs here and there when I needed money, but I was not interested in things. I had no real ambition. As long as I was not absolutely broke, I was OK.'
Brian Jones and Keith Richards spend most of the day playing guitar and listening to records. No money comes in. Ian Stewart's and Keith Richards' mothers provide food and cash. It is during this period that they name themselves 'The Rollin' Stones', suggested by Brian Jones from a Muddy Waters number, 'Rollin' Stones'. For a short time they toy with the name 'Silver Rollin' Stones', just as the Beatles had called themselves the Silver Beatles for a while. It soon evolves into the Rolling Stones.

JULY
The BBC books Blues Incorporated for a radio appearance on *Jazz Club.* The band features seven members, but the BBC will only pay six, so Alexis Korner and the rest decide to turn down the gig. Mick Jagger won't let them, agreeing to stand down. After all he is not the only singer in the band and he wants them to appear in the show even without him.
Since the programme is planned for 12 July, a Thursday, Blues Incorporated has to be replaced at the Marquee that night. The early nucleus of the Rolling Stones is booked to fill the gap.

JULY 12
The Rolling Stones play at the Marquee Club for the first time. The line-up features Mick Jagger on vocals, Brian Jones on guitar and harmonica, Keith Richards on guitar, Dick Taylor on bass, Ian Stewart on piano and Mick Avory on drums.
Numbers include 'Kansas City', 'Honey What's Wrong', 'Confessin' The Blues', 'Bright Lights Big City', 'Dust My Blues', 'Down The Road Apiece', 'I Want To Love You', 'I'm A Hoochie Coochie Man', 'Ride 'Em On Down', 'Back In The USA', 'I Feel A-Kind Of Lonesome', 'Blues Before No More', 'Big Boss Man', 'Don't Stay Out All Night', 'Tell Me That You Love Me' and 'Happy Home'. They earn £20 and, more importantly, Alexis Korner gives them regular bookings at the Ealing Jazz Club and at the Marquee.

AUGUST/SEPTEMBER
The Rolling Stones continue to play at the Ealing Jazz Club and the Marquee, adding new numbers to their repertoire. Their audience grows at each appearance as word of their unique style spreads.
Meanwhile Mick Avory (later with the Kinks) leaves the band. He is replaced by Tony Chapman. Keith Richards says of Mick Avory: 'He was terrible. Couldn't find that off beat.' But the Rolling Stones really need a good drummer and have their eye on Charlie Watts. However, he already has a good job in a central London advertising agency and is only interested in doing weekend gigs.
Charlie Watts has played with various bands, just for the love of it: apart from Blues Incorporated, he has often played in the mainly folk music orientated Troubadour Club in Chelsea and, while in Denmark on business in late 1961, he had played with the Don Byas band, returning to London in February 1962.
In September, it is Dick Taylor's turn to leave the band, as he prefers to continue studying at the Royal College of Art.

OCTOBER
For the first time in their career, the Rolling Stones (Mick Jagger, Brian Jones, Keith Richards, Ian Stewart and Tony Chapman) record three tracks at the Curly Clayton Sound Studio. They cut 'Soon Forgotten', 'You Can't Judge A Book (By Looking At The Cover)' and 'Close Together'. The tape is sent to Neville Skrimshire at EMI Records, but without success. Several fans write to record companies telling them how great the Rolling Stones are, but there is still no response.
Tony Chapman works as a travelling salesman and misses a lot of rehearsals and dates, so another drummer, Steve Harris, sits in occasionally.
In the meantime, the Rolling Stones advertise in the music press for a bass player to fill Dick Taylor's vacancy.

Left: *Mick Jagger at the Marquee Club, backed by Alexis Korner on guitar, Cyril Davies on harmonica, and Charlie Watts (out of shot) on drums.*

OCTOBER 31
Jazz News publishes a letter by Brian Jones.

NOVEMBER
Bass player Bill Wyman (William Perks), married and working as a technician in Streatham, South London, sees the Rolling Stones' ad. in Melody Maker. A friend of Tony Chapman, he has been playing in a South London band called the Cliftons. Tony introduces him to the Rolling Stones.

DECEMBER
The Rolling Stones rehearse with Bill Wyman at the Wetherby Arms. He has more equipment than the rest of them. Says Bill Wyman: 'They didn't like me, but I had a good amplifier, and they were badly in need of amplifiers at that time! So they kept me on. Later, when they were going to get rid of me, I think I clicked or something, and I stayed. I must have fitted in... I didn't like the name Rolling Stones because it seemed a bit pointless and silly.'
In early December Tony Chapman quits the band, due to work commitments, but his days had been numbered anyway. Says Keith Richards: 'Terrible. One of the worst... cat would start a number and end up either four times as fast as he started it or three times as slow.' Steve Harris also has trouble finding time to play with the Rolling Stones so yet another drummer, Carlo Little, from the Cyril Davies band, plays with them occasionally. But they really want a good, permanent drummer: they want Charlie Watts.

IT appears there exists in this country a growing confusion as to exactly what form of music the term 'Rhythm & Blues' applies to.

There further appears to be a movement here to promote what would be better termed 'Soul Jazz' as Rhythm & Blues.

Surely we must accept that R & B is the American city Negro's 'pop' music — nothing more, nothing less.

Rhythm & Blues can hardly be considered a form of jazz. It is not based on improvisation as is the latter. The impact is, and can only be, emotional. It would be ludicrous if the same type of pseudo-intellectual snobbery that one unfortunately finds contaminating the jazz scene were to be applied to anything as basic and vital as Rhythm & Blues.

It must be apparent that Rock 'n' Roll has a far greater affinity for R & B, than the latter has for jazz, insofar as Rock is a direct corruption of Rhythm & Blues, whereas jazz is Negro music on a different plane, intellectually higher, though emotionally less intense.

BRIAN JONES
London, SW 10

(Brian Jones plays guitar with The Rollin' Stones)

Above: *The letter by Brian Jones to* Jazz News *which was published in the edition of 31 October 1962.* Right: *Mick Jagger singing at the Ealing Jazz Club.* Over page: *The original line-up with Ian Stewart on the left next to Keith, Charlie and Bill in the front row; Brian and Mick behind.*

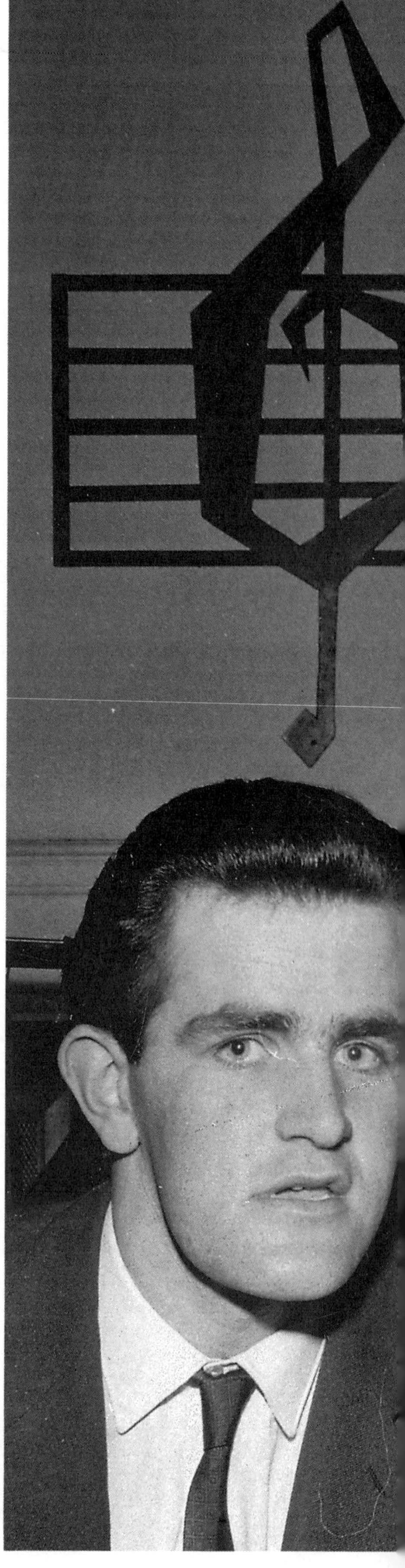

JANUARY 3
Blues Incorporated has its debut gig at the Flamingo Club in Wardour Street, Soho. It is immediately followed by their first recording session, at 1am on 4 January, at Decca's West Hampstead Studios. The main track recorded is 'Early In The Morning'.

JANUARY
In early January, Charlie Watts is playing with a band called Blues By Five (later Six) without much satisfaction. He has left Blues Incorporated because he doesn't want to play professionally and is replaced by Ginger Baker.
Now the Rolling Stones ask Charlie Watts to join the band and after thinking about it for a few days he finally agrees. He says:
'Honestly I thought they were mad. I mean they were working a lot of dates without getting paid or even worrying about it. And there was me, earning a pretty comfortable living, which obviously was going to nose-dive if I got involved with the Rolling Stones. But I got to think about it. I liked their spirit and I was getting very involved with rhythm'n'blues. So I said, OK, yes, I'd join. Lots of my friends thought I'd gone raving mad.'
Before the end of the month the Rolling Stones are ready to take the world by storm. The line-up now consists of: Mick Jagger, vocals and harmonica, Brian Jones, guitar, harmonica and vocals, Keith Richards, guitar and vocals, Bill Wyman, bass and vocals, Charlie Watts, drums, Ian Stewart, piano.
During the early part of the year, the Rolling Stones are playing semi-regular gigs at the Flamingo Club in Wardour Street on Mondays, sometimes at the Marquee on Thursdays (supported by Cyril Davies), at the Red Lion in Sutton, Surrey, on Friday nights, and at the Ealing Jazz Club on Saturdays. Cyril Davies has now formed his own band, and two of its members - drummer Carlo Little and pianist Nicky Hopkins - have occasionally played with the Stones. Nicky Hopkins will become a regular sessions musician with the Stones later, playing on several albums and touring with them in the late sixties and early seventies.

JANUARY 28
First recording session at the IBC Studios in Portland Place. The Rolling Stones cut five tracks with the help of Glyn Johns as engineer. They are: 'Roadrunner', 'Honey', 'What's Wrong', 'Diddley Diddley Daddy', 'I Wanna Be Loved' and 'Bright Lights Big City'. But they still can't find a label to release their tapes.
They begin a regular residency at the Crawdaddy, Station Hotel, Richmond, Surrey, owned by Giorgio Gomelsky. For the third gig, drummer Carlo Little replaces Charlie Watts, and bass-player Ricky Fenson, also from the Cyril Davies band, joins the line-up for this one occasion. The first of many rumours about the Rolling Stones reports that Brian Jones tried to get Carlo Little instead of Charlie Watts.

APRIL 13
First ever newspaper report on the Rolling Stones appears in *The Richmond and Twickenham Times.* Meanwhile, they go into the R.G. Jones studio in London to work on the soundtrack of a 20-minute film shot by Giorgio Gomelsky during one of their gigs at the Crawdaddy. The tracks - 'Pretty Thing' and 'It's All Right Babe' - are mastered by R.G. Jones Junior. They will never be released.

APRIL 21
The Beatles go to Richmond to see the Rolling Stones. Afterwards they join them at the Edith Grove flat.

APRIL 28
The Stones' reputation has caught the attention of nineteen-year-old publicist Andrew Oldham and agent Eric Easton. They go to Richmond to see the Rolling Stones play.

APRIL 29
Oldham and Easton sign a management deal with the Rolling Stones after buying their IBC tapes for £90. They form a new company, Impact Sound, so that Andrew Oldham and Eric Easton can manage the group and supervise their recordings.
Andrew Oldham persuades Ian Stewart to drop out of the official line-up and become the Rolling Stones' road manager. Although he still accompanies them on keyboards he is out of sight at the back of the stage because Oldham doesn't think Stewart's looks fit in with the Stones' image.

At about this time Keith Richards drops the 's' from his surname, probably at the suggestion of Andrew Oldham.

MAY 4
The Rolling Stones play at a *News of the World* charity gig at Battersea Fun Fair.

MAY 10
First official recording session at Olympic Studios, produced by Andrew Oldham. The Rolling Stones cut a Chuck Berry number, 'Come On', and 'I Wanna Be Loved' by Willie Dixon. Andrew Oldham tells engineer Roger Savage: 'Look, I'm the producer and this is the first recording session that I've ever handled. I don't know a damn thing about recording, or music for that matter.' Decca are not satisfied with the tapes, so the Rolling Stones immediately recut the numbers at the Decca Studios in West Hampstead.

MAY 11
During April, Giorgio Gomelsky has called *Record Mirror* journalist Peter Jones to come and see the Rolling Stones at the Crawdaddy. Jones is impressed by them and the following week returns with fellow-journalist Norman Jopling, who writes an article about them, published in the issue of 11 May. Jopling's piece is the first ever written about the Rolling Stones in a music paper. Jopling writes: 'At the Station Hotel, Kew Road, the hip kids throw themselves about to the new "jungle music" like they never did in the more restrained days of trad. And the combo they writhe and twist to is called the Rolling Stones... The Rolling Stones are destined to be the biggest group in the R&B scene... Three months ago only fifty people turned up to see the group. Now promoter Gomelsky has to close the doors at an early hour with over five hundred fans crowding the hall... Fact is that, unlike the other R&B groups worthy of the name, the Rolling Stones have a definite visual appeal.'

JUNE 7
The first single, 'Come On/I Wanna Be Loved' is released on Decca, and produced by Impact Sound (Andrew Oldham and Eric Easton). The A-side is written by Chuck Berry, the B-side by Willy Dixon. It reaches a highest position of Number 20 in the British charts where it remains for seven weeks. They also make their first television appearance, on ABC-TV's *Thank Your Lucky Stars*. For this one and only occasion they all dress the same, in dark trousers, jackets with velvet half-collars, and ties.

JUNE 8
Norman Jopling writes a feature review of the new single in *Record Mirror*: 'It's good, catchy, punchy and commercial, but it's not the fanatical R&B sound that audiences wait hours to hear. Instead it's a bluesy very commercial group that should make the charts in a smallish sort of way.'

JUNE 13
Gig in Middlesborough.
The first British national daily newspaper plaudit, from Patrick Doncaster, appears in

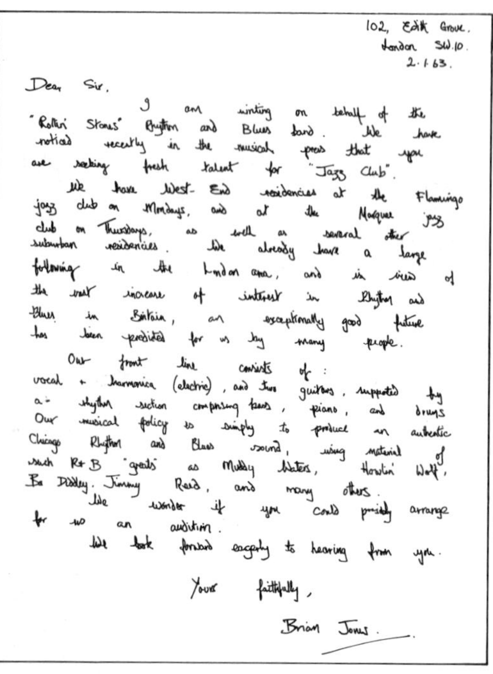

102, Edith Grove.
London SW.10.
2.1.63.

Dear Sir,

I am writing on behalf of the "Rollin' Stones" Rhythm and Blues band. We have noticed recently in the musical press that you are seeking fresh talent for "Jazz Club".

We have West-End residencies at the Flamingo jazz club on Mondays, and at the Marquee jazz club on Thursdays, as well as several other suburban residencies. We already have a large following in the London area, and in view of the vast increase of interest in Rhythm and Blues in Britain, an exceptionally good future has been predicted for us by many people.

Our front line consists of: vocal + harmonica (electric), and two guitars, supported by a rhythm section comprising bass, piano, and drums. Our musical policy is simply to produce an authentic Chicago Rhythm and Blues sound, using material of such R+B "greats" as Muddy Waters, Howlin' Wolf, Bo Diddley, Jimmy Reed, and many others.

We wonder if you could possibly arrange for us an audition.

We look forward eagerly to hearing from you.

Yours faithfully,

Brian Jones.

Above: *Brian's letter to BBC Radio's* Jazz Club.
Left: *The* News of the World *charity gig.*

Richmond and Twickenham Times, Saturday, April 13, 1963 — 15

Barry May writes about the 'new' rhythm and blues

JAZZ

Nowadays it means the music that goes round and around—or the Rollin' Stones are gathering them in

A MUSICAL magnet is drawing the jazz beatniks away from Eel Pie Island, Twickenham, to a new mecca in Richmond.

The attraction is the new Craw-Daddy Rhythm and blues Club at the Station hotel, Kew Road—the first club of its kind in an area of flourishing modern and traditional jazz haunts.

Rhythm and blues, gaining more popularity every week, is replacing "traddypop" all over the country, and even persuading the more sedate modernists to leave their plush clubs. The deep, earthy sound produced at the hotel on Sunday evenings is typical of the best of rhythm and blues that gives all who hear it an irrisistible urge to "stand up and move."

Akin to both rock 'n' roll and the skiffle music that raced up and down the charts of three and four years ago, rhythm and blues has been described as "pepped-up" blues and "original American Negro pop-music." But the sound also has its modernistic leaning a fact apparent from some of the material used by the thriving rhythm and blues groups.

Traditional jazz as a commercial enterprise is played out, and modern jazz has never been able to command major audiences in this country.

One of the founders of the jazz club, Eelpiland, as it is called, where attempts at presenting both traditional and modern jazz have been made, Arthur Chisnell admitted that "things have been quiet." The four and five nights of jazz every week on the island has dwindled to only two—at the weekend.

Rhythm and blues can claim to provide almost a happy medium for young jazz fans. Modernists and "traddies" can be seen side by side at the Station hotel, listening to resident group, the Rollin' Stones.

Drummer Charles Watts in action, with pianist Ian Stuart in the background, taking a break on the maracas.

From a meagre 50 or so on the club's first night, less than two months ago, attendances have rocketed by an average of 50 a week to last Sunday's record of 320. And the membership book lists more than 700 names of rhythm and blues devotees from all parts of London and West Surrey.

Club promoter, bearded Italian film director, Giorgio Gomelsky, is thrilled with the success of the club—but fears he may have to close the membership list if its popularity continues to rise.

Jazz-lover Giorgio first visited Richmond in August, 1961, when he produced a film featuring the Chris Barber jazz band at the first National Jazz Festival held at the Athletic ground, Old Deer Park.

The Rollin' Stones, a six-piece group, were formed just 10 months ago.

Since then they have played in more than a dozen London rhythm and blues clubs, as well as appearances at the West End Marquee Club.

Semi-professionals now, although the average age of the group is only 20, the daytime occupations of its members are as varied as the instruments they play.

Driving force behind the group is London School of Economics student Mick Jagger, vocal and harmonica. He is backed by architect Brian Jones (guitar, harmonica, maracas), guitarist Keith Richards, an art student, bass guitarist Bill Wyman, a representative, drummer Charles Watts, a designer, and on piano, Ian Stewart.

The line-up of the Rollin' Stones, with vocalist Mick Jagger, guitarist Keith Richards, and extreme left, guitarist Brian Jones.

Although "pop" numbers are sometimes played, songs written and recorded by the American rhythm and blues guitarist Bo Diddley are the Rollin' Stones' favourites. Their appreciation of him is carried to the extent of naming the club after a dance Bo Diddley has invented, the "craw-daddy."

The 300 and more in their late teens and early 20s who pack the club on Sunday nights do a dance similar to the craw-daddy. But most improvise on a wildly remote form of the hully-gully, similar to the twist.

For those less inclined to express their feelings for the music physically, the Rollin' Stones also provide visual entertainment.

Hair worn Piltdown-style, brushed forward from the crown like "The Beatles" pop group—"we looked like this before they became famous"—the rhythm section, piano, drums and bass guitar provide a warm, steady backing for the blues of the harmonicas and lead guitars.

Save for the swaying forms of the group on the spotlit stage, the room is in darkness. A patch of light from the entrance doors catches the sweating dancers and those who are slumped on the floor where chairs have not been provided.

Outside in the bar the long hair, suede jackets, goucho trousers and Chelsea boots rub shoulders with the Station hotel's "regulars," resulting in whispered mocking, though not unfriendly remarks about the "funny" clothes.

Few regulars have taken exception to the pub's new customers, and only a small number have chosen to no longer drink there on Sunday nights.

The Rollin' Stones and the Craw-Daddy Club have put the Station hotel on the map, as far as youngsters are concerned.

How sad and unfortunate that it is destined to be soon wiped off the map. Demolished, flattened to the ground and replaced with a brand new public-house.

THE CRAW - DADDY CLUB WILL BE FORCED TO LOOK FOR ANOTHER WEEKLY STAGE —AND THE ROLLIN' STONES WILL GO ON ROLLIN'.

the *Daily Mirror*. He describes the Rolling Stones, the scene at the Station Hotel and the 'new dance... which you will see nowhere in the world but in Richmond... all you need is a crowded room - the Rolling Stones' new record ''Come On''... or maybe you just like to listen to the music which is very exciting anyway'.

JUNE 22
Record Mirror announces that the Stones are to start a regular Thursday night spot at the Scene Club in Ham Yard, off Great Windmill Street in Piccadilly. They have wound up the Sunday night sessions at the Station Hotel, Richmond.

JUNE 29
The Stones visit Alexis Korner's recently opened Mojo Club in Soho.

JULY 6
Gig in King's Lynn, Norfolk.

JULY 7
They tape an appearance on *Thank Your Lucky Stars*.

JULY 11
Gig at the Scene Club, Ham Yard, off Great Windmill Street in Piccadilly.

JULY 13
Taped appearance on *Thank Your Lucky Stars* is broadcast. Gig in Middlesborough.

JULY 15
Gig at Ken Colyer's Jazz club in the afternoon and at the Richmond Athletic Club in the evening.

JULY 16
Another gig at Ken Colyer's Jazz Club.

JULY 18
Second appearance at the Scene.

JULY 19
They play at a party held by Lord and Lady Killernan for their daughter Roxanna in Hastings.

JULY 20
Gig at the Corn Exchange, Wisbech, Cambridgeshire.

JULY 25
Final gig at the Scene.

JULY 27
Gig in Dunstable, Bedfordshire.

JULY 28-AUGUST 1
Recording sessions at the Decca Studios.

AUGUST 2
New Musical Express: 'The Rolling Stones first burst into prominence as the long-haired London group with a twitch that was a kind of dance, who appeared on ''Thank Your Lucky Stars'' recently. From there, the number they did, Chuck Berry's ''Come On'', progressed steadily and this week entered the NME chart. Says Mick Jagger, lead vocal and harmonica with the Rolling Stones: ''The twitch business really comes from a regular club session we do at Richmond, near London. It gets so crowded that all fans can do is stand and twitch. They can't dance because there isn't much room. We believe that there is a lot of room for the rhythm'n'blues sound broadly patterned on the type of music put down by Chuck Berry.'' '

AUGUST 3
Gig at Horsham, Sussex.

AUGUST 5
Gig at Botwell House, Hayes, Middlesex.

AUGUST 6
Gig at the Thames Hotel, Windsor, Berkshire.

AUGUST 9
Gig at the California Ballroom, Dunstable, Bedfordshire.

AUGUST 10
Gigs at the Handsworth and Oldhill Plazas, Birmingham.

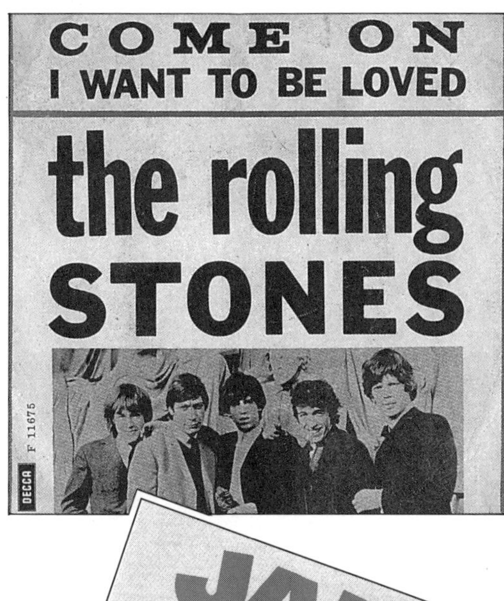

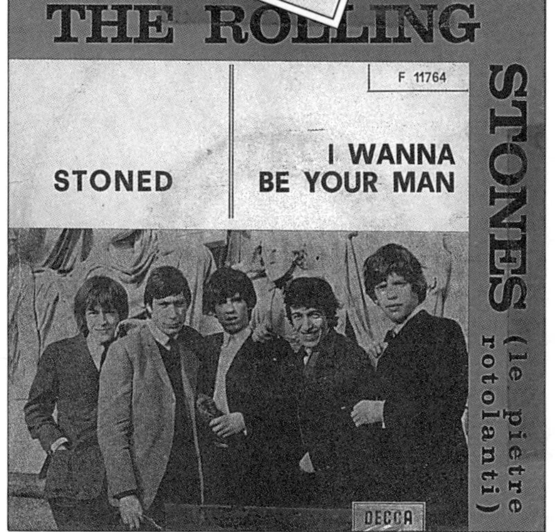

Top: *'Come On', the Stones' first single. In 1963 the Stones appeared both at the Richmond Jazz Festival and on tour with the Everly Brothers and Bo Diddley.* Bottom: *The Italian version of 'Stoned'.*

AUGUST 11
Gig at the Third National Jazz Festival at the Richmond Athletics Association ground.

AUGUST 15
Gig at Dreamland, Margate, Kent.

AUGUST 23
'Come On' reaches Number 20, its highest position in the British charts. Brian Jones says: 'We believe that we sound like ourselves and no one else.'

AUGUST 29
The Rolling Stones appear on Granada TV's *Scene at 6.30*.

AUGUST 30
Gig at the Tower Ballroom, New Brighton, Lancashire.

SEPTEMBER
Recording sessions at the Kingsway Studios throughout the month.

SEPTEMBER 14
The Rolling Stones appear on *Thank Your Lucky Stars* again.

SEPTEMBER 27
'Come On' is included on a Decca compilation album. *Thank Your Lucky Stars, Vol. 2*.

SEPTEMBER 29
Their first major British tour, with Bo Diddley and the Everly Brothers, opens at the New Victoria Theatre, London. The Rolling Stones will play 30 dates between now and 3 November. The Rolling Stones announce new dates for November and December.

OCTOBER 1
Gig at Streatham Odeon, London.

OCTOBER 2
Gig at the Regal, Edmonton, London.

OCTOBER 3
Gig at the Odeon, Southend, Essex.

OCTOBER 4
Gig at the Odeon, Guildford, Surrey.

OCTOBER 5
Appearance at the Gaumont, Watford. Little Richard joins the tour.

Top left: *Gene Pitney and Phil Spector drop in at the recording session for 'Not Fade Away' at the Regent Sound Studios. Pitney quipped, 'When I first saw them I didn't know whether to say hello or bark.' Left to right are Andrew Oldham, Brian, Mick, Keith, Phil Spector and Gene Pitney.* Left: *The Rolling Stones appear on ITV's* Ready, Steady, Go!

OCTOBER 6
Concert at the Capitol, Cardiff, South Wales.

OCTOBER 8
Concert at the Odeon, Cheltenham.

OCTOBER 9
Concert at the Gaumont, Worcester.

OCTOBER 10
Concert at the Gaumont, Wolverhampton.

OCTOBER 11
Concert at the Gaumont, Derby.

OCTOBER 12
Concert at the Gaumont, Doncaster.

OCTOBER 13
Concert at the Odeon, Liverpool.

OCTOBER 16
Concert at the Odeon, Manchester.

OCTOBER 17
Concert at the Odeon, Glasgow.

OCTOBER 18
Concert at the Odeon, Newcastle-upon-Tyne.

OCTOBER 19
Concert at the Gaumont, Bradford.

OCTOBER 20
Concert at the Gaumont, Hanley.

OCTOBER 22
Concert at the Gaumont, Sheffield.

OCTOBER 23
Concert at the Odeon, Nottingham.

OCTOBER 24
Concert at the Odeon, Birmingham.

OCTOBER 25
Concert at the Gaumont, Taunton.

OCTOBER 26
Concert at the Gaumont, Bournemouth. First appearance on BBC Radio's *Saturday Club*.

OCTOBER 27
Concert at the Gaumont, Salisbury.

OCTOBER 29
Concert at the Gaumont, Southampton.

OCTOBER 30
Concert at the Odeon, St. Alban's.

OCTOBER 31
Concert at the Odeon, Lewisham, London.

NOVEMBER 1
Concert at the Odeon, Rochester, Kent. The new single, 'I Wanna Be Your Man/Stoned', produced by Impact Sound at Kingsway Studios, London, is released by Decca. Side One is a Lennon/McCartney composition, while 'Stoned' is written by all five Rolling Stones. The record is planned for release in America as the first Rolling Stones single there, but is cancelled because of its drug-related subject matter.

NOVEMBER 2
Concert at the Gaumont, Ipswich.

NOVEMBER 3
The Rolling Stones finish their first British tour at the Odeon, Hammersmith, in London.

NOVEMBER 8
'I Wanna Be Your Man' enters the Top 30 at Number 30. It will stay in the charts for thirteen weeks, with a highest position of Number 9.

NOVEMBER 15
Derek Johnson writes in *New Musical Express*: '... the invisible barrier which has for so long divided London and Liverpool [has finally been penetrated by] the Rolling Stones. The boys first visited the Cavern Club a few weeks ago, when a group called the Big Three was recording there. The Rolling Stones, who had been playing a date in Manchester, dashed to Liverpool to watch the session as members of the audience and found themselves hailed as celebrities. ''We were really chuffed,'' said lead singer Mick Jagger. ''We only went there to relax, not to perform. But as soon as the word got around that we were there, we were swamped with requests for autographs.'' The explanation for the Rolling Stones' widespread popularity in the North undoubtedly lies in their style - which is raw, exciting, down-to-earth, and strongly R&B flavoured.'

NOVEMBER 28
The *Daily Mirror* reports: 'Gene Pitney meets the Rolling Stones.' He is quoted as saying: 'When I first saw them I didn't know whether to say hello or bark. But then I got to know them. They are something, really something.'

DECEMBER 13
Gene Pitney's British-waxed single, 'That Girl Belongs To Yesterday' is to be released during the next week. It is written by Mick Jagger and Keith Richard, and produced by Andrew Oldham.

DECEMBER 20
The Rolling Stones are voted sixth in the British small group category of the *New Musical Express* Pop Poll.

DECEMBER 27
Richard Green writes in the *New Musical Express*: 'The Rolling Stones create a sound so exciting and gripping that few other groups can come within shouting distance of it.'

JANUARY 6
The Rolling Stones start their second British tour at the Harrow Granada. Also on the bill are the Ronettes, Marty Wilde, the Swinging Blue Jeans, Dave Berry and the Cruisers, Al Paige and the Cheynes.

JANUARY 7
Cyril Davies dies of leukaemia in London. Concert at the Adelphi, Slough, Berkshire.

JANUARY 8
Concert at the Granada, Maidstone, Kent.

JANUARY 9
Concert at the Granada, Kettering, Northamptonshire.

JANUARY 10
Concert at the Granada, Walthamstow, London.
Release date of eighteen-year-old girl singer Cleo's single, 'To Know Him Is To Love Him/There Are But Five Rolling Stones'. It is produced by Andrew Oldham and backed by the Rolling Stones. *New Musical Express* reports: 'Plenty of vocal volume and body action in George Cooper's "Group Scene 1964" when it opened at Harrow Granada on Monday. Two packed houses greeted with cheers, screams and scarf-waving, the "local" lads who had made good, the Rolling Stones... This group certainly is different. Members wear what they like, from shirts to leather jackets, but they have long hair in common.'

JANUARY 12
Concert at the Granada, Tooting, London.

JANUARY 14
Concert at the Granada, Mansfield, Yorkshire. Decca releases a *Ready Steady Go* album, which includes 'Come On' and 'I Wanna Be Your Man'.

JANUARY 15
Concert at the Granada, Bedford.

JANUARY 17
The first EP is released, entitled *The Rolling Stones*, produced by Impact Sound. Tracks include 'You Better Move On', 'Poison Ivy', 'Bye Bye Johnny' and 'Money'. It was recorded at Kingsway Studios.

JANUARY 20
Concert at the Granada, Woolwich.

JANUARY 22
Concert at the Granada, Shrewsbury, Shropshire.

JANUARY 24
Appearance on the BBC show, *Go Man Go*. *The Rolling Stones* EP enters the NME charts at Number 28. It will stay in the chart for eleven weeks, with a highest position of Number 15.

JANUARY 25
The *Saturday Club* album is released by Decca. It includes the Rolling Stones' 'Poison Ivy' and 'Fortune Teller'.

JANUARY 26
Concert at the De Montfort Hall, Leicester.

JANUARY 27
The Rolling Stones finish their British tour at the Colston Hall, Bristol.

JANUARY (late)
The Rolling Stones start recording sessions at the Regent Studios in London. Phil Spector, Gene Pitney, Graham Nash and Allan Clarke all sit in on the sessions, which continue into February, and will form the basis of the first Rolling Stones album.
Decca release a single by George Bean, produced by Andrew Oldham, featuring the first recorded numbers written by Mick Jagger and Keith Richard - 'Will You Be My Lover Tonight' and 'It Should Be You'.

JANUARY 31
Mick Jagger says: 'From the time we first started at Richmond, everything we have done has been spontaneous. Nobody has had to suggest things to us. If we go on stage without a uniform, it is because we want to do it. We just act ourselves.'

FEBRUARY 8
A previously recorded session is broadcast on BBC Radio's *Saturday Club*.
The Rolling Stones start another British tour, promoted by Robert Stigwood, at the Regal, Edmonton. In the evening, they play at the Club Noreik in Tottenham. They are accompanied by John Leyton, Mike Berry, the

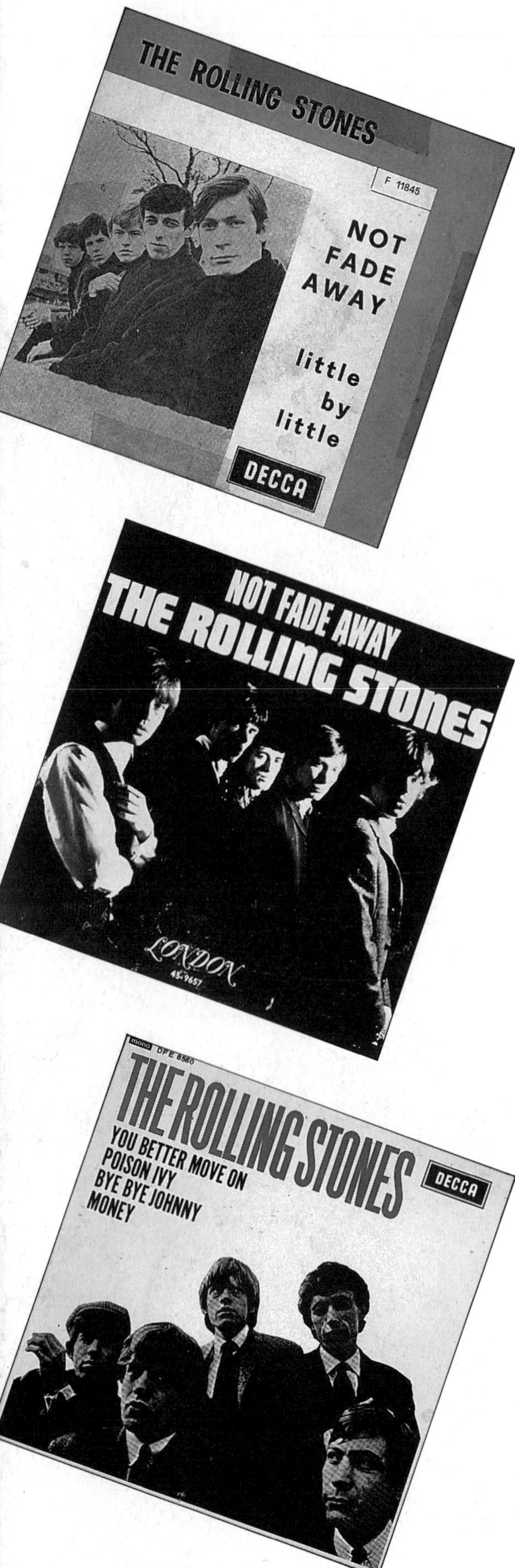

Innocents, Jet Harris, Don Spencer, Billie Davies, the LeRoys and Billy Boyle. *New Musical Express* reports: 'Welcomed by a tremendous barrage from boys and girls alike, the Rolling Stones opened with "Talkin' About You", but it was almost lost in the noise from the fans... The Rolling Stones' guitar noise came far nearer the Chuck Berry original on "Roll Over Beethoven" than the Beatles do on record... The screams did not let up for the slower "You'd Better Move On" or "I Wanna Be Your Man", with which the caveman-like quintet ended.'

FEBRUARY 9
Concert at the De Montfort Hall, Leicester.

FEBRUARY 11
Concert at the Granada, Rugby.

FEBRUARY 12
Concert at the Odeon, Guildford.

FEBRUARY 13
Concert at the Granada, Kingston.

FEBRUARY 14
Concert at the Gaumont, Watford.

FEBRUARY 15
Concert at the Odeon, Rochester.

FEBRUARY 16
Concert at the Guildhall, Portsmouth.

FEBRUARY 17
Concert at the Granada, Greenford.

FEBRUARY 18
Concert at the Rank Cinema, Colchester.

FEBRUARY 19
Concert at the Rank, Stockton-on-Tees.

FEBRUARY 20
Concert at the Rank, Sunderland.

FEBRUARY 21
Concert at the Gaumont, Hanley.
'Not Fade Away/Little By Little' released by Decca. It is produced by Impact Sound, and features Phil Spector on maraccas on the flip-side, of which he is co-writer. Ian Stewart plays piano, not Gene Pitney as rumours suggest.

FEBRUARY 22
Concert at the Winter Gardens, Bournemouth.

FEBRUARY 23
Concert at the Hippodrome, Birmingham.

FEBRUARY 24
Concert at the Odeon, Southend.

FEBRUARY 25
Concert at the Odeon, Romford.

FEBRUARY 26
Concert at the Rialto, York.
'Not Fade Away' enters the British charts at Number 10. It will stay in the charts for twelve weeks, with a highest position of Number 3.

FEBRUARY 27
Concert at the City Hall, Sheffield.

FEBRUARY
During February Decca releases a novelty single of the Andrew Oldham Orchestra, '365 Rolling Stones (One For Every Day Of The Year/Oh, I Do Like To See Me On The B-Side'. The flip-side is co-written by Oldham, Charlie Watts and Bill Wyman.

FEBRUARY 28
Concert at the Sophia Gardens, Cardiff.
Judith Simons writes in the *Daily Express*: 'They look like boys who any self-respecting mum would lock in the bathroom! But the Rolling Stones, five tough young London-based music-makers with doorstep mouths, pallid cheeks and unkempt hair are not worried what mums think! For now the Beatles have registered with all age groups, the Rolling Stones have taken over as the voice of the teens.'

FEBRUARY 29
Concert at the Hippodrome, Brighton.
Appearance on *Thank Your Lucky Stars*.

MARCH 1
Concert at the Empire, Liverpool.

MARCH 2
Concert at the Albert Hall, Nottingham.

MARCH 3
Concert at the Opera House, Blackpool.

MARCH 4
Concert at the Gaumont, Bradford.

MARCH 5
Concert at the Odeon, Blackburn.

MARCH 6
Concert at the Gaumont, Wolverhampton.

MARCH 7
The Rolling Stones finish their British tour at the Morecambe Winter Gardens and go on holiday.

MARCH
Andrew Oldham produces a Decca single by Adrienne Poster of a Jagger/Richard composition, 'Shang A Doo Lang'.
London Records releases 'Not Fade Away'/'I Wanna Be Your Man' as the first Rolling Stones single in the United States.

MARCH 13
The Rolling Stones, Georgie Fame and the

Blue Flames and Long John Baldry record a 30-minute show for the BBC. It will be broadcast as an experimental stereophonic transmission on Saturday 9 May.

APRIL 10
Appearance on *The Joe Loss Show* on TV.

APRIL 16
The first Rolling Stones album is released by Decca. Called *The Rolling Stones,* it features twelve tracks recorded earlier in the year at the Regent Studios, produced by Andrew Oldham and Eric Easton.

APRIL 18
Appearance on BBC Radio's *Saturday Club.* The Rolling Stones play at the Mad Mod Ball at the Empire Pool, Wembley in front of an audience of 8,000. Thirty fans are arrested for riotous behaviour.

APRIL 20/21
The Rolling Stones take part in the international TV festival at Montreux, Switzerland.

APRIL 24
The Rolling Stones album reaches Number 1 in the British charts after only eight days on sale. It will stay in the Top 30 for 40 weeks, eleven of them at Number 1.

APRIL 26
The Rolling Stones take part in the *New Musical Express* Poll Winners' concert at the Empire Pool, Wembley. The show includes the Beatles, the Dave Clark Five and other lesser-known bands. The concert is filmed for two 90-minute TV shows to be transmitted on May 3 and 10.

MAY 1
The Rolling Stones open another British tour at the Imperial, Nelson.
Details of their first movie, produced by Border Films, are confirmed: they will shoot for about 8-10 weeks starting in July, with a Lionel Bart screenplay. The Rolling Stones will contribute the soundtrack music, produced by Andrew Oldham. They also announce that they will tour the USA in June.

MAY 2
'Not Fade Away' enters the US Top 100 at Number 98. It will stay in the chart for 13 weeks, but only makes a highest position of Number 48.
Appearance at the Spa Royal, Bridlington.

MAY 8
Keith Richard says: 'R&B is a bit of a giggle. It's hard to say what R&B is. So many people

Right: *The Stones performing in front of a packed audience at the Montreux International TV festival.*

say Chuck Berry is R&B, then he says he is rock'n'roll, so where do you go from there?... Still I don't mind what you call it at the moment and for the next ten years. I'm happy.'

MAY 9
Concert at the Savoy Rooms, Catford. A previously recorded session is broadcast on the radio show, *Blues In Rhythm.*

MAY 10
Appearance at the Colston Hall, Bristol. Disc jockey Jimmy Saville writes in *The People*: 'The Rolling Stones are a great team for having a laugh and dress very clean and smart when they relax, contrary to what lots of people think.'

MAY 11
Mick Jagger says: 'I wash my hair myself once a week.' Co-manager Eric Easton flies to New York to discuss the forthcoming tour of America, while a further British tour is announced for August.
Appearance at City Hall, Newcastle.

MAY 12
Daily Express headline: 'The Rolling Stones gather no lunch'. The Stones are refused lunch at a Bristol hotel because they are not wearing ties.

MAY 14
The latest issue of *Billboard* in the US, features a full-page advertisement from London Records: 'Watch out USA... Here they are! The Rolling Stones! They're Great! They're outrageous! They're rebels! They sell! They're England's hottest - but hottest - group!'

MAY
The first album, *The Rolling Stones,* is released in the USA by London Records. It is sub-titled 'England's Newest Hitmakers'. The US album features 'Not Fade Away' instead of 'Mona'. The album will reach Number 11 in the US chart, remaining in the chart for a total of 35 weeks.

MAY 15
Gig at the Trentham Gardens, Stoke-on-Trent.

MAY 17
Concert at the Odeon, Edmonton.

MAY 18
Concert at the Odeon, Glasgow.

MAY 19
Riots in Hamilton, Scotland when police try to prevent 4,000 fans, many with forged tickets, from gatecrashing a Stones gig at the Chantingall Hotel.

MAY 21
Decca's *Fourteen* album is released, including one Rolling Stones track, 'Surprise, Surprise'.

MAY 22
It is reported in the press that Lionel Bart has completed the script for the Rolling Stones' movie, which is also to star Peter Sellers. Production is postponed to October when director Clive Donner will be available.
Mick Jagger says: 'We know a lot of people don't like us 'cos they say we're scruffy and don't wash. So what? They don't have to come and look at us, do they?'.

MAY 23
Gig at the University of Leicester.

MAY 25
The Rolling Stones end their British tour at the Granada, East Ham, with Peter and Gordon also on the bill. Richard Green in the *New Musical Express*: 'It became even more obvious that [the Rolling Stones] are approaching the Beatles' popularity and could even overtake the Mersey group... From the moment Mick Jagger picked up his maraccas and the Rolling Stones burst into action it was a battle between them and the teenagers as to who could make the most noise.'

MAY 27
The Rolling Stones begin recording sessions at the Regent Sound Studios.
The *Daily Mirror* reports that a Coventry headmaster suspended eleven schoolboys because they wore their hair like Mick Jagger.

MAY 28
BBC TV has its biggest ever demand for studio tickets when over 8,000 postal applications are received for the Rolling Stones' appearance on *Juke Box Jury* on 27 June.

JUNE 1
The Rolling Stones fly to New York for their first American tour. More than 500 fans await them at New York's Kennedy Airport.

JUNE 3
The *Daily Mirror* reports: 'Teenaged girl fans armed with scissors are keeping the Rolling Stones "prisoners" in a Broadway hotel, for the fans have caught a "curl for a souvenir" fever.'
The Rolling Stones appear on the Hollywood Palace TV show. Dean Martin quips: 'Their hair isn't long. It's just smaller foreheads and higher eyebrows.' Of a trampoline artist also appearing on the show, Martin also says: 'That's the Rolling Stones' father. He's been trying to kill himself ever since.'

Top left: *The Stones pose for a publicity shot on the shores of Lake Geneva during the Montreux Festival.* Left: *Brian's wide-ranging musicianship is reflected in his use of this unusually shaped Vox guitar.*

JUNE 5
The Rolling Stones open their American tour in San Bernardino, California.

JUNE 6
New Rolling Stones single, produced by Andrew Oldham, is released in the USA: 'Tell Me' (written by Jagger and Richard)/'I Just Wanna Make Love To You'. It will reach a highest position of Number 24 in the US Top 100, with ten weeks in the charts.

JUNE 7
The Rolling Stones flop in San Antonio, Texas, where the *Daily Mirror* reports that 'Local singers were cheered wildly. A tumbling act and a trained monkey were recalled to the stage for an encore. But the long-haired Rolling Stones were booed. After the show, at the Teen Fair of Texas, one seventeen-year-old girl said: ''All they've got that our own school groups haven't is hair.'' Only three thousand of the twenty thousand seats were filled.'

JUNE 10
The first issue of the monthly publication, *The Rolling Stones Book,* goes on sale in London. Charlie Watts: 'If someone asks me a direct question, I give a direct answer. Anyway, it's becoming a tradition that beat-group drummers shouldn't be the greatest talkers.'

JUNE 10-11
Recording sessions at the Chess Studios in Michigan Avenue, Chicago. Chuck Berry, Willie Dixon and Muddy Waters visit the sessions.

JUNE 12
Gig at Minneapolis, Minnesota.
The *Daily Telegraph* reports that police had to break up a press conference given by the Rolling Stones the previous day in the middle of Michigan Avenue in central Chicago, bringing traffic to a standstill. 'A senior police chief shouted angrily: ''Get out of here or we will lock up the whole bunch''. The Rolling Stones adjourned to the pavement.'

JUNE 13
Gig in Omaha, Nebraska.

JUNE 14
Concert in Detroit, Michigan.

JUNE 16
The Rolling Stones fly back from the States to play at Magdalen College, Oxford, which had booked them at a fee of £100 for their Commemorative Ball ('Commem') a year

---

Top left: *Mick and Brian mobbed by fans outside the New Elizabeth Ballroom in Manchester.* Left: *Brian, Mick and Andrew Oldham at London Airport.*

earlier when the band wasn't well known.

JUNE 17
Gig at Pittsburgh, Pennsylvania.

JUNE 19
Gig at Harrisburgh, Pennsylvania.

JUNE 20
The Rolling Stones play two concerts at the Carnegie Hall, New York, introduced by Murray the K. Mick Jagger says: 'I give the Rolling Stones about another two years. I'm saving for the future. I bank all my song royalties for a start.'

JUNE 23
Fans riot at the airport as the Rolling Stones arrive back in London.

JUNE 24
The Rolling Stones are voted Best British Vocal Group in the *Record Mirror* Pop Poll, and Mick Jagger is voted the most popular Individual Group Member. The poll awards are presented at the Savoy Hotel, London.

JUNE 26
Decca releases a new single, 'It's All Over Now'/'Good Times Bad Times', produced by Impact Sound. The A-side is a B. & S. Womack composition, recorded at the Chess Studios in Chicago; the B-side a Jagger/Richard composition recorded in London in May.
All-night 'Welcome Home Stones' concert at the Alexandra Palace, with Alexis Korner supporting the Rolling Stones.

JULY 1
'It's All Over Now' enters the British Top 30 at Number 7. It stays in the charts for thirteen weeks, making the Number 1 position in the *Melody Maker* chart. Brian Jones says: 'Some groups give performances. We have a rave, a mad, swaying, deafening, sweating half-hour of tension and excitement which gives us just as big a kick as the kids.'

JULY 4
Appearance on *Juke Box Jury*, (pre-recorded on 27 June), is broadcast.

JULY 8
'It's All Over Now' reaches Number 1 in the *Melody Maker* chart, Mick Jagger says: 'I don't care a damn if our new record has reached Number 1... What's it matter anyway? ''It's All Over Now'' has reached the top, that's great. But I can tell you none of us has been worrying about it.'
Keith Richard, Brian Jones and Bill Wyman go to a party at the Dorchester Hotel, London, celebrating the premiere of the Beatles' film, *A Hard Day's Night*.

JULY 11
Gig at the Spa, Bridlington.

JULY 12
Gig at the Queen's Hall, Leeds. Radio Luxembourg broadcasts a Rolling Stones special called *This Is Their Life*.

JULY
'It's All Over Now'/'Good Times Bad Times' is released in US by London Records.

JULY 15
Appearance on BBC TV's *Top Of The Pops*.

JULY 17
The Rolling Stones appear on the BBC Light Programme's *Joe Loss Pop Show*.

JULY 23
Appearance on BBC Radio's *Top Gear*.

JULY 24
The Stones' British tour opens with a concert at the Empress Ballroom, Blackpool in front of 7,000 fans. Two policemen and 30 fans are injured, and four fans will appear in court the next day charged with assault and carrying offensive weapons. Keith Richard kicks a fan who spits at the Stones during the performance, starting a riot which results in damage amounting to more than £4,000. Following this, another gig at the same venue scheduled for 11 August is cancelled.

JULY 25
Gig at the Imperial, Nelson. *The Rolling Stones* album reaches Number 11 in the US Top 100, its highest position. 'It's All Over Now' comes in to the singles chart at Number 100. It will stay in the chart for ten weeks, with a highest position of Number 26.

JULY 26
The Rolling Stones record a set for ITV's *Thank Your Lucky Stars*.

JULY 31
Gig at the Boom Boom Room in Belfast is stopped after twelve minutes when hysterical girls are carried out in strait-jackets.

AUGUST 2
The Rolling Stones top the bill at the third open-air pop concert to be held at Longleat House, home of the Marquess of Bath. There is an audience of 25,000, of which 200 are taken ill after being crushed against crash barriers as fans surged forward on the appearance of the Stones. The Marquess of Bath says: 'A delightful day... So few hospital cases, the fans were wonderful.'

AUGUST 3
Second concert at Longleat.

AUGUST 6
The Rolling Stones record a spot for the US TV *Red Skelton Show*, which will be networked on 22 September.

AUGUST 7
The Rolling Stones appear at the Richmond Jazz and Blues Festival, then on ITV's *Ready Steady Go!*

AUGUST 8
Concert at the Kurhaus, The Hague, Netherlands. Two girls in the audience have their clothes ripped off. Fans unable to get seats do more than £1,000-worth of damage.

AUGUST 9
Concert at the New Elizabeth Ballroom, Belle Vue, Manchester. The *Daily Telegraph* reports: 'Two policewomen fainted, another was taken to hospital with rib injuries and barmen helped more than 50 policemen control 3,000 screaming teenagers.'

AUGUST 10
Concert at the Tower Ballroom, New Brighton.
Mick Jagger's first conviction. He is fined £32 in Liverpool for driving without insurance, failing to produce his driving licence and exceeding the speed limit. His solicitor explains that he had been on 'an errand of mercy', driving to hospital to see two fans injured in a car crash.

AUGUST 13
Concert at the Palace Ballroom, Douglas, Isle of Man, with an audience of 7,000.

AUGUST 14
The Rolling Stones play at Wimbledon Palais. A new EP, *Five By Five*, is released by Decca. Recorded at the Chess Studios in Chicago the previous June and produced by Andrew Oldham, it has advance orders of 200,000.

AUGUST 15
Mick Jagger and Keith Richard attend a party given in London for Brian Epstein.

AUGUST 18-20
The start of a Channel Islands tour, with six shows at the New Theatre Ballroom, Guernsey. British United Airways have banned the Stones from travelling with them.

AUGUST 21
Five By Five enters the British Top 30 at Number 13. It will stay in the chart for seven weeks, reaching a highest position of Number 7.

AUGUST 21-22
Concerts at the Springfield Hall, St Helier, Jersey, Channel Islands. At the second concert running fights break out between bouncers and fans, and one girl is seen with a flick knife, but is overpowered.

AUGUST 23
The Rolling Stones tour the West Country, starting with a gig at the Gaumont Theatre, Bournemouth.

Important releases during 1964. Top: The EP, 'The Rolling Stones, Vol.2' featured four tracks; centre: *The single 'It's All Over Now';* and bottom: *The US album,* 12 x 5. Top right: *The first official biography of the Rolling Stones.* Right: *The Stones photographed by top photographer Norman Parkinson for* Queen *magazine.*

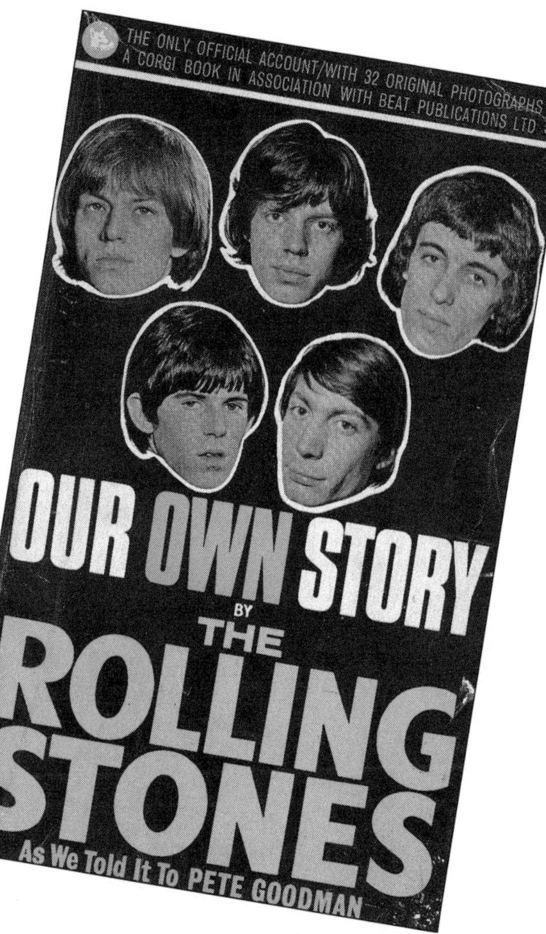

AUGUST 24
Concert at the Gaumont Theatre, Weymouth.

AUGUST 25
Concert at the Odeon, Weston-super-Mare.

AUGUST 26
Concert at the ABC, Exeter.

AUGUST 27
Concert at the ABC, Plymouth.

AUGUST 28
Concert at the Gaumont, Taunton.

AUGUST 29
Concert at the Town Hall, Torquay.

AUGUST 30
Return concert at the Gaumont, Bournemouth.

AUGUST
Decca releases two singles written by Mick Jagger and Keith Richard and produced by Andrew Oldham. The first is Marianne Faithfull's 'As Tears Go By', the second is the Mighty Avengers' 'So Much In Love'.

SEPTEMBER 4
The Rolling Stones announce plans to tour South Africa in December.

SEPTEMBER 5
The Rolling Stones begin another major British tour at the Finsbury Park Astoria, supported by the Mojos, Inez and Charlie Foxx, Mike Berry, Billie Davis, Simon Scott.

SEPTEMBER 10
The Rolling Stones are voted Britain's most popular rock group in the *Melody Maker* Pop Poll, while 'Not Fade Away' is voted best song of the year.

SEPTEMBER 13
At a concert at the Liverpool Empire, two dozen rugby players hired as a 'human crash barrier' disappear under a wave of 5,000 hysterical fans when the Rolling Stones appear on stage.

SEPTEMBER 14
Concert at the ABC, Chester.

SEPTEMBER 15
TV appearance on *Scene at 6.30*. Police fight with 3,000 screaming fans at a concert later at the Manchester Odeon.

SEPTEMBER 16
Concert at the ABC, Wigan.
Twenty-year-old Rolling Stones manager Andrew Oldham marries eighteen-year-old painter Sheila Klein in Glasgow.

SEPTEMBER 17
Police dog patrols are called in to control 4,000 fans at a concert in Carlisle.

SEPTEMBER 18
Concert at the Odeon, Newcastle-upon-Tyne. Marianne Faithfull's 'As Tears Go By' reaches Number 9 in the British charts.

SEPTEMBER 19
After a concert at Edinburgh's Usher Hall, an armoured security van is used to rescue the Rolling Stones from screaming fans.

SEPTEMBER 20
Concert at the ABC, Stockton-on-Tees.

SEPTEMBER 21
Concert at the ABC, Hull.

SEPTEMBER 22
Concert at the ABC, Lincoln.
The *Daily Mirror* reports that at a recent concert a screaming girl fan managed to break through the bouncers and grab at Mick Jagger on the edge of the stage, pulling him into the empty orchestra pit.

SEPTEMBER 24
Concert at the Gaumont, Doncaster.

SEPTEMBER 25
Concert at the Gaumont, Hanley.
'Time Is On My Side'/'Congratulations' is released in America on London Records. Produced by Andrew Oldham, the A-side was recorded at the Chess Studios in Chicago, the B-side at the Regent Studios in London. British blues singer Long John Baldry says: 'Before meeting Memphis Slim I thought R&B came from Dartford.'

SEPTEMBER 26
Concert at the Odeon, Bradford.

SEPTEMBER 27
Concert at the Hippodrome, Birmingham.

SEPTEMBER 28
Concert at the Odeon, Romford.

SEPTEMBER 29
Concert at the Guildford Odeon.

OCTOBER 1
Concert at the Colston Hall, Bristol. The Rolling Stones are banned from the Strand Hotel because of the way they are dressed.

OCTOBER 2
Concert at the Odeon, Exeter.

OCTOBER 3
Appearance on ITV's *Thank Your Lucky Stars*, followed by a concert at the Regal, Edmonton.

OCTOBER 4
Concert at the Gaumont, Streatham, London.

OCTOBER 5
Concert at the Gaumont, Wolverhampton.

OCTOBER 6
Concert at the Gaumont, Watford.

OCTOBER 8
Concert at the Odeon, Lewisham, London.

OCTOBER 9
Concert at the Gaumont, Ipswich. The Rolling Stones cancel their South African tour because of the Musicians' Union opposition to Apartheid.
Andrew Oldham, on a business trip to New York, acquires a new film script which, if the Stones agree, will go into production in the New Year. A new album is also released in the US this month by London Records, entitled *12 x 5.* Produced by Andrew Oldham, it includes tracks recorded in London and Chicago.

OCTOBER 10
Concert at the Odeon, Southend.

OCTOBER 11
The Rolling Stones' British tour winds up at the Hippodrome, Brighton.

OCTOBER 14
Charlie Watts marries Shirley Ann Shephard in Bradford.

OCTOBER 16-17
The Rolling Stones travel to Berlin for a TV show.

OCTOBER 17
'Time Is On My Side' enters the US Top 100 at Number 80. It will stay in the chart for thirteen weeks.

OCTOBER 18
The Rolling Stones travel from Berlin to Brussels for another TV show. The airport is besieged by 5,000 fans and the Minister for the Interior refuses to allow them to perform until persuaded otherwise by TV producer Frans Romeyn. The Stones are filmed on stage at the American Theatre in the Brussels World Fair ground.

OCTOBER 20
First show at the Paris Olympia. 2,000 fans break windows and wreck seats in the hall, and the riot spills out into the streets. 150 fans are arrested and the damage amounts to over £1,400.

OCTOBER 23
The Rolling Stones fly to New York for their second American tour. Marianne Faithfull's

---

Top: *Mick and Brian mournfully toast their success.* Left: *The Stones during their European tour.*

new single is released by Decca. It is 'Blowin' In The Wind', featuring Keith Richard on acoustic guitar.

OCTOBER 24
Two shows at the New York Academy of Music, with audiences of 8,000. The Stones are interviewed by Murray the K.

OCTOBER 25
The Rolling Stones make their debut appearance on the *Ed Sullivan Show*, and the fans riot. Sullivan tells the *Newark Evening News* afterwards: 'I promise you they will never be back to our show... If things can't be handled, we will stop the whole business. We won't book any more rock'n'roll groups and we'll ban teenagers from the theatre if we have to. Frankly, I didn't see the group until the day before the broadcast... I was shocked when I saw them.'

OCTOBER 26
Concert in Sacramento, California.

OCTOBER 27
Recording session at the RCA Studios, Hollywood.

OCTOBER 28-29
Concert at the Santa Monica Civic Auditorium. The Rolling Stones appear in the filmed Electronovision TAMI (Teen Age Music International) Show, with Chuck Berry, the Beach Boys, the Supremes, Marvin Gaye, James Brown, Smokey Robinson and the Miracles, Billy J. Kramer and the Dakotas, Gerry and the Pacemakers, the Barbarians, Jan and Dean and Lesley Gore. Afterwards this show will be known as *Gather No Moss*.

OCTOBER 31
Concert at San Bernardino, California. In the UK, the BBC transmits a previously recorded session on their *Rhythm and Blues Show*, featuring a very short and obscure number called 'Dust My Pyramids' which is credited to Richard and Jones. This is the only number in the whole Stones catalogue credited to Brian Jones.

NOVEMBER 1
Concerts at Long Beach and San Diego, California.

NOVEMBER 2
In Los Angeles, the Rolling Stones record for the TV show, *Shindig*, produced by Jack Good, and return to the RCA Studios for more recording sessions. Co-manager Eric Easton flies back to England with pneumonia.

NOVEMBER 3
A concert in Cleveland, Ohio. All future pop concerts are banned by the mayor after a seventeen-year-old girl falls from the balcony. The mayor states: 'Such groups do not add to the community's culture or entertainment.'

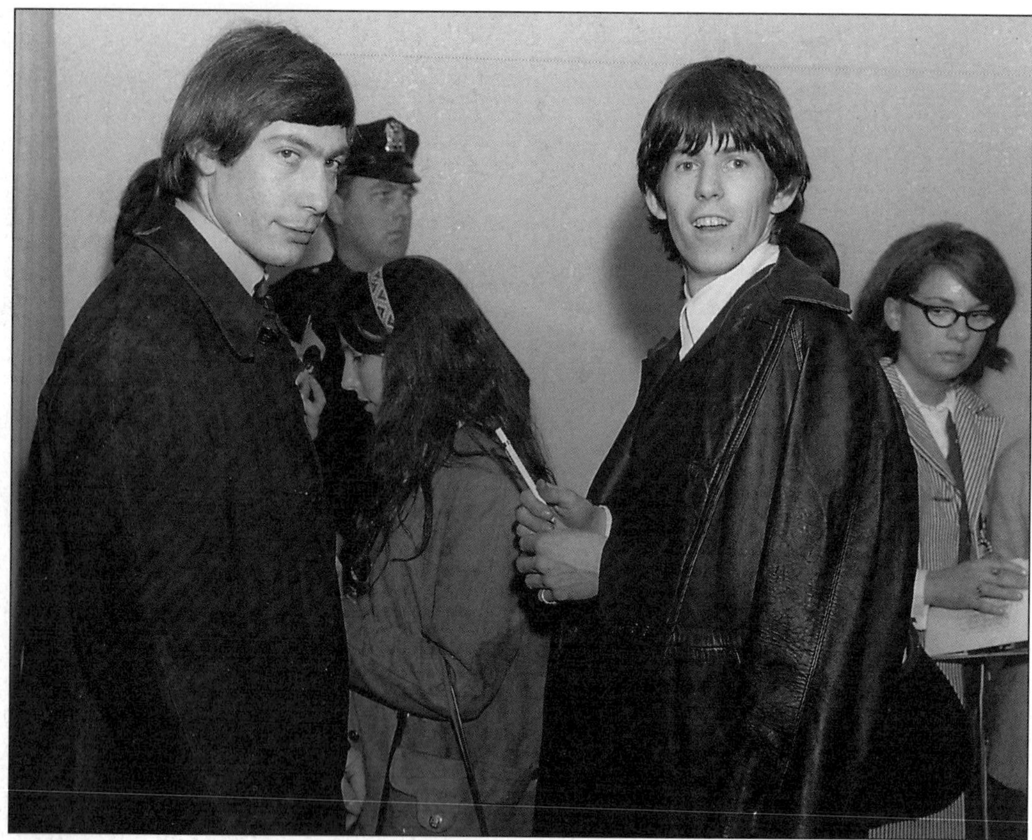

NOVEMBER 4
Concert at Providence, Rhode Island.

NOVEMBER 5
The Rolling Stones fly to Milwaukee for a concert, after which they fly on to Chicago to cut new material in the Chess studios.

NOVEMBER 8
The Rolling Stones complete their recording session in Chicago.

NOVEMBER 11
Concert in Minneapolis, Minnesota.

NOVEMBER 12
Concert at the Coliseum, Fort Wayne, Indiana.

NOVEMBER 13
Concert in Dayton, Ohio. The new single, 'Little Red Rooster'/'Off The Hook', is released by Decca in the UK. Recorded in Chicago last June and produced by Andrew Oldham, there are advance orders of 300,000. The A-side is by Willy Dixon, the B-side is credited to Nanker Phelge.

NOVEMBER 14
Concert in Louisville, Kentucky. *12 x 5* enters the US charts; it will stay there for 33 weeks, with a highest position of Number 3.

NOVEMBER 15
The Rolling Stones travel to Chicago. While there Brian Jones is admitted to the Passavant Hospital with a temperature of 105°F. Although the US press implies Jones has taken an overdose, in England he is reported to have pneumonia. Either way he misses the last three days of the tour. Stones production manager Mike Dorsey reports: 'I was in the next room to Brian Jones and he called me in the middle of the night to say he felt really grim... He was admitted with a temperature of 105 and was delirious - he had to be fed through his veins. He had been complaining for a few days of generally feeling ill, faint and sick. He made the most of a bad situation on stage, though, and even at the end didn't want to go into hospital.'

NOVEMBER
Decca releases an Andrew Oldham produced single by the Greenbeats, of 'You Must Be The One', written by Jagger and Richard. In the *News of the World*, Alan Whittaker reports on Oldham's odd sense of humour - in Paris Airport he staged a fake faint, while at Brussels Airport he pretended to be disabled.

NOVEMBER 20
All five Stones appear on *Ready Steady Go!*. 'Little Red Rooster' goes straight to Number 1 in the British Top 30.

NOVEMBER 23
The Rolling Stones are banned from

appearing on the BBC after failing to turn up to record for *Saturday Club* and *Top Gear*. Mick Jagger says: 'I understand that the bookings were made on our behalf but we never consented to them. That is partly the reason we didn't turn up.'

NOVEMBER 27
Mick Jagger is fined £16 for driving offences at Tettenhall, Staffs. His solicitor, Dale Parkinson, tells the court: 'The Duke of Marlborough had longer hair than my client and he won some famous battles. His hair was powdered, I think because of fleas. My client has no fleas.'

DECEMBER 4
Keith Richard has teamed with Andrew Oldham to write a number for American singer Bobby Jameson, 'All I Want Is My Baby', which will be released in the New Year.

DECEMBER 5
Appearance on ITV's *Thank Your Lucky Stars*.

DECEMBER
A new single is released in America: 'Heart of Stone'/'What A Shame' are both Jagger/Richard compositions and produced by Andrew Oldham. The A-side was recorded in October at the RCA Studios in Hollywood, while the flip side was recorded in Chicago in November.

DECEMBER 12
Brian Jones denies rumours that he is leaving the group. The Rolling Stones are voted second world vocal group in the *New Musical Express* Pop Poll, first R&B group, and Mick Jagger is voted best new disc and TV singer.

DECEMBER 21
Ode To A Highflying Bird, written and illustrated by Charlie Watts, is to be published by Beat Publications in January 1965. Virginia Ironside reports in the *Daily Mail*: 'He explained that he had written the book in 1961. "It doesn't matter if you don't know anything about Charlie Parker, because it's just about this little bird. In fact it's the kind of book you can buy for a kid." '

DECEMBER
London rumour of the year claims that an extraordinary jam session has been held in a recording studio during which Rod Stewart sang a Carole King number backed by P. P. Arnold on vocals, Nicky Hopkins and Keith Emerson on keyboards, Ronnie Wood on guitar, the entire Georgie Fame brass section, and Keith Richard on bass.

Left: *The Rolling Stones arrive in New York for their second American tour. London Records herald them in advance as 'England's newest hitmakers' for the launch of their first album.*

JANUARY 3
In the *New Musical Express* points table the Rolling Stones are the third best-selling artists of the year (1964) and their first album was the best-selling album of the year.

JANUARY 6
The Stones fly to Ireland.

JANUARY 7
Concert in Dublin.

JANUARY 8
Concert in Cork.

JANUARY 10
Concert at the Commodore, Hammersmith.

JANUARY 11-12
Recording sessions at the Regent Sound Studios, London, in preparation for a new US album due for release next February.

JANUARY
Bill Wyman produces a Columbia-released single for the Cheynes, 'Down And Out'/'Stop Running Around', the latter being a Wyman composition.

JANUARY 13
The Rolling Stones pre-record an appearance on *Thank Your Luck Stars*.

JANUARY 15
Decca releases *Rolling Stones No. 2*, the Rolling Stones' second album, in the UK. It was recorded in London, Chicago and Hollywood and produced by Andrew Oldham. The Rolling Stones appear on *Ready Steady Go!*
It is announced that they will begin their next US tour on 19 April. There are visa problems to overcome because the US government have refused to grant permission for British groups to tour. Yet more film plans are announced too, this time for a project beginning in June 1965 produced by a company called Impact Films, of which Andrew Oldham, Eric Easton and the five Stones are directors.

JANUARY
Decca releases a single produced and co-written by Bill Wyman for Bobby Miller, entitled 'What A Guy'/'You Went Away'.

JANUARY 17
The Rolling Stones fly to Los Angeles for recording sessions.

JANUARY 18
The group records a new single for release on 26 February.

JANUARY 19
The Rolling Stones fly from Los Angeles to Sydney, Australia, via Honolulu and Fiji.

JANUARY 21
The group arrives at Sydney Airport to a riot of 3,000 fans. The *Daily Mirror* reports next day: 'About 300 (girls) tore through a chain wire fence... and then smashed into a quarantine area ripping a steel Customs Hall rail.'
The tour of Australia and New Zealand will include Roy Orbison, Rolf Harris and Dionne Warwick.

JANUARY 22
The new album enters the British charts at Number 1. It will stay in the Top 10 for twenty weeks. Charlie Watts' book, *High Flying Bird*, is published in London while the Stones' Australian tour opens with two shows at the Manufacturers' Stadium, Sydney, each attended by 10,500 fans.

JANUARY 23
Two shows at the Agricultural Hall, Sydney.

JANUARY 24
The Stones fly to Brisbane.

JANUARY 25/6
Concerts at the Town Hall, Brisbane, and TV filming. At one show 40 fans storm the stage. Mick Jagger says: 'I almost got torn to pieces and Keith's shirt was torn so much that it looks as though he has been living in it on a desert island for two years.'

JANUARY 27
Two more gigs in Sydney, at the Agricultural Hall.

JANUARY 28
The Stones go on to Melbourne and play at the Palais Theatre. All nine concerts

scheduled in the city are sold out before they arrive. Andrew Oldham says: 'We've been knocked by the newspapers who keep trying to dig up scandal stories and run banner headlines about the Rolling Stones having all night parties. We wish we were!'

JANUARY 29-30
Shows at the Palais Theatre, Melbourne.

JANUARY 31
The Rolling Stones fly to New Zealand.

FEBRUARY 1
Concert at the Theatre Royal, Christchurch. In the *Daily Express* in London, John Drew reports from Christchurch that the Stones complain their hotel has too few bathrooms. Mick Jagger says: 'You can't blame us if we smell.'

FEBRUARY 2
Concert at the Civic Theatre in Invercargill, New Zealand's southernmost town and the one closest to the South Pole.

FEBRUARY 3
Concert at the Town Hall, Dunedin.

FEBRUARY 4
The group flies to Auckland for three concerts at the Town Hall.

FEBRUARY 6
Concert in the Town Hall, Auckland.

FEBRUARY 8
The Rolling Stones are refused entry by the Midland Hotel in Wellington after unruly crowd behaviour elsewhere, so they fly back to Christchurch for a meal at the Black Cat Restaurant.

FEBRUARY 10
Two more shows at the Palais Theatre in Melbourne.

FEBRUARY 12
Two shows at the Centennial Hall, Adelaide.

FEBRUARY 13
Concert at the Capitol Theatre, Perth.

FEBRUARY
The Mighty Avengers release a single on Decca, 'Blue Turns To Grey'/'I'm Lost With You', produced by Andrew Oldham and the A-side written by Jagger and Richard.

FEBRUARY 15
The Rolling Stones fly to Singapore. They are voted Best R&B Band of the Year in the *Melody Maker* Poll.

FEBRUARY 16
Two concerts in Singapore.

FEBRUARY 17
Concert in Hong Kong, the final date of their tour. The Stones fly to Los Angeles, via Tokyo and Honolulu.

FEBRUARY 18
In Los Angeles, Brian Jones rests in Hollywood, while Mick, Keith and Charlie put the final touches to the material recorded at the RCA Studios earlier.

FEBRUARY 21
Charlie Watts flies to Miami for a short holiday. In London Mick Jagger and Keith Richard have started the search for a new home as fans have discovered the whereabouts of their Hampstead flat.

FEBRUARY
Parlophone releases a single by the Toggery Five, entitled 'I'd Much Rather Be With The Boys'/'It's So Easy'. The A-side is written by Andrew Oldham and Keith Richard.
A new Stones album is released in the US called *The Rollings Stones Now*, produced by Andrew Oldham and recorded in Chicago, Hollywood and London.

FEBRUARY 26
A new single, 'The Last Time'/'Play With Fire' is released in Britain by Decca. The A-side is a Jagger/Richard composition, the B-side, attributed to 'Nanker Phelge', is in fact by all five Stones. It was recorded at the RCA Studios in January and produced by Andrew Oldham.
At an appearance on *Ready Steady Go!* Mick is mobbed by fans and injures his ankle. He says: 'I thudded down on the floor and a

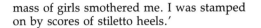

mass of girls smothered me. I was stamped on by scores of stiletto heels.'

FEBRUARY 28
Brian Jones celebrates his twenty-second birthday on *The Eamonn Andrews Show* on TV. Former Everly Brothers guitarist Joey Paige is staying with Brian at his rented Chelsea house. Paige is in England to promote his single which features a Bill Wyman composition, ''Cos I'm In Love With You', to be released by Fontana in March. Keith Richard and Andrew Oldham travel to Paris for a brief holiday.

MARCH 2
Appearance on ITV's *Pop Inn*.

MARCH 4
Appearance on BBC TV's *Top Of The Pops*.

MARCH 5
The Rolling Stones begin a two-week British tour supported by the Hollies and Dave Berry at the Regal, Edmonton. Part of the show is recorded for a projected live EP and album. 'The Last Time' goes into the British charts at Number 8. It will stay in the charts for nine weeks, making the Number 1 spot for four weeks.

MARCH 6
Concert at the Liverpool Empire, which is recorded, plus an appearance on BBC Radio's *Top Gear*.

MARCH 7
Concert at the Palace Theatre, Manchester. A girl falls fifteen feet from the dress circle during the concert onto the people below, fortunately only breaking a few teeth. The Stones are ordered out of the Midland Hotel, Manchester, because they are not wearing ties.

MARCH 8
Gig at the Futurist Club, Scarborough.

MARCH 9
Concert at the Odeon, Sunderland.

MARCH 10
'The Last Time'/'Play With Fire' is released in the US on London Records. The Rolling Stones play at the ABC, Huddersfield.

MARCH 11
Appearance on Granada TV's *Scene at 6.30*, followed by a concert at the City Hall, Sheffield. Keith Richard says: 'I reckon there are three reasons why American R&B stars don't click with British teenage fans. One, they're old; two they're black; three, they're ugly.' Charlie Watts says: 'Money is very useful stuff to have; actually, the more you earn the less you seem to handle.'

MARCH 12
Concert at the Trocadero, Leicester. 'The Last Time' reaches Number 1 in Britain, joining their second album which is Number 1 in the album chart. The album will stay in the Top 10 for twenty weeks.

MARCH 13
Concert at the Granada, Rugby.

MARCH 14
Concert at the Odeon, Rochester.

MARCH 15
Concert at the Odeon, Guildford.

MARCH 16
Concert at the Granada, Greenford.

MARCH 17
Concert at the Odeon, Southend.

MARCH 18
The Rolling Stones end their British tour at the Romford ABC. There is an incident at a filling station when Bill Wyman, Brian Jones and Mick Jagger are refused use of a toilet, and urinate against a wall instead.

MARCH 19
The tailoring trade magazine, *The Tailor and Cutter*, appeals to the Rolling Stones to wear ties, to stop tie manufacturers and retailers from going out of business. Mick Jagger's reaction in the *Daily Mirror* is: 'The trouble with a tie is that it could dangle in the soup... It is also something extra to which a fan can hang when you are trying to get in and out of a theatre.'

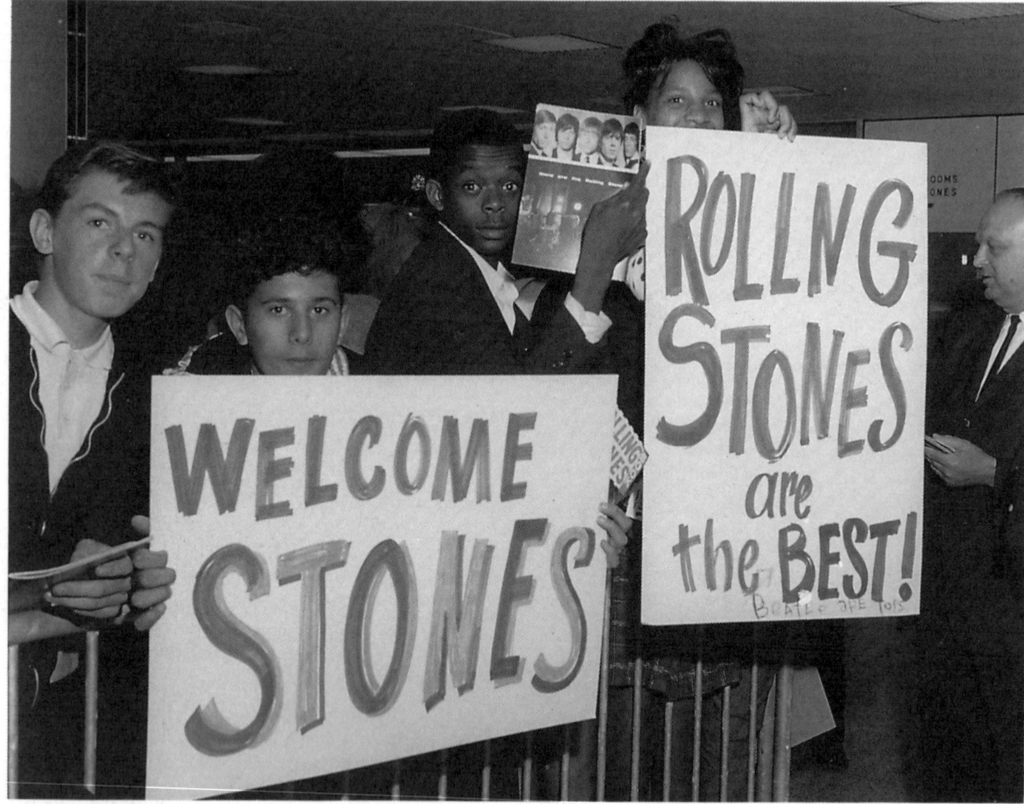

MARCH 20
The Rolling Stones Now enters the US charts. it will reach a highest position of Number 5 in the Top 200.

MARCH 24
The Rolling Stones fly to Denmark.

MARCH 26
Bill Wyman is knocked unconcious by a 220 volt electric shock in Odense, Denmark.

MARCH 27
Concert at the K. B. Hallen, Copenhagen. 'The Last Time' enters the US charts at Number 79. It will stay in the chart for ten weeks, with a highest position of Number 9.

MARCH 28
Second concert in Copenhagen.

MARCH 30
Third concert in Copenhagen.

MARCH 31
Concert in Göteborg, Sweden.

APRIL 1
Concert in Stockholm.

APRIL 2
After being filmed in Stockholm for Swedish TV, the Rolling Stones fly back to London.

APRIL 3
Bill Wyman has an eye operation.

APRIL 9
Live appearance on *Ready Steady Go!*

APRIL 11
The Rolling Stones play at the Empire Pool, Wembley during the *New Musical Express* poll-winners concert.

APRIL 13-16
The group travels to West Germany for a short tour and TV filming, after which they travel to Paris.

APRIL 17-18
Three concerts at the Paris Olympia.

APRIL 19
The Rolling Stones return to London, where they refuse to appear on the TV variety show, *Sunday Night at the London Palladium.*

APRIL 20
Brian Jones says: 'I play a lot of lead guitar and I am not really interested in rhythm guitars... In the Stones we have two lead guitar patterns going and we never use straight rhythm guitar as in the old Shadows days. We also use a heavy bass riff pattern... a Chuck Berry thing.'

APRIL 22
The group flies to Montreal to start their third North American tour.

APRIL 23
First concert in Montreal.

APRIL 24
Concert at the Y Auditorium, Ottawa.

APRIL 25
Concert at the Maple Leaf Gardens, Toronto, in front of an audience of 16,000, the largest of this tour. Glaswegian singer Lulu releases a Jagger/Richard song, 'Surprise, Surprise', as her new single on Decca.

APRIL 26
During their date in London, Ontario the house-lights are turned on and the stage power is turned off by the police. The Stones try to continue without power, Mick singing and playing the maraccas, Charlie Watts drumming, Brian on the tambourine and Keith and Bill hand-clapping. But the police refuse to turn the power back on, so after apologising to the audience, the Stones leave the stage.

APRIL 29
Concert in Albany, New York State.

APRIL 30
Concert in Worcester, Massachusetts. Andrew Oldham and Eric Easton leave London to join the Stones in New York.

MAY 1
Concerts at the New York Academy of Music and the Convention Hall, Philadelphia.

MAY 2
In spite of his previous remarks, the Rolling Stones appear on the *Ed Sullivan Show* in New York. Nat Hentoff writes that they are 'just incredible'. The doors of the TV studio are locked for twelve hours as they record four numbers for the show, and afterwards a party is given for them by London Records.

MAY 4
Concert in Statesboro, Georgia. The police are called by motorists who complain of women indecently exposing themselves at a hotel, but it is only the Rolling Stones, sunbathing.

MAY 5
Concert at the Municipal Auditorium, Atlanta, Georgia.

MAY 6
Concert in Clearwater, Florida.

MAY 7
Concert in Birmingham, Alabama.

MAY 8
Concert at the Coliseum, Jacksonville, Florida. During the day Brian slips while doing karate

Left: *Enthusiastic fans welcome the Stones at the start of their North American tour. Hysteria for the group matched that for the Beatles.* Right: *Keith Richard starts the denim trend.*

exercises beside a swimming pool and breaks two ribs.

MAY 9
Concert at the Aire Crown Theatre, Chicago.

MAY 10-11
In seventeen hours of recording at the Chess Studios, they cut four tracks for a new album.

MAY 11
The Stones fly to Los Angeles.

MAY 12-13
More recording sessions, this time at the RCA Studios in Hollywood, where they cut a further three tracks, including 'Satisfaction'.

MAY 14
Concert in the Civic Auditorium, San Francisco.

MAY 15
Concert in the Swing Auditorium, San Bernardino.

MAY 16
Concert at the Civic Hall, Long Beach. The Stones' limo is besieged by fans who cave in the roof by standing on it. The group has to try to hold up the roof while their chauffeur drives off with bodies still swarming over the car.

MAY 17
Concert in the Convention Hall, San Diego.

MAY 20
TV appearance in Los Angeles on Jack Good's *Shindig*.

MAY 21
Concert at the Civic Auditorium, San Jose. In London, Decca releases a single by Vashti of a Jagger/Richard composition called 'Some Things Just Stick In Your Mind'.

MAY 22
Concerts at the Radcliff Convention Hall, Fresno, and the Municipal Hall, Sacramento.

MAY 25
The Rolling Stones fly to New York.

MAY 27
Further film news: Eric Easton reports that scriptwriters are working on ideas and it is hoped that shooting can start in July. The new single, 'Satisfaction'/'Under Assistant West Coast Promotion Man', is released in the United States on London. Both are Jagger/Richard compositions, produced by Andrew Oldham and were recorded only two weeks previously at the RCA Studios.

MAY 28
Decca release a single by Thee, produced by Andrew Oldham's chauffeur, Reg King, of a

Jagger/Richard composition, 'Each And Every Day'.

MAY 29
Concert at the New York Academy of Music.

MAY 30
A final concert of the tour at the New York Academy of Music. Promoter Sid Bernstein has booked three extra dates in New York, as the tour has been a sell-out. The Stones also tape six numbers for future editions of the *Clay Pole TV Show*. Now the tour is over the Stones go on holiday. Brian Jones and Bill Wyman fly back to Los Angeles; Charlie Watts goes to Gettysburg to further his studies of American history; and Mick Jagger and Keith Richard take a car through the Arizona desert.

JUNE
In Los Angeles, the Rolling Stones come top in a major pop poll, with the Beatles second and Herman's Hermits third. They return from holiday in early June.

JUNE 10
Appearance on BBC Radio's *Top Gear*.

JUNE 11
The EP *Got Live If You Want It*, recorded live during March in London, Liverpool and Manchester, is released in the UK on Decca, produced by Andrew Oldham. Gossip hints at the possible marriage between Mick Jagger and model Jean Shrimpton's sister Chrissie.

JUNE 12
Appearance on ITV's *Thank Your Lucky Stars!* 'Satisfaction' enters US charts at Number 67 and stays in for eighteen weeks. It is their first US Number 1.

JUNE 15
The Rolling Stones begin a short Scottish tour at the Odeon, Glasgow.

JUNE 16
Concert at the Usher Hall, Edinburgh. *Got Live If You Want It* enters the British charts at Number 13. It will stay in the chart for six weeks, with a highest position of Number 7.

JUNE 17
Forty girls faint during a concert at the Caird Hall, Dundee.

JUNE 18
Last Scottish date at the Odeon, Aberdeen.

JUNE 23
The Rolling Stones fly to Norway for the start of a short Scandinavian tour.

JUNE 24
Concert in Oslo. The Stones' first visit to Norway is greeted by baton-wielding policemen battling with rioting fans, and an audience of 3,000 screaming 'We want the Rolling Stones'. One girl manages to climb onto the stage and kiss Charlie Watts, after which she faints.

JUNE 25
Concert in Poeri, Finland.

JUNE 26
Concert at the K. B. Hallen, Copenhagen, Denmark,

JUNE 27
The Rolling Stones visit the pirate radio station, Syd.

JUNE 29
The tour ends in Mälmo, Sweden. Meanwhile Charlie Watts has bought a sixteenth century mansion in Sussex from Lord Shawcross, former British Attorney General. Charlie's father, a parcels truck driver at King's Cross Railway Station says: 'We are proud of Charlie, but we can't understand why he prefers an old place like this to something modern.'

JULY 1
The Rolling Stones arrive back in London to face the majesty of the law. In Glasgow, Stipendiary Magistrate Mr James Langmuir, of Glasgow Central Juvenile Court, calls them 'animals, clowns and morons' after one of their fans is arrested for breaking a window. Two Members of Parliament publicly defend the group. Meanwhile in London the *Evening News* reports that private summonses have been issued against Bill Wyman, Mick Jagger and Brian Jones for alleged 'insulting behaviour' at an all-night filling station in Romford Road, Stratford, on the night of 18 March.

JULY 7
'Satisfaction' goes to Number 1 in the US charts. The Rolling Stones fly to Los Angeles for recording sessions and to mix their forthcoming album, *Out Of Our Heads*.

JULY 10
In a 'Battle of the Giants' poll conducted by Radio Luxembourg, the Rolling Stones receive 3,001 votes, 161 more than the Beatles. The Stones announce that there will be no more 'Nanker Phelge' songs - all compositions will be individually credited in future.

JULY 13
The Rolling Stones return to London.

JULY 16
Concert at the Odeon, Exeter, supported by

the Walker Brothers and Steam Packet.

JULY 17
Concert at the Guildhall, Portsmouth.

JULY 18
Concert at the Gaumont, Bournemouth.

JULY
Decca releases another Mighty Avengers single written by Jagger and Richard, called 'Walkin' Thru The Sleepy City'.

JULY 22
Brian, Mick and Bill are fined £5 each plus costs at West Ham Magistrates' Court after being found guilty of insulting behaviour at the filling station. The Magistrate says: 'Just because you have reached an exalted height in your profession, it does not mean you can behave in this manner.'

JULY 23
Mary Malone in the *Daily Mirror* reports on the previous day's hearing, at which the court was told of the night the Stones' Daimler pulled into the petrol station in Romford Road, West Ham, with several friends inside:. 'Wyman asked if he could go to the lavatory, but was refused. A mechanic, Mr Charles Keeley, asked Jagger to get the group off the forecourt of the garage. He brushed him aside, saying: "We will piss anywhere, man." This was taken up by the group as a chant as one of them danced. Wyman, Jagger and Jones were seen to urinate against a wall of the garage. The car drove off with people inside sticking their hands through the windows in a well-known gesture.'

JULY
The Rolling Stones' third album, *Out Of Our Heads*, is released in America on London Records. Produced by Andrew Oldham, it was recorded in London, Chicago and Hollywood.

JULY 25
Concert in Great Yarmouth. The Rolling Stones cancel a proposed date in Blackpool on 11 August because of the riots there in 1964. In Richmond, the Crawdaddy Club closes down.

JULY 28
The Rolling Stones record a special insert at the Twickenham Studios for the US TV show, *Shindig*.

JULY 30
Rumours circulating in London suggest that the Rolling Stones will stay with Decca for UK and foreign releases, except the US. It is also suggested that they are quitting London Records, and that their US representative, Allen Klein, is negotiating a new record deal there.

AUGUST 1
The Rolling Stones play two shows at the London Palladium, supported by Steam Packet, the Walker Brothers, the Moody Blues, the Quiet Five, the Fourmost and Julia Grant. After the show, the Rolling Stones go on holiday. Bill Wyman, who now has a £12,000 house in Beckenham Kent, forms a new company with Shel Talmy called Mossy Music.

AUGUST 4
Andrew Oldham forms his own record company, Immediate Records, to be distributed by Philips. The first three singles announced for release on 20 August are 'I'm Not Saying' by Nico, 'Hang On Sloopy' by the McCoys and 'The Bells of Rhymney' by Fifth Avenue.

AUGUST 7
Out Of Our Heads goes into the US charts. It will remain there for sixty-five weeks, with three weeks at Number 1.

AUGUST
Bill Wyman produces a Columbia released single for the Preachers, called 'Hole In My Soul'/'Too Old In The Head'.

AUGUST 14
Mick, Keith and Andrew Oldham fly to New York. Mick Jagger says: 'The whole British music scene is dead boring now. There hasn't been anything new or exciting for ages... First there was the Beatles, then us, now there's nothing.'
Brian Jones' girlfriend eighteen-year-old Linda Lawrence, who has gone on holiday with him to Tangier, is also seeking a court order against him as the father of her year-old son, Julian Brian.

AUGUST 20
'Satisfaction'/'Spider And The Fly', produced by Andrew Oldham, is released in the UK on Decca. The B-side is the last track attributed to 'Nanker Phelge', as previously announced. The group appears on BBC 1's *Top Of The Pops*, and also tapes a set to be broadcast on 30 August during the Bank Holiday special, *Yeh! Yeh!*.
An album called *The Rolling Stones Songbook* by the Andrew Oldham Orchestra is released by Decca.

AUGUST 21
Out Of Our Heads goes to Number 1 in the States.

Left: *The Stones are driven to the Odeon, Manchester in a closed van to protect them from violent fans.* Right, top: *David Bailey's cover shot for* The Rolling Stones No.2 *album.* Centre: New Musical Express *leads with the Stones' tour dates for Autumn 1965.* Bottom: *A rare bootleg EP of the Stones'* Saturday Club *sets.*

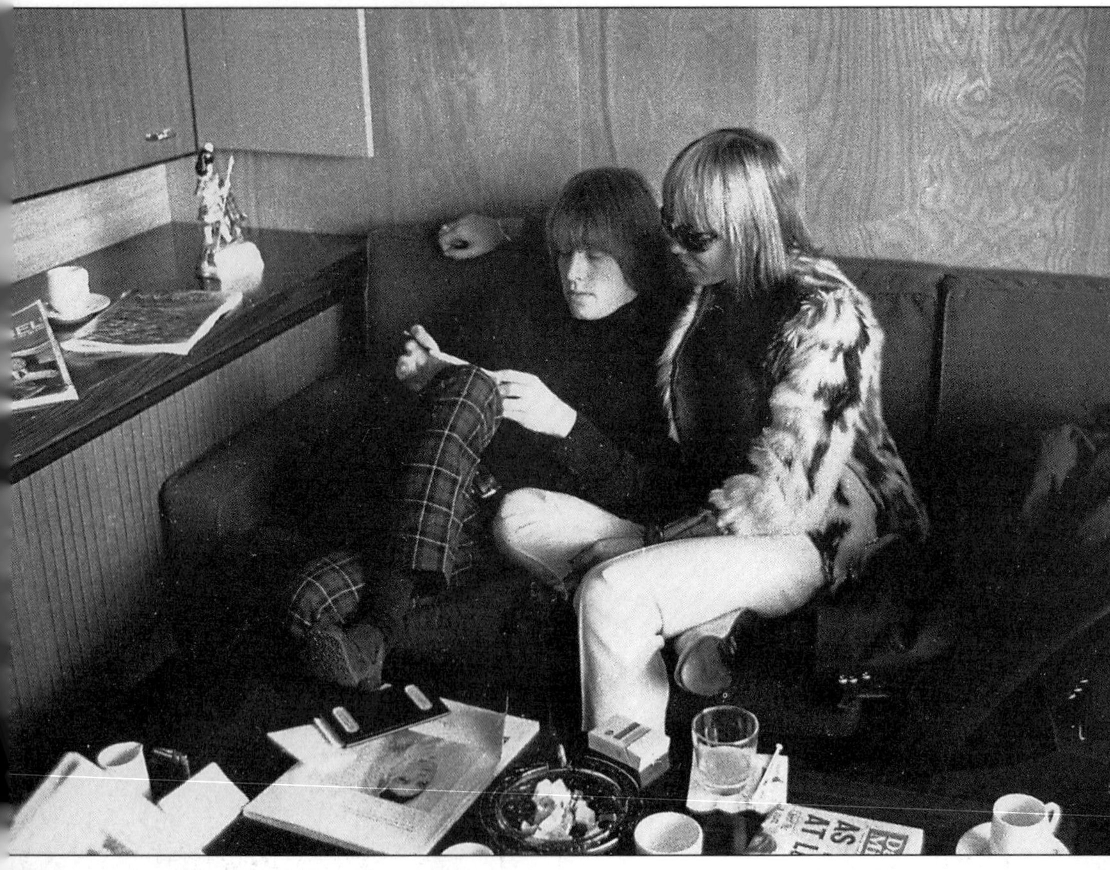

AUGUST 22
Concert at the Futurist, Scarborough.

AUGUST 23
Security guards spray 200 fans with a fire hose as they break through a barrier at a Manchester TV studio while waiting for the Stones to arrive.

AUGUST 24
The Rolling Stones meet Allen Klein at the Hilton Hotel, London.

AUGUST 27
'Satisfaction' enters the British charts at Number 3. It will stay in the charts for nine weeks, three of them at Number 1. The Stones appear live on *Ready Steady Go!*

AUGUST 28
The *Evening Standard* reports that the Rolling Stones have a new agent, Tito Burns, who also represents Bob Dylan in the UK; that they have a new co-manager, Allen Klein; and that they have signed a new five-year contract with Decca.

AUGUST 29
Judith Simons in the *Daily Express* reports that the Stones will stay with London Records in the States. Andrew Oldham says: 'Under the terms of a deal concluded with our American business manager, Mr Allen Klein, the Stones are guaranteed three million dollars over the next five years.' The *Express* continues: 'Expenses are high. Each guitarist owns about eight instruments, and the total cost of their present equipment is £4,000. When the Stones are on tour, hotel bills are about £700 a week. Salaries for secretarial and other staff accounts for £200 a week.'

AUGUST 30
TV appearance on *Yeh! Yeh!* is transmitted.

SEPTEMBER 2
The Rolling Stones record an appearance for *Ready Steady Go!* It is confirmed that London Records will continue to distribute the Stones' records in America. Another American tour starting on 29 October is announced, as well as a film to begin shooting in January 1966. Mick Jagger says: 'We are recording in the US solely because we believe we can produce our best work there. We can record right through from 6 o'clock in the morning over there without so much as a tea break, and the engineers are first class.' Brian Jones counters rumours that the Stones are planning to live in the US: 'I think this got started because I've just bought a house in Los Angeles. It's purely a business investment and neither I

Top left: *Anita Pallenberg and Brian Jones in the VIP lounge at London Airport, setting off on the US tour.* Left: *The Stones arrive in New York.* Right: *Mick on stage during the tour.*

nor any of the others have plans to settle out there.'

SEPTEMBER 3
Two shows in Dublin, during the second of which 30 young men get onto the stage and riot. *Melody Maker* reports: 'The youths swarmed all over the stage. Mick Jagger was dragged to the floor. Brian Jones was wrestling with three punching teenagers and Bill Wyman was forced back against a piano at the side of the stage. Keith Richard managed to escape off stage, and implacable Charlie Watts carried on playing stone faced as bedlam raged around him.'

SEPTEMBER 4
A concert in Belfast doesn't fare much better. Fans smash about 80 seats and hurl pieces onto the stage. The injury toll is two serious leg injuries, several faintings and a head injury.
The Stones appear on *Lucky Stars Summer Spin* TV show and 'Satisfaction' reaches Number 1 in the British charts.

SEPTEMBER 5
Final concert in Dublin. The Rolling Stones fly to Los Angeles for two days of recording sessions at the RCA Studios, Hollywood.

SEPTEMBER 8
They fly directly to the Isle of Man for a ballroom appearance in Douglas.

SEPTEMBER 10
The Stones appear on *Ready Steady Go!* Their second album re-enters the British Top 10, at Number 10.

SEPTEMBER 11
The Rolling Stones fly to Dusseldorf for a tour of West Germany and Austria. Thousands of fans go berserk at Dusseldorf Airport, with 200 breaking through a police cordon, attacking the police and smashing doors. The main hotels in Dusseldorf refuse to accommodate the Stones.
Concert at the Halle Munsterland, Munster.

SEPTEMBER 12
Concert at the Grughalle, Essen.

SEPTEMBER 13
2,000 fans riot at a concert at the Ernst Merck-Halle, Hamburg.

SEPTEMBER 14
Concert at the Olympiahalle, Munich. When asked what he would do if the beat wave died, Brian Jones answers: 'Oh, I suppose I'll become a criminal again.'

SEPTEMBER 15
The Hilton Hotel cancels their reservations in West Berlin. During the concert at the Waldbuhne, three fans smash 50 rows of seats, and after the show they smash up

coaches of a railway train and attack a conductor. Rumours that they smashed up an East German train as well cause a political incident, as East Germany sues the West Germans. 400 policemen armed with rubber truncheons battle with fans after the concert; 70 fans are injured and 32 of them, plus six policemen, are detained in hospital.

SEPTEMBER 17
The Rolling Stones wind up their tour at the Stadthalle, in Vienna.

SEPTEMBER 18
Appearance on BBC Radio's *Saturday Club*.

SEPTEMBER
Another new single is released by London Records in the US. It is 'Get Off Of My Cloud'/'I'm Free'. Written by Jagger and Richard, it was recorded at the RCA Studios in Hollywood earlier in the month and produced by Andrew Oldham.

SEPTEMBER 23
Appearance on *Top Of The Pops*.

SEPTEMBER 24
The Rolling Stones start a 22-date British tour at the Astoria, Finsbury Park, London. Support comes from the Spencer Davies Group, Mike Sarne, Unit 4 Plus 2, the Checkmates, Charles Dickens, Habbit, the End, and Ray Cameron. The tour coincides with the release of *Out Of Our Heads* in Britain on Decca.

SEPTEMBER 25
Concert at the Gaumont, Southampton. Bill Wyman has formed another company called Freeway Music with Glyn Johns to develop new talent. Their first discovery is the End, now touring with the Stones.

SEPTEMBER 26
Concert at the Colston Hall, Bristol.

SEPTEMBER 27
Concert at the Odeon, Cheltenham.

SEPTEMBER 28
Concert at the Capitol, Cardiff.

SEPTEMBER 29
Concert at the Granada, Shrewsbury.

SEPTEMBER 30
Concert at the Gaumont, Hanley.

OCTOBER 1
Out Of Our Heads enters the British charts at Number 3. It will stay in the Top 10 for eighteen weeks, with a highest position of Number 2.
Rumours circulate that Bill Wyman is about to leave the group. He tells *Disc Weekly*: 'I don't know if any of the rest of the boys know about it. I'm certainly not quitting. If I'm

thrown out I still get my money, but if I leave of my own accord, I don't. I'm not stupid.' Meanwhile he has produced a new Bobbie Miller single, 'Every Beat Of My Heart'/'Tomorrow', out on Decca.
The Stones play a concert at the ABC, Chester.

OCTOBER 2
Concert at the ABC, Wigan.

OCTOBER 3
Concerts at the Odeon, Manchester. These are the wildest shows of the tour - during the first fans smash twelve seats trying to get to the stage and police have to form a human barrier in front of the stage. Keith Richard is knocked out for five minutes by a flying missile and has to be carried off for treatment, while Mick Jagger is cut near the eye.

OCTOBER 4
Concert at the Gaumont, Bradford.

OCTOBER 5
Concert at the ABC, Carlisle.

OCTOBER 6
Concert at the Odeon, Glasgow.

OCTOBER 7
Concert at the City Hall, Newcastle-upon-Tyne.

OCTOBER 8
Concert at the ABC, Stockton-on-Tees. Immediate Records releases a Jimmy Tarbuck single, the B-side of which is a Jagger/Richard composition, 'We're Wasting Time'.

OCTOBER 9
'Get Off Of My Cloud' enters the US Top 100 at Number 64. It will stay in the chart for twelve weeks with two weeks at Number 1. The Rolling Stones play at the Odeon, Leeds.

OCTOBER 13
Concert at the De Montfort Hall, Leicester.

OCTOBER 14
Concert at the Odeon, Birmingham.

OCTOBER 15
Concert at the ABC, Cambridge.

OCTOBER 16
Concert at the ABC, Northampton.

OCTOBER 17
Final concert of the British tour at the Tooting Granada in South London.

OCTOBER 21
Appearance on *Top Of The Pops*.

OCTOBER 22
'Get Off Of My Cloud'/'The Singer Not the

Song' is released in the UK on Decca. The Rolling Stones appear on ITV's *Ready Steady Go!*

OCTOBER 25
Andrew Oldham flies to New York prior to the US tour, where 'Get Off Of My Cloud' is named record of the week by local radio stations.

OCTOBER 26
It is announced that Mick Jagger, Keith Richard and Andrew Oldham have formed an independent record production company called We Three Producers. Their first product is an EP by Chris Farlowe, called *Farlowe In The Moonlight Hour*, to be released by Immediate Records on 19 November.

OCTOBER 27
The Rolling Stones arrive in New York to be greeted by a hundred foot illuminated picture of themselves in Times Square. The Stones have hired a private plane to transport them from city to city, and their headquarters are two floors of the Warwick Hotel in New York.

OCTOBER 29
The Stones open their fourth sell-out North American tour in the Forum, Montreal. 440 fans rush the stage, and 40 girls need hospital treatment. When the Stones finish the set, they try for a quick getaway, but Charlie's jacket is ripped to pieces, Brian sustains a cut on the forehead and Bill and Keith are trapped on stage for twenty minutes.
'Get Off Of My Cloud' enters the British charts at Number 3. It will stay in the charts for nine weeks, with three weeks at Number 1. The Rolling Stones overtake the Beatles in the *New Musical Express* points table.

OCTOBER 30
Two concerts in New York State, at the Barton Hall, Ithaca and the War Memorial, Syracuse. Bob Dylan visits Brian Jones at their New York hotel. Earl Wilson reports that the Stones are carried to a Hilton Hotel press conference in their limo via the freight elevator: 'Hilton security officials said they were the only personalities to be taken inside the hotel in a car, save for the late President Kennedy who visited the hotel in mid-1963.'

OCTOBER 31
Concert in the Maple Leaf Gardens, Toronto, before a crowd of 15,000.

NOVEMBER 1
Concert at the Auditorium, Rochester, New York. Police stop the concert after 3,000 fans try to storm the stage.

NOVEMBER 3
Concert at Providence, Rhode Island.

NOVEMBER 4
Concert at New Haven, Connecticut.

NOVEMBER 5
Concert in the Boston Garden. The Stones out-gross the Beatles. 'Get Off Of My Cloud' is simultaneously at Number 1 in the UK and US.

NOVEMBER 6
Concerts at the New York Academy of Music and the Convention Hall, Philadelphia. Promoter Sid Bernstein adds a further concert at the Academy of Music. Andrew Oldham says: 'On this tour every concert is a sell-out... During this six-week period of concerts and TV appearances we will gross an unprecedented $1,500,000.'

NOVEMBER 7
Concert at the Mosque Theatre, Newark, New Jersey.

NOVEMBER 10
Concert at the Reynolds Coliseum, Raleigh, N. Carolina.

NOVEMBER 11
Appearance on the *Hullaballoo* TV show in New York,

NOVEMBER 12
Concert at the War Memorial, Greensboro, North Carolina.

NOVEMBER 13
Concerts at the Arena, Washington, D.C., and at the Civic Center, Baltimore, Maryland.

NOVEMBER 14
Concert at the Auditorium, Knoxville, Tennessee. Wild rumours fuelled by the US magazine *Blast* say that Mick Jagger is leaving the Rolling Stones.

NOVEMBER 15
Andrew Oldham returns to London to edit an hour-long documentary about the Rolling Stones shot in Ireland in September, called *Charlie Is My Darling*. The Rolling Stones play at the Charlotte Coliseum, North Carolina.

NOVEMBER 16
Concert at the Auditorium, Nashville, Tennessee.

NOVEMBER 17
Concert at the Coliseum, Memphis, Tennessee.

NOVEMBER 19
Concert in Jackson, Mississippi.

NOVEMBER 20
Concert in Shreveport, Louisiana.

Left: *The Stones appear on the* Hullaballoo *TV show in New York.* Right: *Keith and Charlie take time out from their North American tour in Colorado for a Western-style ride on horseback.*

NOVEMBER 21
Concerts at the Will Rogers Coliseum, Fort Worth, Texas, and in Dallas.

NOVEMBER 23
Concert at the Assembly Hall, Tulsa, Oklahoma.

NOVEMBER 24
Concert at the Civic Arena, Pittsburgh, Pennsylvania.

NOVEMBER 25
Concert in Milwaukee, Wisconsin.

NOVEMBER 26
The Rolling Stones, playing at the Cobo Hall in Detroit, Michigan, are invited to attend a Tamla Motown session.

NOVEMBER 27
Concerts in Dayton and Cincinnati, Ohio.

NOVEMBER
A new album is released in America on London Records, called *December's Children*. Produced by Andrew Oldham, it was recorded in London, Chicago and Hollywood.

NOVEMBER 28
Concert at the McCormack Place, Chicago.

NOVEMBER 29
Concert at the Coliseum, Denver, Colorado. Governor John A. Love of Colorado declares a Rolling Stones Day throughout the State.

NOVEMBER 30
Concert at the Red Fox Ball Park in Scottsdale, Arizona. The Rolling Stones win the United Europe Pop Contest with 'Get Off Of My Cloud'.

DECEMBER 1
Concert at the Auditorium, Vancouver, British Columbia. A rumour circulates in London that Brian Jones is to marry twenty-year-old German actress Anita Pallenberg in Chelsea and that Bob Dylan is to be the guest of honour.

DECEMBER 2
Concert at the Coliseum, Seattle, Washington.

DECEMBER 3
Concert at the Auditorium, Sacramento, California. An electric shock knocks Keith unconscious. Keith had predicted to *Melody Maker* on 8 February, 'I'll probably die of an electric shock.'

Left: *Mick, Keith and Andrew Oldham in the RCA studios during the recording of 'Satisfaction'.* Right: *The 1965 albums.* Top: December's Children; centre: The Rolling Stones Now, *another US release;* bottom: Out Of Our Heads.

December's Children enters the US charts and goes gold. It reaches a highest position of Number 2.

DECEMBER 4
Concert at the Auditorium, San Jose, California. Brian Jones denies that he is to marry Anita Pallenberg.

DECEMBER 5
Concert at the Auditorium, San Diego, California.
The Stones end their American tour with a concert at the Los Angeles Sports Arena in front of 14,000 fans. Anita Pallenberg flies from London to be there.

DECEMBER 6
The Rolling Stones begin recording sessions at the RCA Studios in Hollywood.

DECEMBER 10
The recording sessions end. They have recorded ten new tracks, then take a holiday. In the *New Musical Express* Poll Winner's Poll, 'Satisfaction' is voted best disc of the year, with 'Get Off Of My Cloud', third. The Rolling Stones are voted best British R&B group, second British vocal group, and second world vocal group.

DECEMBER
A new single, 'As Tears Go By'/'Gotta Get Away' is released in the US. Recorded in Hollywood, it is written by Jagger and Richard and produced by Oldham.

DECEMBER 17
It is announced that a film, *Back, Behind And In Front*, starring the Rolling Stones, will start shooting in Britain on 10 April, and will also be shot in four East European countries. Music will be by Jagger and Richard, and it will be produced by Andrew Oldham and Allen Klein.

DECEMBER 21
US music business magazine *Cash Box* gives 'Satifaction' as the single to score most points in the US charts for the year.

DECEMBER 25
Brian Jones spends Christmas in the Virgin Islands with Anita Pallenberg. 'As Tears Go By' enters the US charts at Number 79. It will stay in the charts for nine weeks, with a highest position of Number 6.

DECEMBER 27
Brian Jones arrives back in London suffering from a tropical virus he has picked up in the Virgin Islands.

DECEMBER 31
The Rolling Stones appear on Rediffusion TV's *The New Year Starts Here*. They are Number 1 on the *New Musical Express* Point Table of the Year.

JANUARY 1
Appearance on the New Year's Day *Ready Steady Go!*

JANUARY 14
A new album entitled *Could You Walk On The Water?* will be released on 10 March. A Decca spokesman says: 'We would not issue it with this title at any price!'
Immediate issue a single by Chris Farlowe, called 'Think', written by Mick and Keith, and produced by Keith and Andrew Oldham.

JANUARY 25
The *Daily Mirror* reports a poser for the Munich tax authorities. The question being argued is whether the Rolling Stones make music or just noise? 'That's not music. It's just noise', they said, and handed concert organizer Karl Bauchmann a £1,200 bill for amusement tax.

FEBRUARY 4
'19th Nervous Breakdown'/'As Tears Go By' is released. The American release has 'Sad Day' as the flip side. Written by Jagger and Richard, it was recorded at the RCA Studios in Hollywood last December, and produced by Andrew Oldham. 'As Tears Go By' was recorded in London.

FEBRUARY 5
Immediate release a single by the group Charles Dickens, called 'So Much In Love', written by Jagger and Richard. The Herd have released the same song on Parlophone.

FEBRUARY 6
The Rolling Stones appear on the *Eamonn Andrews Show*.

FEBRUARY
Keith Richard produces an album called *Today's Pop Symphony* featuring numbers written by Jagger and Richard, Lennon and McCartney, Wilson Pickett, Steve Cropper.

FEBRUARY 12
The Rolling Stones fly to New York. The *Daily Mail* reports: 'The Rolling Stones refused to be photographed when they flew into New York tonight. After one of the group shouted at photographers, a cameraman yelled: "Say that again and we'll take your picture lying down".'

FEBRUARY 13
The Rolling Stones appear on the *Ed Sullivan Show*. '19th Nervous Breakdown' enters the British charts at Number 2. It remains in the Top 30 for seven weeks, with a top position of Number 1.

FEBRUARY 14
The Rolling Stones leave New York and fly to Sydney, Australia via Los Angeles.

FEBRUARY 18
The Rolling Stones open their tour in Sydney, at the Show Ground.

FEBRUARY 19
Second concert at the Sydney Show Ground.

FEBRUARY 20
'19th Nervous Breakdown' reaches Number 1 in the British charts.

FEBRUARY 21
Concert at the Town Hall, Brisbane.

FEBRUARY 22
Concert at the Centennial Hall, Adelaide.

FEBRUARY 23
The group flies to St Kilda, New Zealand.

FEBRUARY 24
Concert at St Kilda. As fans storm the stage Keith receives a cut eye and needs hospital treatment.

FEBRUARY 26
Second concert at St Kilda.
'19th Nervous Breakdown' enters the US charts at Number 46. It will reach the Number 1 position, with a total of ten weeks in the charts.

FEBRUARY 28
Concert at the Town Hall, Wellington.

MARCH 1
The Rolling Stones finish the tour with a concert at the Town Hall in Auckland.

MARCH
Cliff Richard and the Shadows release a new single 'Blue Turns To Grey' written by Mick and Keith.

new MUSICAL EXPRESS

WORLD'S LARGEST CIRCULATION OF ANY MUSIC PAPER

No. 1009 EVERY FRIDAY PRICE 6d. MAY 13, 1966 Registered at the G.P.O. as a Newspaper

HOW MERSEYS MAKE GIRLS CRY

Keith Richard's new mansion

DAVE DEE · TROGGS
DYLAN · BEACH BOYS
MAMA'S & PAPA'S

TOP POP NEWS

I LOVE A RAINBOW
sings
LORNE GREENE
on R.C.A. 1517

GALLICO MUSIC LTD., 21 Denmark St., W.C.2 TEM 3856

a different kind of single from the rolling stones

PAINT IT, BLACK

THE ROLLING STONES

F 12395

DECCA

produced by andrew loog oldham

MARCH 3
The Rolling Stones begin recording sessions at the RCA Studios, LA.

MARCH 4
Mick, Keith and Andrew Oldham produce the first Chris Farlowe album *14 Things To Think About* released on Immediate.

MARCH 11
Bill Wyman produces a Bobbie Miller single 'Everwhere I Go'. The flip side is a composition by Bill and Ian Stewart called 'Stu Ball', featuring Bill on bass, Keith on guitar, Ian Stewart on piano and Tony Meehan on drums; it is released by Decca.

MARCH 12
The Stones finish their recording sessions at the RCA Studios on Sunset Boulevard. They have cut 21 new tracks.

MARCH 21
The Rolling Stones win the Carl Alan Award for the most outstanding group of 1965.

MARCH 22
'19th Nervous Breakdown' reaches Number 1 in the USA.

MARCH 25
The group flies to Amsterdam for a two-week European tour.

MARCH 26
Concert at the Brabanthal Danbosche, Amsterdam.

MARCH 27
Concert in Brussels.

MARCH 28
Appearance on a French TV show in Paris.

MARCH 29
Concert at the Paris Olympia. Charlie Watts is suffering with food poisoning, but goes on stage against doctor's orders. 3,000 fans riot and ten policemen are injured, while 57 fans are arrested. After the concert a party is held at the George V Hotel, where Francoise Hardy and Brigitte Bardot meet the Rolling Stones. Rumours circulating in Paris say that Brigitte Bardot asked them to write her a song.

MARCH 30
Concert at the Musicorama, Marseille. Mick says afterwards: 'They were ripping the seats apart and beating up the gendarmes. The kids were going bonkers. Even hitting the police with their own truncheons. I kept out of it as much as possible. I don't like seeing police being thumped.'
Mick is hit in the eye by a chair thrown from the auditorium and has to have eight stitches. The *Daily Worker* reported in London: 'Police

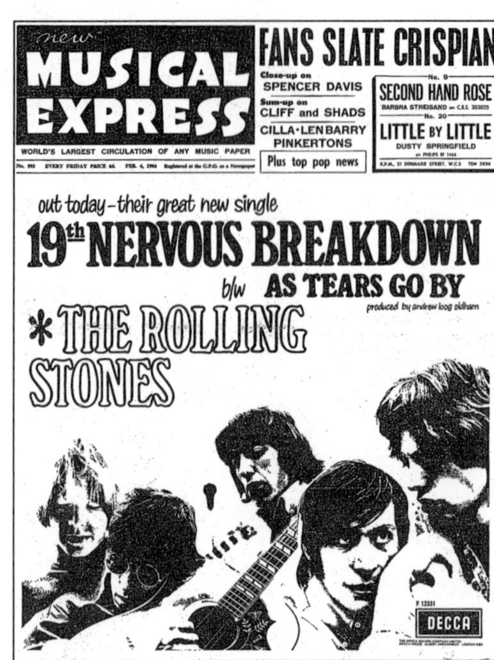

new MUSICAL EXPRESS
WORLD'S LARGEST CIRCULATION OF ANY MUSIC PAPER
EVERY FRIDAY PRICE 6d. FEB. 4, 1966 Registered at the G.P.O. as a Newspaper

FANS SLATE CRISPIAN

Close-up on SPENCER DAVIS
Sum-up on CLIFF and SHADS
CILLA · LEN BARRY PINKERTONS
Plus top pop news

No. 9 SECOND HAND ROSE BARBRA STREISAND on C.B.S.
No. 20 LITTLE BY LITTLE DUSTY SPRINGFIELD

out today – their great new single
19th NERVOUS BREAKDOWN
b/w AS TEARS GO BY
produced by andrew loog oldham
* THE ROLLING STONES
DECCA

Top: *the Stones, minus Charlie who is suffering from food poisoning, at a press conference in the Georges V Hotel before their concert at the Paris Olympia.* Above: *once again* New Musical Express *gives front page prominence to the Stones' latest release.*

held 85 fans but released them all except one this morning. He had bitten a policeman. Said one of the Stones afterwards: ''It's one of the best nights we ever had''.'

MARCH
A new anthology album is released in America by London Records, called *Big Hits (High Tide and Green Grass)*.

MARCH 31
Concert at the Palais D'Hivers, Lyon.

APRIL 2
The Rolling Stones fly to Stockholm.

APRIL 3
Concert at the Tunlinga Tennishallen, Stockholm.

APRIL 5
The Rolling Stones finish their European tour at the K.B. Hallen, Copenhagen.

APRIL 6
Brian Jones says: 'I've been insulted by more Texans than anyone else in the world.'

APRIL 13
The Searchers release a single called 'Take It Or Leave it' written by Jagger and Richard.

APRIL 14
The Rolling Stones appear on *Top Of The Pops*.

APRIL 15
The new album *Aftermath* is released in England. Produced by Andrew Oldham, it was recorded in December 1965 and March 1966 at the RCA Studios in Los Angeles. The album features fourteen new tracks all written by Mick Jagger and Keith Richard. One of the tracks, 'Goin' Home', runs for eleven minutes and 45 seconds, the first time in rock'n'roll history a track lasts more than the normal four minutes. The album was originally titled *Could You Walk On The Water*, but Decca Records refused to release it with that title.
Gene Latter covers 'Mother's Little Helper', while Wayne Gibson's new single is 'Under My Thumb'. Garrick and Tony Merrick record a version of 'Lady Jane'.

APRIL 16
Big Hits enters the US charts. The album remains in the American charts for ninety-nine weeks, with a highest positon of Number 2.

Top: *Mick Jagger with his long-term girlfriend Chrissie Shrimpton, sister of top model Jean Shrimpton.* Right: *The Italian version of 'As Tears Go By', overdubbed in Italian.* Far right: *the Italian sleeve for '19th Nervous Breakdown'; the label reads 'Number 1 all over the world'.*

THE
ROLLING
STONES
Live and in Person
Sacramento Memorial Auditorium
FRI. JULY 22
2 SHOWS 6:30 pm & 9:30 pm
PLUS the McCOYS, the STANDELLS, and the TRADEWINDS

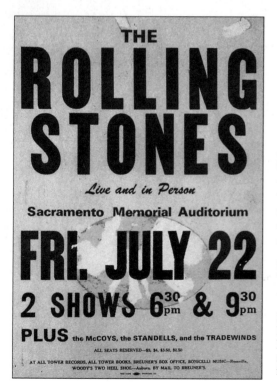

APRIL 20
Mick holidays in Paris with Chrissie Shrimpton.

APRIL 22
Aftermath enters the British charts at Number 2. It will stay in the charts for a total of nineteen weeks, with seven weeks at the Number 1 position.

APRIL
Otis Redding smashes the US charts with a version of 'Satisfaction'.

APRIL 24
Brian Jones and Anita Pallenberg are among the guests at Guinness heir Tara Browne's 21st birthday party.

APRIL
A new single is released in America on London, called 'Paint It Black'/'Stupid Girl'. Written by Jagger and Richard, and produced by Andrew Oldham, it was recorded early in March in Hollywood.

APRIL 29
Aftermath reaches Number 1 in the British charts.

APRIL 30
Brian Jones and Mick Jagger spend the weekend in Ireland with Tara Browne.

MAY 1
The Stones appear in *New Musical Express* Poll Winners concert at the Wembley Empire Pool.

MAY
Twice As Much cut a version of 'Sittin' On A Fence', by Jagger and Richard and produced by Andrew Oldham, released on Immediate.

MAY 10
It is officially announced that the movie *Back, Behind And In Front* will not be made. Instead the Stones will shoot another film based on a British novel *Only Lovers Left Alive*, by Dave Wallis, probably shooting some time next August. In the novel, the adults commit suicide, and teenagers turn Britain into a Fascist jungle. Andrew Oldham says: 'The book could have been written for the Stones.' The Rolling Stones will play the main roles, but they will not appear as a group. They will receive $1 million for the film and will cut the soundtrack in Los Angeles at the end of the American tour.

MAY 11
The Rolling Stones appear on *Thank Your Lucky Stars!*

MAY
Keith Richard buys a country house called Redlands in West Wittering, Sussex. Keith says: 'It's gorgeous and has a moat around it.'

MAY 12
Brian flies to Marbella in Spain for a week's holiday.

MAY 13
The single 'Paint It Black'/'Long Long While' is released in the UK by Decca.

MAY 14
'Paint It Black' enters the US charts at Number 48. It remains in the charts for eleven weeks, with a highest position of Number 1.

MAY 20
'Paint It Black' enters the British charts at Number 5. It will stay in the chart for six weeks, with a highest position of Number 1.

MAY 26
The Rolling Stones go to Bob Dylan's first 'electric' concert at the Royal Albert Hall.

MAY 27
The Rolling Stones appear on *Ready Steady Go!*. 'Paint It Black' reaches Number 1 in the UK. Mick Jagger tells the *Daily Express* 'When I was sixteen I wanted to be a journalist. But it seemed too much like hard work. When I went to university to study politics and economics I thought of going into politics. But I believe it is harder initially to get into politics and then get to the top than it is in the pop world. There are parallels one can draw between the two fields. In selling yourself as a politician, like selling records, not so much depends on what you have to say but on how you say it. The last election has proved the selling power of an image on television.'

MAY 29
Brian flies off to Marbella again for a short holiday.

JUNE 9
'Paint It Black' reaches Number 1 in the USA.

JUNE 14
Mick collapses from exhaustion at his new home near Regent's Park.

JUNE 15
Mick appears on the TV show, *A Whole Scene Going*.

JUNE 17
Immediate releases Chris Farlowe's new single 'Out Of Time', produced by Mick Jagger.

JUNE
Aftermath is released in America on London Records. The American version includes

---

Top left: *Brian with his girlfriend, Anita Pallenberg.* Left: *A poster for the US tour.*

'Paint It Black'. A single taken from the album 'Mother's Little Helper'/'Lady Jane' is also out in the US on London.

JUNE 21
The *Daily Mirror* reports that the Stones are suing fourteen of New York's top hotels for £1,750,850 because they turned down their bookings. They also file a damages suit alleging that the hotels had injured their reputation and claiming that the refusal of bookings amounts to 'discrimination on account of national origin', violating New York's civil rights laws.

JUNE 23
The Rolling Stones arrive in New York for their fifth North American tour. They use the sailing yacht *SS Sea Panther*, anchored in New York harbour, as their headquarters.

JUNE 24
The Stones open their sell-out North American tour at Lynn, Massachusetts. In New York, custom-built Vox electronic equipment is stolen from them only hours after the tour opens. The equipment includes Brian Jones' electronic dulcimer, the world's first.

JUNE 25
Concerts in Cleveland and Pittsburgh Civic Arena.

JUNE 26
Concerts in the Arena, Washington, D.C., and the Baltimore Civic Center.

JUNE 27
Concert at the Civic Center, Hartford, Connecticut.

JUNE 28
Concert in Buffalo, New York State.

JUNE 29
Concert at the Maple Leaf Gardens, Toronto.

JUNE 30
The concert at the Montreal Forum is stopped because of riots.

JULY 1
Concert at the Stadium, Atlantic City, New Jersey.

JULY 2
Concert in Forest Hill, New York.

JULY 3
Concert in Asbury Park, New Jersey.

JULY 4
Concert at Virginia Beach.

JULY 6
Concert at the War Memorial Hall, Syracuse, New York.

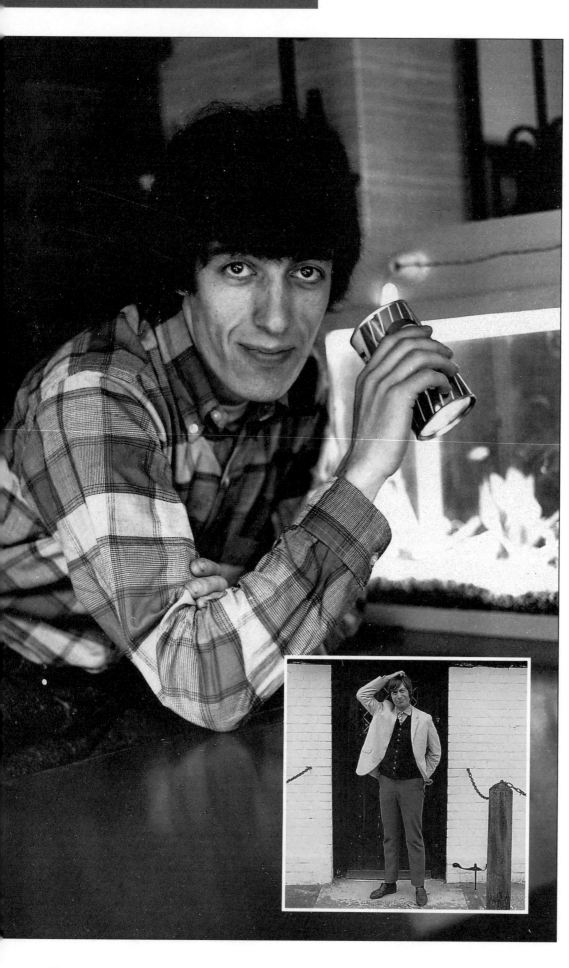

JULY 8
Concert at the Cobo Hall, Detroit, Michigan. The *Daily Telegraph* reports that police investigated today a report by angry residents that a member of the Rolling Stones dragged an American flag along the floor of the War Memorial Hall on their way to the stage. 'According to witnesses, one of the group snatched the flag from a chair where it had been spread to dry. During a brief scuffle it was grabbed by a member of the staff. Police said today the singer wanted the flag as a souvenir, and had apologised for the incident.'

JULY 9
Concert at the Convention Center, Indianapolis.
'Mother's Little Helper' enters the US charts at Number 70. It remains in the charts for nine weeks, with a highest position of Number 8. *Aftermath* also enters the American album charts. It will remain in the charts for 50 weeks, with its highest position as Number 1.

JULY 10
Concert in Chicago.

JULY 11
Concert in Houston, Texas. An audience of 11,000 fans.

JULY 12
Concert at the Krawalle, St Louis, Missouri.

JULY 14
Concert at Winnipeg, Canada.

JULY 15
Concert at Omaha, Nebraska.

JULY 19
Concert in Vancouver, Canada.

JULY 20
Concert in Seattle, Washington.

JULY 21
Concert in Portland, Oregon.

JULY 22
Concert in the Auditorium, Sacramento, California.
Mick says: 'One thing I will say about the American Press this time, is that, in spite of the rubbish written by the usual idiots who come back to the dressing room and say: ''Which one of you is Ringo'', we are getting great reviews.'

Left: *Bill Wyman at home. He pursued his own interests in parallel with his work with the Rolling Stones.* Inset: *Charlie Watts found all the paraphernalia of press interest in his private life difficult to take seriously.*

JULY 23
Concert at Salt Lake City, Utah.
'Lady Jane' enters the US charts at Number 83. It will stay in the charts for six weeks, with a highest position of Number 24. *Aftermath* reaches Number 1.

JULY 24
Concert at Bakersfield, California.

JULY 25
Concert at the Hollywood Bowl, Los Angeles. A group of young radicals welcome the Rolling Stones thus: 'We welcome the Rolling Stones, they themselves are our fellows in the desperate struggle against the mad people who got the power. We fight in guerilla groups against the imperialist invader in Asia and South America. We make noise at every rock'n'roll concert. In Los Angeles we set on fire and raid everywhere and the bulls know that our guerillas will be going back there... Fellows, you'll come back to this land when it is free from state tyranny and play your wonderful music in the factories which will be led by workers among one million red flags fluttering above an anarchic community of two million people. Rolling Stones, the young people of California listen to your message. Long live the revolution!' Says an English politician: 'Our relationship with the United States runs the risk of getting considerably worse as soon as the Rolling Stones arrive in America. What kind of image of English youth will they propagate there? A very, very bad one! Americans will believe that English young people have attained a new degree of degeneration and that this country is being recklessly ruined.'

JULY 26
Concert at San Francisco. Mick Jagger is 23.

JULY 28
The Rolling Stones finish their North American tour at the International Sports Center in Honolulu, Hawaii.

AUGUST 3
The Rolling Stones start an eight-day recording session at the RCA Studios in Hollywood.

AUGUST 10
Appearance on the *Ed Sullivan Show*.

AUGUST 12
The Stones finish their recording sessions in Los Angeles and go on holiday. Mick goes to Mexico, Keith flies to New York, Bill and Diane fly to Palm Springs, Florida.

Keith Richard relaxing at his home, Redlands, near West Wittering in Sussex. Redlands became a focus for the Stones and their entourage, a place where they thought they were free from interference from fans and press alike.

AUGUST 13
Charlie arrives in London from Los Angeles and, after a brief stay, flies to a Greek island with Shirley.

AUGUST 14
Brian arrives from Los Angeles and flies off to Tangier.

AUGUST
While in Tangier Brian Jones breaks two bones in his left hand, so he flies back to London to consult a specialist.

AUGUST 25
Mick is involved in a car crash with his Aston Martin DB6, near his flat in Marylebone, London. Neither he nor Chrissie Shrimpton, who is with him, is hurt. Damage to the car is valued at £700.

AUGUST 27
Rumours circulating the rock world report that Brian will be unable to play for at least two months, because of the trouble with his left hand.

SEPTEMBER 2
The Rolling Stones work at the IBC studios with producer Mike Leander and an orchestra.

SEPTEMBER 7
Mick and Keith fly to Los Angeles to finish mixing the tracks for a new single.

SEPTEMBER 9
Mick and Keith fly from Los Angeles to New York to meet Brian, Charlie and Bill.

SEPTEMBER 10
The Rolling Stones appear on the *Ed Sullivan Show* in New York without Brian Jones, and on *Ready Steady Go!* in London, to present their new single 'Have You Seen Your Mother Baby, Standing In The Shadow?' which will be released within a couple of weeks.

SEPTEMBER 22
Appearance on *Top Of The Pops*.

SEPTEMBER 23
'Have You Seen Your Mother Baby, Standing In The Shadow'/'Who's Driving Your Plane' released simultaneously in Britain and America. Both tracks were written by Mick Jagger and Keith Richard, and recorded last August in Los Angeles, produced by Andrew Oldham. The sleeve picture of the record features the Rolling Stones in drag, and, for the occasion, they have changed their names: Mick is Sara, Brian is Flossie, Bill is Penelope, Charlie is Millicent and Keith is Milly. The picture was taken in New York's Park Avenue by Jerry Schatzberg. A promotional film is produced by Peter Whitehead. It will be banned by *Top Of The Pops*.
The Rolling Stones open their two-week British tour at the London Royal Albert Hall. Five thousand fans attend and many of them storm the stage: Brian and Bill run off, chased by fans, while Mick is nearly strangled and Keith knocked down by girls who jump on him. More than 50 girls are taken to hospital. The show is recorded for a possible live album, and is described by the press as the rock event of the year. Keith Moon, John Entwistle and Jonathan King are in the audience. The Rolling Stones are supported by Ike and Tina Turner, the Ikettes, and the Yardbirds. An after-concert reception is held at the Kensington Hotel, where the Rolling Stones receive an award for the US record sales of their last four albums: 22 Gold Discs for a total of $22 million. The party is filmed for *Top Of The Pops*.

SEPTEMBER 24
Concert at the Odeon, Leeds.

SEPTEMBER 25
Concert at the Liverpool Empire.

SEPTEMBER 28
Concert at the ABC, Manchester.

SEPTEMBER 29
Concert at the ABC, Stockton.

SEPTEMBER 30
Concert at the Odeon, Glasgow.
'Have You Seen Your Mother Baby, Standing In The Shadow?' enters the British charts at Number 10. It stays in the charts for six weeks, with a highest position of Number 5.

OCTOBER 1
A concert at the Newcastle City Hall is recorded for a live album.

OCTOBER 2
Concert at the Gaumont, Ipswich.

OCTOBER 4
'Have You Seen Your Mother Baby, Standing In The Shadow?' enters the US charts at Number 40. It will remain in the chart for eight weeks, with a highest position of Number 9.

Left and right: *The Albert Hall, 23 September 1968. As girl fans storm the stage to the cheers of the 5,000 strong audience, an hysterical fan leaps on Mick. The Stones had to be hustled to safety and the concert abandoned.*

OCTOBER 6
Concert at the Odeon, Birmingham.

OCTOBER 7
The concert at the Colston Hall, Bristol is recorded.
Appearance on *Ready Steady Go!*.
The long-awaited Rolling Stones film, *Only Lovers Left Alive*, will go into production next November at MGM's Borehamwood Studios, and shooting will continue till Christmas.

OCTOBER 8
Concert at the Capitol, Cardiff.

OCTOBER 9
The Rolling Stones finish their British tour at the Gaumont in Southampton.

OCTOBER 14
Brian Jones says: 'A new generation came to see us on tour. Youngsters who had never seen us before, from the age of about twelve, were turning up at the concerts. It was like three years ago, when the excitement was all new.' Keith Richard says: 'We were in danger of becoming respectable! But now the new wave has arrived, rushing the stage just like old times!'
Immediate releases a new Chris Farlowe single in the UK, 'Ride On Baby', by Mick and Keith.

OCTOBER 25
In London, Mick and Keith attend a party for Bobby Darin.

NOVEMBER 4
A new album is released in America called *Got Live If You Want It*. Although the cover states that it was recorded live at the Royal Albert Hall in London last September, the tracks were in fact recorded at concerts in Newcastle, Manchester and Bristol. It is produced by Andrew Oldham, and released on London Records. Although not officially released in the UK, Decca have pressed a few copies, entitled *Have You Seen Your Mother Live?* However Decca releases a compilation album called *Big Hits (High Tide and Green Grass)*.
Immediate releases a Chris Farlow EP called *Farlowe In The Midnight Hour*, featuring a version of 'Satisfaction'. It is produced by Oldham, Jagger and Richard. Mick Jagger also produces a Chris Farlowe album, *The Art Of Chris Farlowe*, out on Immediate. Tracks include versions of 'Paint It Black', 'I'm Free', 'Out Of Time', and 'Ride On Baby'.

NOVEMBER 10
The Official Rolling Stones Book, after two and a half years and 30 editions, ceases publication in London. For the first time in two and a half years the Rolling Stones cut new material in London, at the Olympic Studios in Barnes.

NOVEMBER 11
Big Hits enters the British charts at Number 6. It will stay in the charts for thirteen weeks, its highest position being Number 4.
Keith Richard, Charlie Watts, Mick Jagger, John Lennon, George Harrison, Donovan and Eric Burdon are all at a party for the Four Tops.

NOVEMBER 19
Got Live If You Want It enters the US charts where it remains for 48 weeks, with a highest position of Number 6.

NOVEMBER
Brian Jones poses with Anita Pallenberg for a historic photo session. He is dressed in a Nazi SS uniform, a chivalry cross at his neck, and jack boots, crushing a doll beneath his foot.

NOVEMBER 25
They cut more material at the Olympic Studios.

DECEMBER 6
The Stones complete their recording sessions.

DECEMBER 10
The Rolling Stones are voted second best British vocal band, and second British R&B group, in the *New Musical Express* Pop Poll.

DECEMBER 13
Andrew Oldham flies to New York to edit the final tracks for a new album and single to be released early in the New Year. Keith and Brian fly to Los Angeles for the Christmas holidays.

DECEMBER 20
Despite denials all around, rumours still report that Brian Jones is to marry Anita Pallenberg.

DECEMBER
After three years, Mick Jagger and Chrissie Shrimpton break up. Mick says: 'Three years is a long time to be spent with somebody, but although we were unofficially engaged we hadn't set any date for a wedding.' Says Chrissie: 'We were very much in love but we argued all the time. As time goes on you begin to feel different about life and each other. There wasn't a row. We broke by mutual agreement.' Not long before Christmas she attempts suicide.

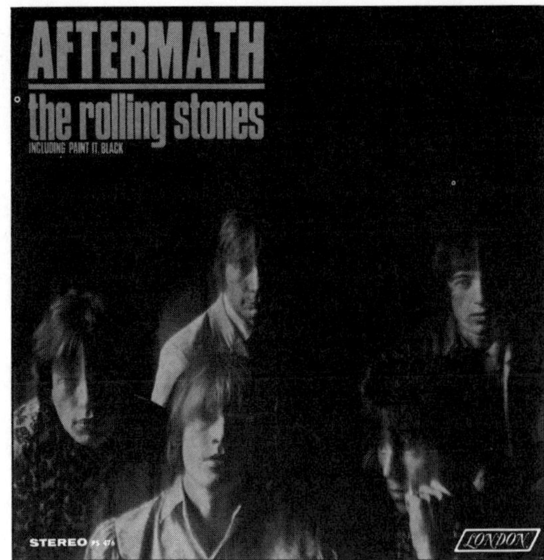

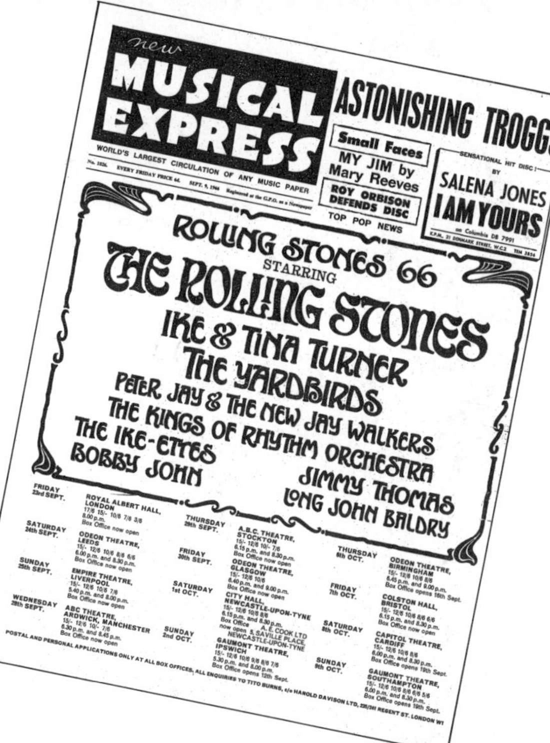
new MUSICAL EXPRESS
WORLD'S LARGEST CIRCULATION OF ANY MUSIC PAPER
No. 1026 EVERY FRIDAY PRICE 6d. SEPT. 9, 1966 Registered at the G.P.O. as a Newspaper
ASTONISHING TROGGS
Small Faces
MY JIM by Mary Reeves
ROY ORBISON DEFENDS DISC
TOP POP NEWS
SENSATIONAL HIT DISC! BY SALENA JONES I AM YOURS on Columbia DB 7991

ROLLING STONES 66
STARRING
THE ROLLING STONES
IKE & TINA TURNER
THE YARDBIRDS
PETER JAY & THE NEW JAY WALKERS
THE KINGS OF RHYTHM ORCHESTRA
THE IKE-ETTES
BOBBY JOHN
JIMMY THOMAS
LONG JOHN BALDRY

FRIDAY 23rd SEPT. ROYAL ALBERT HALL, LONDON 17/6 15/- 10/6 7/6 3/6 8.00 p.m. Box Office now open
SATURDAY 24th SEPT. ODEON THEATRE, LEEDS 15/- 12/6 10/6 8/6 6/6 6.00 p.m. and 8.30 p.m. Box Office now open
SUNDAY 25th SEPT. EMPIRE THEATRE, LIVERPOOL 15/- 12/6 10/6 7/6 5.40 p.m. and 8.00 p.m. Box Office now open
WEDNESDAY 28th SEPT. ABC THEATRE, ARDWICK, MANCHESTER 15/- 12/6 10/- 7/6 6.30 p.m. and 8.45 p.m. Box Office now open
THURSDAY 29th SEPT. A.B.C. THEATRE, STOCKTON 15/- 12/6 10/- 7/6 6.15 p.m. and 8.30 p.m. Box Office now open
FRIDAY 30th SEPT. ODEON THEATRE, GLASGOW 15/- 12/6 10/6 6.40 p.m. and 9.00 p.m. Box Office now open
SATURDAY 1st OCT. CITY HALL, NEWCASTLE-UPON-TYNE 15/- 12/6 10/6 8/6 6.15 p.m. and 8.30 p.m. Box Office now open A. E. COOK LTD 5, SAVILLE PLACE, NEWCASTLE-UPON-TYNE
SUNDAY 2nd OCT. GAUMONT THEATRE, IPSWICH 15/- 12/6 10/6 9/6 8/6 7/6 5.30 p.m. and 8.00 p.m. Box Office opens 12th Sept.
THURSDAY 6th OCT. ODEON THEATRE, BIRMINGHAM 15/- 12/6 10/6 8/6 6.45 p.m. and 9.00 p.m. Box Office opens 16th Sept.
FRIDAY 7th OCT. COLSTON HALL, BRISTOL 15/- 12/6 10/6 8/6 6/6 6.15 p.m. and 8.30 p.m. Box Office now open
SATURDAY 8th OCT. CAPITOL THEATRE, CARDIFF 15/- 12/6 10/6 8/6 6.00 p.m. and 8.30 p.m. Box Office opens 19th Sept.
SUNDAY 9th OCT. GAUMONT THEATRE, SOUTHAMPTON 15/- 12/6 10/6 8/6 6/6 5/6 6.00 p.m. and 8.30 p.m. Box Office opens 19th Sept.
POSTAL AND PERSONAL APPLICATIONS ONLY AT ALL BOX OFFICES, ALL ENQUIRIES TO TITO BURNS, c/o HAROLD DAVISON LTD, 235/241 REGENT ST. LONDON W1

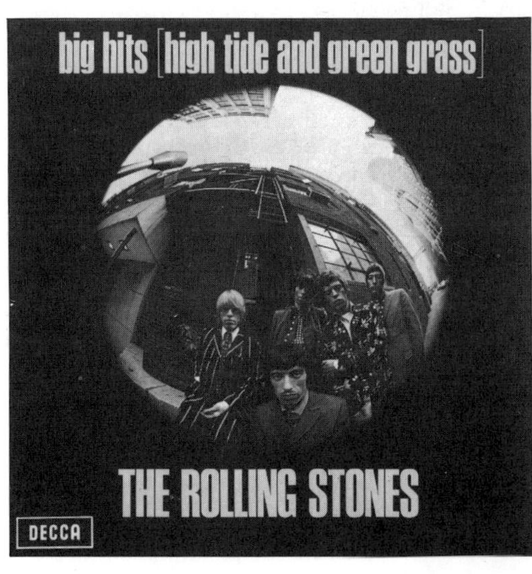

Left: *The cover photo by Jerry Schatzberg for 'Have You Seen Your Mother Baby, Standing In The Shadow'. Taken in New York's Central Park, the photo features, left to right, 'Flossie' (Brian), 'Milly' (Keith), 'Sara' (Mick), 'Millicent' (Charlie), and 'Penelope' (Bill) in the wheelchair.* Top right: Aftermath, *released in April 1966.* Centre right: New Musical Express *sets out the 1966 UK tour dates.* Right: *UK cover for the compilation album* Big Hits.

JANUARY
The Rolling Stones mix their new album at the London Olympic Studios.

JANUARY 13
A new single is released in Britain and America called 'Let's Spend The Night Together'/'Ruby Tuesday'. Written and composed by Mick Jagger and Keith Richard, and produced by Andrew Oldham, it was recorded at the Olympic Studios in London last Novemeber.
While appearing on the *Ed Sullivan Show* in New York to promote their new single, The Rolling Stones are forced to change the words from 'Let's Spend The Night Together' to Let's Spend Some Time Together'. Several US radio stations ban the record.

JANUARY 20
The new album is released in the UK, called *Between The Buttons*. All the tracks are written by Mick and Keith and produced by Andrew Oldham. Recorded at the Olympic Studios, London and RCA Studios, Los Angeles, in November and December 1966, the back of the album cover features drawings by Charlie Watts.
It is rumoured that one track, 'Miss Amanda Jones' is inspired by fashion moel Amanda Lear, a friend of Brian's. 'Let's Spend The Night Together' enters the UK charts at Number 17; it will stay in the charts for eight weeks with a highest position of Number 2. 'Ruby Tuesday' also goes in, at Number 29, remaining in the charts for twelve weeks, with a highest position of Number 22.

JANUARY 21
'Ruby Tuesday' enters the US charts at Number 78, and 'Let's Spend The Night Together' at Number 86. 'Ruby Tuesday' will reach Number 1 and stay in the charts for twelve weeks, whereas 'Let's Spend The Night Together' only makes Number 55, and is only in the charts for eight weeks.

JANUARY 22
The Stones appear on the TV variety Show *Sunday Night At The Palladium*. They mime to pre-recorded music and refuse to appear on the traditional roundabout of stars at the end of the show, causing a press sensation. The show's director says: 'They're insulting me and everyone else.'
Mick Jagger tells the *New Musical Express*: 'The only reason we did the show at the Palladium was because it was a good national plug - anyone who thought we were changing our image to suit a family audience was mistaken.'

JANUARY
Mick produces the new Chris Farlowe single, 'My Way Of Giving', written by Steve Marriott of the Small Faces, which will be released by Immediate. Mick also produces a version of 'Backstreet Girl' sung by Nicky Scott, on a single released by Immediate.

JANUARY 24
The Rolling Stones record more material at the Olympic Studios.

JANUARY 26
They pre-record for *Top Gear* (BBC radio).

JANUARY 27
Between The Buttons enters the British charts at Number 4. It will stay in the charts for eleven weeks, with a highest position of Number 3. *Between The Buttons* is released in America on London Records. The American version includes 'Let's Spend The Night Together' and 'Ruby Tuesday'.
Mick and Marianne Faithfull fly off to the South of France for a short holiday. Marianne Faithfull appears at the Italian Song Festival in San Remo.

FEBRUARY 2
Appearance on *Top Of The Pops*.

FEBRUARY 4
Mick Jagger and Marianne Faithfull attend the International Record and Music Publishing Market in Cannes. The Rolling Stones are nominated the best selling British act from 1 July 1965 to 30 September 1966, and receive a special award.
Brian Jones says: 'Our generation is growing up with us and they believe in the same things we do. Nearly all of them think like us and are questioning some of the basic immoralities which are tolerated in present

day society; the war in Vietnam, persecution of homosexuals, illegality of abortion, drug taking. All of these things are immoral. We are making our own statement, others are making more intellectual ones. We believe there can be no evolution without revolution. I realise there are other inequalities; the ratio between affluence and reward for work done is all wrong. I know I earn too much, but I'm still young and there's something spiteful inside me which makes me want to hold on to what I've got.'

FEBRUARY 5
The *News Of The World* reports that Mick Jagger took LSD at the Moody Blues' home in Roehampton; the same night, while appearing on Eamonn Andrews' TV show, Jagger announces he is suing the newspaper. The newspaper has in fact mis-reported almost a year later on a conversation a journalist had with Brian Jones in May 1966. According to the article, Mick is supposed to have said: 'I don't go much on it [LSD] now the cats have taken it up. It'll just get a dirty name. I remember the first time I took it. It was on our tour with Bo Diddley and Little Richard.' The article went on: 'Later at Blases, Jagger showed a companion and two girls a small piece of hash and invited them to his flat for "a smoke".' In Los Angeles, a radio station announces Mick Jagger's death in London.

FEBRUARY 7
Mick Jagger's libel suit is served against the *News Of The World*.

FEBRUARY 10
Mick Jagger, Keith Richard, Marianne Faithfull and Donovan, sit in on Beatles recording sessions in London.
Bill Wyman produces Hamilton and the Movement's first single 'I'm Not The Marrying Kind' written by Bill and Peter Gosling, released on Decca.

FEBRUARY 11
Between The Buttons enters the US charts, where it remains for 47 weeks, reaching a highest position of Number 2.

FEBRUARY 12
Fifteen police officers, armed with a warrant issued under the Dangerous Drugs Act, raid Redlands, Keith Richard's home at West Wittering, Sussex, during a weekend party. Mick Jagger, Keith Richard, Marianne Faithfull and other guests are searched and samples are taken away for tests.

FEBRUARY 19
The *News Of The World* carries a veiled report of the Redlands raid. No names are mentioned but it is headlined 'Drug Squad Raids Pop Stars' Party'.

FEBRUARY 23
Mick Jagger and Marianne Faithfull arrive eight minutes late at the Royal Opera House, Covent Garden, for the world premiere of Roland Petit's ballet, *Paradise Lost*, starring Rudolph Nureyev and Margot Fonteyn. This causes a scandal as the performance is in the presence of H.R.H. Princess Margaret.

FEBRUARY
As a result of the pressure building up due to the West Wittering bust, some of the Stones decide to go to Morocco. Keith Richard, Brian Jones, Anita Pallenberg and another girl called Deborah Dixon leave London by car. Keith says later: 'Everybody felt, "Oh, what a bring-down. Let's all go to Morocco, take a load off, and cheer up." '

MARCH 4
'Ruby Tuesday' reaches Number 1 in the USA. Mick flies to Morocco.
Brian Jones has written and composed the soundtrack for a movie starring his girlfriend Anita Pallenberg. It was recorded at the IBC Studios in London with the assistance of Mike Leander.

MARCH 6
On the way to Morocco through France, Brian has a serious asthma attack and is admitted to hospital in Alby in the South of France with 'respiratory trouble'. Keith Richard and Anita

Pallenberg continue their trip to Morocco. While Brian is in hospital Keith begins an affair with Anita.

MARCH 9
Marianne Faithfull flies from Naples to Tangier to join Mick. During their stay in Morocco, Cecil Beaton takes a now famous photograph of Mick.

MARCH 10
Brian Jones flies back to London from Nice, and goes into the West London Hospital. An official press release announces Brian's new role as film composer for Volker Schlondorff's film *Mord Und Totschlag* (A Degree of Murder) starring Anita Pallenberg. The film is chosen to be Germany's entry for the 1967 Cannes film Festival.

MARCH
Bill Wyman produces a single for the Moon's Train called 'Deed I Do'.

MARCH 15
Brian Jones flies to Morocco to rejoin Keith Richard, Mick Jagger, Anita Pallenberg and Marianne Faithfull in Marrakesh.

MARCH 16
While Brian is out recording ethnic Moroccan music, Anita, Keith, Mick and Marianne fly out of Tangier to Madrid from where they return to London, abandoning Brian without even leaving a note. This is the end of Anita's affair with Brian.

MARCH 18
Brian Jones returns to London from Morocco. The *Daily Mirror* reports: 'Two of the Rolling Stones pop group, Mick Jagger and Keith Richard, have been accused of offences against the drug laws. Summonses against the two men, both aged 23, were issued after a police raid on Richard's £20,000 farmhouse at West Wittering, Sussex. The summonses, due to be dealt at Chichester magistrates court on 10 May, are expected to be served next week. Two other men, not yet named, are also to be summoned.'

MARCH 25
The Rolling Stones open a three-week European tour in Orebro, Sweden.
The *Evening News* reports: 'Swedish Customs Officers have searched the Rolling Stones from head to toe for drugs. The pop group, arriving from Copenhagen, said they were delayed for nearly an hour as officers inspected sixteen pieces of luggage. ''They were looking for pot,'' said Mick Jagger, ''and they went through every bit of clothes we had, even our underclothes''.'

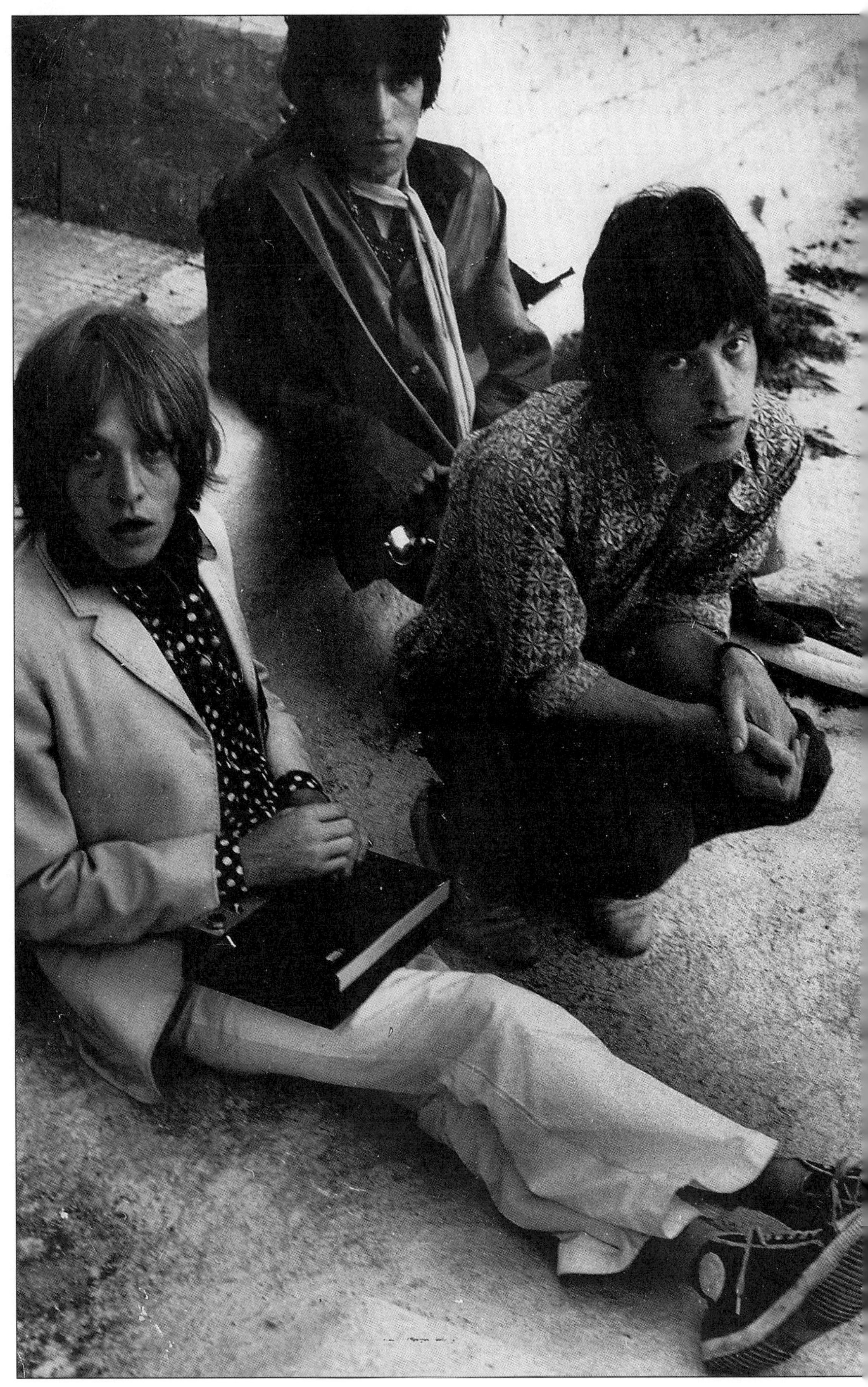

Left: *Backstage at the London Palladium.* Right: *Brian, Keith and Mick photographed in Morocco by Cecil Beaton.*

MARCH 26
Concert at Helsingborg, Sweden. 2,000 fans throw bottles, chairs and fireworks at the stage, and police use dogs and batons to stop the riot. Says Mick Jagger: 'Why do you have to hit girls on the head with batons?'

MARCH 29
Concert at the Stadhalle, Bremen.

MARCH 30
Concert at the Sporthalle, Cologne.

MARCH 31
Concert at the Westfalenhalle, Dortmund.

APRIL 1
Concert at the Ernst Merck-Halle, Hamburg.

APRIL 2
Concert at the Stadhalle, Vienna. Trouble starts when someone throws a smoke bomb - a riot breaks out and 154 Austrian fans are arrested.

APRIL 5
The Rolling Stones arrive in Italy and play at the Palazzo dello Sport, Bologna.

APRIL 6
Concert at the Palazzo dello Sport, Rome. Jane Fonda, Brigitte Bardot and Gina Lollobrigida are all in the audience.

APRIL 8
Concert at the Palazzo dello Sport, Milan. Girls try to storm the stage and fans throw sandwiches at Mick Jagger.
Olympic gold medallist Lynn Davies complains to the press about the Stones' behaviour in a German hotel: 'I felt sick and ashamed to be British as they poured out swear words at the breakfast table. They are tarnishing the name of their country in a foreign land'. Mick Jagger replies: 'The accusations are disgusting and completely untrue. We deny that we were badly behaved. I cannot remember when we have behaved better. We hardly used the public rooms in this hotel. They were crammed with athletes behaving very badly.'

APRIL 9
Concert in the Palazzo dello Sport in Genoa.

APRIL 10
As the Rolling Stones arrive in Paris, they are searched by Customs. Mick Jagger says: 'I feel as if I am being treated as a witch.'
Mick Jagger tells *Melody Maker*: 'Since the peak of the Beatles and the Rolling Stones there have been a lot of big groups but none with any real flair, except for the Who and the Jimi Hendrix Experience.'
About police and drugs: 'There are only about a thousand real addicts in Britain and nobody is going to make a fortune peddling heroin because the addicts can get it on

prescription. But if we stop this, the Mafia will move in and we're going to have the same problem as America.'

APRIL 11
Concert at the Paris Olympia. 200 policemen try to control more than 5,000 screaming fans but there are riots in the streets.

APRIL 12
Mick Jagger is punched by an airport official during a row at Le Bourget Airport. The Stones were being searched for drugs and it takes such a long time that they miss their flight to Warsaw, so Mick loses his temper. However, he comes off worst in the ensuing fracas. Eventually they get away for their first visit to Eastern Europe.

APRIL 13
In Warsaw police use batons and tear-gas to break up a crowd of 3,000 teenagers trying to storm the Palace of Culture, where the Rolling Stones are appearing. Hundreds of police, some wearing steel helmets, seal off the square, but when the Stones' bus draws into the square, trouble erupts. About 1,000 teenagers angry at not being able to get tickets for the concert, break down the crash barriers and charge the iron gates of the building. The police draw batons and wade into the crowd, then fire tear-gas, to be met by a barrage of bottles and stones. About 30 people are arrested, after which a crowd of about 2,000 tries to force its way into the building through an entrance at the other side of the square. After breaking up the crowd the police bring in two water cannons ready for the second performance.

APRIL 14
Concert at the Hallenstadion, Zurich, before an audience of 12,000.
Mick Jagger is thrown to the ground by a fan who breaks through a cordon of 300 policemen. The *Daily Mirror* reports: 'The youth hoisted himself onto a twenty foot high stage, specially built to keep fans at bay, and rushed Jagger from behind. He grabbed Jagger by the lapels of his floral jacket and flung him to the floor. Then he began jumping on the singer. Detectives rushed to Jagger's rescue but the Stones' road manager, Tom Keylock, yelled at them to stand aside. He waded in with an uppercut at the youth's jaw, and broke his hand.'

APRIL 15
A reasonably uneventful concert at the Hautreust Hall, the Hague.

Top left: *Mick arrives late for the ballet with his girlfriend, singer Marianne Faithfull, for whom he and Keith have written several songs. Their late arrival causes quite a stir at the Royal Opera House.* Left: *Mick and Brian on stage at the Paris Olympia in April 1967.*

APRIL 17
The Stones' concert in the Athens Football Stadium is the last of their European tour and they go on holiday. Brian flies to Cannes with Anita for the International Film Festival, later joined by Keith who drives across Europe for a week. Bill stays in Greece for a week, while Charlie and Mick fly to London.

APRIL 22
Mick says: 'It was our idea to go to Poland. I wanted the kids there to have the chance to listen to us. I think our records will be on sale in the East in a few years. I'd love to go to Leningrad... We shall never tour America again. It's very hard work and one bring down after another. You have no idea of how terrible it is unless you've been through it. Every place you go there is a barrage of relentless criticism, and after about the fourth week you just start lashing out.'

APRIL
Mick tells the *Daily Mirror*: 'I see a great deal of danger in the air... teenagers are not screaming over pop music any more, they're screaming for much deeper reasons. We are only serving as a means of giving them an outlet. Teenagers the world over are weary of being pushed around by half-witted politicians who attempt to dominate their way of thinking and set a code for their living. They want to be free and have the right of expression; of thinking and living aloud without any petty restrictions. This doesn't mean they want to become alcoholics or drug-takers or tread down on their parents. This is a protest against the system. I see a lot of trouble coming in the dawn.'

MAY
Bill Wyman produces a single for the Warren Davis Monday Band called 'Wait For Me', written by Bill Wyman and Peter Gosling. Mick produces a single for Chris Farlowe called 'Yesterday's Papers', written by Jagger and Richard and out on Immediate.

MAY 10
Mick, Keith and art gallery owner Robert Fraser, appear in court at Chichester, Sussex, to face drug charges relating to the raid at Keith's home, Redlands, in February. Released on £100 bail each, they are all remanded for trial at the West Sussex Quarter Sessions at Chichester on 22 June. The Stones' American manager Allen Klein attends the hearing.
On the same day, Brian Jones is arrested in his flat in South Kensington, and charged with possession of drugs. Brian and his friend Prince Stanislaus Klossowski are taken to Chelsea Police Station. Brian is remanded on £250 bail.

MAY 11
Brian Jones appears at Marlborough Street Magistrates' Court.

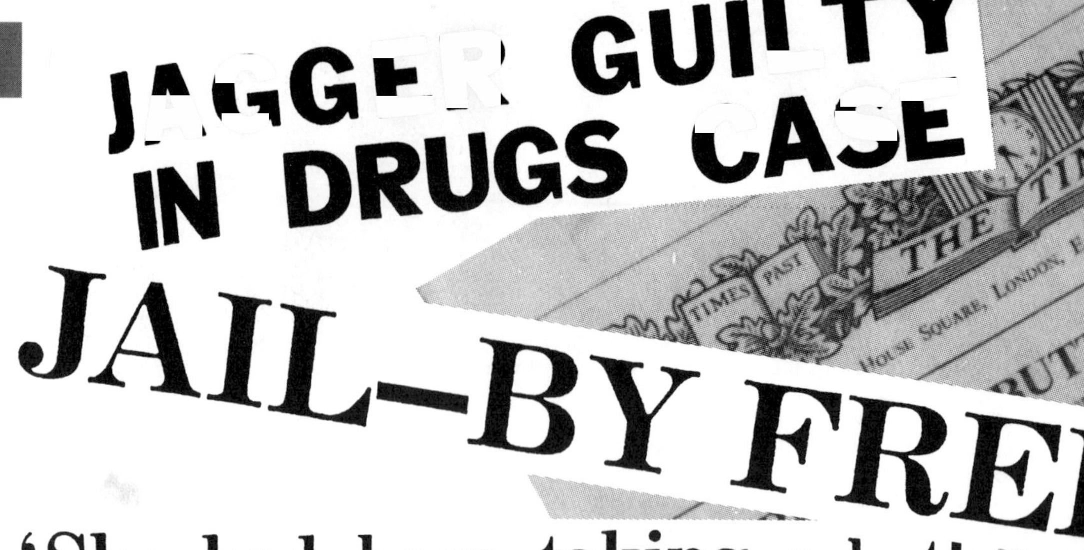

'She had been taking a bath when police arrived'

MICK JAGGER A
'MILANO DRUG

The police raid at Redlands, Keith's home in Sussex, in February 1967 erupted into a press free-for-all in June, as Mick and Keith are both found guilty of drugs-related offences and given prison sentences. These are later quashed on appeal. Above: *Mick and Keith on bail, pending appeal.* Right: *Mick leaving the court hearing in handcuffs.*

'NUDE GIRL AT STONES PARTY'

STONES

JAGGER IS ... D OVER DRUGS

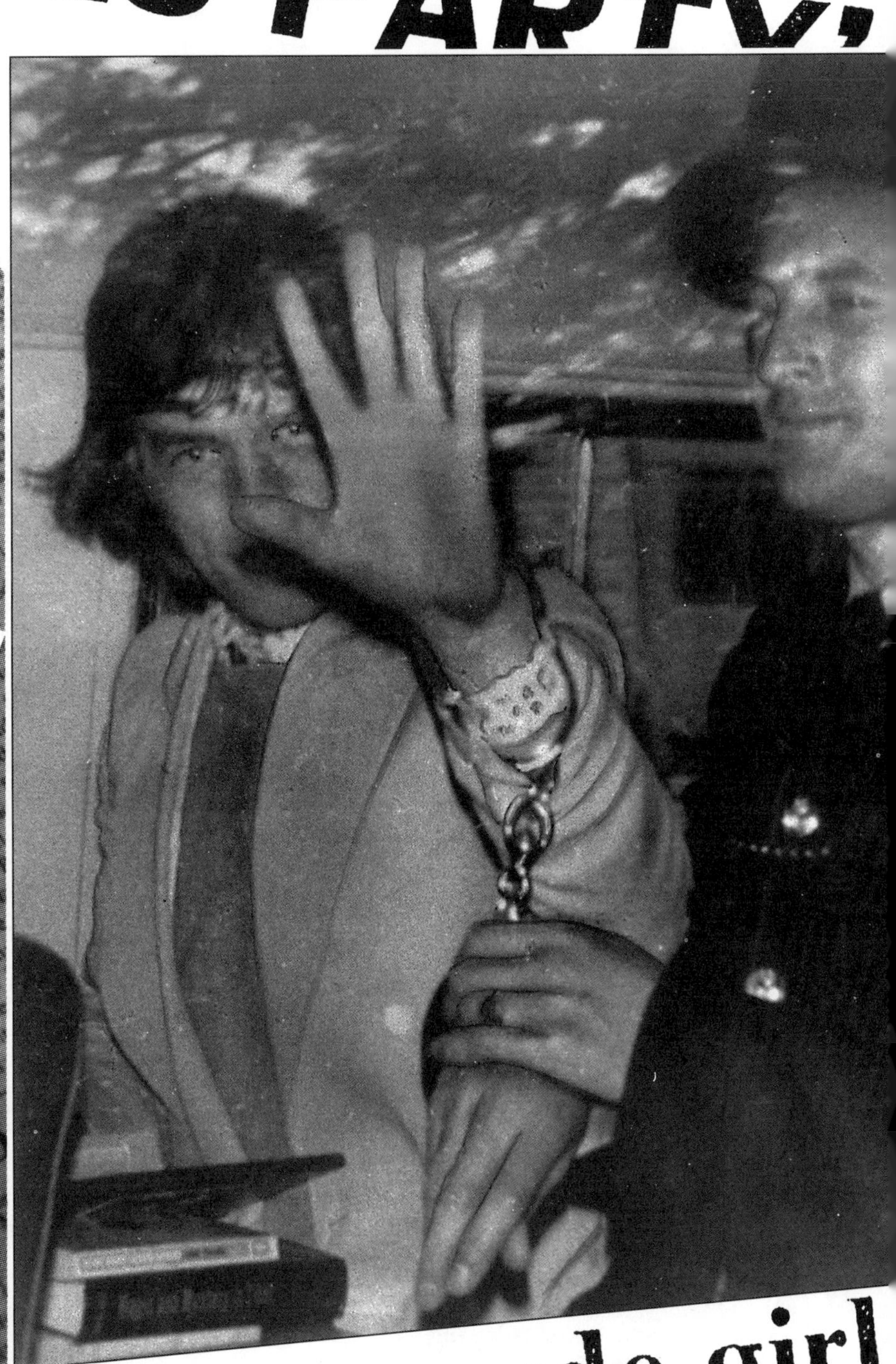

Keith Richard says nude girl came down from bath

MAY 12
Brian adds soprano saxophone to a Beatles track, 'Baby You're A Rich Man', at the Olympic Studios in London.

MAY 16-19
The Stones have four days of recording sessions at the Olympic Studios.

MAY 21
Mick Jagger appears on BBC TV's *Look Of The Week* with Professor John Cohen of Manchester University, to discuss the relationship between performers and audiences.

JUNE 3
Marianne Faithfull collapses on stage at the Royal Court Theatre in Sloane Square, London, during a performance of Chekov's *Three Sisters*.

JUNE 15
Mick and Keith add backing vocals to the Beatles' 'All You Need Is Love' at the Olympic Studios.

JUNE 16-18
Brian Jones goes to the Monterey Pop Festival in California. He introduces Jimi Hendrix's set.

JUNE
A new compilation album is released in America on London, called *Flowers*. Produced by Andrew Oldham, it features three previously unreleased tracks: 'My Girl', which was recorded on March 1966 at the RCA Studios in Los Angeles, 'Ride On Baby', and 'Sitting On A Fence', both recorded in December 1965 at the RCA Studios in Hollywood.

JUNE 27/28
The trials of Mick Jagger, Keith Richard and Robert Fraser take place at the West Sussex Quarter Sessions in Chichester Crown Court, under Mr Justice Block. Mick's case is heard first. He is accused of the possession of amphetamines; his defence is that he obtained them legally in Italy to overcome airsickness. The jury take five minutes to return a guilty verdict. Mick is held on remand in Brixton Prison to await his sentence (he is Prisoner Number 7856). He requests books on Tibet and modern art, and two packs of Benson & Hedges. Keith's charge is more serious - that of allowing drugs (cannabis) to be consumed on his premises. The prosecuting counsel says: 'That there was a strong, sweet, unusual smell in these premises will be clear from the evidence, and you may well come to the conclusion that the smell could not fail to have been noticed by Keith Richard.' It becomes clear during the trial that the *News Of The World* has played a major part in setting up the raid, particularly in planting a 'Mr X' as a spy - probably Keith's driver. There is also much innuendo about a certain 'Miss X' (it was no secret that this was Marianne Faithfull) whose presence, wearing nothing but a fur rug, is presented as 'evidence' of misconduct of some sort. Keith is also found guilty. Robert Fraser is found guilty of possessing heroin.
Keith is remanded to Wormwood Scrubs (Prisoner Number 5855). All three are brought back into the dock in Chichester together for sentencing. Judge Block says: 'The offence of which you have been properly convicted by the jury carries with it a maximum sentence of as much as ten years, which is a view of the seriousness of this offence which is taken by Parliament.' He then sentences Keith to one year in prison, plus £500 costs. Mick is sentenced to three months plus £100 costs, and Fraser to six months plus £200 costs.

JUNE 30
Mick and Keith are granted bail in the High Court for the sum of £7,000 each, pending appeal against their sentences. The *Evening Standard* reports: 'The Who consider Mick

Jagger and Keith Richard have been treated as scapegoats for the drug problem and as a protest against the savage sentences imposed upon them at Chichester yesterday, the Who are issuing today the first of a series of Jagger/Richard songs to keep their work before the public until they are again free to work before the public themselves. The Who's single features ''Under My Thumb'' and ''The Last Time''.'
Two fans are arrested when several of them protest outside the *News Of The World* offices in Fleet Street calling for the release of Mick and Keith. The police disperse the fans who scream: 'Free the Stones!' At Piccadilly Circus, fans meet around the statue of Eros demanding their release.

JULY 1
The Times publishes a leading article criticising the severity of the sentence passed on Mick Jagger. The article, headed 'Who Breaks a Butterfly on a Wheel?' (echoing the trial of Oscar Wilde) accuses the judiciary of treating Mick Jagger with severity just because he is famous. It concludes 'It should be the particular quality of British justice to ensure that Mr Jagger is treated exactly the same as anyone else, no better and no worse. There must remain a suspicion in this case that Mr Jagger received a more severe sentence than would have been thought proper for any purely anonymous young man.'

JULY 2
John Gordon writes in the *Sunday Express*: 'Was Jagger convicted of taking one of the evil drugs like heroin or cocaine? Or LSD with which some of the Beatles confess they have been experimenting? Not at all. Did he smoke marijuana which some experts say is evil but others, equally expert, say is not so evil? That wasn't alleged against him. He merely had four benzedrine tablets, legally purchased abroad, which, with the knowledge and approval of his doctor, he took to keep him awake while he worked.'

JULY 6
Brian is admitted to hospital suffering from nervous strain.

JULY 7
The Rolling Stones start a two-week recording session at the Olympic Studios, where they cut a new single and material for a new album.
The Beatles' single 'All You Need Is Love'/'Baby You're A Rich Man' is released. The A-side features Mick and Keith on vocals, plus Marianne Faithfull, the flip side features Brian on soprano saxophone.

JULY 12
Brian joins the other Rolling Stones in the studio.

JULY 20
The recording sessions end.

JULY 22
Flowers enters the American album charts, where it remains for 35 weeks, with a highest position of Number 2.

JULY 23
Brian flies to Marbella for a short holiday with Suki Potier and Nicky Browne, widow of Tara Browne who was killed in a car crash last year.

JULY 31
At the Appeal Court, Mick Jagger is given a conditional discharge, and Keith Richard's conviction for permitting his house to be used for the purpose of smoking cannabis resin is quashed. However the Appeal Judges remind Mick of his responsibilities as a pop idol.
At a press conference afterwards Mick says: 'I simply ask for my private life to be left alone. My responsibility is only for myself. I had prepared myself mentally, physically and business-wise for the possibility of going to jail. It felt lovely to be sure of freedom.'

Far left: *Mick and Keith at Redlands on their way to court in May 1967.* Left: *Mobbed by a crowd of 500 fans, Mick and Keith are helped to a waiting limousine in Chichester after electing trial by jury for drugs charges arising from the Redlands raid in February.* Above: *A compilation album entitled* Flowers, *released worldwide, except in the UK.* Right: *Brian emerges from the West London Court in June 1967 after being sent for trial at Inner London Sessions on drugs charges.*

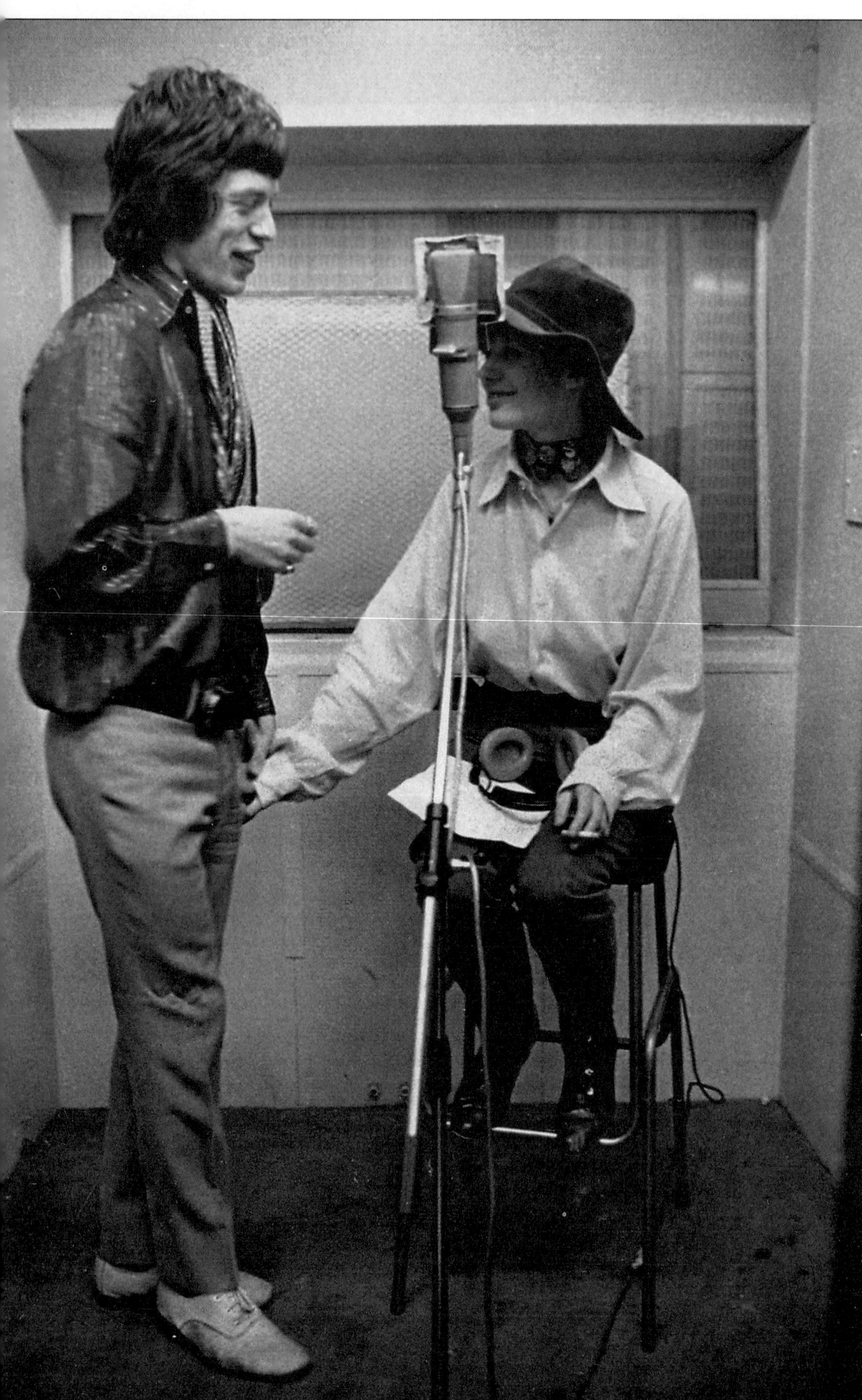

Mick appears on ITV's *World In Action* in a special discussion with William Rees-Mogg, editor of *The Times*, Lord Stow Hill, Dr John Robinson, the Bishop of Woolwich, and Father Thomas Corbishley, a leading Jesuit priest. Mick says: 'I am a rebel against society, but not an obvious one. Many people like me feel that things are wrong. Society has pushed me into this position of responsibility.'

AUGUST 1
The Times reports: 'The Court quashed the conviction of Keith Richard for permitting, as an occupier, his house at West Wittering to be used for the purpose of smoking cannabis resin, contrary to section 5 (1) of the Dangerous Drugs Act, 1965, because the chairman of West Sussex Quarter Sessions (Judge Block), did not warn the jury that there was only tenuous evidence which could make them sure that a girl at the house, dressed only in a rug, smoked cannabis resin and that Mr Richard must have known it.'

AUGUST 5
Mick produces two tracks for Marianne Faithfull, including the Beatles' 'When I'm 64'.

AUGUST 12
A new single 'We Love You' will be released on 18 August. The Rolling Stones have filmed a short promotional film but it is banned by the BBC, since Mick, Keith and Marianne Faithfull act scenes from *The Trials Of Oscar Wilde*.
Mick and Marianne go on holiday in Ireland.

AUGUST
The Rolling Stones start a week of recording sessions at the Olympic Studios.

AUGUST 18
'We Love You'/'Dandelion' is released in the UK and US.
Written by Mick Jagger and Keith Richard and produced by Andrew Oldham, the A-side was recorded in July at the Olympic Studios. 'Dandelion' was recorded in November 1966 in London. The single is intended as a 'thank you' from the Rolling Stones to their fans who supported them during the recent trials.
Rumours say that John Lennon and Paul McCartney appear as back-up vocals on 'We Love You'.
Press reports hint that Andrew Oldham may no longer produce the Rolling Stones' records, as their relationship is deteriorating.

AUGUST 25
'We Love You' enters the British charts at

Left: *Mick in the studio with Marianne Faithfull. During August 1967 he produced two tracks for her latest album.*

Number 13. It will stay in the charts for six weeks, with a highest position of Number 9.

AUGUST 26
Mick and Marianne join the Beatles on a visit to the Maharishi Mahesh Yogi's seminar at the Teacher Training College in Bangor, North Wales.

SEPTEMBER 1
Keith arrives from Rome where he was staying with Anita Pallenberg. Brian arrives from Marbella for a three day recording session.

SEPTEMBER 2
Mick says: 'I like entertaining... I suppose performing is an aid. It helps me as a person, as an individual, to get rid of my ego. It's a better process than others. If I get rid of the ego on stage, then the problem ceases to exist when I have left there. I no longer have a need to prove myself continually to myself.'

SEPTEMBER 3
Brian Jones announces he is applying for a pilot's licence.

SEPTEMBER 5-7
Recording sessions at the Olympic Studios, London. After the session Brian flies to Marbella and Keith to Rome.
Rumours say Mick is producing the new Marianne Faithfull single.

SEPTEMBER 8
Keith is granted permission to build a nine-foot high brick wall around Redlands.

SEPTEMBER 9
'Dandelion' enters the US charts at Number 74. It will stay in the charts for eight weeks with a highest positon of Number 14.

SEPTEMBER 14
Mick Jagger arrives in New York from Paris, while Brian, Keith, Bill and Charlie come from London. As they arrive at New York's Kennedy Airport, Mick and Keith are questioned by immigration officers. The following day they appear at the immigration offices on Broadway to answer further questions about their drug trials in England, but are later allowed to leave when the British authorities inform the officials of their successful appeals.

SEPTEMBER 16
'We Love You' enters the US charts at Number 86. It stays in the charts for six weeks, with a highest position of Number 50. The Rolling Stones discuss business in New York with Allen Klein and work on the cover of their new album.

Above: *Brian on holiday in Marbella with his Portuguese-born girlfriend, Suki Potier.*

SEPTEMBER 29
The Rolling Stones return from New York. After months of rumour and speculation, the Rolling Stones and their producer/manager Andrew Oldham part company. The Rolling Stones will produce all their future records themselves.

OCTOBER 1
Jewellery and furs belonging to Marianne Faithfull are stolen from Mick Jagger's Cheyne Walk flat.

OCTOBER 3
Keith's guard dogs are shot at and wounded for worrying local livestock.
The new album is tentatively titled *Cosmic Christmas*.

OCTOBER 5
Keith joins Anita Pallenberg in Rome.

OCTOBER 15
The *People* reports a proposed Beatles/Stones business venture: 'They are looking for new studios in London, probably to record unknown pop groups. And they may make films together. There is no question of the two pop groups merging.'
Bill applies for membership of the Royal Horticultural Society.

OCTOBER 17
An official press release from the Stones' office refutes the newspaper report: 'Mr Jagger states that preparatory conversations of a purely exploratory nature were held between him and Mr Paul McCartney... These conversations have not been resolved and any assumption to the contrary should be considered premature.'

OCTOBER 20
Brian flies to the Spanish Costa del Sol to relax before his court appearance.

OCTOBER 30
At the Inner London Sessions, Brian Jones admits possession of cannabis and allowing his flat to be used for the smoking of the drug. His plea of 'Not guilty' to a charge of possessing methedrine and cocaine is accepted. Brian is sentenced to nine months' imprisonment and taken to Wormwood Scrubs.

OCTOBER 31
Rolling Stones fans demonstrate in King's Road, Chelsea, for nearly two hours against Brian's sentence. Seven fans plus Mick Jagger's brother, Chris, are arrested and charged with obstructing the police and abusive behaviour. Brian Jones is released from Wormwood Scrubs on £750 bail pending an appeal. Brian will appear in court again in December.

NOVEMBER 1
A spokesman for the Rolling Stones says that they will continue as a four-member band for some time if Brian has to have medical treatment. Allen Klein says from New York: 'There is absolutely no question of bringing in a replacement.' Mick and Keith are in New York on business. The new album, now possibly titled *Her Satanic Majesty Requests And Requires*, will be released later this month. Chris Jagger and the other Stones fans appear at Marlborough Street Magistrates' Court charged with obstructing the police, abusive behaviour and damaging a police van. They are all released on £25 bail each.

NOVEMBER 12
The Rolling Stones' office issues a press release objecting to comments in a speech made by Judge Leslie Block at a dinner given by the Horsham Ploughing and Agricultural Society. He had been reported as saying, and did not deny in subsequent interviews, 'We did our best, your fellow countrymen, I, and my fellow magistrates, to cut these Stones down to size, but alas, it was not to be, because the Court of Criminal Appeal let them roll free.' He continued: 'I can only suppose that the Court of Criminal Appeal was influenced by the words of Shakespeare when he wrote his own epitaph in these words, "Blest be the man who spares these stones".' Leslie Perrin, on behalf of the Stones, questions the Judge's words in view of Brian's forthcoming appeal and asks whether the Stones can get an unbiased hearing as a result.

NOVEMBER 19
A new single, taken from the forthcoming album, is released in America on London Records. Called 'In Another Land'/'The Lantern', the A-side is written and sung by Bill Wyman, and the flip side is a Jagger/Richard composition. Both are produced by the Rolling Stones.

NOVEMBER 27
Their Satanic Majesties Request is released in America on London. Another single from the album is also released. 'She's A Rainbow'/'2,000 Light Years From Home', written by Jagger and Richard, was recorded earlier in the year at the Olympic Studios and is the first single to be produced by the Stones themselves. The album is also the first to be produced by the Stones, and is the first to feature a 3D picture sleeve, manufactured in New York at a cost of more than £10,000. All tracks are by Jagger and Richard, except 'In Another Land'. It was recorded at the Olympic Studios and Bell Sound in London. In America, the album goes gold before its release, grossing $2,000,000 in its first ten days on sale.

DECEMBER 2
The Rolling Stones have nearly completed plans to open their own TV and recording studio in London. They plan to shoot their first film next February.

DECEMBER 8
Their Satanic Majesties Request is released in Britain.

Allen Klein assists Mick and Keith when they are questioned by US immigration officers in New York, about their UK drug convictions.

DECEMBER 9
Brian says of the new album: 'Yes, of course the album is a very personal thing. But the Beatles are just as introspective. You have to remember that our entire lives have been affected lately by socio-political influences. You have to expect these things to come out in our work'.

DECEMBER 12
Brian Jones appears in court. His prison sentence is set aside when three psychiatrists describe him as 'an extremely frightened young man', (with suicidal tendencies, asserts one). Brian gets three years' probation and a £1,000 fine instead. Lord Justice Parker says to him: 'Remember, this is a degree of mercy which the court has shown. It is not a let-off. You are still under the control of the court. If you fail to co-operate with the probation officer, or you commit another offence of any sort, you will be brought back and punished afresh.' Probation officer William Hornung says: 'I will not treat him as a celebrity. To me, Brian Jones is the same as any other offender who has been placed on probation.' The Rolling Stones are voted best British R&B group of the year in the *New Musical Express*, and second British vocal group.

DECEMBER 14
Brian collapses and is rushed to St George's Hospital, London. A doctor reports: 'There is no cause for alarm. He is just tired and suffering from over-strain. He has also had some teeth out.' *Their Satanic Majesties Request* enters the British charts at Number 10. It will stay in the charts for nine weeks, with a highest position of Number 3.

DECEMBER 16
Rumours report that the Rolling Stones will form their own label called 'Mother Earth', to be distributed by Decca. It is said that Mick Jagger will supervise and produce all material and that Marianne Faithfull will be the first artist to sign with them. *Their Satanic Majesties Request* reaches Number 2 in America, where it remains for six weeks, with a total of 30 weeks in the charts.
Mick and Marianne Faithfull will spend Christmas in South America.

DECEMBER 27
Proceeds from US sales of *Their Satanic Majesties Request* now exceed $2,500,000.

DECEMBER 30
'She's A Rainbow' enters the US charts at Number 77. It will stay in the charts for seven weeks, with a highest position of Number 25.

Right: *Mick and Marianne at a party in Kilkenny Castle, Ireland, while they were staying with members of the Guinness family.* Inset: *This back cover photo for* Their Satanic Majesties Request *was reproduced in 3D on some versions.*

NINETEEN 68

JANUARY 4
At the University of California in Los Angeles, students taking music degrees must now study the Rolling Stones, as one of the music professors feels they have made an important contribution to modern music.

JANUARY 20
Brian is in a London recording studio with Paul McCartney, contributing saxophone on a track to be included in a solo album by Paul's brother Mike McGear, formerly with the Scaffold. The LP will be released in 1971 by Warner brothers, called *Mike McGear*.

JANUARY
Mick Jagger produces a track for P.P. Arnold, called 'Though It Hurts Me Badly', released on Immediate Records.

FEBRUARY 28
Brian Jones spends his 26th birthday in Paris. It is announced that American Jimmy Miller is the Rolling Stones' new producer. He is invited to produce several tracks for their new album. Jimmy Miller says: 'Mick contacted me and said he likes the things I did with Traffic. *He* had been producing the Rolling Stones but he says he doesn't want to be on two sides of the control room window now.'

MARCH 8
Bill Wyman produces a single for the End, called 'Shades Of Orange'/'Loving Scared Loving' (both Wyman/Gosling compositions).

MARCH 9
Mick Jagger says: 'We're rehearsing because we've forgotten how to do it. We've forgotten how to put the plugs in the amplifier. We're just having a good time.'

MARCH 15
The Rolling Stones cut material for a new album at the Olympic Studios in London, with Jimmy Miller.

MARCH 16
Brian Jones' girlfriend, Linda Keith, collapses in her flat in Chesham Place, Belgravia.

MARCH 17
A second session at the Olympic Studios with Jimmy Miller. During the night, Charlie Watts learns that his wife Shirley is in labour.

MARCH 18
A daughter, Serafina, is born to Charlie and Shirley Watts.

APRIL
The Rolling Stones continue to work on their new album until 18 April.

APRIL 20.
Mick Jagger and Marianne Faithfull holiday in Ireland.

APRIL 28
The Rolling Stones tape three promotional films for their new single.

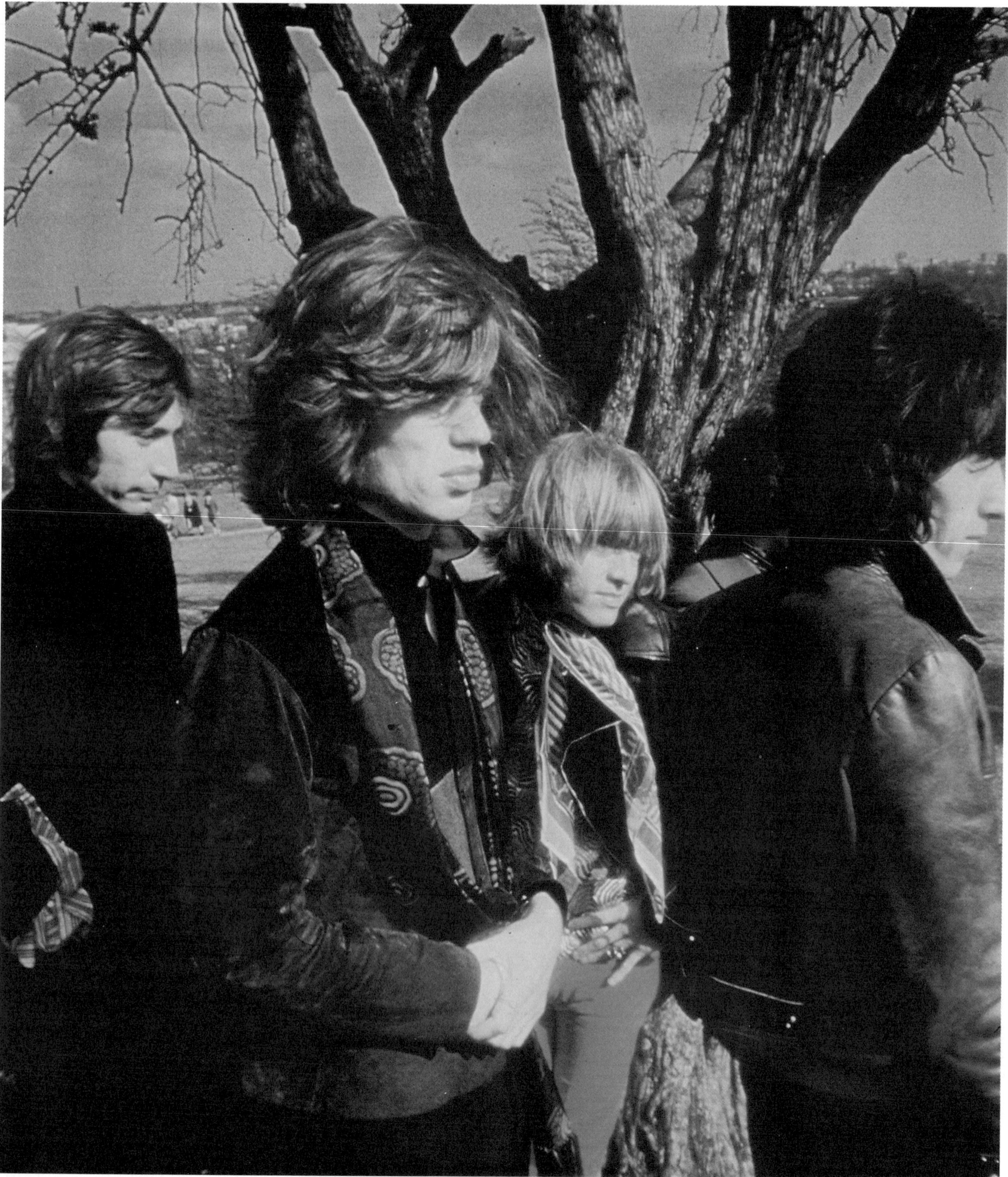

MAY 11
It is officially announced that Mick Jagger will star opposite James Fox in a film called *The Performers*, to be directed by Nicholas Roeg and Donald Cammell. Anita Pallenberg will also appear in the film, for which shooting will start in mid-July, and Mick Jagger will write the soundtrack music.

MAY 12
The group plays at the *New Musical Express* Poll Winners' concert at the Empire Pool, Wembley. Mick Jagger says afterwards: 'It was just like old times. In fact, it was better than old times. One of the best receptions we have ever had. We were all delighted.'
The performance is covered by Southern TV for the programme *Time For Blackburn*.

MAY 13
The Rolling Stones are in the Olympic studios again to work on the new album.

MAY 17
Mick Jagger in *IT (International Times)*: 'Many lyrics in pop music are very good, at least as good as the popular lyrics of the last century.'

MAY 21
Brian Jones is arrested again and charged with possessing cannabis at his flat in Royal Avenue House, King's Road, Chelsea. He appears at Marlborough Street Magistrates' Court and is remanded for three weeks on £2,000 bail. Brian Jones denies the charge.

MAY 25
'Jumpin' Jack Flash'/'Child Of The Moon' is released by Decca. Both tracks are by Jagger and Richard and it is the first Stones single produced by Jimmy Miller and recorded at the Olympic Studios in London.

MAY 29
'Jumpin' Jack Flash' enters the British charts at Number 12. It will stay in the charts for ten weeks, reaching the Number 1 spot.

JUNE 1
The Rolling Stones reveal that their new album is to be called *Beggars' Banquet* and will be released on 26 July. Charlie Watts says: 'You can't bring back an era that is dead. If the Beatles went back to Liverpool now there would be no need to cordon off blocks to prevent the thousands of fans getting at them. The times have changed and it's going to be a long time before they change again.'

Top right: Melody Maker *announces the new single 'Jumpin' Jack Flash' and Mick's acting debut.* Centre right: *The banned cover for* Beggars' Banquet. *The record was re-released in 1984 with this original sleeve design.* Bottom right: *Front page prominence in the* Record Mirror.

JUNE 5
The Rolling Stones begin work on Jean-Luc Godard's film, *One Plus One*. Mick Jagger says: 'We are very excited about this. We have been great admirers of Godard's work for a long time, and have a great respect for him.'

JUNE 8
'Jumpin' Jack Flash' enters the US charts at Number 63. It will stay in the charts for twelve weeks, also reaching the Number 1 position.

JUNE 11
While the Rolling Stones are in the Olympic Studios in Barnes shooting an all-night session for *One Plus One*, the studio catches fire at 4.15am. The Stones, Marianne Faithfull, Godard and his film crew have to be evacuated from the building. Firemen soon get the blaze under control and the studio only suffers minor damage. Mick Jagger says: 'The fire brigade was so thorough that our Hammond organ and all the electrical equipment was completely drenched.'
Brian Jones is committed for trial at the Inner London Sessions.

JUNE 14
It is announced that Mick Jagger will start working on his first film, now retitled *Performance*, on 29 July.

JUNE 19
'Jumpin' Jack Flash' reaches Number 1 in the UK.

JUNE 22
A message from the Rolling Stones to their fans appears in the *New Musical Express*: 'Dear readers of NME. Jumpin' Jack Flash is really gassed that he made Number 1. So are the Rolling Stones. Thank you. We are slaving over a hot album which is coming out next month. Until then...'

JUNE
The Rolling Stones tape three tracks at Keith's home, Redlands.

JULY 7
Mick Jagger, Keith Richard, Marianne Faithfull, Anita Pallenberg and Jimmy Miller fly to Los Angeles for the final mix of the new album.

JULY 8
Charlie Watts and Shirley join Mick and Keith in Los Angeles.

JULY 16
Mick Jagger will now start work on *Performance* in mid-September due to the Rolling Stones' recording commitments. He is working on the album sleeve design with Tom Wilkes of A&M Records. Mick Jagger will stay in Los Angeles until the end of the

month. *Beggers' Banquet* will be released next September and not later this month as previously announced.

JULY 20
Immediate records releases a Chris Farlowe single featuring 'Paint It Black', produced by Mick Jagger.

JULY 23
'Jumpin' Jack Flash' reaches Number 1 in the US charts. Mick Jagger goes to a Doors concert in Hollywood, and to the following party with Jim Morrison. Brian Jones is on holiday with his girlfriend Suki Potier in Morocco, where he tapes some local music.

JULY 26
The Rolling Stones release their new single in America. Taken from the forthcoming album, it is called 'Street Fighting Man'/'No Expectations', written by Jagger and Richard and produced by Jimmy Miller, and released by London Records. Mick Jagger is 25 today.

AUGUST 3
Mick Jagger and Marianne go on holiday in Ireland.

AUGUST 17
Rumours circulate in London that Eric Clapton will join the Rolling Stones later in the year, when Cream disbands.

AUGUST 24
The sleeve of the new Stones album is the subject of a dispute between the band and their record companies. The cover shows a lavatory wall inscribed with graffiti which Decca and London say would cause offence, and they refuse to release it.

SEPTEMBER 3
'Street Fighting Man' is banned in Chicago after the recent riots at the Democratic Convention there.

SEPTEMBER 4
Mick Jagger says: 'I'm rather pleased to hear they have banned ''Street Fighting Man'', as long as it's still available in the shops. The last time they banned one of our records in America, it sold a million.'

SEPTEMBER 5
Giant billboards advertising *Beggars' Banquet* have been erected in London, Manchester and Birmingham, in spite of the dispute over the album sleeve. Mick Jagger says: 'We have

---

Top left: *French film director Jean-Luc Godard (centre) meets Bill and Mick on the set of* One Plus One (Sympathy For The Devil). Left: *Supported by Keith, Mick and Suki Potier, Brian emerges from court with a fine after being found guilty of possession of cannabis.* Right: *David Bailey's 1968 portrait of the Stones.*

tried to keep the cover within the bounds of good taste. I mean we haven't shown the whole lavatory. That would have been rude... I don't think it's offensive. And I haven't met anyone, apart from two people at the record company, who finds it offensive. I even suggested that they put it out in a brown paper bag with "Unfit for children" and the title of the album on the outside, if they felt that bad about it.' Keith Richard says: 'The job of the record company is to distribute. All they've got to do is put it in the shops, not dictate to people what they should or should not have.' Producer Jimmy Miller adds: 'There's nothing really wrong with it. It all seems so silly to me.'

SEPTEMBER 7
'Street Fighting Man' enters the US charts at Number 84. It only reaches Number 48 with six weeks in the charts.

SEPTEMBER
Bill Wyman produces an album for the End, called *Introspections*, released on Decca. Charlie Watts appears on the album, together with Nicky Hopkins.

SEPTEMBER 12
Mick starts work on *Performance* in London. On the same evening the film *Girl On A Motorcyle*, starring Marianne Faithfull and Alain Delon, is premiered in London. It causes a press sensation as Marianne appears in one scene totally nude.

SEPTEMBER 14
Mick Jagger says of the disputed cover: 'No, we did not deliberately go out to produce a cover of this kind for "sensationalism" or to offend "Them". It was simply an idea that had not been done before and we chose to put the writing on a lavatory wall because that's where you see most writing on walls. There's really nothing obscene there except in people's minds.' Keith Richard says of 'Street Fighting Man': 'The fact that a couple of American radio stations in Chicago banned the record just goes to show how paranoid they are. Yet they want us to make live appearances. If you really want us to cause trouble we could do a few stage appearances. We are more subversive when we go on stage.'

SEPTEMBER 21
It is announced that the Rolling Stones will star in a major film, *Maxigasm*, to be made in Hollywood and directed by Carlo Ponti. Work will begin in late December in North Africa. Mick Jagger is reportedly to play the main role, supported by Brian and Keith, together with Anita Pallenberg and Marianne Faithfull.

Top left: *The Stones in rehearsal for* The David Frost Show. Left: *The album* Beggars' Banquet *is launched with a mock medieval banquet.*

'Jumpin' Jack Flash' is voted best single of the year by *Melody Maker* readers.

SEPTEMBER 26
Brian Jones is fined £50 with £105 costs at Inner London Sessions after being found guilty of possessing cannabis. He says: 'It's great not to be in jail. I was sure I was going to jail for at least a year. I never expected that I would be going home. It was such a wonderful relief... This summer has been one long worry to me. I knew I was innocent, but everything seems to happen to me.'
Mick Jagger, Keith Richard and Brian's girlfriend Suki Potier attend the hearing. Mick Jagger says: 'We are pleased that Brian didn't have to go to jail. Money doesn't matter.'

OCTOBER 3
The *Daily Mail* reports that the Rolling Stones have lost their battle over the sleeve design of their new album, which has delayed its release for over three months. Mick Jagger says: 'I don't find it at all offensive. Decca has put out a sleeve showing an atom bomb exploding. I find that more upsetting.'

OCTOBER 4
Marianne Faithfull reveals she is expecting a baby. Mick Jagger comments: 'I'm happy about Marianne having our baby. It's real groovy. We'll probably have another three. But marriage? Can't see it happening. We just don't believe in it.' Marianne says: 'Why should we marry? We've got along fine together so far. The baby is not going to change the way we feel about each other.'

OCTOBER 12
Instant Records releases the soundtrack album of *Tonite Let's All Make Love In London*, which features interviews with Mick Jagger and Andrew Oldham among others. The movie of the same name was produced last year by Lorrimer Films, and includes the Rolling Stones, Mick Jagger, Michael Caine, Vanessa Redgrave, Julie Christie, Lee Marvin, Eric Burdon and the New Animals, Donyale Luna and Pink Floyd. Mick Jagger says in *Rolling Stone*: 'Pop concerts are just gatherings of people who want to have a good time and I don't really think they have a higher meaning... On record we can be quite musical, but when you get to the stage, it's no virtuoso performance. It's a rock'n'roll act, a very good one, but nothing more.'
Mick appears on *The David Frost Show* on TV.

OCTOBER
Immediate Records releases *Blues Anytime*, an album featuring Jimmy Page, Eric Clapton, Mick Jagger, Bill Wyman and Ian Stewart.

Right: *The 'Beggars' Banquet' at the Kensington Gore Hotel soon degenerates into slapstick as foam custard pies are liberally distributed.*

NOVEMBER 1
Mick Jagger says: 'The visual impact of the Rolling Stones is one of the most important parts. The song ''Jumpin' Jack Flash'' was made a hit by the film we did to promote it. Straight performance, nothing else, no freakin' about on the heath and that whole trip. That was what really helped the record, made it commercial, 'cos it was shown all over the world.'

NOVEMBER 9
Mick Jagger and Decca executives work on a compromise sleeve for *Beggars' Banquet*, showing an invitation card. The album will be released this month in America and in early December in Britain. Mick Jagger admits that he has lost interest in the situation concerning the sleeve: 'It is an unnecessary loss of time.' All the Stones go to the Tiny Tim concert at the Royal Albert Hall in London.

NOVEMBER 11
Mick finishes working on *Performance*.

NOVEMBER 17
Mick Jagger appears on Radio 1's *Top Gear* in an interview with John Peel. Mick reveals that the Rolling Stones have plans to undertake a major world tour. He says: 'We may possibly do some shows in January round the world, with the last few in Europe, finishing up in the mother country.'

NOVEMBER 19
Marianne Faithfull is admitted to a North London nursing home.

NOVEMBER 20
Marianne loses her baby at five and a half months of pregnancy. Mick Jagger says: 'Marianne has lost the baby following pregnancy complications. She is all right, but we are both very upset.'

NOVEMBER 21
Brian Jones buys Cotchford Farm, once owned by A. A. Milne. The house is near Hartfield, Sussex.

NOVEMBER 27
Rumours report that the Rolling Stones may split up, on the grounds that Mick Jagger is more interested in films than music and Brian is reported to be working with an advertising agency founded by himself. *Beggars' Banquet* is released in the US on London Records.

NOVEMBER 29
Premiere of *One Plus One* at the London Film Festival.

The Rolling Stones' Rock'n'Roll Circus. Top left: *Bill Wyman, Pete Townshend, Keith Moon and Charlie Watts watch the set building* and below: *John Lennon, Yoko Ono, Keith, Mick, Brian and Eric Clapton.*

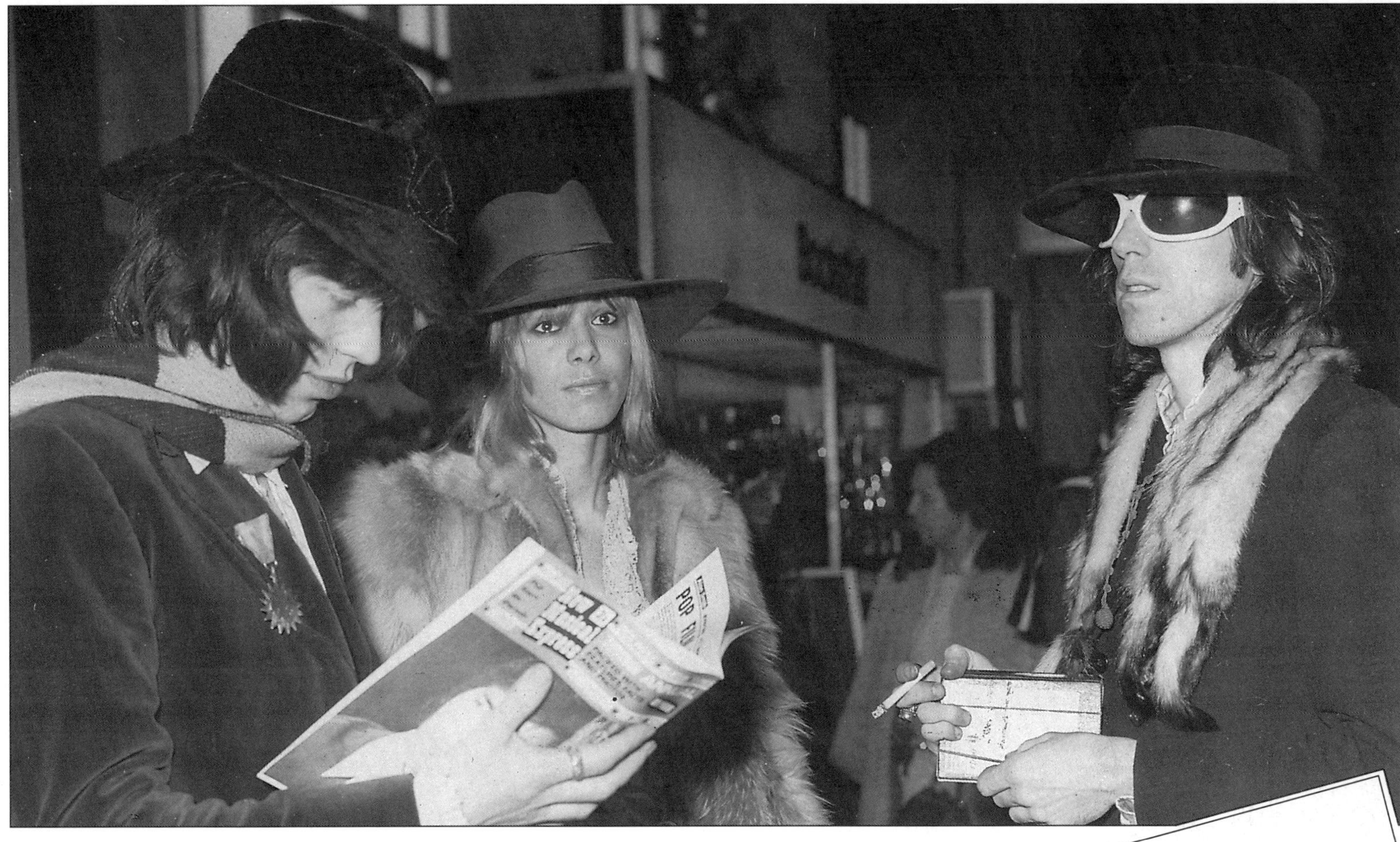

DECEMBER 4
The Rolling Stones appear on *The David Frost Show*.

DECEMBER 5
Beggars' Banquet is released in the UK on Decca. All tracks are written by Mick Jagger and Keith Richard and were recorded at the Olympic Studios in London, and produced by Jimmy Miller. A lunch party is held in the Elizabethan Rooms at the Kensington Gore Hotel in London. Guests include Les Perrin, Lord Harlech, Decca executives, reporters and various 'beautiful people'. The lunch ends with all concerned being pelted with comic custard pies. *Beggars' Banquet* enters the US charts.

DECEMBER 7
The Rolling Stones are voted best British R&B band of the year in the *New Musical Express* Pop Poll.

DECEMBER 8
The *Sunday Express* reports that Mick Jagger and Keith Richard are off to Rio de Janeiro to consult a magician. Keith says: 'We have become very interested in magic and we are very serious about this trip. We are hoping to see this magician practise both white and black magic. He has a long and difficult name which we cannot pronounce. We just call him ''Banana'' for short.'

DECEMBER 11
Beggars' Banquet enters the British Albums Top 20 at Number 3, its highest position. It will stay in the charts for twelve weeks.

DECEMBER 12
The Rolling Stones' TV show *The Rock'n'Roll Circus* is shot at the Intertel Studios, Wembley, with the Who, Eric Clapton, John Lennon, Yoko Ono, Mitch Mitchell, Taj Mahal, Marianne Faithfull, Jethro Tull and black fashion model Donyale Luna.

DECEMBER 17
Beggars' Banquet reaches Number 2 in the US album charts, its highest position. It will stay in the charts for a total of 26 weeks.

DECEMBER 18
Mick Jagger, Keith Richard, Marianne Faithfull and Anita Pallenberg leave for Brazil. Keith Richard is 25 today. Mick starts writing the soundtrack for the film *Performance*, using a synthesiser.

Above: *Mick, Keith and Anita at Heathrow Airport on their way to Rio de Janeiro.*

Rolling Stones
Beggars Banquet

Sympathy for the Devil
No Expectations
Dear Doctor
Parachute Woman
Jig-Saw Puzzle

Street Fighting Man
Prodigal Son
Stray Cat Blues
Factory Girl
Salt of the Earth

Written by Mick Jagger and Keith Richard
Produced by Jimmy Miller
Recorded at Olympic Studios
Engineers Glyn Johns, Eddie and Gene
All selections Mirage Music Ltd
We are deeply indebted to Nicky Hopkins and to many friends

DECCA

NINETEEN 69

JANUARY 4
Brian Jones is said to be 'furious' at several hotel managers in Kandy on the island of Ceylon (now Sri Lanka) who have refused him accommodation. They have accused him of being a penniless beatnik'. Wearing a tight-fitting pink suit and a psychedelic scarf, Brian pulls out a bundle of banknotes as he tells journalist: 'I am not a beatnik. I work for my living. I have money and I do not wish to be treated as a second class citizen.'

JANUARY 8
The *Daily Sketch* reports: 'Mick Jagger and Keith Richard have been barred from an exclusive hotel for wearing ''op art'' pants and nothing else. They were asked to leave the Hotel Crillen in Lima, Peru, after refusing the manager's pleas to change clothes. Last night the two Rolling Stones were staying in the equally exclusive Hotel Bolivar.'

FEBRUARY 1
Mick Jagger says: 'We chose Jimmy Miller because unlike so many other record producers he does not have an ego problem.'
Keith says: 'Subversive, of course we're subversive. But if they really believe you can start a revolution with a record they are wrong.'

FEBRUARY 22
Marianne Faithfull's new single is released on Decca. Called 'Something Better'/'Sister Morphine', it is credited to Jagger, Richard and Faithfull, and is produced by Mick Jagger.

MARCH
Early in the month the Rolling Stones go back into the Olympic Studios in London to cut a new LP.
During the month it is announced that Mick is providing the soundtrack music for a Kenneth Anger movie called *Invocation Of My Demon Brother*.

MARCH 8
Jimmy Miller: 'The Rolling Stones are easy to work with. They know what they're after but it sometimes takes days to get it right. Mick Jagger sees just what he wants and won't settle for anything less.'
Marianne Faithfull: 'My relationship with Mick Jagger is very important. What he gives me doesn't matter. It is enough that he gives.'

MARCH 29
Mick Jagger: 'I don't think I shall live to a very old age anyway. I've always had that feeling. But if you can stop your body falling apart, you've won half the battle. Degeneration of a physical nature is half the problem.'

APRIL
Mick Jagger and Keith Richard are on holiday in Rome and Positano where they collaborate on new tracks. Later in the month the Stones

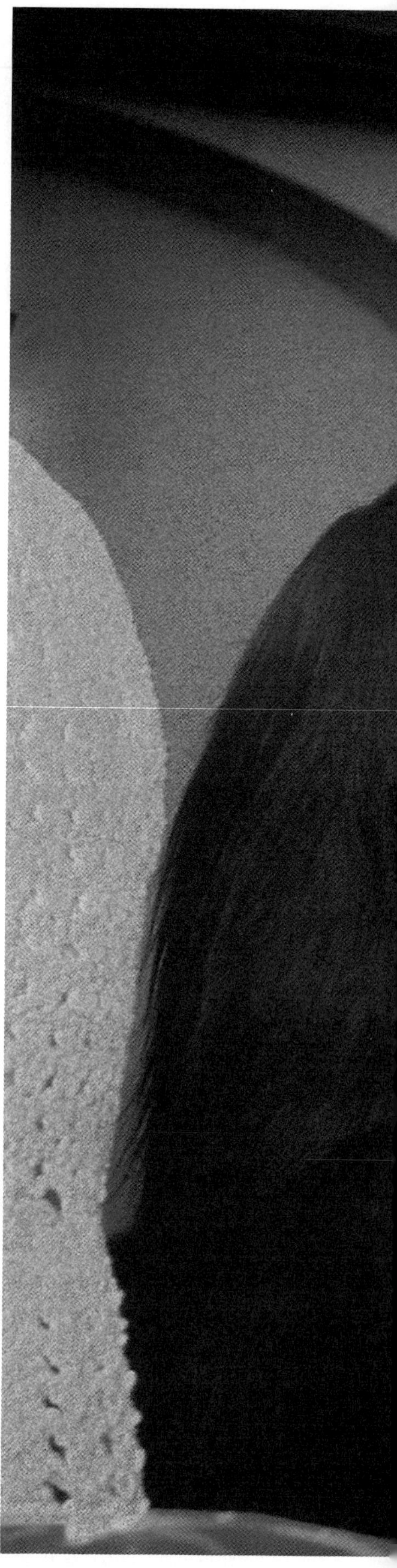

are back at the Olympic Studios.

MAY 24
It is announced that Mick Jagger and Marianne Faithfull are to star in *Ned Kelly* to be made on location in Australia. Shooting will start in July.

MAY 28
Mick Jagger and Marianne Faithfull are arrested for possession of cannabis resin following a police raid on Jagger's house in Cheyne Walk, Chelsea. They are taken to Chelsea police station and released on £50 bail. Mick says: 'The police, about six or seven of them, arrived at about a quarter to eight, just after Marianne and I had our tea. They were in the house for about an hour. We went in my car, not a police car.'

MAY 29
Mick and Marianne appear at Marlborough Street Magistrates' Court where they are remanded until 23 June.

JUNE 4
The *Evening Standard* reports that more than 500 people have already signed a petition in Glenrowan, near Melbourne, Australia, protesting against the casting of Mick Jagger in the role of the Australian folk hero, Ned Kelly, who made his last stand at this settlement.

JUNE 7
Keith Richard and Anita Pallenberg are involved in a car crash near Keith's home in Sussex. Anita, seven months pregnant, breaks her collar-bone and is taken to hospital in Chichester. No other cars are involved, but their car is a write-off.

JUNE 8
After a meeting with the other members of the group at Cotchford Farm, Brian Jones parts company with the Rolling Stones.
Jagger explains: 'Brian wants to play music which is more to his taste rather than always playing ours. So we decided that it's best that he's free to follow his own inclinations. We've parted on the best of terms. Obviously friendships like ours don't break up just like that.'
Brian says: 'The Rolling Stones' music is not to my taste any more - I want to play my own kind of music. Their music has progressed at a tangent to my own musical tastes.'

JUNE 10
A virtually unknown guitarist named Mick Taylor is to replace Brian Jones; a photo session is arranged in Hyde Park to introduce him.

JUNE 14
Mick Taylor: 'I was invited to do a session with the Rolling Stones. It puzzled me. I had never met Mick Jagger in my life and here he was phoning me. I went down and played on some tracks and thought little more about it. Then they asked me if I wanted to be a Stone. I was amazed. I said I'd love to be a Stone and that was that.'
Mick Jagger: 'He doesn't play anything like Brian. He's a blues player and wants to play rock'n'roll, so that's okay.'
Later Taylor admits: 'I just assumed I was the best guitarist available at the time.'

JUNE 16
The Rolling Stones tape a session for David Frost's TV series.

JUNE 21
Mick Jagger: '*The Rock'n'Roll Circus* was done ages ago and has never been seen. It'll probably be shown in the autumn to coincide with the album. It'll blow your mind, baby. TV is so appallingly bad, this is just what it needs.'

JUNE 24
The Stones rehearse at the Beatles' Apple Studios.

Left: *Keith and Anita in Rome, where she was working for a time, partly in order to escape from the problems she was having with British immigration authorities. Anita would give birth to their son, Marlon, in September 1969*

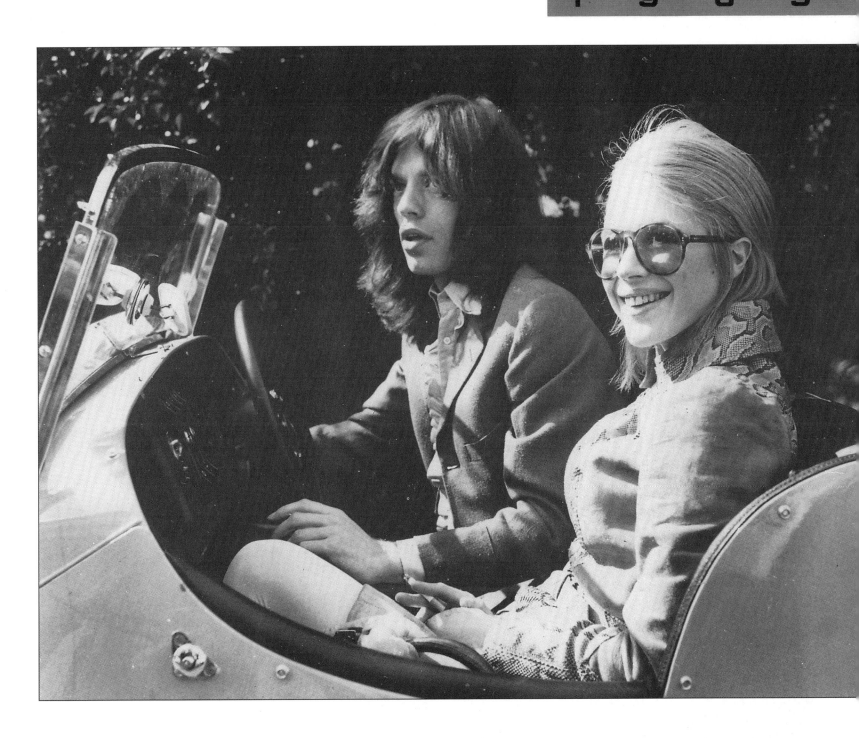

JUNE 28
Apple releases a Billy Preston single 'That's The Way God Planned It', produced by George Harrison and featuring Keith Richard on guitar.

JULY 1
The hearing of drug charges against Mick and Marianne is adjourned until 29 September.

Above: *Mick and Marianne, (wearing a characteristic snakeskin blouson) outside their house in Cheyne Walk, Chelsea in May 1969 en route to Marlborough Street Magistrates Court to face charges of possessing Marijuana. They were remanded until 23 June.*

JULY 2-3
Shortly after midnight Brian Jones is found at the bottom of the swimming pool at his home, Cotchford Farm. His Swedish girlfriend Anna Wohlin, a nurse, gives mouth to mouth resuscitation while Frank Thorogood, a builder renovating the house, and his friend Jenny Lawson, another nurse, call an ambulance. By the time the doctor arrives Brian Jones is dead. He was 27. At the inquest in East Grinstead, Anna Wohlin says: 'He suffered from asthma and hay fever and always carried an inhaler.' She had been living with him for six weeks. Jenny Lawson: 'I attempted conversation but his speech was somewhat garbled. I didn't think either Frank or Brian were in a fit condition to swim. I felt very strongly about this and mentioned it to both of them. They disregarded my warning and I saw Brian climb onto the diving board. He was a bit unsteady on his feet and Frank had to help him... I left him swimming for a few minutes but when I returned I saw him lying face-down at the bottom of the pool. Frank had gone into the house to fetch a towel.'
Frank Thorogood: 'Brian had some difficulty on the springboard but he swam quite normally.'
Dr Albert Sachs, of the Royal Victoria

Hospital, East Grinstead who conducted the Post Mortem reported: 'For a man of his age, his heart was a bit bigger than it should have been. It was fat and flabby. His liver was twice the normal weight. It was in an advanced state of fatty degeneration and not functioning properly. I could find no evidence microscopically that he had had an attack of asthma. His urine contained 1,200 microgrammes of an amphetamine, which indicated he'd had a fairly large quantity of the drug.' The coroner's verdict on the death was that Brian Jones drowned while under the influence of alcohol and drugs. That night the other Stones were in the studios working on new tracks, one of which was 'I Don't Know Why'.

After wild rumours about murder, Keith Richard tells *Rolling Stone* two years later: 'There was no one there that would want to murder him. Somebody didn't take care of him. And they should have done, because he had somebody there who was supposed to take care of him.. Everyone knew what Brian was like, especially at a party. Maybe he did just go in for a swim and have an asthma attack. I never saw Brian have an attack although I know he was asthmatic. He was a good swimmer. He was a better swimmer than anybody else around me. He could dive off rocks straight into the sea. He was really easing back from the whole drugs thing. He wasn't hitting them like he had been, he wasn't hitting anything like he had. Maybe the combination of things, it's one of those things I just can't find out. We were completely shocked. He was a goddamn good swimmer and it's just very hard to believe he could have died in a swimming pool... It's the same feeling with who killed Kennedy. You can't go to the bottom of it.' Anita Pallenberg agrees: 'They think he was really down but he was really up.'

JULY 4

Mick Jagger counters rumours that the Stones' Hyde Park concert will be cancelled saying, 'Brian would have wanted it to go on. We will now do the concert for him. I hope people will understand that it's because of our love for him that we are still doing it.'

The Rolling Stones appear on *Top Of The Pops* to mark the release of their new single 'Honky Tonk Woman'/'You Can't Always Get What You Want'. It is written by Mick Jagger and Keith Richard, produced by Jimmy Miller and recorded at the Olympic Studios in London.

The *Daily Mirror* reports that two of Brian's former girlfriends are planning to claim against his estate (estimated at about £150,000). Pat Andrews and Linda Lawrence, who both have sons (Mark aged seven and Julian aged five) by Brian, complain that they have had little or no support for their children. Pat Andrews says: 'All we have received is 50 shillings (£2.50) a week from Brian under the court order and we are

HOW BRIAN JONES WAS DESTROYED
Brian Jones Dies in Pool; Was 'Rolling Stones' Star
BRIAN JONES DIES IN POOL TRAGEDY
Rolling Stone Jones Found Dead in Pool
BRIAN JONES–WASTED LONG BEFORE I GOT THERE
BLACKHILL ENTERPRISES
IN ASSOCIATION WITH
THE ROLLING STONES
Photographer
PRESS
NON TRANSFERABLE
DESIGNED AND PRINTED BY BLUE EGG LTD. 01-586-2595
HYDE PARK
JULY 5 1969

Above: *Only three weeks after being replaced in the Rolling Stones by Mick Taylor, Brian Jones drowns in his swimming pool at Cotchford Farm, Sussex. Sacked because he was in no fit state to tour, Jones was apparently pulling himself together at the time of his death.*

having to live in a London hostel because we have no other money.' Linda Lawrence's father says: 'Brian made a settlement of £1,000. But this only paid some bills he left behind.'

JULY 5
The Rolling Stones play before an audience of around 300,000 in Hyde Park as a tribute to Brian Jones. The concert is filmed for worldwide distribution. Mick Jagger: 'I am just so unhappy about Brian's death. I am so shocked and wordless and so sad. Something has gone. I really lost something. I hope he is finding peace.'

JULY 8
In Sydney, Australia, Marianne Faithfull collapses in her bedroom at the Chevron Hotel. She is taken unconscious to St Vincent's Hospital where she will spend five days in a coma. She is replaced in *Ned Kelly* by Diane Craig. Marianne Faithfull is reported as having suffered from a drugs overdose.
'Honky Tonk Woman' enters the British charts at Number 15, and the US Top 100 at 79. It will stay in the UK charts for thirteen weeks, with five weeks at Number 1, and in the US it stays in the charts for sixteen weeks, with four weeks at Number 1.

JULY 9
It is announced that Bill and Diane Wyman are divorced.

JULY 10
Brian Jones is buried in his home town of Cheltenham. Canon Hugh Hopkins, Rector of the church where Brian once sang as a choirboy, read Brian Jones' own epitaph: 'Please don't judge me too harshly.' Bill Wyman, Keith Richard and Charlie Watts attend the funeral.
Later Pete Townshend wrote and recorded a personal tribute to Brian at Eel Pie Island Studios. The track has never been released:
'I used to play my guitar as a kid
Wishing that I could be like him
But today I changed my mind
I decided I don't want to die
But it was a normal day for Brian
Rock'n'Roll that's the way
It was a normal day for Brian
A man who died every day.'

JULY 13
Mick starts work on *Ned Kelly* on location around Melbourne, Australia.

JULY 23
'Honky Tonk Woman' reaches Number 1 in the UK.

Right, top and bottom: *Before 300,000 people on 5 July 1969, Mick Jagger reads a poem by Shelley to dedicate the free open-air concert in Hyde Park to Brian Jones who died two days previously.*

AUGUST
Keith Richard joins the line-up of George Harrison, Eric Clapton, Ginger Baker, Klaus Voorman and Doris Troy on Billy Preston's album *That's The Way God Planned It*, produced by George Harrison.

AUGUST 9
Mick Jagger: 'We really must finish *The Rock'n'Roll Circus* soon.'

AUGUST 10
A son, Marlon, is born to Anita Pallenberg and Keith Richard at King's College Hospital.

AUGUST 12
'Honky Tonk Woman' reaches Number 1 in the US.

AUGUST 18
Mick Jagger is accidentally shot in the hand while handling a gun on the set of *Ned Kelly*. Doctors say the injury is not permanent. He is back at work within a few days.

SEPTEMBER 1
Charlie Watts admits: 'I don't know what happened about *The Rock'n'Roll Circus*. We liked it except for our bit in it. We wanted to reshoot our scenes in the Coliseum in Rome, the first circus the world ever knew. But they got frightened off in Rome.' Mick Jagger explains: 'I never expanded the Rolling Stones into an Apple because I'm just not interested in being a businessman. I wouldn't get any satisfaction out of creating a Mary Hopkin.'

SEPTEMBER 2
Through The Past Darkly (Big Hits Volume 2) is released in America on London. Produced by Andrew Oldham and Jimmy Miller, the LP is dedicated to the memory of Brian Jones. Granada TV's film *Stones In The Park* is broadcast.

SEPTEMBER 12
Through The Past Darkly (Big Hits Volume 2) is released in the UK on Decca.

SEPTEMBER 13
Big Hits Volume 2 enters the US charts, grossing more than $1,000,000 in two weeks. It stays in the charts for 32 weeks, with a highest position of Number 2.

SEPTEMBER 14
Immediate releases a Chris Farlowe album called *The Last Goodbye* featuring an unreleased track titled 'Looking For You' produced by Mick Jagger.

Brian Jones' funeral. Left: *Leaving the church in Cheltenham are Canon Hugh Hopkins, Brian's parents, sister and ex-girlfriend Suki Potier.* Top left and right: *A floral tribute from Mick and Marianne who were unable to attend as they*

SEPTEMBER 17
Big Hits Volume 2 enters the British charts at Number 14 and stays in the charts for sixteen weeks reaching a highest position of Number 1.

SEPTEMBER
Mick Jagger finishes filming on *Ned Kelly* and flies from Sydney to Indonesia for a two week holiday.

OCTOBER
Decca releases a limited edition of 200 copies of *The Promotional Album* specially made for radio stations. The album covers the Rolling Stones' output from 1963 to date, including the track 'Love In Vain' from their forthcoming album.

OCTOBER 7
In East Berlin at least 50 youths are arrested by police when it is rumoured the Rolling Stones are playing on the roof of a building owned by millionaire publisher Axel Springer, which overlooks the Berlin Wall. A riot erupts as police move in to disperse the crowds.

OCTOBER 16
Mick Jagger arrives in London from Indonesia.

OCTOBER 17
The Rolling Stones fly to Los Angeles to work on the upcoming American tour and mix the new album. Mick and Keith are guests on an estate near Laurel Canyon with Stephen Stills; Bill Wyman and Mick Taylor stay at the Beverly Wilshire while Charlie Watts and family rent a mansion previously owned by the Du Pont family overlooking Sunset Strip which the group uses as its headquarters while on the West Coast.

OCTOBER 28
The Rolling Stones rehearse in Warner Brothers' studios and Stephen Stills' basement. They also cut material for the new album at Elektra Studios which they intend mixing before the tour begins.

NOVEMBER 1
In spite of adding a fourth concert at Madison Square Garden and a second at the Los Angeles Forum, the tour is a complete sell out within hours of tickets going on sale.

NOVEMBER 7
The Stones open their sixth American tour at the State University, Fort Collins, Colorado.

---

were in Australia to shoot Ned Kelly. Right top: *The poster for the 1969 US tour which highlights the influence of Art Nouveau on late-sixties graphics.* Far right, top and bottom: *The unusual octagonal cover and sleeve for the Stones' second compilation album,* Through The Past, Darkly.

NOVEMBER 8
Concert at the Los Angeles Forum with an audience of 18,000 that grosses the Stones $230,000 breaking the venue's previous record established by the Beatles in 1966. It is now clear the tour will gross more than $2,000,000. In the *San Francisco Chronicle* Ralph Gleason complains of the high ticket prices. 'Are the Rolling Stones really able to use all that money? If they really admire black musicians as much as every note they play, every note they sing would indicate, wouldn't it be possible to make a show with, say Ike and Tina Turner and one of the old persons like Howlin' Wolf and give a share to them? How much can the Rolling Stones take to England after the deduction of taxes? How much profit do the British manager, the American manager and the agency have to make?'

NOVEMBER 9
Concert at the Oakland Coliseum. The *Daily Express* reports: 'The Rolling Stones on their first American tour for three years relax on a hot Sunday afternoon in a closely guarded ranch-style mansion near Hollywood. A dreamy-eyed little blonde admirer in a maxi length knitted dress saunters by as the group pose for cameraman Terry O'Neill. "Get your clothes off and get into the picture," says head Stone, Mick Jagger, with all the enthusiasm of a man ordering a British Railways cup of tea. The young lady promptly obliges...'
The Management of the Royal Albert Hall in

London refuses to accept the Rolling Stones' booking for a major concert on their return from the US. The Stones will now play two shows at the Saville Theatre on 14 December and two more at the Lyceum Ballroom on 21 December. The new album, titled *Let It Bleed* and not *Sticky Fingers* as previously reported, will be released on 28 November. Advance sales mean that even before it is issued it is already certified gold in the US. With both *Big Hits Volume 2* and 'Honky Tonk Woman' also certified gold, this gives the Stones three gold discs within two months.

NOVEMBER 10
Concert at the Sports Arena, San Diego.

NOVEMBER 11
Concert at the Coliseum, Phoenix, Arizona. 'Honky Tonk Woman' is voted the record of the year in BBC Radio One's European Pop Jury.

NOVEMBER 13
Concert at the Moddy Coliseum, Dallas. *Michael Kohlhass - Der Rebell*, a film directed by Volker Schlondorff, opens at London's New Victoria cinema. For his role in the film Keith Richard has had to cut his hair for the first time in two years. Anita Pallenberg also has a role in the film. Warner Brothers' studio executives are reported as describing Nicholas Roeg and Donald Camell's *Performance* as 'unintelligible'.

NOVEMBER 14
Concert at the Coliseum, Auburn, Alabama.

NOVEMBER 15
Concert at the University of Illinois.

NOVEMBER 16
Concert at the International Amphitheatre, Chicago.

NOVEMBER 17-23
Apart from one date at the Los Angeles Forum on 20 November, the Stones take a

Above: *Mick Taylor joins the line up in a publicity photo for the American fan club.* Left: *The brilliant album cover for* Let It Bleed. Right: *Mick at the Los Angeles Forum, November.*

week off to cut new tracks at the Muscle Shoals Studios, Alabama.

NOVEMBER 24
Concert at the Olympia Stadium, Detroit.

NOVEMBER 25
Concert at the Philadelphia Spectrum.

NOVEMBER 26
Concert at the Baltimore Civic Center.

NOVEMBER 27
Two shows at Madison Square Garden. Leonard Bernstein joins them backstage.

NOVEMBER 28
Another two concerts at Madison Square Garden. Jimi Hendrix goes backstage. All four shows have been recorded for live material and filmed for a rock documentary. Each show has grossed $100,000 and it is estimated that 55,000 New Yorkers have seen them. During this current tour the Rolling Stones have broken attendance records at every arena they've played. They have also broken all records for fastest sellout time. At a press conference they announce they will play a free open air concert in San Francisco on 6 December as a 'thank you' to their American fans. In the meantime another Stones album *Rolling Stones Now* originally released in 1965 is certified gold. The new album *Let It Bleed* goes on sale in the States. All tracks are written and composed by Mick Jagger and Keith Richard with the exception of 'Love In Vain' an old blues number by Woody Payne. The album, which features both Mick Taylor and the late Brian Jones, is produced by Jimmy Miller and recorded last Spring in London at the Olympic Studios.

NOVEMBER 29
Concert at the Boston Garden.

NOVEMBER 30
Concert at the International Raceway, Palm Beach, with an audience of 55,000. The right wing John Birch Society fail in their attempt to stop the show, claiming it will corrupt the moral character of youth.

DECEMBER 5
Let It Bleed is released in Britain on Decca. The Rolling Stones fly to San Francisco.

DECEMBER 6
At the Altamont Speedway, Livermore, California the Rolling Stones give a free open air concert before more than 500,000 fans. Traffic jams build up for twenty miles in all directions. The Stones arrive by helicopter. The concert is being filmed and Santana, Jefferson Airplane, the Flying Burrito Brothers, Crosby Stills Nash and Young appear as supporting acts. Hell's Angels have been engaged as guards and paid with beer but, unable to control the crowd they resort

SAN JOSE

to violence and by the time the Stones arrive on stage they go berserk and are beating fans with billiard cues. As the group go into 'Under My Thumb' eighteen-year-old Meredith Hunter tries to jump onto the stage, a Hell's Angel pulls a knife and right in front of the Stones the black youth is stabbed to death. It is claimed he pulled a gun, but it is never found. After a brief interruption the show goes on. Two fans are killed when a Plymouth convertible runs through the crowd. Both victims are 22. Another fan, under the influence of drugs, falls into an irrigation channel and drowns. A girl has her ankle broken as a Hell's Angel rides his motorbike into the crowd near the stage. At least twenty serious accidents are reported. Nineteen doctors and six psychiatrists treat hundreds of people for injuries and drug overdoses. Festival promotor Rock Scully, manager of the Grateful Dead who suggested employing the Hell's Angels says: 'The Rolling Stones signed the contract. They've got what they paid for. Let it bleed, man!' *Rolling Stone* reports: 'Altamont was the result of diabolic egoism and, most of all, a lack, a fundamental lack of humanity.' Two years later Keith Richard is to add: 'One really got the feeling that they really wanted to suck you out.'

Altamont is the final date of the Rolling Stones' American tour.

Let It Bleed enters the US charts. It will stay in the charts for nineteen weeks, reaching a highest position of Number 2. In the UK, it will reach the Number 1 spot, with sixteen weeks in the charts.

DECEMBER 8

Keith Richard and Charlie Watts arrive back in London. Anita Pallenberg tells Keith that the Home Office has given her an ultimatum, either to marry or get out of England. They have been holding her Italian passport since July when they turned down a request for an extension to her visa. Anita says: 'It's just like living in a police state. It's disgraceful. I'm not going to get married just to suit them.' Keith agrees. 'I refuse to get married because some bureaucrat says we must. Rather than do that I would leave Britain and live abroad. But if I want to continue to live in England, and if that's the only way Anita can stay, we will marry, but I don't know when.'

Bill Wyman and Mick Taylor stay on in America for a few days while Mick Jagger flies to Switzerland on business. He admits: 'I don't really like singing very much. I'm not really a good enough singer to enjoy it, but I am getting into it a little bit. I enjoy playing the guitar more than I enjoy singing and I can't play the guitar either. But I know that if I keep on playing guitar, I can get better, whereas I can't improve much as a singer.'

Left: *Hell's Angels bludgeon a young black man, Meredith Hunter, to death with billiard cues in front of the stage during the free show at the Altamont Speedway.* Top right: *Mick winds the Altamont audience into a frenzy.* Right: *A promotional copy of 'Satisfaction'.*

DECEMBER 11

Marianne Faithfull who, with her son Nicholas, has been staying in Rome during the American tour with film producer Mario Schifano, meets up with Mick at London's Heathrow airport.

DECEMBER 14

The Rolling Stones give two shows at the Saville Theatre.

DECEMBER 18

Keith Richard on Altamont: 'I thought the show would have been stopped, but hardly anybody seemed to want to take any notice. The violence just in front of the stage was incredible. Looking back I don't think it was a good idea to have the Hell's Angels. But the Grateful Dead who've organised these shows before thought they would be the best. I believe the alternative would have been the Black Panthers. I wouldn't like to say whether they would have been more vicious.' On Brian Jones: 'There are some people you know aren't going to get old. There was a friend of Brian's and mine called Tara Browne who died about three years ago and, at the time, Brian and I agreed that he, Brian, wouldn't live very long either. I remember saying "You will never make thirty, man", and he said "I know".'

On drugs: 'Even though I was foolish enough to get caught and in doing so advertised the fact that I smoked pot, I feel no responsiblilty for what anybody else may do with their bodies or what they may put into them.'

DECEMBER 19

Mick Jagger is fined £200 plus 50 guineas (£50 + 50 shillings) costs at Marlborough Street Magistrates' Court for being found in possession of cannabis resin. Marianne Faithfull is acquitted.

DECEMBER 21

The Rolling Stones play two Christmas shows at the Lyceum Ballroom in the Strand. Fans are covered with artificial snow as they enter.

JANUARY 15
A bootleg Rolling Stones album, illegally recorded live at the Oakland Coliseum during the recent US tour, is circulating in America. Called *Liver Than You'll Ever Be,* it is the first Stones bootleg.

JANUARY 20
The Stones have a mobile recording studio built into an articulated truck, known as 'the Mighty Mobile'.

JANUARY 31
It is reported that the Rolling Stones have filed a £4,580,000 law suit against Sears Point International Raceway for breach of contract and fraud, claiming they had to move at the last moment to Altamont Raceway nearly 40 miles away for the disastrous concert on 6 December 1969.
A Stones spokesman subsequently denies this: 'The festival promoters may be suing, but the Rolling Stones are not involved.'

FEBRUARY 7
A track from *Let It Bleed* called 'You Got The Silver' will be included in the soundtrack of *Zabriskie Point,* directed by Michelangelo Antonioni, to be released by MGM.

FEBRUARY
Transatlantic Records release an album called *The People Band,* produced by Charlie Watts, and featuring Charlie Watts and eight session musicians.
In London, the Stones mix live tracks at the Olympic Studios, recorded during the recent American tour.

MARCH 2
London Records files a suit in the British High Court, claiming $1,000,000 damages against four Hollywood stores for selling the bootleg, *Liver Than You'll Ever Be.*

MARCH 9
The bootleg album of the Oakland Coliseum concert is being imported into England in large quantities. The Mechanical Copyright Protection Society and Essex Music take legal steps to ban its sale.

MARCH 14
The Rolling Stones announce their European tour which will start in The Hague on 8 May and after fourteen shows in seven countries will end in Helsinki on 7 June.

APRIL
The Flying Burrito Brothers' new album *Deluxe,* features a version of 'Wild Horses'.

MAY
The British press report that Brian Jones was in debt to the tune of $400,000 when he died. His assets are put at $75,000. A spokesman for the Rolling Stones says that vast sums in royalties are due to the estate.
Bill Wyman and Charlie Watts appear on Leon Russell's first album, *Leon Russell.*

JUNE 8
Detective-Sergeant Robin Constable issues a writ claiming he has been libelled in a statement made by Mick Jagger to Scotland Yard.

JUNE 18
Allen Klein is discussing a new Rolling Stones recording deal.

JUNE 24
Ned Kelly is premiered at the London Pavilion. The soundtrack is released today on Liberty. Mick sings a number called 'Wild Colonial Boy'.

JUNE 28
A note book, a guitar and clothes are stolen from Mick's Bentley parked in Chelsea.
It is rumoured that Polydor are to distribute Rolling Stones' records in Europe and Atlantic Records in the US. Mick Jagger is reportedly dating American actress Patti D'Arbanville.

JULY
The Stones cut tracks for the new album at the Olympic Studios in London, and in the Mighty Mobile.

JULY 11
It is rumoured that Warner Brothers plan to shelve *Performance.* The studio claim it is because Jagger's cockney accent is too thick, that it is unintelligible to an American

THE ROLLING STONES
EUROPEAN TOUR 1970
A SBA PRESENTATION
Design John Pasche

audience. The truth however is that they are concerned at the highly contentious drug element in the film. They are contractually committed to a charity premiere in aid of the drug charity 'Release'.
The album, provisionally called *Get Your Ya Yas Out*, is now ready but is not released as their contract with Decca is about to run out.

COMING SOON
MICK JAGGER
AS "NED KELLY"
A film by TONY RICHARDSON Color by DeLuxe®
GP ALL AGES ADMITTED Parental Guidance Suggested
Original motion picture score available on United Artist Records
United Artists
Entertainment from Transamerica Corporation

JULY 20
Decca release a new single in the UK, called 'Street Fighting Man'/'Surprise Surprise'.

JULY 28
Premiere of *Ned Kelly* in Glenrowan, near Melbourne, Australia.

JULY 30
The Rolling Stones start legal proceedings against Allen Klein: 'Neither he, ABKCO Industries Inc, nor any other company have any authority to negotiate recording contracts on their behalf in the future.'

JULY 31
The Stones' contract with Decca expires, but before they are actually released from the contract they have to deliver one more song. They comply with this condition and present Decca with 'Cocksucker Blues'. Decca are shocked by its crude lyrics and the track is never released.

AUGUST 15
The Rolling Stones are to launch their own record label to be headed in the States by Marshall Chess with Trevor Churchill handling the London end.

AUGUST 19
Mick Jagger on *Ned Kelly*: 'That was a load of shit. I only made it because I had nothing else to do. I knew Tony Richardson was a reasonable director and I thought he'd made a reasonable film. The thing is, you never know until you do it whether a film will turn out to be a load of shit and if it does all you can say is, ''Well, that was a load of shit,'' and try to make sure you don't do anything like it again.'
On marriage: 'I don't envisage a time when I shall ever get married and settle down. I might have kids and I might get married, but I'll never settle down. I'm not the type.'

AUGUST 29
Mick Jagger on the new label: 'We want to release the odd blues record and Charlie Watts wants to do some jazz; what we're not interested in is bubble gum material. We want to control prices to stop the price of records going up. I'd like to find new ways of distribution. I don't want to do any production. We haven't a name yet. As long as the band swings we won't split.'
Charlie Watts: 'I'm not amazed that the band is still going, just amazed they get anything together. That's our claim to fame.'

Rumour has it that the Stones' *Rock'n'Roll Circus* will be broadcast on US TV. The band fly to Helsinki stopping in Copenhagen to give a press conference for the start of their European tour.

SEPTEMBER 2
Concert at the Olympic Stadium, Helsinki. They open their first sell-out European tour in three years with a brand new set designed by Chip Monk which needs two lorries and a forklift truck to move it. The set includes a huge proscenium arch which supports six rows of curtains and several banks of lights. The staging is described by the Stones' management as 'a new milestone in the presentation of pop music on the road'.
It is rumoured that hotels in Copenhagen are refusing to accept bookings for the band.

SEPTEMBER 3
Concert at Malmo, Sweden.
Mick Jagger is cited when Marianne Faithfull is sued for divorce by her husband John Dunbar.

SEPTEMBER 4
Concert at the Royal Tennis Hall, Stockholm. Hundreds of fans storm the stage.

SEPTEMBER 6
Get Yer Ya Yas Out! is released on Decca in Europe and London in America. Recorded live at Madison Square Garden in New York last November, it is produced by the Rolling Stones and Glyn Johns.
Despite rumours to the contrary, the band plan to tour England early in the New Year.

SEPTEMBER 9
Concert at the Tennis Stadium, Aarhus, Denmark.

SEPTEMBER 12
Concert at the Forum, Copenhagen. *Get Yer Ya Yas Out!* enters the British Top 30 at Number 28. It will stay in the charts for thirteen weeks, with a highest position of Number 1.

SEPTEMBER 13
Press conference in Hamburg.

SEPTEMBER 14
Concert at the Ernst Merck Halle, Hamburg. Before the start 200 police mount a massive security check for 1,000 forged tickets.

SEPTEMBER 16
Concert at the Deutschlandhalle, Berlin. 50 fans are arrested in clashes outside the hall before the show.

SEPTEMBER 18
Concert at the Festhalle, Cologne.

SEPTEMBER 19
The *Performance* soundtrack album is released on Warner Brothers and features Mick Jagger, Ry Cooder, Randy Newman and Buffy St Marie. The Rolling Stones are interviewed on Radio Luxembourg.

SEPTEMBER 20
Concert at Killesberg, Stuttgart.

SEPTEMBER 22
Concert at the Olympia, Paris. Before the concert several policemen are injured outside the hall. To satisfy demand two more concerts are added and the venue changed to the Palais des Sports. A post-gig party is held at the Hotel George V.

SEPTEMBER 23
Two concerts at the Palais des Sports, Paris.

SEPTEMBER 27
Concert at the Stadthalle, Vienna.

SEPTEMBER 28
The Rolling Stones arrive in Rome; Mick Jagger punches a reporter at a press conference 'for asking stupid questions'.

SEPTEMBER 29
Concert at the Palazzo dello Sport, Rome.

OCTOBER 1
Concert at the Palazzo dello Sport, Milan. Police use tear gas to disperse a crowd of 2,000 trying to enter the hall when it is

MICK JAGGER: «prendo a calci soltanto i presuntuosi»

LA CONFERENZA STAMPA ROMANA DEI ROLLING STONES SI E' CONCLUSA PRECIPITOSAMENTE, QUANDO MICK JAGGER, IRRITATO DALLE DOMANDE BANALI DI CERTI GIORNALISTI, LI HA SCACCIATI A INSULTI DALLA SALA. CONCLUSO L'INCIDENTE, IL NOSTRO LUIGI COZZI HA AVVICINATO IL CANTANTE CONDUCENDO UNA SERENA E COMPLETA INTERVISTA CHE DIMOSTRA COME I ROLLING STONES NON SIANO AFFATTO INAVVICINABILI, MA SOLTANTO STANCHI DI TROPPA GENTE E GIORNALI CHE PRETENDONO DI SQUADRARLI CON SUFFICIENZA E PRESUNZIONE

di Luigi Cozzi

Che Mick Jagger non giri con il fiore in mano e che non sia abituato a porgere l'altra guancia, lo sanno tutti. O forse non proprio tutti: i giovani, che sono quelli che contano per queste manifestazioni, e i giornalisti specializzati in musica moderna. Invece, alla conferenza stampa dei Rolling Stones (assente il solo Keith Richard), sono intervenute alcune persone che queste cose purtroppo non le sanno, tanto meno sfoggiano comprensione per certe forme di gioventù e non vantano una conoscenza sia pur vaga del mondo pop.

Comunque, Mick Jagger arriva nella sala della conferenza. Gli chiedono subito come si chiama, chi sia. Mick si innervosisce. «Ma come?» grida alla sua segretaria. «Questi signori vengono e non sanno neppure chi sono io? Ma dove vivono? Che professionisti sono? Si informino prima di venire a intervistarmi. Io dovrei chiedere chi sono costoro!».

Ma risponde con pazienza, spiega di chiamarsi Mick Jagger. Poi gli domandano che cosa ne pensa delle recensioni tedesche sul conto del loro spettacolo: orribili. Mick è perplesso, dice che non ci sono state recensioni orribili. Il giornalista insiste e Mick gli chiede su quale giornale tedesco è apparso il pezzo denigratorio. Non ottiene risposta, ma soltanto una nuova domanda: è vero che sono stati scacciati dall'albergo per via degli abiti? Mick è visibilmente seccato, dice: «Sì, dieci anni fa».

L'atmosfera è tesa. Mick chiede di nuovo alla segretaria perché sono venuti questi giornalisti e non dei critici specializzati che sappiano che cosa sono e che cosa rappresentano gli Stones, gente con la quale si potrebbe discorrere proficuamente. Non ottiene risposta, ma un giornalista gli rivolge una nuova, secca domanda. «Che

Roma, domenica 27 settembre 1970: arrivano i Rolling Stones da Vienna. Nella foto qui sopra, Anita Pallemberg con Marlon, il bambino avuto da Keith Richard. Nella foto sotto, Bill Wyman con Astrid, sua attuale compagna. La ragazza alle loro spalle, vestita di nero, sta attualmente con Mick Jagger.

37

Top right: *A rare bootleg EP,* Cocksucker Blues. Centre: Get Yer Ya Yas Out *the album of live concert tracks from the 1969 US tour.* Right: *An Italian magazine features the Stones' arrival in Rome for the Italian leg of the tour.*

already full. Seven police and several fans are injured. 63 fans are taken into custody.

OCTOBER 3
Concert at the Palais des Sports, Lyon.

OCTOBER 6
Concert at the Festhalle, Frankfurt.

OCTOBER 7
Concert at the Grughalle, Essen.

OCTOBER 9
Concert at the Rai Halle, Amsterdam.

OCTOBER 10
Get Yer Ya Yas Out! enters the US Top 30 at Number 27. It will stay in the charts for eleven weeks with a highest position of Number 5. Mick Jagger arrives back in London with a new Nicaraguan girlfriend named Bianca Perez Morena de Macia.

OCTOBER 11
The European tour ends with a concert at the Olympiahalle, Munich.

OCTOBER 26
Mrs Alpha May Anderson, whose 18-year-old son Meredith Hunter was killed at the Altamont Concert last year, is suing the Rolling Stones, the Hell's Angels, the Promoters and the security staff for £28,000.

OCTOBER 30
John Dunbar is granted a decree nisi from Marianne Faithfull. Mick Jagger, cited as co-respondant, is ordered to pay costs of £200.

OCTOBER 31
The Rolling Stones have recorded eight new tracks at Olympic. A spokesman denies rumours that they are planning a concert at the Roundhouse in Camden Town on 22 Novemeber.

NOVEMBER 7
A Mick Jagger solo single 'Memo From Turner' (Jagger/Richard) is released on Decca. Produced by Jack Nitsche, the flip side features an instrumental written by Nitsche, 'Natural Magic'. It was recorded in November 1968 at the Olympic Studios.

NOVEMBER 24
Mick Jagger and Bianca fly to Nassau for a two-week holiday.

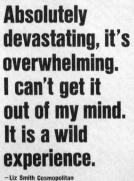

DECEMBER 6
The documentary *Gimme Shelter* is premiered at the Plaza Theatre, New York. Covering the Rolling Stones American tour it includes several sequences of the band at Altamont.

DECEMBER 18
Keith Richard holds a party at Olympic Studios. Among the guests are Eric Clapton and Al Kooper.

DECEMBER 20
The new album from Alexis Korner's band CCS features a version of 'Satisfaction'.

DECEMBER 22
Eric Burdon's new album *The Black Man's Burdon* will include a new version of 'Paint It Black'.

Absolutely devastating, it's overwhelming. I can't get it out of my mind. It is a wild experience.
—Liz Smith Cosmopolitan
The Rolling Stones
GIMME SHELTER
Directed by David Maysles, Albert Maysles, Charlotte Zwerin · A Maysles Films, Inc. Production
PRINTED IN U.S.A.

Left: *Mick at the Palazzo dello Sport, Rome.* Top right: *An advertisement for the film* Gimme Shelter, *which documented the ill-fated US tour of 1969.* Below left: *The soundtrack for the film* Performance.

NINETEEN 71

JANUARY 4
Keith Richard attends the British premiere of *Performance* at the Warner West End Cinema held in aid of Release, a charity devoted to helping drug addicts and offenders. Warner Brothers, unhappy about their involvement in the drug orientated film, withdraw the film after a West End run of only a few weeks. It is never put on general release.

JANUARY 6
A daughter, Chloe, is born to Mick Taylor and Rose Miller at Wimbledon Hospital, London.

JANUARY 7
The US magazine *Billboard* places the Rolling Stones as third best-selling artists in the US from 1960 to 1970.

JANUARY 29
Rumours suggest the Stones intend to leave England and move to France very soon.

FEBRUARY 6
The Rolling Stones announce a farewell British tour confirming their decision to move to France, thus becoming the first British rock'n'roll tax exiles. Bill Wyman attends the London premiere of the rock movie *Mad Dogs And Englishmen* starring Joe Cocker, Leon Russell and others.

FEBRUARY 16
The Stones are sued for invasion of privacy by the Hell's Angel who was charged with the murder of Meredith Hunter at Altamont.

FEBRUARY 22
Hundreds of fans sleep rough on Glasgow's Sauchiehall Street waiting for tickets to go on sale for the concert on 8 March.

FEBRUARY 26
Decca Records announce that a new 'oldie' Rolling Stones album will be released next month.

MARCH 1
Fans queueing for tickets at the Liverpool Empire stampede the box office and the police are called.

MARCH 2
'A Story Of Our Time - Brian Jones, The Rolling Stones', a documentary by Michael Wale, is broadcast on BBC Radio 4.

MARCH 4
The Rolling Stones begin their sell-out British tour at the Newcastle City Hall.

MARCH 5
Concert at the Manchester Free Trade Hall. The *Daily Telegraph* reports that the Rolling Stones have grossed an estimated £83,000,000 during their careers so far and suggests that they could gain personal taxation advantages by becoming French residents. The Stones' publicist, Les Perrin, said the move was not a

case of running away from the taxman but that the main reason for the move is that they like France tremendously, and they will be retaining British citizenship and will continue to record in England.

MARCH 6
Concert at the Coventry Theatre, Coventry. Decca release a new 'oldie' album called *Stone Age* in Britain and Europe.

MARCH 8
Concert at Green's Playhouse, Glasgow.

MARCH 10
Concert at the Big Apple, Brighton. *Stone Age* enters the British Top 30 at Number 22. It will reach a highest position of Number 5, with a total of eight weeks in the charts.

MARCH 12
Concert at the Liverpool Empire.

MARCH 13
Concert at the University of Leeds. An advertisement issued by the Rolling Stones' office and signed by Mick Jagger appears in all the British music magazines: 'Comment, I feel, on behalf of the Rolling Stones should be made on reports which estimate that the Rolling Stones' fortune from recordings alone is reckoned to be £83,000,000... The sum mentioned is ludicrous; in our opinion it most probably exceeds the collective recording earnings of the Beatles, Elvis Presley, ourselves and others.'

MARCH 14
The Rolling Stones round off their British tour with two concerts at the Roundhouse in London in front of a capacity crowd of 4,000 for each show. In the audience are Eric Clapton, the Faces, Jim Gordon, Jim Keltner, the Family, Edgar Broughton, Chris Jagger, John Peel and Tom Donahue. Tickets are sold for up to £10 on the black market.

MARCH 20
The Rolling Stones advertise in the British music press that they were not consulted about Decca's release of the *Stone Age* album. 'It is, in our opinion, below the standard we try to keep up, both in choice of content and cover design.' The advertisement is signed Mick Jagger, Keith Richard, Charlie Watts, Bill Wyman and Mick Taylor.

MARCH 22
It is rumoured that Atlantic Records will almost certainly distribute the Rolling Stones' own label in America.

Left: *Bianca Jagger wears a see-through top at a party at the Canto Club House in St Tropez to launch the new label, Rolling Stones Records.*

MARCH 26
The Rolling Stones record two televison shows at the Marquee Club, their first appearance there for nearly eight years. Keith Richard swings his guitar at club owner Harold Pendleton's head but misses and so escapes a charge of grievous bodily harm. The Rolling Stones play before an invited audience. One show for British TV is 28 minutes long, a second, for various European TV stations, runs for 52 minutes. In *The Tailor and Cutter* magazine, Mick Jagger is voted one of the world's hundred best dressed men.

MARCH 30
The Rolling Stones give a farewell party for friends at Skindles Hotel, Maidenhead, before leaving for the South of France. Guests include John Lennon, Yoko Ono, Eric Clapton and photographers Patrick Lichfield.

APRIL 1
It is announced that Marshall Chess, son of Chess Records' founder Leonard will be running the Rolling Stones new label.

APRIL 6
In Cannes the Rolling Stones sign a distribution contract with the Kinney Group to release all the future Rolling Stones recordings on their new label, Rolling Stones Records. In the States they will be distributed by Atlantic Records. Mick Jagger says: 'By signing this contract we are guaranteeing to produce six new albums over the next four years; this includes *Sticky Fingers*. Additionally perhaps there may be some solo albums projecting the Rolling Stones individually over this period.'
The Stones arrive by yacht at Port Pierre, in the bay of Cannes and throw a party at the Canto Club House. Among the guests are Stephen Stills, and Atlantic Records President Ahmet Ertegun. Mick Jagger says they plan to release a new single in mid-summer, a new album in Autumn and another single just before Christmas. He also plans to write a book about the band.
From now on the Rolling Stones can spend no more than 90 days a year in the UK. They have all moved to France. Mick has a house in Mougins, home of Pablo Picasso, Keith Richard lives in a spacious old villa called Nellcot in Villefranche-sur-Mer and this will be used as the band's permanent base. Bill Wyman has a house at La Bastide Saint-Antoine nearby, Charlie Watts has a small farmhouse at Cevennes and Mick Taylor lives in Grasse.
In England Mick Jagger's country house at Stargrove that incorporates a recording studio

Right: *Mick during a concert in Newcastle-upon-Tyne.* Inset right: *It's trousers off and sticky fingers on for the sleeve for 'Brown Sugar'* and left, *1920s graphics on the poster for the 1971 UK tour.*

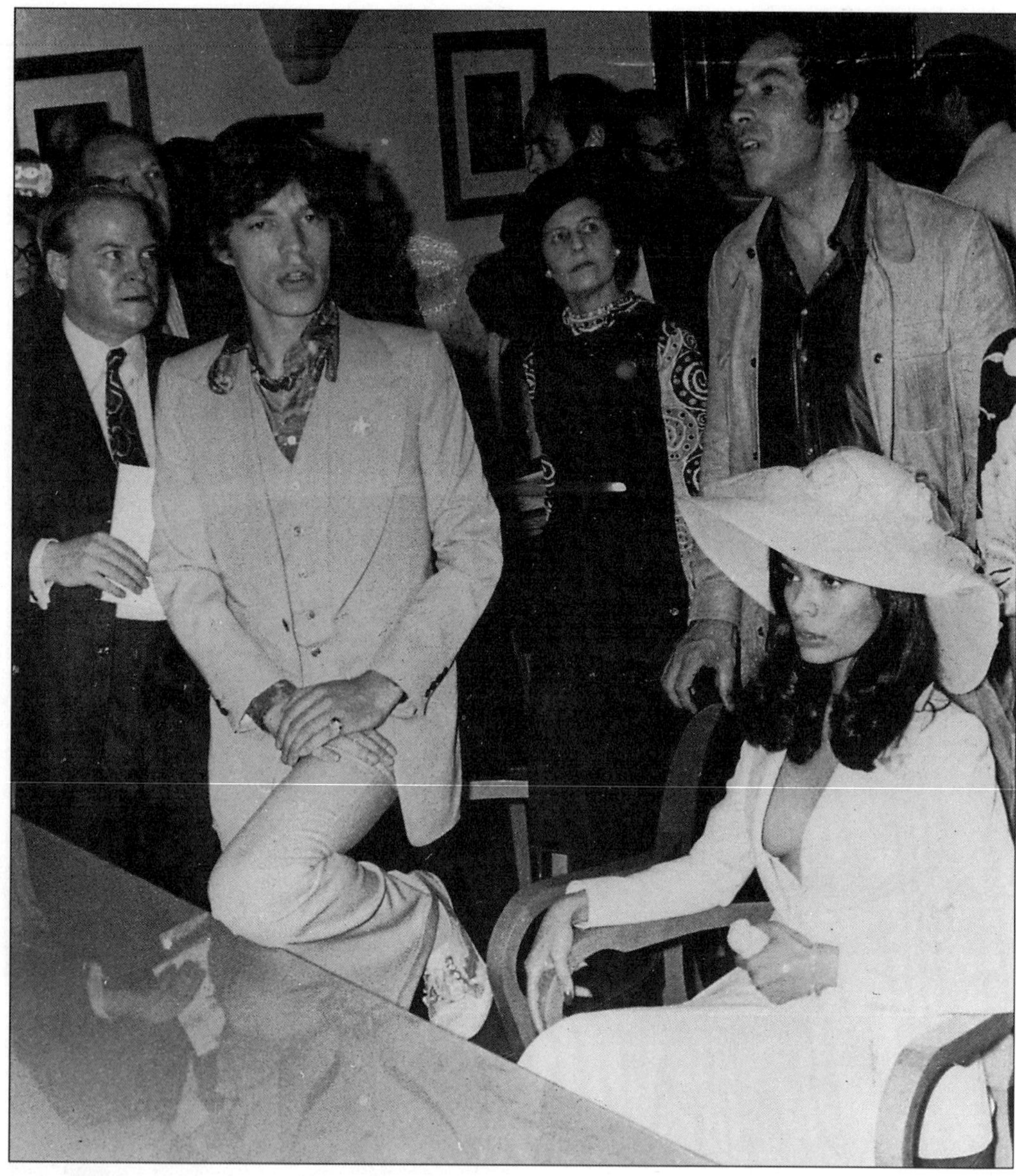

with all facilities is available for rent of $6,200 a week. The Mighty Mobile can also be leased for $3,750 a week.

APRIL 12
Mick Taylor is to feature on the new John Mayall album *Back To The Roots*.

APRIL 15
The Rolling Stones appear on *Top Of The Pops* to promote 'Brown Sugar', the soon-to-be-released single taken from their forthcoming album. The *Daily Mirror* reports from St Tropez: 'A familiar sight on the French Riviera [is] Rolling Stones' Mick Jagger dining out in uncommonly conventional style with society girl Bianca Perez Morena de Macias. All the signs are that the couple plan to marry very soon... 26-year-old Jagger meanwhile is saying little. At the Byblos Hotel, trendiest place in town, he admitted yesterday: "It's quite true that I have been seeing this girl for some time. But I'm not the sort of bloke who would make a big fuss of announcing a date, am I?" Bianca, an exotic 21-year-old South American graduate of the Sorbonne, full-lipped like Mick Jagger, is a former girlfriend of actor Michael Caine and one-time fiancée of record producer Eddie Barclay.'
Mick Jagger on the band's future: 'The band is not retiring just because we're going away. We'll remain a functioning group, a touring group, and a happy group. We're not going to stay in the South of France for a whole year, we're going on the road. I couldn't live in France for a whole year.'

APRIL 16
The single, 'Brown Sugar'/'Bitch', with 'Let It Rock' on the UK version, is released on both sides of the Atlantic by Rolling Stones Records. 'Let It Rock' is an old Chuck Berry number recorded live at Leeds in March. The two Jagger/Richard tracks were recorded at Muscle Shoals Studios in Alabama in December 1969 and at Olympic Studios in London last year, and produced by Jimmy Miller.

APRIL 18
Mick Jagger and Bianca are pictured leaving the Yves St Laurent boutique in St Tropez and deny rumours that they are to marry.

APRIL 22
'Brown Sugar' enters the British Top 30 at Number 18. It will stay in the charts for eleven weeks, making the Number 1 position.

APRIL 23
The new album *Sticky Fingers* is released, recorded at the Muscle Shoals Studios in Alabama in 1969, and in the Mighty Mobile and Olympic Studios in London in 1970. All the tracks are written by Mick Jagger and Keith Richard except for 'You Got To Move' by Fred McDowell. This first album for the new label is produced by Jimmy Miller and the cover, showing a pair of trousers, a real zipper and underneath a pair of Y-fronts, was designed by Andy Warhol.

APRIL 27
'Brown Sugar' enters the UK Top 30 at Number 28. It will stay in the charts for ten weeks, reaching the Number 1 position. In the States, it will also reach Number 1, with eleven weeks in the charts.

MAY 2
Bianca's birthday. Mick Jagger flies from Nice to Paris to give her a £4,000 diamond bracelet and a dinner party in her honour.

MAY 7
The *Daily Mirror* reports: 'Pop star Mick Jagger and his beautiful South American girlfriend are planning a secret wedding in France. They have applied for a special dispensation to marry without having their banns posted - which would allow the ceremony to go ahead without anyone but local officials knowing. Jagger called on a senior magistrate yesterday at Draguignan in Southern France to make his application. Only two days ago Bianca said: "There's not going to be a wedding this week, next week or ever. Mick and I are very happy together. We don't need to get married. Why should we?" '

MAY 8
Mick goes to Paris to collect two specially designed wedding rings.

Above left: *The civil ceremony in St Tropez to legalize Mick and Bianca's marriage. Like everything else connected with their relationship the occasion turns into a chaotic media circus.*
Above right: *Anita Pallenberg passes a joint to*

MAY 11
Mick's parents and several friends fly from London to Nice in a chartered plane.

MAY 12
Mick Jagger marries Bianca Perez Morena de Macias in St Tropez in a civil ceremony in the 17th century St Anne Chapel. The wedding is performed by Father Lucien Baud. The groom has been taking Roman Catholic religious instruction for the past few weeks from the Bishop of Fréjus and Father Baud. Witnesses are Nathalie Delon and Roger Vadim. In addition to both families and other members of the Stones, guests include Paul and Linda McCartney, Ringo and Maureen Starr, Ronnie Wood, Ian McLagan, Ronnie Lane, Kenny Jones, John Walker, Ahmet Ertegun, Marshall Chess, Donald Cammell, Ossie Clark, Jimmy Miller and Lord Lichfield.
At the reception at the Café des Arts Mick joins in a jam session put together by Stephen Stills, Bobby Keys, Nicky Hopkins, Doris Troy, P.P. Arnold with Davis Brown and Michael Shrieve of Santana. The party ends at 4.00 am.

MAY
Mick's mother says: 'I hope my other son doesn't become a superstar.'
'Brown Sugar' and *Sticky Fingers* are at Number 1 in Britain. *Sticky Fingers* will stay in the UK charts for a total of 27 weeks. It will also make Number 1 in the US, with a total of 25 weeks in the charts.

MAY 13
Mick and Bianca leave Cannes by yacht.

MAY 16
Mick and Bianca change yachts at Micinaggio and make for a nearby chateau accessible only by sea.
In Britain the Rolling Stones are heard on the *Dave Lee Travis Show* with material specially recorded during their recent tour.

MAY 21
Elton John says: 'Mick Jagger is the perfect pop star. There's nobody more perfect than Jagger. He's rude, ugly-attractive, he's brilliant. The Rolling Stones are the perfect pop group. The Beatles were a bit show-biz, but the Rolling Stones, they don't give a shit.'

MAY 23
Mick Taylor appears on the new B.B. Blunder album *Worker's Playtime*, playing bottleneck guitar.

Mick on the set of Performance. Right: *The sleeve for* Sticky Fingers. *Designed by Andy Warhol some versions featured a working zipper which opened to reveal a pair of Y-fronts.* Inset: *In Franco's Spain it was considered too subversive and this stickier version was substituted.*

MAY 24
Granada TV's *Stones In The Park* is televised.

MAY 26
Keith Richard drives his Jaguar into a car driven by an Italian tourist at Beaulieu sur Mer. A dispute follows and the police are called. Keith is charged with assault and battery and will appear in court in June to put his case. Meanwhile he attends the Cannes Film Festival, where *Gimme Shelter* is being screened.

MAY 29
Mick Jagger is reported to be considering a starring role in the film *Ishtar* to be directed by *Performance* director Donald Cammell with Norman Mailer as co-star. Shooting is scheduled to begin on location in North Africa this summer.
Marshall Chess claims that *Sticky Fingers* is the fastest-selling Rolling Stones album ever in the US.

MAY 30
Mick and Bianca return to St Tropez. The band are heard on John Peel's *Sunday Concert* on BBC Radio 1 with live material recorded during their last British tour.

JUNE 1
The Rolling Stones are at Number 1 in both album and singles charts in the US with *Sticky Fingers* and 'Brown Sugar'.

JUNE 3
Bill Wyman produces an album for John Walker. In Nice, Charlie Watts' wife Shirley is sentenced, *in absentia*, to six months' imprisonment and a £30 fine for abusive language and assaulting customs and airport officials.

JUNE 5
The Rolling Stones' TV special, filmed at the Marquee on 26 March, has been turned down by the BBC and two ITV companies. The longer European version has already been televised in several European countries.

JUNE 12
A new single taken from *Sticky Fingers* is released in America. 'Wild Horses'/'Sway' (Jagger/Richard), produced by Jimmy Miller is released on the Rolling Stones Records label.

JUNE 26
Decca release a new 'oldie' maxi-single 'Street Fighting Man'/'Surprise Surprise'/'Everybody Needs Somebody To Love'. It marks the first appearance in Britain of 'Surprise Surprise' which featured on *Rolling Stones, Now* released only in America in February 1965. Keith's court case is adjourned until December.

JULY 6
'Wild Horses' reaches Number 20 in the US. It will stay in the charts for three weeks, with a highest position of Number 18.

JULY 7
The maxi-single enters the British charts at Number 27. It will stay in the charts for six weeks, with a highest position of Number 17.

JULY 10
Using the Mighty Mobile, recording sessions get underway at Keith's home, known affectionately as Keith's Coffee House, in Villefranche sur Mer. The band are joined by Bobby Keys, Jim Price, Nicky Hopkins, Gram Parsons and many others.

JULY 26
Mick Jagger spends his 28th birthday recording in Villefranche. In the States a $7,500,000 suit is filed against ex-manager Allen Klein.

JULY 30
At London's Heathrow airport Mick and Bianca Jagger announce they are expecting a baby. They are en route to Ireland to stay at Leixlip Castle as guests of the Guinness family.

JULY 31
The British premiere of *Gimme Shelter* at the Rialto Cinema, London, is attended by Keith Richard and Anita Pallenberg.

AUGUST 5
At Aix-en-Provence Shirley Watts' six-month jail sentence is reduced to fifteen days suspended.

AUGUST 20
Rolling Stones Records release an album called *The London Howlin' Wolf Sessions*, featuring Howlin' Wolf, Eric Clapton, Steve Winwood, Ian Stewart, Ringo Starr, Charlie Watts and Bill Wyman. Recorded in London at Olympic Studios, and produced by Norman Dayron, it is released in America on Chess Records.

AUGUST 27
Decca Records release a new 'oldie' album called *Gimme Shelter*. Side One features previously released material. Side Two is part of the *Got Live If You Want It* album, which was recorded at the Royal Albert Hall in London in 1966 but has never before been released in Britain. *Gimme Shelter* is not released in America.

AUGUST 28
Mick Jagger appears on the Doctor John album *Sun, Moon and Herbs*.

AUGUST 31
Mick Jagger, Keith Richard, Bill Wyman, Charlie Watts and Lewis Jones, father of Brian, file a High Court writ against ex-Stones manager Andrew Oldham and Eric Easton, charging that they made a secret deal with Decca Records in 1963 to deprive the group of record royalties. The suit alleges that Oldham persuaded Brian Jones to accept six per cent of the wholesale record price as the Rolling Stones' share while Decca was giving Oldham and Easton fourteen per cent. At the same time Oldham had a 25 per cent management contract with the Stones themselves. The four original Rolling Stones, plus Lewis Jones are also suing Allen Klein for $29,000,000, alleging he failed to represent their best financial interests. They state that Klein persuaded them to sign over all North American rights to their songs to a company called Nanker Phelge Music Inc. The band claim that they were led to believe they ran the company when in truth it was controlled by Klein.

OCTOBER 1
Eleven guitars are stolen from Keith's villa in Villefranche sur Mer in France. He offers a 'reasonable' reward for information leading to their return.

OCTOBER 8
Rolling Stone Records release a Brian Jones album, *Joujouka*. It was recorded in Morocco in 1968 and features a local group called the Pipes of Pan.

OCTOBER 20
Twenty new numbers are now recorded but not yet mixed. The band hopes to release this new album to coincide with their planned US tour next April.

OCTOBER 21
Bianca Jagger gives birth to a daughter, Jade, at the Belvedere Nursing Home in Paris.

OCTOBER 26
Mick Jagger appears on *Beaton by Bailey*, a documentary on photographers Cecil Beaton and David Bailey.

OCTOBER 30
Rolling Stones Records release 'Rockin' Daddy', a single from the *Howlin' Wolf London Sessions*.

NOVEMBER 7
Bill Wyman produces Tucky Buzzard's second album *Loudwater House* to be released on 4 February.

NOVEMBER 23
The recording sessions in Villefranche end and provide enough material for a double album. The Stones plan to release the tentatively named *Tropical Disease* in February.

NOVEMBER 24
Mick Jagger details plans for the 40-venue tour of the States set for the spring. He admits that he really wants to play in Russia and indicates that negotiations are underway.

NOVEMBER 30
Keith Richard and Mick, Bianca and Jade Jagger leave for America, Keith to Nashville to collect guitars ordered to replace those stolen, before joining Mick in LA to finish work on the new album. In mid-air a row breaks out. The Stones party is asked to move as they are sitting in the wrong first class seats. Mick Jagger refuses and air hostess Pauline Lough claims afterwards that he swore at her: 'I asked him not to use bad language. Then I turned around and started to walk away. He came up behind me and grabbed me by the arm and swung me roughly around.' Mick denies grabbing Pauline: 'I'd like to give her a good slap in the face because she deserves it.' Pan American are to hold an enquiry.

DECEMBER 3
French magistrates accept Keith Richard's claim of self defence and drop charges of assault and battery against him following the incident in Beaulieu last summer.

DECEMBER 4
The Rolling Stones are in Los Angeles working on the new album at the Sunset Sound Studios.

DECEMBER 11
Mick and Bianca are looking for a house on the West Coast. It is expected that they will stay in California till the US tour starts in the spring.
Nicky Hopkins says: 'Well, I'm just about a permanent member of the Rolling Stones these days. There are no contracts or anything, it just happens.'

DECEMBER 12
The Montreux Casino catches fire while Frank Zappa is playing. The Mighty Mobile, which is there while being rented by Deep Purple, escapes damage.

DECEMBER 15
Decca releases another anthology album, *Milestones*, in Europe but not in Britain. In America London release *Hot Rocks 1964-1971*, a double anthology album.

DECEMBER 20
The Stones go to a B.B. King concert in Las Vegas.

DECEMBER 28
Mick Jagger attends a reception in Los Angeles to celebrate the Who's latest Gold disc.

Right: *Mick and Bianca take a motorbike ride into St Tropez. In the South of France they found the freedom denied them in England but continued their decadent and glittery lifestyle.*

JANUARY 10
The Rolling Stones continue to work on the new album and upcoming tour in Los Angeles.

JANUARY 18
Hot Rocks reaches Number 9 in the US albums Top 30. It will stay in the Top 20 for seventeen weeks with a highest position of Number 4.

JANUARY 21
The Rolling Stones are suing ex-manager Allen Klein for releasing the *Hot Rocks* album without their agreement.

JANUARY 22
The Rolling Stones are voted second best British band and second best vocal band in the World in the *New Musical Express* pop poll for 1971.

JANUARY 29
Mick, Keith and Ian Stewart join Chuck Berry on stage at the Hollywood Palladium but leave after only three numbers as Chuck is unhappy about the sound.

FEBURARY 15
The Stones are back in Los Angeles for more recording.

FEBRUARY 18
The Los Angeles Radio station, KDAY, plays two new Rolling Stones' tracks non-stop for eighteen hours. The band succeed in stopping the broadcast. The tape has been stolen from Marshall Chess's home.

FEBRUARY 20
Decca release the Rolling Stones anthology album *Milestones* in Britain.

FEBRUARY 26
Allen Klein's ABKCO Records has been granted a preliminary injunction by the New York State judiciary restraining Atlantic Records from releasing an album entitled *Hot Rocks 1964-71*. The Court decided that ABKCO had adequately shown that Atlantic's proposed identical *Hot Rocks* album had appropriated performances from ABKCO's version.

MARCH 25
Milestones reaches Number 17 in the UK, its highest position. It will stay in the charts for nine weeks.

APRIL 14
A new single is released on Rolling Stones Records, 'Tumbling Dice'/'Sweet Black Angel'. Both numbers are written by Jagger and Richard and are taken from the new album recorded in the summer of 1971 in Villefranche-sur-Mer and produced by Jimmy Miller.

APRIL 17
Anita Pallenberg gives birth to Keith Richard's daughter, Dandelion, in Geneva, Switzerland.

APRIL 24
Mick Jagger returns from holiday and joins the rest of the band in London.

APRIL 29
The *New Musical Express* gives away a maxi-single to promote the Stones new album now re-titled *Exile On Main Street*. More than 300,000 copies of their magazine are sold. Keith Richard says: 'We're not exactly old just because we've got a few kids these days.'

MAY 6
'Tumbling Dice' goes into the British charts at Number 13. It will stay in the Top 30 for six weeks, with a highest position of Number 5.

MAY 9
'Tumbling Dice' goes into the US Top 30 at Number 26. It will stay in the Top 30 for seven weeks with a highest position of Number 10.

MAY 10
The release of *Exile On Main Street* is delayed. It is rumoured that Allen Klein has put an injunction on its release but Marshall Chess says the delay is caused by production problems with the cover.
The Rolling Stones, ABKCO records and Allen Klein jointly announce the settlement of all outstanding differences. In addition the

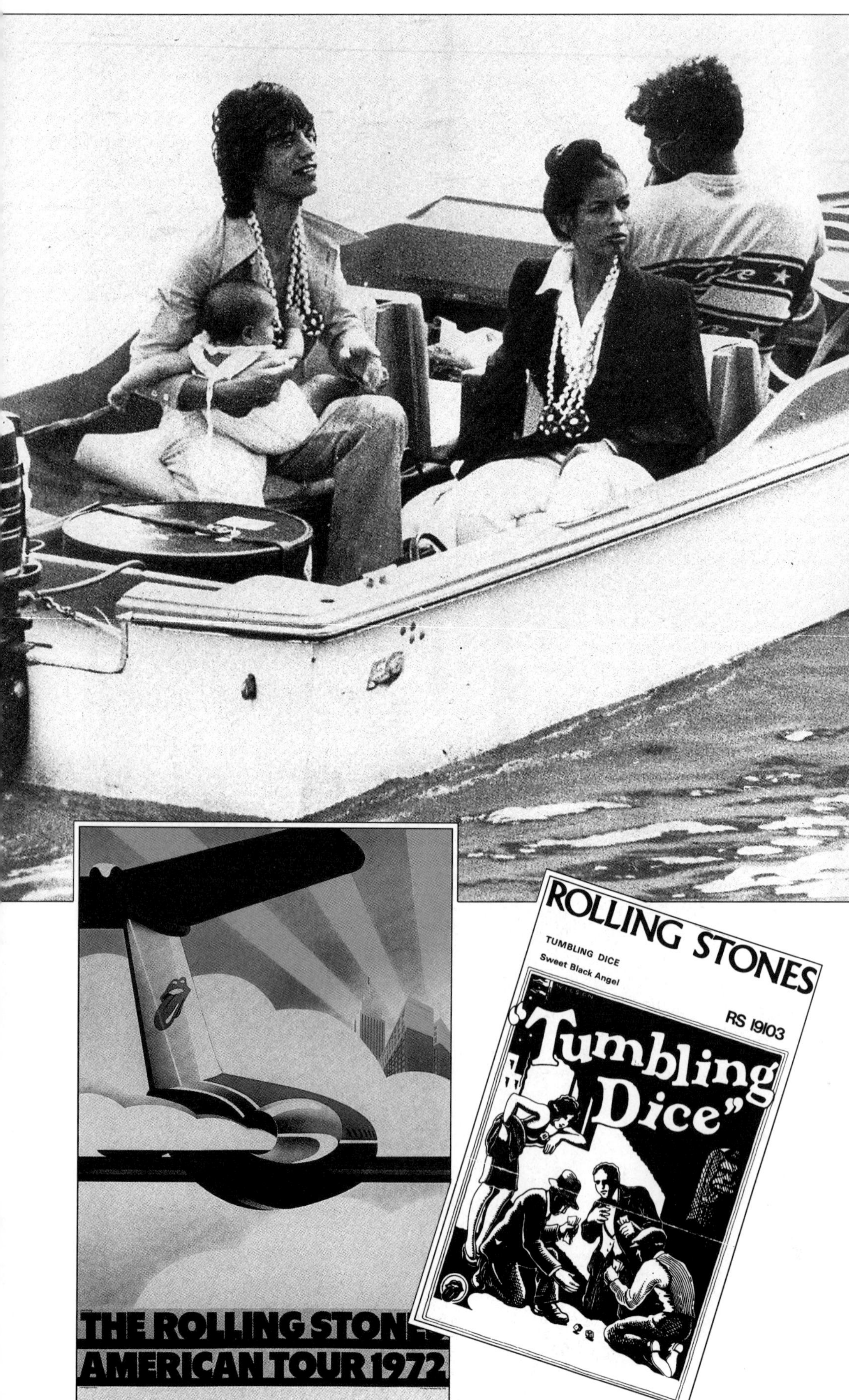

group have assigned their claims against Eric Easton to ABKCO and will cooperate with them against him.

MAY 12
Mick Jagger goes to Los Angeles where he lunches with Rudolph Nureyev at Sardi's before sitting in on John and Yoko's sessions at the Record Plant.

MAY 17
The Rolling Stones travel to Montreux, Switzerland to rehearse. While there they receive a gold disc for German sales of *Sticky Fingers*.

MAY 22
Peter Rudge, the Stones' tour manager, flying from New York to Los Angeles says: 'I feel a bit like Montgomery before Alamein - it's not like a rock'n'roll tour, more like the Normandy landing.'

MAY 23
The Stones go in person to the US Embassy in London to collect their work permits and all, except Bill Wyman, miss their flight to the States.

MAY 26
Exile On Main Street is released by Rolling Stones Records. The double album features eighteen tracks, all written by Jagger and Richard except for 'Shake Your Hips', an old blues number by James More, 'Stop Breaking Down' another blues classic rearranged by all the Stones and 'Ventilator Blues' in which Mick Taylor collaborated with Jagger and Richard.
Produced by Jimmy Miller, the album was recorded last year in Villefranche-sur-Mer and early this year in Hollywood. The cover is designed by film-maker Robert Frank, who will film the American tour for a possible documentary. Meanwhile they rehearse at Warner Brothers studios.

MAY 30
Exile On Main Street enters the UK Top 30 at Number 2. It will stay in the charts for fourteen weeks, with a highest position of Number 1.

JUNE 3
The seventh North American tour opens at Vancouver's Pacific Coliseum with an audience of 17,000. 30 policemen are injured as 2,000 fans try to gatecrash the concert. Eight are arrested.

JUNE 4
Concert at the Coliseum, Seattle.

Top left: *Mick and Bianca on holiday on the Pacific Island of Bora Bora with baby Jade.* Far left: *The North American tour poster.* Left: *Poster for 'Tumbling Dice'.*

JUNE 6
Concert at the Winterland, San Francisco. DJ Emperor Rosko joins them to record a special radio show.
Exile On Main Street enters the US Top 30 at Number 14. It will stay in the charts for sixteen weeks, with a highest position of Number 1.

JUNE 8
Concert at Winterland, San Francisco.

JUNE 9
Concert at the Hollywood Palladium, Los Angeles.

JUNE 11
Concert at the Forum, Los Angeles.
Billy Preston, Ike and Tina Turner, the Ikettes, John Phillips, Jack Nicholson, Dean Stockwell, Karen Black, Britt Ekland and Lou Adler are all there. The Stones add an extra concert the same day.

JUNE 13
Concert at the International Sports Arena, San Diego. 60 people are arrested and fifteen injured. *Exile On Main Street* reaches Number 1 in the UK.

JUNE 14
Concert at the Civic Arena, Tucson, Arizona. Police use tear-gas to disperse 300 gatecrashers.

JUNE 15
Concert at the University of New Mexico, Albuquerque. Six people faint when 200 ticket-holders push into the arena to claim seats because of a forged ticket scam.

JUNE 16
Concert at the Coliseum, Denver, Colorado.

JUNE 18
Concert at the Sports Center, St. Paul, Minnesota.

JUNE 19
Concert at the International Amphitheatre, Chicago, Illinois.

JUNE 20
Concert at the International Amphitheatre in Chicago. 25 fans are arrested. Tom Fitzpatrick of the *Chicago Sunday Times* writes: 'They were famous; now they are a legend.'
Exile On Main Street reaches Number 1 in the US.

JUNE 22
Concert at the Municipal Auditorium, Kansas

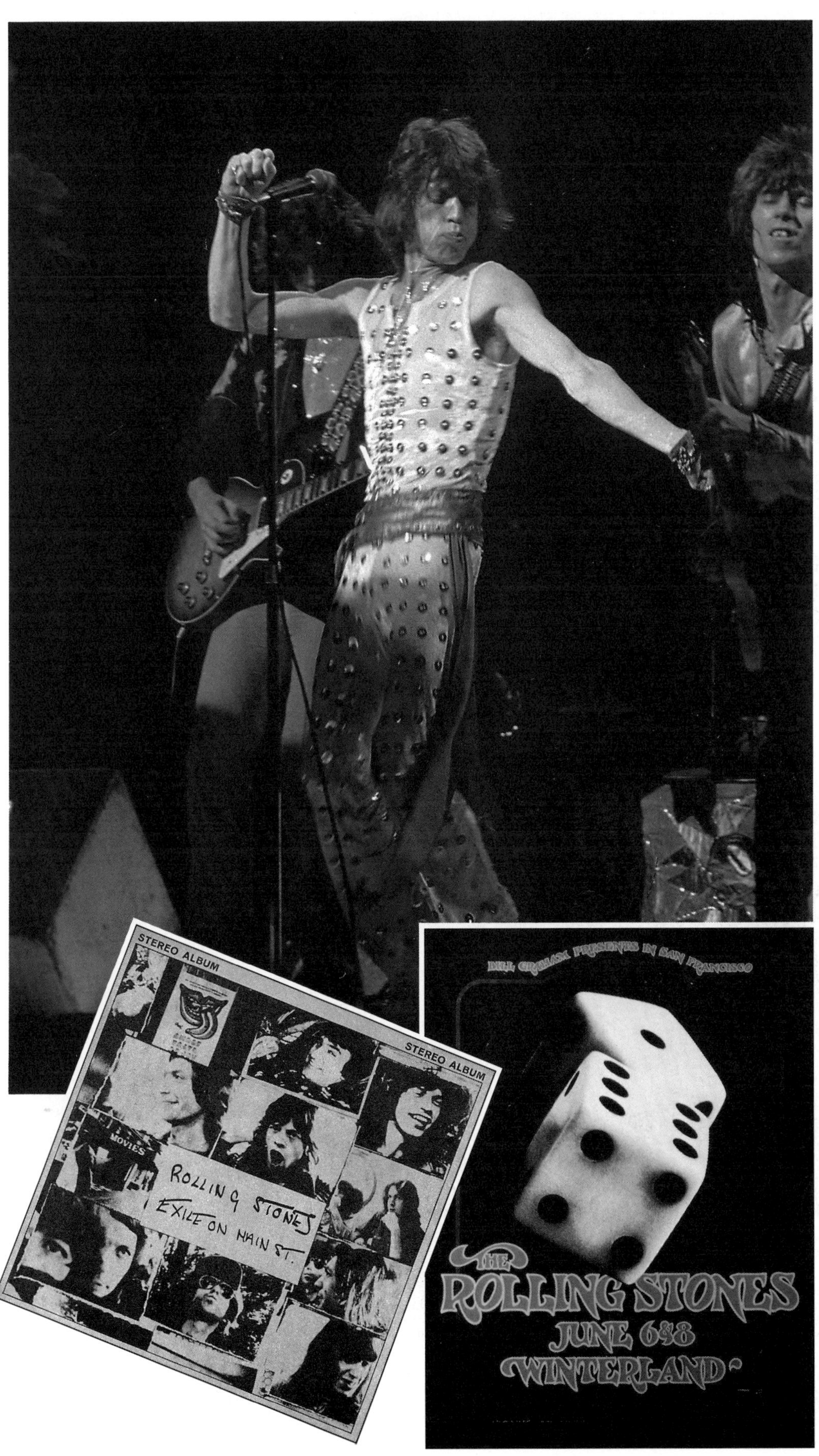

Top right: *On stage during the 1972 North American tour.* Far right: *Poster advertising the Stones' concert at Winterland, San Francisco.* Right: *Album cover for* Exile On Main Street.

City. Truman Capote and Princess Lee Radziwill, Jackie Kennedy's sister, are in the audience.

JUNE 24
Two concerts at Fort Worth, Texas which are recorded and filmed for a live album and documentary.

JUNE 25
Two concerts at the Hoffeinz Pavilion, Houston. In the UK, *Exile On Main Street* causes British television clean-up campaigner Mary Whitehouse to complain to the BBC regarding alleged obscenities on two tracks 'without actually hearing them'.

JUNE 27
Concert at the Auditorium, Mobile.

JUNE 28
Concerts at the University of Alabama, Tucaloosa. A fourth concert is added at Madison Square Garden on 25 July.

JULY 4
Concert at the Robert Kennedy Stadium, in Washington, D.C. There is an audience of 48,000, and Robert Kennedy Jr is one of them.

JULY 5
Concert at the Scope, Norfolk, Virginia.

JULY 6
Concert at the Coliseum, Charlotte, North Carolina.

JULY 7
Concert at the Civic Arena, Knoxville.

JULY 9
Concert at Keil Auditorium, St Louis, Missouri.

JULY 11
Concert at the Rubber Bowl, Akron, Ohio. The Stones are seen on BBC2's rock show *The Old Grey Whistle Test* with material taped in the South of France and Montreux.

JULY 12
Concert at the Convention Center, Indianapolis.

JULY 13
Concert at the Cobo Hall, Detroit.

JULY 14
Second concert at the Cobo Hall, Detroit.

JULY 15
Two concerts at the Maple Leaf Gardens, Toronto, Canada.
'Happy'/'All Down The Line', a single taken from *Exile On Main Street*, is released in America.

JULY 17
Concert at the Forum, Montreal. A bomb planted under a truck by French-Canadian separatists destroys the Stones' equipment. Replacements have to be flown in from Los Angeles and the show starts 45 minutes late. Outside the Forum fans riot after 3,000 forged tickets are sold. Inside Mick Jagger is hit by a flying bottle.

JULY 18
Concert at the Boston Garden.
Because of fog en route from Montreal to Boston, the Stones are forced to land in Warwick, Rhode Island. As two local reporters start to take photographs, two of the Stones party try to push them away and a scuffle breaks out. The police are called and Keith Richard is arrested for assault. Mick Jagger, Marshall Chess and Robert Frank are charged with obstructing a police officer. Their release is quickly arranged by Boston's mayor Kevin White but the show opens two hours late. The three are to appear in court on 23 August.

JULY 19
Another concert at the Boston Garden.
T-Bone Walker and his manager Robin Hemingway meet Keith, Mick and Marshall Chess at the Boston Sheraton Hotel to discuss the possibility of signing with Rolling Stones Records.

CHICAGO DAILY NEWS Tuesday, June 20, 1972 Want ads in this section Section Three ☆ Page 25

everyday / for and about people

The Stones did their part for 11,000 excited fans. . . .Folks had arrived wide-eyed and stoned out of their minds. Little pretty girls, no more than 14-year-olds. . . .The arena itself was too hot, sticky and smoke-filled and . . . often the only way to determine exactly what song was being played was to plug your ears.

Frenzy for 5 Stones

By Marshall Rosenthal and Jack Hafferkamp

Mick Jagger and the Rolling Stones, the biggest pop music attraction in the world, barnstormed into the International Amphitheatre Monday night. But for Anthony DiCaro, it was not a good scene.

"These kids don't buy nothin'," DiCaro complained as he stood behind a rickety folding table, hopelessly hawking Rolling Stone T-shirts ($4), posters ($2) and pendants ($3).

"Most of these acid shows are a bummer for business. Know what I mean? These kids are all freaked out!"

FREAKED OUT, indeed. DiCaro pulled in only $20 at the concert in the International Amphitheatre, but the Stones, led by Jagger — an androgynous 28-year-old with Marilyn Monroe's lips, David Cassidy's body and Bette Midler's campy wardrobe—grossed about $60,000 for the first of three Chicago appearances.

The Stones, for their part, did their best for the 11,000 excited young fans, playing about 15 songs (including "Brown Sugar," "Tumbling Dice," "Gimme Shelter," "Love in Vain," "Midnight Rambler," "Jumpin' Jack Flash" and "Street Fighting Man,") in the 1½ hours they were onstage.

But, in spite of the best sound and lighting systems ever used in the Amphitheatre, the monumental limitations of the hall finally proved more powerful than the electric incantations of the world's most influential rock band. For people seated in the hall's distant regions, this long-awaited Stones show simply wasn't much fun.

THE INCREDIBLE expectations aroused by the Stones' arrival were topped only by the security measures used for the event — certain police and private security forces in the history of rock concerts here.

The crowd, it seemed, had little choice but to be orderly. The Halsted St. sidewalk was split down the middle by wooden barricades. People with tickets queued up between the barricades and the wall of the building. Those who were not within the barricade were asked by policemen, stationed every 10 feet, if they had tickets. If they didn't have tickets, they were asked to leave. If they argued, they were herded into a paddy wagon.

Once a ticket-holder reached the gate in the fast-moving procession, an usher inspected the ticket with an ultraviolet lamp. Joe Maiorella, Midwest regional manager for Ticketron, explained:

"When each ticket was issued, the operator stamped it with an invisible ink caricature of Jagger. This is what the usher is looking for."

But no counterfeit ticket was found Monday night, and so the fans filed into the hall without incident.

FOLKS HAD ARRIVED wide-eyed and stoned out of their minds. Little pretty girls, no more than 14-year-olds. They walked out into the corridor for a breath of air, and the air there hung heavy with the smell of the Royal Lipizzan Stallions, the act that had played the Amphitheatre last weekend.

In the corridors, kids were selling pills to other kids. Uppers, downers, acid, whatever you wanted. Buy it and gulp it down.

The stage door, heavily secured, framed a group of stage-door Johnnies, young men hoping to get a glimpse of their Mick, who would soon be onstage, sequined from head to toe.

Young people who did not have tickets were outside the hall, casing it for an easy break-

and was quickly apprehended and handcuffed.

"It's impossible to secure the whole building," an Andy Frain usher said, "and tomorrow will be worse, because the crashers came tonight to find the weak points here."

In the first aid station, everything was normal, the nurse in attendance said. "There has been nothing serious, just the usual (for a rock concert) headaches, heat exhaustion, vomiting and cut feet."

THE ARENA ITSELF was too hot, sticky and smoke-filled, and the sound (although plenty loud) was far too echo-muddy. Jagger's between-song comments were completely unintelligible and often the only way to determine exactly what song was being played was to plug your ears.

For many fans the only solution (in fact, for many the only *intention*) was to move forward, resulting in a very heavy body jam in front of the stage. It was so heavy during the last third of the show that several people climbed on stage to escape the crunch. (They were quickly hustled backstage and out the door by the security forces.)

There were other small incidents of discomfort. Like the man in the wheelchair caught in the stage-front crush, who had to be lifted onstage so that he would not be trampled.

Or the young girl who wandered, like an automaton, into the men's washroom looking for her contact lens.

WHAT THOSE who didn't mind the super-crowding saw was the first Chicago appearance of the five Stones (plus Bobby Key and

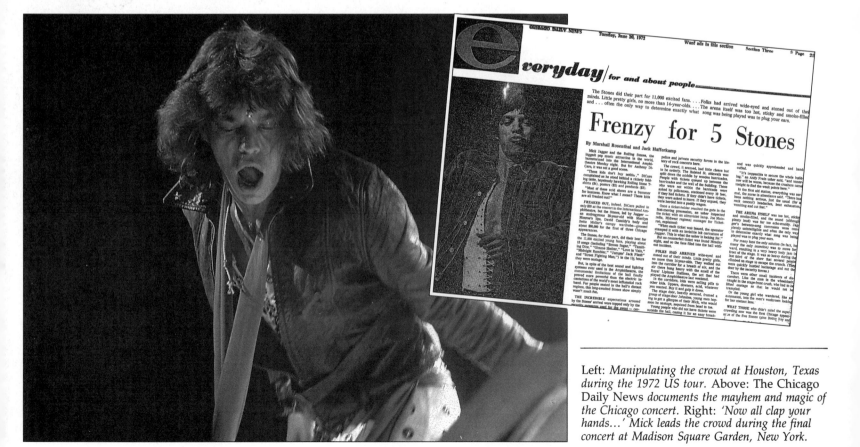

Left: *Manipulating the crowd at Houston, Texas during the 1972 US tour.* Above: The Chicago Daily News *documents the mayhem and magic of the Chicago concert.* Right: *'Now all clap your hands...' Mick leads the crowd during the final concert at Madison Square Garden, New York.*

JULY 20
Concert at the Spectrum, Philadelphia.
Kid Jenson of Radio Luxembourg and Bill Fowler of WEA Records fly from London to Philadelphia to tape material to be broadcast on a planned Rolling Stones special.

JULY 21
Two more shows at the Spectrum, Philadelphia.

JULY 22
Concert at the Civic Arena, Pittsburgh.

JULY 24
Concert at Madison Square Garden. Two policemen are injured and ten people are detained. A party is held at the Four Seasons restaurant, attended by Orson Welles.

JULY 25
The second and third concerts at Madison Square Garden.

JULY 26
Final concert at Madison Square Garden. As it is Mick Jagger's birthday, he is presented with a cake and a giant panda. At the end of the concert he retaliates with rose petals and custard pies. Guests at the party afterwards at the St Regis Hotel include Bob Dylan, Carly Simon, Andy Warhol, Truman Capote, Princess Lee Radziwill, Dick Cavett and many others. Count Basie and Muddy Waters provide the music. Rock Promoter Bill Graham says: 'New York is New York. Till you do it there it hasn't happened. They could have sold the Garden out for a year. They are the biggest draw in the history of mankind. Only one other guy ever came close; Ghandi.'

AUGUST 1
'Happy' enters the US Top 30 at Number 23. It will stay in the charts for five weeks, with a highest position of Number 14.

AUGUST 5
Mick Jagger says: 'When I'm 33, I'll quit. That's the time when a man has to do something else. I can't say what it will definitely be. It's still in the back of my head - but it won't be in show business. I don't want to be a rock star all my life. I couldn't bear to end up as an Elvis Presley and sing in Las Vegas with all those housewives and old ladies coming in with their handbags. It's really sick.'

AUGUST 9
Keith Richard, Anita Pallenberg and their two children move to Montreux.

AUGUST 28
Mick and Bianca travel to Ireland to stay with Lord Gowrie near The Curragh for a few weeks' holiday.

SEPTEMBER 11
Following their arrest last July, Mick Jagger and Keith Richard are now set to appear before the Rhode Island Court on 13 December.

SEPTEMBER 15
Alexis Korner is to narrate *The Rolling Stones Story* which will be broadcast on BBC Radio 1 next year.

SEPTEMBER 22
Mick and Bianca Jagger, Charlie and Shirley Watts, Mick Taylor and Elton John attend a farewell party for their personal secretary Shirley Arnold who is leaving to join the Faces. Having started the first Stones Fan Club she has been with them for nine years.

OCTOBER 7
Mick Jagger is working at the Olympic Studios editing live tapes recorded during the US tour.
Mick says: 'Allen Klein would probably sue me if I told you my opinion of him. He's a person to be avoided as far as I'm concerned. He's just interested in himself.'

OCTOBER 10
In the High Court it is announced that Eric Easton is suing Andrew Oldham, Allen Klein, Decca Records, London Records and Nanker Phelge Music. Mick Jagger and all the above are counter-suing.

OCTOBER 15
Asked to explain Britain's apparent decadence by Belgian rock magazine *Extra*, Mick Jagger says: 'Since I left, there hasn't been any.'

NOVEMBER 6
At Chelmsford Magistrates' Court, Bill Wyman is banned from driving for six months and fined £20 for speeding in his Mercedes on the A12 near Chelmsford.

NOVEMBER 18
Cocksucker Blues, Robert Frank's film of the tour is scheduled to open at the Plaza Theatre in Manhattan around Christmas. However, due to several 'hard scenes' the film, shot partly in colour and partly in black and white, runs into trouble and is never released.

NOVEMBER 20
Mick is a guest artist on Carly Simon's single 'You're So Vain'.

NOVEMBER 25
The Rolling Stones arrive in Kingston, Jamaica for four weeks' recording sessions at the Dynamic Sound Studios.

NOVEMBER 30
Mick Jagger, Keith Richard and Mick Taylor fly to Los Angeles to plan their forthcoming Far Eastern tour.

DECEMBER 2
Warrants are issued in Nice against Keith Richard and Anita Pallenberg for drug offences.

DECEMBER 3
Rumour suggests that Leon Russell, now on holiday in Jamaica will play with the Stones on their new album. Keith buys a house at Point of View, Ocho Rios, Jamaica.

DECEMBER 4
The other Stones fly to Nice to clarify matters relating to the alleged drug violations both at Keith's house in Villefranche and aboard his yacht *Mandrax*. They return to Jamaica to continue work on the new album.

DECEMBER 6
Mick Jagger says: 'Charlie Watts, Bill Wyman, Mick Taylor and myself deny categorically that we have been charged by the French police with the buying and use of heroin. It has never been suggested that we used or bought heroin. The four of us were not freed on "provisional liberty", because we had never been arrested on any charge... at no time did we hold drug parties in our homes.' Keith Richard comments: 'The first I heard of the warrant for my arrest was when I read it in the newspaper this morning.' Sergeant Maurey of the French police states: 'We have been investigating the case in secret for the past thirteen months and three arrests have been made in connection with drugs. No other members of the group have been involved - they were given a thorough going over in Nice recently and are clean.' The action against the Stones followed the arrest of a number of young Frenchmen on drug charges. They were all described as Rolling Stones' fans and one was said to have been a cook at Keith's house.

DECEMBER 9
Carly Simon's single 'You're So Vain' is said to have been inspired by Mick Jagger.

DECEMBER 11
Because of a contractual dispute between the Rolling Stones, Decca Records and Allen Klein, the double live album recorded during the US tour last summer may never be released.
Keith Richard says: 'Allen Klein and Decca are grabbing all they can because, being a live album, it has three old songs to which they have the rights. No doubt they won't let us put it out unless we give them the earth.'

DECEMBER 12
The Stones may be forced to cancel their record-breaking Japanese tour (55,000 seats

sold in five hours) due to the drug problems with the French police.

DECEMBER 13
Keith Richard says: 'All you hear about me is when the warrants are out. What I resent is that they tried to drag my old lady into it, which I find particularly distasteful.' Dynamic Sound Studios' owner says that Mick Jagger has written a reggae song called 'Man Eating Woman'.

DECEMBER 14
Speaking about the Rolling Stones' projected live album, Allen Klein says: 'I met Mr Jagger a month ago, personally assured him that I had no objection to the album being released, and told him to go ahead and put it out. I cannot speak for Decca Records.' In London a spokesman for Decca says: 'We would be happy to come to some arrangement and do an intelligent deal with the Rolling Stones. We have been very easy with them in the past, some of us feel too easy. But the time has come when we feel that we should have a bit of a fight back.'

DECEMBER 17
The Trials of Oz with songs by John Lennon, Buzzy Linhard, Yoko Ono and Mick Jagger opens in the New York East Village.

DECEMBER 20
A double anthology album called *More Hot Rocks (Big Hits And Fazed Cookies)* is released in America on London Records.

DECEMBER 22
The Stones' tour manager Peter Rudge returns exhausted to London after a 35,000 miles journey negotiating and finalising details for the Far East tour with both governments and promoters.

DECEMBER 23
A serious earthquake devastates Managua, Nicaragua, home of Bianca Jagger's parents.

DECEMBER 26
Mick and Bianca leave London en route for Nicaragua to search for her mother and relatives.

DECEMBER 28
Mick and Bianca Jagger charter a jet in Kingston and fly to Managua. With them they take 2,000 anti-typhoid vaccine syringes.

DECEMBER 31
In Managua Bianca is safely reunited with her parents.

Left: *From 1972 on Mick and Bianca were the media's hottest property, uncrowned king and queen of the 'me decade'.* Far right: NME *lead on the story of the Stones' dispute with Allen Klein and Decca.*

NINETEEN 73

JANUARY 3
Both Mick and Bianca Jagger are amongst the best dressed men and women of 1972 in an American poll of 2,000 international fashion editors.

JANUARY 4
After being reported missing in Managua, Mick and Bianca Jagger are now safe.
One of the Stones is reported to have been refused entry to Australia. Neither name nor reason is given.

JANUARY 6
A Decca Records spokesman says the company has decided to issue no more Rolling Stones material, 'because we're all so tired of it; after all, we've heard it many times before'.

JANUARY 8
Mick Jagger is banned from entering Japan because of his drug conviction six years ago.

JANUARY 9
Albert Grassy of the Australia Immigration Ministry announces that there is no longer any ban on the entry of any member of the Rolling Stones.

JANUARY 10
The US music magazine *Billboard* votes the Rolling Stones the best band in 1972. Mick Jagger announces his plan to give a benefit concert for Nicaraguan Earthquake victims.

JANUARY 11
It is confirmed that the Stones' Japanese tour has been cancelled despite record breaking ticket sales.

JANUARY 14
The Rolling Stones are in Los Angeles rehearsing for their Australian tour.

JANUARY 18
The Rolling Stones play a benefit concert at the Los Angeles Forum for Nicaraguan earthquake victims. They raise over $516,810, the highest grossing charity rock concert to date, outdoing even the 1971 concert for Bangladesh organised by George Harrison, and are presented with a commemorative plaque by the Nicaraguan Ambassador.

JANUARY 19
To raise more money for Nicaragua, the radio station KMET in Hollywood auctions Rolling Stones' memorabilia. *The Village Voice* reports that Marshall Chess says the Stones are considering marketing their own 'Rolling Stones Beer' to be packaged in a can with a red lips logo.

JANUARY 20
The Rolling Stones fly to Honolulu.

JANUARY 21/22
The Stones start their Australasian tour with two shows at the International Sports Centre, Honolulu.

JANUARY 23
The band return to Los Angeles. In an interview with Lou Irvin of Radio network KDAY, Mick Jagger says: 'I believe that every man should be able to move around the world without any hindrance. I don't believe in these barriers and passports and work permits and visas.' Meanwhile their double anthology *More Hot Rocks* enters the US Top 30 at Number 26. It will stay in the charts for seven weeks with a highest position of Number 9.
Mick Taylor cuts tracks for Nicky Hopkins' new album.

JANUARY 28
Bette Midler on the Rolling Stones' Concert at Madison Square Garden last summer: 'I got outta my seat, and I stood in the aisle and I saw just what that Mick Jagger was doing. I saw just what he was *doing*. You know what I mean, he was doing *it*, right on stage.' (Doing what?) 'It, my darling - oh the *nerve*. I stood there and I shouted "*please....oh please.*" Oh, how I wanted him!'

JANUARY 29
Radio KMET in Hollywood closes the bidding on the Stones paraphernalia including a personally autographed costume belonging to Mick Jagger, a large 'tongue' cushion, a pillow autographed by Mick Taylor and a bottle of vodka with one shot remaining inscribed 'Have a drink with me, Bill Wyman'.

FEBRUARY 5
The Stones play two shows at the Football Stadium in Hong Kong.

FEBRUARY 8
The Rolling Stones arrive in Sydney.

FEBRUARY 9
A press reception is held in Sydney.

FEBRUARY 10
The Stones fly to Auckland, New Zealand.

FEBRUARY 11
Concert at Western Springs Stadium, Auckland. £500 is raised for a local boys recreation centre when sixteen sheets and pillowcases used by the group are auctioned by enterprising local fundraisers.

FEBRUARY 13
Concert at the Milton Park Tennis Courts, Brisbane.
When asked about reports that Bianca is to do a film for Andy Warhol, Mick says: 'Andy Warhol? We work well together. When girls get together there's always talk but they never get anything done.'

FEBRUARY 14
Second concert at Milton Park, Brisbane.

FEBRUARY 17/18
Concerts at the Kooyong Tennis Courts, Melbourne. Press Conference at Montsalvat Castle.

FEBRUARY 20
Concert at Memorial Park Drive, Adelaide.

FEBRUARY 21
Concert at Memorial Park Drive, Adelaide. 5,000 fans clash with 300 policemen and 21 people are arrested.

FEBRUARY 24
Concert at the Western Australia Cricket Ground, Perth. Immigration Minister Albert 'Little Al' Grassby, says: 'The Rolling Stones are an excellent example to Australia Youth. I told them I was putting my faith in them and they would do the right thing. I have no regrets that I let them in. Yes, I went out on a limb to give them visas. To give a man a bad name and hang him is immoral and un-Australian.'

FEBRUARY 26/27
The Stones wind up their Australian tour with concerts at the Royal Randwick Racecourse, Sydney.

FEBRUARY 28
The Rolling Stones go their separate ways on holiday. Bill Wyman flies to the States, Charlie Watts to France, Keith Richard to Jamaica, Mick Taylor to Indonesia and Mick Jagger to the States via Jamaica.
It is rumoured that the Stones have been banned from entering the US. Although they continue to travel back and forth, they do not perform in the States until after the matter is resolved in August 1974.

MARCH 3
The *Daily Mirror* quotes Mick Jagger on why he has cut his hair: 'Because I had begun to feel an old tart with long hair.'

MARCH 6
Mick, Keith and Bill are in Los Angeles mixing the new album.

MARCH 26
An advertisement for the new Lex Hotel at Heathrow Airport appears in the *Times*. It

---

Above left: *At odds with Mick's prancing, the others' static style looked dangerously like a backing band.*

features portraits of Prime Minister Edward Heath, David Frost, Barbra Streisand, Olympic swimmer Mark Spitz and the Rolling Stones. Heath complains about the use of well-known personalities in advertisements without their permission. Mick Jagger says the Stones have no objection to standing beside Mr Heath and they hope he doesn't object to standing beside them.

APRIL 4
The *Radio Times* heralds the six-week Radio One series *The Rolling Stones Story* with Mick Jagger in colour on the cover and interviews with family and friends inside.

APRIL 7
At Warwick, Rhode Island, Judge Orion Orton rejects an action to dismiss charges arising from the incident last July involving the Stones and local photographers. Mick Jagger and Keith Richard will stand trial next time they are in the States.
The Rolling Stones Story starts on Radio 1.

APRIL 11
The School of Literature at California State University is to innovate a degree level rock studies programme. Rock performers to be assessed in Dr James Wheeler's course include Bob Dylan, Jimi Hendrix, Paul McCartney, John Lennon, Neil Young, Grace Slick, Mick Jagger and Keith Richard.

APRIL 13
Atlantic Records throw a 25th anniversary party in Paris. Marshall Chess treats the guests to 'Dancing with Mr D' from the Stones new, yet to be released, album.

APRIL 14
Japanese magazine *Music Life* votes the Rolling Stones best group of the year and Mick Jagger best male vocalist.

APRIL 16
Tucky Buzzard's album, *All Right On The Night* produced by Bill Wyman, is out on Purple Records.

APRIL 28
The *New Musical Express* reports: 'Don't expect any airplay for "Starfucker" from the upcoming Rolling Stones album.'

APRIL
Charlie Watts says: 'I don't know if I could take a solo all on my own.'

APRIL 29
'Sad Day'/'You Can't Always Get What You Want' is released by Decca in Britain and by London Records in the US. 'Sad Day' has never been released as a single in the UK before.

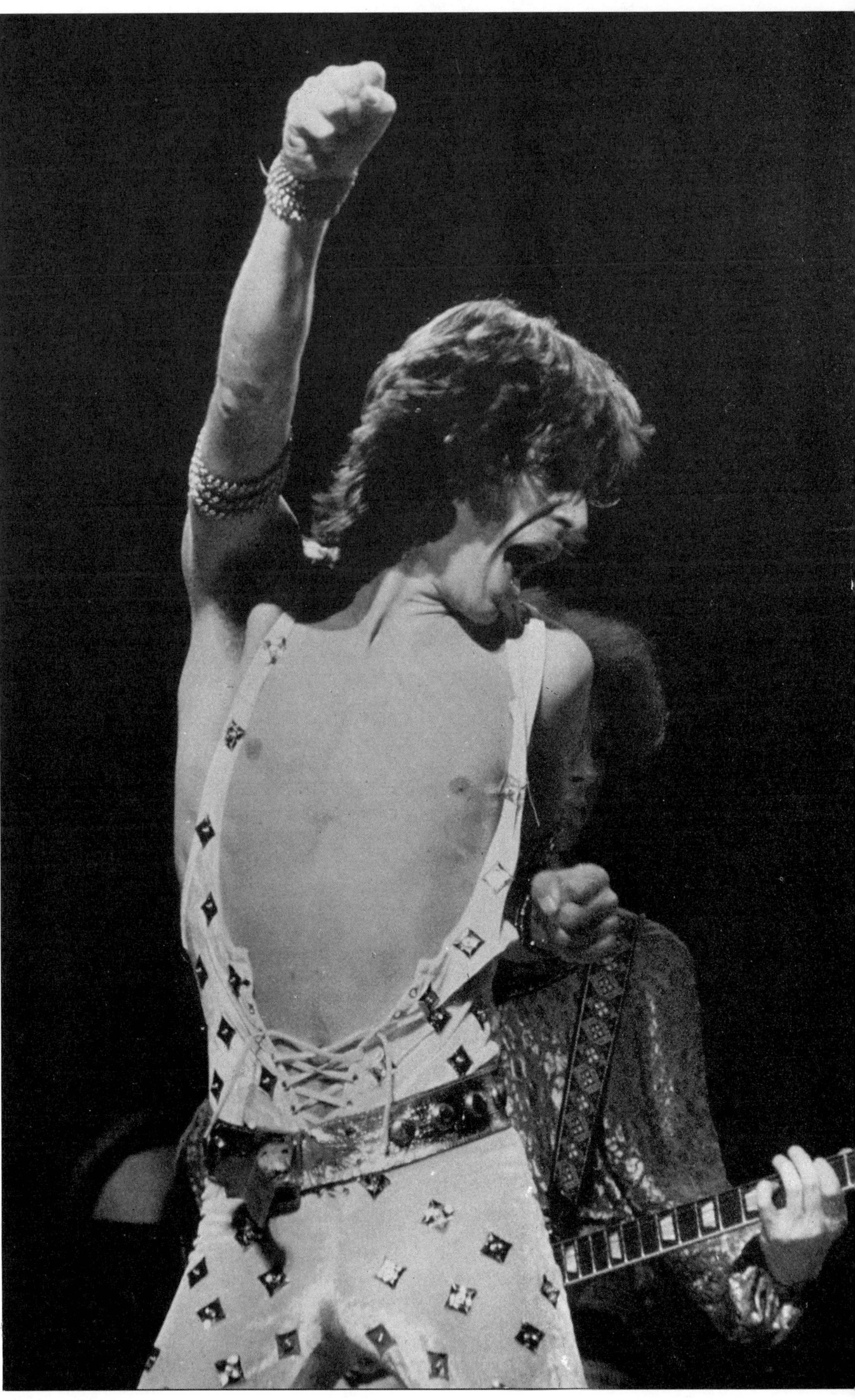

Right: *'Glam Rock' Jagger-style.*

APRIL 30
Mick and Bianca Jagger attend a party in New York given by the magazine *After Dark* to honour Bette Midler, recently voted entertainer of the year.

MAY 2
Cecil Beaton's portrait of Mick Jagger is sold at Sotheby's for £220.

MAY 9
Mick and Bianca Jagger fly from New York to Washington to present the Senate with a cheque for £350,000 for the Pan American Development Fund. In return they receive a Golden Key in appreciation of the Nicaraguan Aid concert in January.

MAY 10
While Mick and Bianca are at the New York Academy of Music at a J. Geils concert, firemen are called to a fire at their English home, Stargrove.

MAY 11
Bianca returns to London to attend the Liza Minnelli midnight concert at the Palladium.

MAY 13
Gram Parsons says: 'I think it was a logical step for the Rolling Stones to get into country music, because they've always been well into the old blues since they first began.'

MAY 15
The Rolling Stones turn down an offer to play at the Lincoln Drill Hall on 16 June. Says promoter Tony Lyne: 'We are offering them 105% of the gross take if they will do a gig for us, and I'm quite sure they've never had an offer like that before.'

MAY 17
Mick and Bianca attend a party at the Ritz in London to launch a new label, G&M Records, one of whose first signings is Mick's brother, Chris Jagger.

MAY 19
Jack Bruce: 'The Rolling Stones are the ultimate rock band.'

MAY 28
The Rolling Stones mix their new album at Island Studios in London. Keith Richard is said to be missing some sessions.

Bianca looks on as Mick talks to brother Chris at the G&M Records launch at the Ritz, London.

JUNE 1
Rumours sweep Los Angeles, New York and London that Keith Richard is leaving the Stones.

JUNE 6
Billy Gaff of G&M Records gives a birthday party at his Fulham home to which Mick and Bianca are invited. Fans storm the house.

JUNE 7
Charlie Watts, Keith Richard, Anita Pallenberg, Mick and Bianca Jagger attend a party after a Wings concert at the Hammersmith Odeon. Other stars present include Eric Clapton, Elton John, the Who, some of the Faces and Chris Jagger.

JUNE 8
In Los Angeles Stones tour manager Peter Rudge says: 'The Rolling Stones will definitely tour Europe this year but won't play in America again, at least not in 1973.

JUNE 9
In the *New Musical Express* Mick Jagger denies rumours that Keith Richard is to leave the group to be replaced by Ronnie Wood of the Faces. 'The report has no basis in fact whatsoever, it's absolutely untrue.' Ronnie Wood also denies that any approach has been made to him.

JUNE 11
Keith Richard joins Mick Jagger in denying the Rolling Stones' split. He says he had been hanging around with Ronnie Wood while in London so the rumour has come as a 'complete shock'.

JUNE 13
The US magazine *Creem* votes the Rolling Stones band of the year, best live act and best album *(Exile On Main Street)*. Bill Wyman is voted top bass player.

JUNE 14
Jimi Hendrix, a documentary including conversations between Hendrix and Jagger, opens in London.

JUNE 15
While at Island Studios mixing the new album, *Goats Head Soup*, Keith Richard confirms that the Stones are planning a major European tour. Now a Jamaican resident, Keith also reveals personal plans to record with a rastafarian band in Kingston.

JUNE 16
The musical press report that Mick Taylor plans to join Nicky Hopkins for an album and that Bill Wyman is to collaborate with Jim Keltner. Ian Stewart says: 'Bill has written a lot of good songs that are fairly gentle and not the sort of things that would suit the group. Mick Taylor has a few as well but he tends to begin more than he finishes.'

JUNE 18
Mick, Bianca and Jade fly to Italy for a short holiday. Meanwhile singer/acress Marsha Hunt files an application order at Marylebone Magistrates Court, London claiming that Mick Jagger is the father of her daughter Karis.

JUNE 19
Following Marsha Hunt's suit, the Court orders blood tests to be taken at the request of Mick Jagger's attorney. The hearing is adjourned. A spokeman for the putative father says: 'This allegation is not admitted. There are discussions between the parties about the merits of the allegations.'

JUNE 23
After a year of negotiations it is announced that the Rolling Stones will tour the Soviet Union next spring becoming the first British rock band to perform there.

JUNE 25
Mick Jagger goes to the Queen Elizabeth Hall to see Mick Taylor play with Mike Oldfield. Mick says: 'There's so much good music being played at the moment. I'd really like to do a concert like this one.'

JUNE 26
Keith Richard is arrested by Drug Squad

Above: *Mick on stage during the UK tour. The whole Stones act was becoming increasingly flamboyant.*

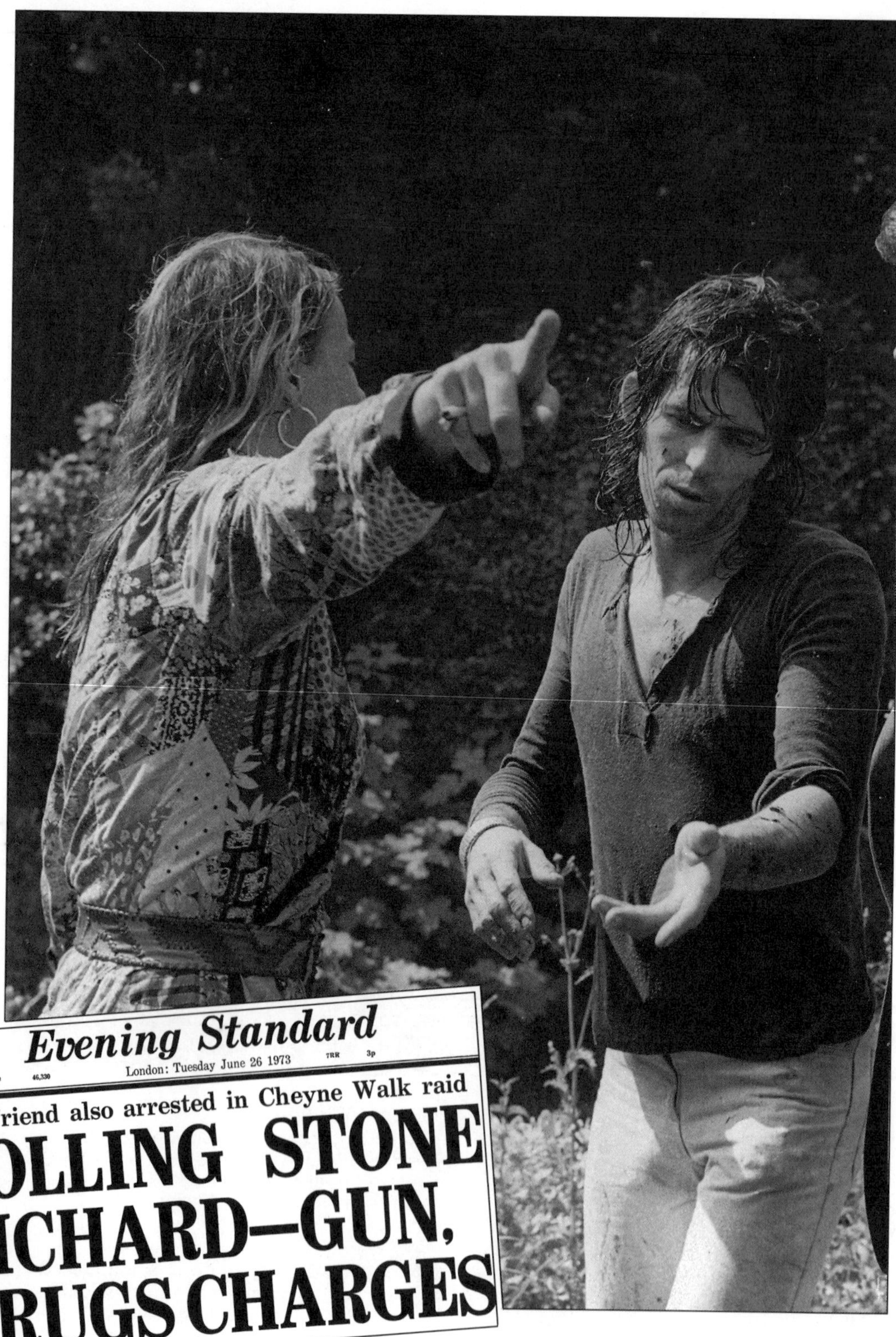

Evening Standard

London: Tuesday June 26 1973 3p

Girl friend also arrested in Cheyne Walk raid

ROLLING STONE RICHARD—GUN, DRUGS CHARGES

officers in a house in Cheyne Walk, Chelsea. Anita Pallenberg and Prince Jean Stanislas Klossowski are also arrested. All three are charged with possession of cannabis. Keith is also charged with possessing a revolver and ammunition without a firearms certificate.

JUNE 27
Keith Richard is remanded on £1,000 bail until 1 August on drug and gun charges but his passport is returned so that he can go ahead with recording commitments abroad.

JULY 10
British newspapers report that Mick and Bianca's marriage is on the rocks as Mick sets off on tour without her. Both deny the story and Mick adds: 'You wouldn't take your wife to the office, would you?'

JULY 17
The Rolling Stones announce their autumn European tour which will open in Vienna on 1 September and end in Berlin on 19 October and take in eight countries, but not in France due to Keith Richard's legal problems. The Stones will be supported by Billy Preston and the American band Cracker, the first signing to the Rolling Stones label.

JULY 24/25
Bianca is in Paris, modelling Yves St Laurent clothes for the *Daily Mirror*. The Stones shoot a promo film for their new single.

JULY 26
Mick Jagger is 30. A party is held in the Stones' London office. Of the new album *Goats Head Soup* Mick says: 'I really felt close to this album and I really put all I had into it... but whatever you do it's always wrong. If you do it rocky, people say ''Oh it's like the same old rock'n'roll'', and if you do slow ballads, they say it's too pretty.'

JULY 28
America is to get BBC Radio's *The Rolling Stones Story*. The series will be syndicated on stations across the States this summer.

JULY 29
The Stones send a huge 'thank you' card to Al Grassby, Australian Immigration Minister, for letting them tour earlier in the year.

JULY 30
Mick Jagger watches the Test Match at the Oval. Rumours are circulating that the Stones and the Faces will join forces. Speculation began when members of both bands, namely Ian McLagan, Ronnie Wood, Mick Jagger and Keith Richard started recording together at Wood's Richmond home studio.

JULY 31
A serious fire breaks out at Redlands, Keith's home in Sussex. Keith, Anita and the children escape but the house is very badly damaged. Some antique furniture, books and equipment are saved.
Marsha Hunt's paternity suit against Mick Jagger is adjourned until 6 November, awaiting a blood test.
At Marylebone Magistrates' Court, Keith Richard and Anita Pallenberg are remanded on bail in their absence in relation to the Cheyne Walk drugs raid.

AUGUST 4
Peter Rudge says: 'It would be very strange to see Keith Richard on top form without the

Above: *A summer of trouble for Anita and Keith who watch helplessly as their 500-year-old Sussex home, Redlands goes up in flames.*

company of a good tequila.'

They're back!...in London for their first British tour after three long years
the ROLLING STONES
Rolling Stones rock Wembley
They're back!
STONED!
STONES—ALREADY A POP LEGEND

AUGUST 6
Crowds queue for tickets as box offices open for the UK tour. A fourth concert has been added at Wembley's Empire Pool following the almost instant sell-out of the original three shows.

AUGUST 13
Several concerts on the forthcoming tour will be recorded for a possible live album to be released just before Christmas. The album could also include studio numbers remaining from their Jamaican sessions.

AUGUST 14
Keith and Anita are further remanded until 12 September. Meanwhile filming continues on a twenty minute segment for the first edition of *Don Kirshner's Rock Concert* which begins network screening in the States in late September and which will mark the Stones' first TV appearance there in ten years. To avoid any problems with the new album the group are forced to change the name of 'Starfucker' to 'Star Star'. Some say the song is Jagger's answer to 'You're So Vain' but groupies insist it's in homage to them.

AUGUST 18
Following a ban by the local Council, the planned open air concert in Cardiff is cancelled and switched to Pembroke Castle, 97 miles away on the Welsh coast. As the venue is smaller, numbers will be restricted to 12,000. 8,000 fans sign a petition protesting at Cardiff Council's action.
The Stones fly to Rotterdam, Holland to rehearse.

AUGUST 20
A new single 'Angie'/'Silver Train' (Jagger/Richard), recorded in Jamaica and produced by Jimmy Miller is released on Rolling Stones Records.

AUGUST 22
The Spanish Government bans all Rolling Stones records throughout Spain, due to remarks allegedly made by Mick Jagger attacking the Franco regime. He denies making any such comments.

AUGUST 25
The proposed Pembroke Castle concert is cancelled because of opposition from the local council, the second time in three weeks the Stones have been prevented from playing in Wales. Organiser John Martin says that local public opinion fears the possibility of 'another Altamont'. 'It is obvious that the council is completely prejudiced against the Rolling Stones. If it had been Tom Jones, or someone like that, there would have been no problems'. Alderman Ernie Morgan comments: 'The castle would not have seen anything like it since Oliver Cromwell forced its surrender. Talk about the Rolling Stones, there would be stones flying everywhere.'

AUGUST 28
'Angie' enters the British Top 30 at Number 28. It will remain in the charts for nine weeks, it highest position Number 2.

AUGUST 31
Goats Head Soup is released on Rolling Stones Records and features ten tracks written by Mick Jagger and Keith Richard. Produced by Jimmy Miller it was recorded at Dynamic Studios, Kingston, Jamaica, last autumn.

SEPTEMBER 1
Opening concert of the European tour at Vienna's Stadthalle in front of 16,000 fans. A representative of the Soviet Union's Ministry of Culture, Yuri Kurinoff, attends the show.

SEPTEMBER 3
Concert at the Eisstadion, Mannheim, West Germany.

SEPTEMBER 4
Concert in the Sporthalle, Cologne, West Germany.

SEPTEMBER 5
The Rolling Stones fly from Cologne to London. Plans to continue the tour behind the Iron Curtain are shelved due to lack of time.

SEPTEMBER 6
The Stones give a big party at Blenheim Palace.

SEPTEMBER 7
Concert at the Empire Pool, Wembley.
The *Daily Mirror* reports: 'Scores of rock fans broke through one of the main doors to the Empire Pool, Wembley, last night in a bid to see the Rolling Stones' sell-out concert. Among the audience last night were actors Ryan O'Neal, Elliot Gould and Donald Sutherland and musicians Peter Frampton, Jeff Beck, Tim Bogert, Carmine Appice and photographer David Bailey.'

SEPTEMBER 8
Concert at the Empire Pool, Wembley.

SEPTEMBER 9
The Rolling Stones' final concert at the Empire Pool. Their total audience over four concerts has been 40,000. Over 15,000 postal requests for tickets were unsuccessful. A Rolling Stones' spokesman said: 'They could have played Wembley for a week.'

SEPTEMBER 10
DJs on BBC Radio 1 and 2 are asked not to play 'Star Star' from the new album.

SEPTEMBER 11
Concert at the Bellevue, Manchester.
Goats Head Soup enters the British Top 30 at Number 7. It will remain in the charts for twelve weeks, including two weeks at Number 1.

SEPTEMBER 12
Concert at the Bellevue, Manchester.
Keith Richard and Anita Pallenberg are now set for trial on 24 October.

SEPTEMBER 13
Concert at Newcastle City Hall.

SEPTEMBER 15
'Angie' enters the US Top 30 at Number 27. It will stay in the Top 30 for ten weeks, reaching the Number 1 spot.

SEPTEMBER 16/17
Two concerts at the Apollo Centre, Glasgow.

SEPTEMBER 19
The final British concert at the Odeon, Birmingham.

SEPTEMBER 23
Concert in Innsbruck, Austria.

SEPTEMBER 25/26
Goats Head Soup reaches Number 1 in the UK.
Concerts at the Festhalle, Berne, Switzerland.

SEPTEMBER 28
Concert at the Olympiahalle, Munich, West Germany.

SEPTEMBER 30
Two concerts at the Festhalle, Frankfurt, West Germany.

OCTOBER 2
Concerts at the Ernst Mercke Halle, Hamburg. The Rolling Stones appear, pre-recorded, on BBC2's *The Old Grey Whistle Test*.
Goats Head Soup enters the US Top 30 at Number 9. It will remain in the charts for 14 weeks, including two weeks at Number 1.

OCTOBER 5
Decca release another 'Oldies' album called *No Stone Unturned*.

OCTOBER 6
Concert at the Scandinavium, Gotheborg, Sweden.
The Rolling Stones are to record a special live concert in Brussels for Radio Luxembourg's French service to be broadcast in full on 18 October.

OCTOBER 7
Two concerts at the Brondby Hallen, Copenhagen, Denmark.

OCTOBER 9/10/11
Concerts at the Grughalle, Essen, West Germany.

OCTOBER 12
Anita Pallenberg is reported to be in hospital in Switzerland.

OCTOBER 13
Concert at the Ahoy Halle, Rotterdam, the Netherlands.

OCTOBER 14
Two more concerts at the Ahoy Halle, Rotterdam.

OCTOBER 15
Concert at the Palais de Sport, Antwerp, Belgium.

Above left: *The overt sexuality of Mick's act spills over into his costume – but even this can't put Keith off his stroke.* Inset: *Ticket for one of the Stones' sell-out concerts at the Empire Pool, Wembley in September 1973.* Below: *Promotional sticker for* Goats Head Soup.

Fines of £500 and twelve months' suspended prison sentences are imposed on Keith Richard and Anita Pallenberg for drug offences in Nice. Stones' saxophonist Bobby Keys also receives a suspended sentence.

OCTOBER 17
Concert at the Forêt Nationale, Brussels, Belgium.

OCTOBER 19
The European tour ends with a concert at the Deutschlandhalle, Berlin.

OCTOBER 23
Goats Head Soup and 'Angie' both reach Number 1 in the USA.

OCTOBER 24
Keith Richard is fined a total of £205 by Marlborough Street Magistrates when he admits possession of cannabis, chinese heroin and Mandrax tablets, plus a revolver, a shotgun and ammunition at his Chelsea home. Anita Pallenberg is given a one year conditional discharge for possessing 25 Mandrax tablets. Their lawyer says the drugs had been left by others who stayed there while the couple were out of the country.

OCTOBER 25
Mick Jagger and Mick Taylor join Billy Preston on stage at the Rainbow Theatre, London. It is rumoured that Mick Taylor is leaving the Stones to tour the States with Mike Oldfield.

NOVEMBER 13
The Rolling Stones fly to Munich to cut a new album at Musicland Studios. However, Mick Taylor does not accompany them as he is suffering from a 'mysterious illness'.

NOVEMBER 24
The band finish their recording sessions at Musicland Studios.

DECEMBER 15
A single, 'Doo Doo Doo Doo Doo (Heartbreaker)'/'Dancing With Mr D', taken from *Goats Head Soup* is released in the USA.

DECEMBER 22
The National Council for Civil Liberties is spearheading a campaign against the Independent Displays Bill now being discussed in Parliament. The clean-up bill threatens to emasculate pop culture, claims Chaz Ball of the NCCL. 'I'm sure Mick Jagger offends the modesty of the average man at certain points in his act. People should know more about this. The implications for the business and for freedom of expression in general are great.'

NINETEEN 74

JANUARY 5
Bill Wyman is in Los Angeles to record a solo album.

JANUARY 12
Rolling Stones Records re-issues the maxi-single, 'Brown Sugar'/'Bitch'/'Let It Rock'.

JANUARY 14
The Rolling Stones fly to Munich for two weeks' recording at Musicland Studios.

JANUARY 22
'Doo Doo Doo Doo Doo (Heartbreaker)' enters the US Top 30 at Number 24. It will remain in the charts for five weeks, reaching a highest position of Number 10.

JANUARY 26
Mick Jagger on the New York Dolls: 'We were almost going to sign them at one point. I went down to the Imperial College gig and didn't think much of them at all. I think all this posing stuff is going to be tolerated until, oh, the middle of 1974 and then it'll be dead.'

FEBRUARY 10
Mick Jagger watches the England v West Indies Test Match in Port of Spain, Trinidad. He and Bianca deny their marriage is on the rocks.

FEBRUARY 13
Keith Richard, Anita Pallenberg and Bobby Keys are banned from entering France.

FEBRUARY 15
Mick Jagger is at the opening of the Bottom Line club in New York,

FEBRUARY 16
US Vice President Gerald Ford admits on TV he has never heard of Mick Jagger.

FEBRUARY 21
Early Stones footage is re-broadcast on TV in Los Angeles.

FEBRUARY 25
Mick Jagger visits David Bowie's recording session in London.

MARCH 1
A film, *Ladies and Gentlemen, The Rolling Stones*, documenting their US tour is previewed in New York.

MARCH 13
Mick Jagger and John Lennon are among the guests for the presentation of a special Oscar to James Cagney.

MARCH 25
Mick Jagger, John Lennon, Harry Nilsson, Bobby Keys and Jesse Ed David cut material at the Record Plant in Los Angeles.

APRIL 14
Ladies and Gentlemen, The Rolling Stones, is premiered at the Ziegfeld Theatre in New York.

MAY 1
Bill Wyman appears on BBC 2's *Old Grey Whistle Test*.

MAY 4
Bill Wyman says: 'People ask me why I don't do more on stage. But I'm a bass player, and when I get up there, the only thing that matters to me is bass, whether the ceiling falls in or anything. I have to listen like mad to hear the beat of those drunks over the kids screaming. That's what I play to. I've been in one of the biggest bands in the world for eight years and I've never seen anything near the money people talk and write about. I never wrote any songs, never got any publishing. That's why Brian Jones died broke as he did, owing money.'

MAY 10
Bill Wyman is among the guests at the launch of Led Zeppelin's Swan Song label at the Bel Air Hotel, New York. His first solo album, *Monkey Grip* which he also wrote, composed and produced, is released on Rolling Stones Records. Bill plays bass, guitar and harmonica and a guest line up includes Dr John, Leon Russell, Dallas Taylor and Betty Wright.

MAY 18
Keith Richard is back in London after several months in Switzerland. He and Ron Wood are in the audience for the Who's concert at Charlton Athletic football stadium.

MAY 20
The Rolling Stones mix their new album at Island Records Studios in Notting Hill.

MAY 28
Mick Taylor, Mick Jagger, George Harrison and Eric Clapton join Ron Wood during sessions for his solo album recorded at his Richmond home, where Keith Richard is living while in London.

JUNE 15
Keith Richard says: 'Rock'n'Roll is only any good when you're confident about it. Hesitate and you're lost, especially on stage... I find it a bit of a drag that certain people feel the need to project their death wishes on me. I've got no preoccupation with death whatsoever... I was nineteen when it started to take off, right, and just a very ordinary guy. Chucked out of night clubs, birds poke their tongues out at me, that kind of scene. And then suddenly, Adonis! And, you know it's so ridiculous, so totally insane. It makes you very cynical. But it's a hell of a thing to deal with. It really is a bugger. Looking back now, happily married an' all that, it seems incrediby funny, but it took me years to get it under control.'
'Monkey Grip'/'What A Blow', a single taken from Bill Wyman's solo album, is released by Rolling Stones Records.

JUNE 28
Bill Wyman plays with Muddy Waters at the Montreux Jazz Festival. He also jams with Buddy Guy and Junior Wells' All Stars.

JULY 3
Brian Jones' fans make a pilgrimage to his grave in Cheltenham.

JULY 9
The Stones appear on BBC TV's *Old Grey Whistle Test* playing the new single 'It's Only Rock'n'Roll, (But I Like It)'.

JULY 13
Keith Richard appears on stage with Ron Wood, Willie Weeks, Andy Newmark and Ian McLagan at the Kilburn State Cinema, London. Mick Jagger is in the audience for Eric Clapton's concert at Madison Square Garden.
The *New Musical Express* publishes an open letter to the Stones from a Brian Jones fan: 'We were so saddened when we went up to Cheltenham last Wednesday evening to take flowers on the anniversary of the death of a close friend, Brian Jones. Although his grave was covered with flowers, which had been brought by fans from all over Europe with their hard-earned money - the founder of the greatest rock'n'roll band in the world had been forgotten not only by Mick Jagger, Bill Wyman, Charlie Watts, Keith Richard and Anita, but by all the people he trusted and called his friends, (with the exception of Shirley [Watts]). Please print this to thank those fans like Margaret Lowe who remembered and filled the spaces of his friends which moved the hearts of a very sad family. Nicholas, Chelsea, London.'

JULY 14
Keith Richard appears again with Ron Wood in Kilburn.

If I could stick my pen in my heart
Spill it all over the stage
Would it satisfy ya?
Bill Wyman
Monkey Grip

Far left: *Striking poster design for* It's Only Rock'n'Roll. *The album topped the US charts.*
Left: Monkey Grip, *Bill Wyman's first solo album*

JULY 27
In the *New Musical Express* Keith Richard is nominated 'The World's Most Elegantly Wasted Human Being'. NME also publishes a letter from Les Perrin replying to the letter about Brian Jones: 'While understanding the sense of hurt which caused an open letter to be written by ''Nicholas of Chelsea'' (I wish he had appended his full name and address because a personal note would be in place). I think I should elucidate concerning the attitudes of other member of the Rolling Stones in connection with the anniversary of the death of Brian Jones. Brian is not forgotten by Mick, Bill, Charlie, Keith or Anita. The reverse is the case and considerable thought was given to sending a floral tribute. After much heartsearching it was decided that, rather than the ephemeral salutation of flowers, that a donation to charity should be made. Knowing as the boys did of Brian's personal contributions to children's funds, it was decided to donate money to the United Nations Children's Fund for relief to refugee children of Bangladesh. Normally, this matter would not be mentioned but it is, because it is felt in this case that an explanation is needed.'

JULY 30
'It's Only Rock'n'Roll' enters the British Top 30 at Number 27. It remains in the charts for a total of six weeks, peaking at Number 10.

AUGUST 10
Mick says he has more than a hundred early Stones tapes and he plans to release some within the year.

AUGUST 17
The Los Angeles premiere of *Ladies and Gentlemen, The Rolling Stones*. Proceeds are donated to the LA Free Clinic.

AUGUST 18
Mick is in LA for the final mastering of the new album.

AUGUST 20
'It's Only Rock'n'Roll' enters the US Top 30 at Number 28. It will stay in the charts for seven weeks, reaching a highest position of Number 18.

AUGUST 24
The Stones videotape three songs for the *Don Kirshner TV Show* in New York.

AUGUST
During the month the Stones approach former US secret service agent Bill Carter (who had worked for Presidents John F.

Right: *Bianca arrives with Austrian actor Helmut Berger at his 'bad taste' 30th birthday party. She was increasingly seen in public without Mick.*

Kennedy and Lyndon Johnson), now a top lawyer from Little Rock, Arkansas, to try to resolve their US immigration problems, imposed in February 1973. He arranges for work permits and visas to be issued to them through the Immigration and Naturalization Service office in Memphis, Tennessee.

AUGUST 31
Keith Richard says: 'As far as I know Brian Jones never wrote a single finished song in his life; he wrote bits and pieces but he never presented them to us. No doubt he spent hours, weeks, working on things, but his paranoia was so great that he could never bring himself to present it to us.'
On reports that he has had total blood transfusions in Switzerland, he says: 'That's beautiful. I love that. I've heard about that thing and I'd love to do it just because I'm sure that eating motorway food for ten years has done my blood no good at all. The only time I've ever been to Switzerland is to ski... I gave up drugs when the doctor told me I had six months to live. If you're gonna get wasted, get wasted elegantly.'

SEPTEMBER 18
Mick Jagger rents a house at Montaux, Long Island, where he and Bianca will stay till early October. They have spent the summer at Andy Warhol's house nearby.

SEPTEMBER 27
Ron Wood's solo album is released by WEA. Called *I've Got My Own Album To Do*, (suggested by Mick Jagger) it includes two tracks written by Jagger/Richard, 'Act Together' and 'Sure The One You Need'. Mick, Keith and Mick Taylor also feature on the album.

SEPTEMBER 29
Mick and Bianca Jagger are in the audience for Eric Clapton's concert at the Nassau Coliseum, New York.

OCTOBER 7
Bianca says Mick married her because he looks like her.

OCTOBER 12
Mick Taylor says: 'Mick Jagger is always talking about doing a solo album. I mean, he could do an amazing record too. He played me some tapes he made in LA with musicians like Jim Keltner and Jack Bruce and they were great. Keith could do one too. I know he doesn't feel the need to, but he could still do it.

OCTOBER 15
Keith Richard says: 'I'm changing my image. I've arranged for a whole series of dental appointments in Switzerland... I only ever get ill when I give up drugs.' Keith, Ron Wood, Jimmy Page, Ian Stewart and Rick Grech are at Olympic Studios in London.

OCTOBER 17
Mick Jagger spends a week in Paris where rumours abound that he is dating Nathalie Delon.

OCTOBER 18
A graffiti publicity campaign throughout London announces the release of the new album, *It's Only Rock'n'Roll*. All tracks are by Jagger and Richard, bar 'Ain't Too Proud To Beg', an old Temptations hit. The album was recorded at Musicland in Munich between last November and January this year. With a cover designed by Guy Peelhaart, the album is produced by the Glimmer Twins. Ron Wood and Kenny Jones appear on the title track.

OCTOBER 22
It's Only Rock'n'Roll enters the British Top 30 at Number 14. It will remain in the charts for seven weeks, peaking at Number 4.
Keith Richard says: '*Goats Head Soup* to me was a marking-time album. I like it in many ways but I don't think it has the freshness that this one has... Rock'n'Roll can't be planned or prepared. You can have a few basic structures though. I'm not the sort of person who sits down at home with a guitar, writes a song and says, "that's how I hear it," because I play in a band and leave it up to them to tell me how it should go for them.'

OCTOBER 25
A new single taken from the album 'Ain't Too Proud to Beg'/'Dance Little Sister', produced by the Glimmer Twins is released in the States on Rolling Stones Records.

OCTOBER 26
Mick and Bianca Jagger attend a party at the Four Seasons restaurant after the premiere of *Night Porter*, given by producer Joe Levine in honour of starring actress, Charlotte Rampling. Mick and Bianca narrowly avoid being thrown out by for being 'scruffy' by Mrs Levine, who relents on discovering who they are.
Meanwhile Radio Station KTIM in San Rafael, California announces that Mick Jagger has been shot on stage in London. Following this, several radio stations broadcast the rumour as hard news.

OCTOBER 29
It's Only Rock'n'Roll enters the US Top 100 at Number 34. It will remain in the charts for thirteen weeks, including one week at Number 1.

OCTOBER 30
Bianca, now reported to be in Jamaica, says that she had wanted to name her baby Jesse James and was disappointed it wasn't a boy.

NOVEMBER
The Rolling Stones and their associates attend

a three-day meeting in Switzerland to discuss future plans which, after the issuing of new visas, could include a major American tour next summer, other European dates and a new album.

NOVEMBER 9
While in Switzerland for his 'dental' appointments, Keith spends some time at the 'Sinus Recording Studios' working on a new number called 'Scarlet'.

NOVEMBER 17
Mick and Bianca are amongst guests at the premiere of the animated film, *Sergeant Pepper's Lonely Hearts Club Band*, and at the party at New York's Hippopotamus Club.

NOVEMBER 22
Mick and Bianca attend a party for Elton John in the Grand Ballroom of the Pierre Hotel.

NOVEMBER 26
It's Only Rock'n'Roll reaches Number 1 in the US while 'Ain't Too Proud to Beg' enters the US Top 30 at Number 21. The single will stay in the charts for five weeks, peaking at Number 15.
Mick and Bianca spend a few days in Nicaragua monitoring the distribution of charity aid.

DECEMBER 4
Mick Jagger and Mick Taylor watch Eric Clapton in concert at the Hammersmith Odeon, London and join the party afterwards.

DECEMBER 7
The Stones start recording at Musicland Studios in Munich.

DECEMBER 12
Mick Taylor officially leaves the Rolling Stones to join the Jack Bruce Band. In Munich Mick Jagger comments: 'After five and a half years, Mick wishes a change of scene and wants the opportunity to try out new ventures, new endeavours. While we are all most sorry that he is going, we wish him great success and much happiness.' Asked about Taylor's replacement Jagger says: 'No doubt we can find a brilliant 6′ 3″ blond guitarist who can do his own make-up.' Rumours sweep the rock world as to who will follow him. Highest on the list of names are Ron Wood, Jeff Beck and Mick Ronson.

DECEMBER 13
Mick Taylor says: 'I'd worked with them in such a way and for so long, that I didn't think I could go much further without some different musicians. So when this chance with Jack Bruce came up, well, I wanted to be with him. I'd known for several months that he wanted to put together a new band. We'd played a lot together lately and we'd really hit it off. It was all purely musical reasons. There was no personal animosity in the split. There was no row, no quibbling or squabbling.'
The Stones finish recording in Munich.

DECEMBER 14
It's Only Rock'n'Roll is voted second best album of the year by *NME* staff.

DECEMBER 21
Talking about rumours that his departure from the Rolling Stones was for financial reasons, Mick Taylor says: 'I'm very disturbed by those rumours... it had absolutely nothing to do with those things. I think the rumours were started by an interview I did in a trade paper, but the things I said were taken out of context. And I never wanted the things I said written, reported or repeated. Whatever I felt about credits on songs has nothing to do with my decision to leave. If Mick Jagger or Keith Richard ever want to do solo albums, I'd like to work with them. And I don't want my friendship with the Rolling Stones jeopardized, or anything I may do with them later.'
Mick Jagger says: 'I don't want to say goodbye to him. I hope I can work with him again. If I do something on my own, I'd like to have Mick Taylor along to play, you know? We've already talked about this, the other day. I don't know really how this break will affect us. I never have known how long we're going to go on. I just can't really say. I mean, we won't go on forever.'

DECEMBER 28
London Records get ready for a special sales promotion on the occasion of the tenth anniversary of their signing the Stones. They are to re-issue seventeen Rolling Stones albums made over ten years to be promoted under the slogan 'The World's Greatest Rock'n'Roll Band - A London Recording Where It All Began'.
Decca are set to release an album called *Rock'n'Roll Circus* recorded during the show of the same name and including Brian Jones. Meanwhile the Rolling Stones are to release a live album of their best known singles hits.

DECEMBER 31
Ron Wood says: 'People obviously would think that I'm joining the Rolling Stones due to my supposed social connections with them. This, however, is just not true - for, though I respect them immensely, my position in the Faces is of far greater personal importance.'

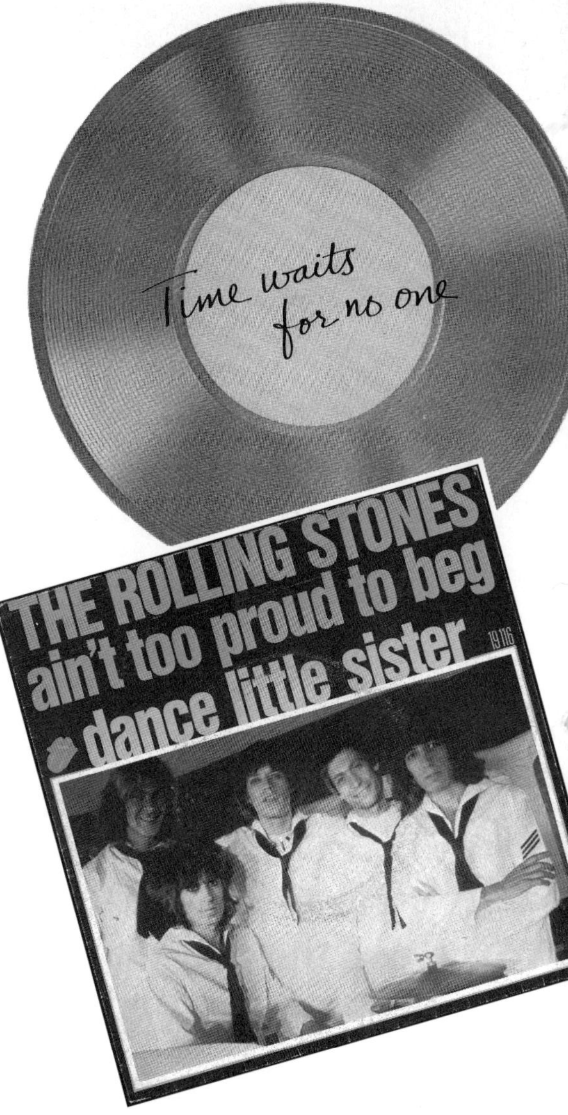

Above left: *In spite of his part-time marriage, Mick still finds time for 3-year-old Jade.* Below: *Mick's toy-boy phase.* Top right: *The Stones opted for the Cecil B DeMille treatment on the cover of* It's Only Rock'n'Roll. Bottom: *Mick Taylor's last single with the Stones.*

NINETEEN 75

JANUARY
US rock magazine *Creem* votes *It's Only Rock'n'Roll* best album of the year: the Rolling Stones, best band; and *Ladies And Gentlemen, The Rolling Stones,* best rock movie.

JANUARY 18
The *Melody Maker* publishes 'the Stones' Shopping List', with names of contenders for Mick Taylor's replacement, including Jeff Beck, Mick Ronson, Robben Ford, Peter Frampton, Ry Cooder, Dave Clempson, Ollie Halsall, Jorma Kaukonen, Steve Hillage.

JANUARY 19
Keith Richard will play guitar and sing on the title track of Alexis Korner's next album *Get Off Of My Cloud.*

JANUARY 22
The Stones fly to Rotterdam to record. Alexis Korner joins them.

FEBRUARY 9
Recording over, Mick Jagger flies to New York while Keith Richard returns to London.

FEBRUARY 15
Keith Richard rehearses with US guitarist Wayne Perkins at Ron Wood's home studio in Richmond. They will continue sessions on and off till the end of the month.

MARCH 6
Allen Klein's company ABKCO is reported to have two live Stones albums ready, one a selection of unreleased tracks, the other the soundtrack of the never seen *Rock'n'Roll Circus*, including a version of 'Yer Blues' featuring John Lennon, Eric Clapton, Mitch Mitchell and Keith Richard.

MARCH 8
Mick Jagger and Peter Rudge, in New York to plan this year's US tour, see John Entwistle's Ox at the Academy of Music.
Jagger denies a new guitarist has been chosen.
In London the *New Musical Express* votes *It's Only Rock'n'Roll* the best designed album cover.

MARCH 11
Mick Jagger flies to Los Angeles to jam at the Record Plant Studios with Ron Wood and members of Wings.

MARCH 15
Marsha Hunt has settled out of court, for an undisclosed sum, the paternity suit she took out against Mick Jagger as father of her daughter, Karis.

MARCH 22
The Rolling Stones fly to Munich to continue recording at Musicland.

MARCH 27
Chris Spedding reports he's been approached

GRETSCH

by the Stones to replace Mick Taylor. He claims he is unable to help out on the new album due to his commitments to the Roy Harper band.

MARCH 30
Ron Wood flies to Munich to join the Stones in the studio.

APRIL 4
Recording over, the Stones return to London. Mick continues on to the States where the others will join him in a few days. They will be rehearsing in Montauk, Long Island, on Andy Warhol's estate.

APRIL 14
It is officially announced that Ron Wood will play with the Rolling Stones for their forthcoming American tour but that he will not be joining them permanently as he is staying with the Faces. Meanwhile he is in Amsterdam recording a solo album with Bobby Womack, Willie Weeks, Andy Newmark, and Ian McLagan.

MAY 1
An astonished crowd of New Yorkers watch as the Rolling Stones bring traffic to a standstill as they drive slowly down Fifth Avenue, playing 'Brown Sugar' from the back of a truck. Angry motorists watch helplessly as delirious fans swarm around them. Pressmen waiting at the Fifth Avenue Hotel are tossed leaflets detailing their '1975 Tour of the Americas'. Starting at the Baton Rouge in Louisiana on 1 June, the tour will wind up on 21 August in Caracas, Venezuela. They will play 58 dates, 42 in the US and Canada and sixteen in South America. 1.5 million people are expected to see them. It is the longest tour ever undertaken by the Stones.

MAY 13
Ron Wood is to leave the Stones line-up for the US tour after their final US concert in Jacksonville as the Faces are scheduled to start a major tour at the same time. It is unclear who will replace him for the South American leg of the tour.

MAY 18
While leaving a restaurant in Montauk, Mick Jagger cuts his right hand on glass from the door, losing a considerable amount of blood and needing twenty stitches. Later he says: 'It's a bit messy but I won't need a cast or anything.'

MAY 21
The Stones unveil their new stage set in a hangar at Stewart Airport, Newburgh, New York State. It is designed by Robin Wagner in

Left: *Mick and Ron Wood of the Faces. Ron is announced as temporary replacement for Mick Taylor on the 1975 tour.*

the shape of a lotus flower with five petals that jut out into the audience. In a more sophisticated version, to be used in New York, Chicago and Los Angeles, the petals will be raised and lowered hydraulically.

MAY 23
Decca release two old tracks as a single in the UK: 'I Don't Know Why' (Wonder/Riser/Hunter/Hardaway)/'Try A Little Harder' (Jagger/Richard). The A-side was produced by Jimmy Miller and the B-side by Andrew Oldham. Both tracks are taken from the *Metamorphosis* album. It is released in the US by ABKCO.

MAY 30
The Rolling Stones fly from Newark, New Jersey to New Orleans.

JUNE 1
The tour opens at the Louisiana State University in Baton Rouge before an audience of 15,000. The show features a twenty-foot-long inflatable penis.
Ron Wood is 28.

JUNE 2
Charlie Watts is 34.

JUNE 3
Concert at the Convention Center, San Antonio, Texas.

JUNE 4
Second concert at San Antonio Convention Center.
A new album by Leslie West called *The Great Fatsby* includes a version of 'Honky Tonk Woman' and a track called 'Highroller' written by Jagger and Richard and featuring Mick Jagger on rhythm guitar.

JUNE 5
Mick Jagger says: 'Ron Wood had to please both me and Keith. I can sort of tell a good guitar player, but probably Keith can tell better than me. Remember he used to be lead guitarist for the Rolling Stones. Ron seems a natural in the respect that both he and Keith are brilliant rhythm guitarists. It allows a certain cross-trading of riffs not previously possible.'

JUNE 6
Concert at Harrowhead Stadium, Kansas City, with an audience of 80,000. In the UK Decca Records release *Metamorphosis* featuring sixteen tracks, all but three never previously released, produced by Jimmy Miller and Andrew Oldham. In the States the album is released on Allen Klein's ABKCO label but features only fourteen tracks.

JUNE 7
Talking about the Press, mid-air, en route to Milwaukee, Mick Jagger says: 'I don't read any of the analytical stuff. Those are the ones I skip. I only look at the front pages or the pictures, actually. Someone asked me if I minded bad reviews and I said no. As long as my picture is on the front page, I don't care what they say about me on page 96.'

JUNE 8
Concert at the Milwaukee County Stadium, with an audience of 60,000.

JUNE 9
Concert at the Civic Center, St. Paul, Minnesota.

JUNE 10
Anita Pallenberg is fined £200 in Jamaica on drugs charges and is deported. From now on, if Keith wants to use his Jamaican house, he will have to go alone. The first hearing, according to the *Daily Express*, was adjourned after she adopted 'an unusual posture' in court.

JUNE 11/12
Concerts at the Boston Garden.

JUNE 13
Peter Rudge at Niagara Falls says: 'Don't let Mick Jagger come here - he'll want it on stage!'
Made In The Shade, a compilation album of tracks produced by Jimmy Miller and the Glimmer Twins, is released on Rolling Stones Records.

JUNE 14
Concert at the Municipal Stadium, Cleveland, Ohio with an audience of 82,500.

JUNE 15
Concert at the Municipal Auditorium, Buffalo, New York.

JUNE 17/18
Concerts at the Maple Leaf Gardens, Toronto.

JUNE 19
In the US newspaper, the *National Star*, under the headline: 'It's Time We Exorcised This Demonic Influence Over Our Children!', Steve Dunleavy writes: 'Mick Jagger should come to America more often because it does us good, really good to look at ourselves squarely in the eye and see where we have failed. Where have we failed that this simple-faced disciple of dirt is a hero, a rootin', tootin' hero to our teenager kids? We have this pale-faced foreigner, this Englishman, getting $10 a seat from our kids to see him perform. And what do they see? They are

Top right: *In an unprecedented move, the 1975 tour was trumpeted to New Yorkers on a giant billboard in Times Square.* Centre: *Keith features on* Hit Parade *cover.* Bottom: *No photo opportunity was turned down on the 1975 tour: the Stones pose in front of the Alamo.*

blitzkrieged by a tightly packaged excess of four-letter words and tacky smut.'

JUNE 22
Concert at Madison Square Garden, New York. Eric Clapton joins the Stones for an encore in 'Sympathy For The Devil'. There's a party afterwards at the home of Atlantic Records' Press Officer Earl McGrath.

JUNE 23
Concert at Madison Square Garden.
Ron Wood says: 'Let's go down and watch Mick put on his make-up. That's always a good laugh.'

JUNE 24
Another concert at Madison Square Garden. *Metamorphosis* enters the UK chart at Number 27. It enters the US Top 30 at Number 19; it will stay in the charts for eight weeks, peaking at Number 8. At the same time *Made In the Shade* enters the US album chart at Number 25 and will stay in the charts for nine weeks reaching a highest position of Number 6, going gold. Bill Wyman says: 'I loved Mick Taylor for his beauty. He was technically really great. But he was shy, maybe like Charlie Watts and I. Mick wasn't so funky but he led us into other things. Ron Wood's a bit like Keith; he takes us back. He's not such a fantastic musician, perhaps, but he's more fun, got more personality.'

JUNE 24
Concert at Madison Square Garden.

JUNE 25
Another concert at Madison Square Garden, where Mick Jagger says to the audience: 'I'd like to introduce you to Billy Preston. He's staying at the St. Moritz Hotel and he likes white boys.'

JUNE 26
Concert at Madison Square Garden. During the day some of the group jam with Eric Clapton at the Electric Lady Studio.

JUNE 27
Sixth and final concert at Madison Square Garden. Carlos Santana joins the Stones for an encore. It is believed that the Rolling Stones have grossed $1.25 million during the six Madison Square Garden shows.

JUNE 27
A party is given by the Rolling Stones for members of the Steel Bands Asssociation to thank them for performing at the opening of the New York shows.

Left: *Mick as a Cherokee Indian, one of the many stage personae he adopted during the 1975 tour.* Right: *Another fine example of Mick's eclectic wardrobe with Inca-style fabric design, Turkish pantaloons and Anglo-Saxon cross-gartering.*

JULY 1
Concert at the Capital Center, Washington, D.C. *Made In The Shade* enters the British Top 30 at Number 17; it drops out after eight weeks, its highest position Number 10.

JULY 2
Second concert at the Capital Center. Bianca, Andy Warhol and fashion designer Guy Laroche visit the White House at the invitation of President Ford's son Jack. But not the Stones. 'They would only do so,' claims Peter Rudge, 'if they could paint the White House black.' Meanwhile all the South American dates are postponed until an expanded tour, rather than just the five cities, can be put together.

JULY 4
Concert at the Memorial Stadium, Memphis, with an audience of 50,000.

JULY 5
Keith Richard is arrested by a Highway Patrol in Fordyce, Arkansas, charged with possessing an offensive weapon. Ron Wood is also held, but not charged. Both are released on $162 bail. Keith says: 'I bent down to change the waveband on the radio and the car swerved slightly. A police patrol vehicle then pulled out from a lay-by and stopped us. I was then questioned about having a ''concealed weapon'', a penknife complete with tin-opener and a device for removing stones from horses' hooves.'

JULY 6
Concert at the Cotton Bowl, Dallas, Texas. The Stones are obliged to take out a $3 million bond against possible damages during their stay at the Continental Hyatt House Hotel in California.

JULY 7
The Rolling Stones arrive in Los Angeles for Ringo Starr's birthday party. News of Mick Taylor leaving the Jack Bruce Band filters through from England and immediately it's rumoured he will rejoin the band for their opening show at the Forum.

JULY 9
Concert at the Los Angeles Forum.
Liza Minnelli, Raquel Welch and countless other personalities are in the audience. Afterwards a party is given by Diana Ross. Billy Preston says: 'The Rolling Stones are a lot more R&B orientated. It feels like I've been playing with them for years. We're a family. Keith is really enjoying playing with Ronnie. The band is doing a lot of things they have never done in America.'

JULY 10
Concert at the L.A. Forum. Keith Richard says: 'This band is less slick and sophisticated sounding than the other one at its best when everybody was in tune and could hear each other. This is a lot funkier, dirtier and rougher and a lot more exciting. The problem for us when Mick Taylor left was whether to replace him or take the opportunity of a break to form a new band and make it different. Mick was a really nice player, but his interest was in melody and harmony and notes.'
Ron Wood says: 'The last show I forgot myself. I went up to the microphone and said: ''They're a great rock'n'roll band aren't they? I wish I was playing with them.'' And then it hit me. ''I am playing with them!''.'

JULY 11
Another concert at the L.A. Forum.
Bill Wyman and Ron Wood go to the Roxy to see Bob Marley and the Wailers.

JULY 12
Concert at the L.A. Forum. The Stones have now beaten the Beatles' record of twenty albums to have reached the Top 30 in the US. *Made In The Shade* gives the Stones 21.

JULY 13
Final show at the Los Angeles Forum.

JULY 15/16
Concerts at the Cow Palace, San Francisco.

JULY 18
Concert at the Coliseum, Seattle, Washington.

JULY 19
Concert at the Hughes Stadium, Denver. Elton John joins the Stones on stage.
Mick Jagger says: 'People always want to know about your sex life. Why? because they've got nothing else to think about. Because they've got empty heads. Because stupid heads print it in newspapers. People like gossiping. Especially women. I am not down on women. I've got a song on the next album that's got a nice bit about them called ''I Love Ladies''.'

JULY 23
Concert at the Chicago Stadium. The Rolling Stones add three dates to their current US tour, increasing their potential gross income by $1,000,000. As a result the Faces have to cancel three shows in Miami, losing $20,000.

JULY 24
Concert at the Chicago Stadium. Howlin' Wolf is there and afterwards has dinner with Bill Wyman.

JULY 26
Concert at the Indiana University Assembly Center, Bloomington. Mick Jagger is 32.

JULY 27/28
Concerts at the Cobo Hall, Detroit, Michigan.

JULY 30
Concert at the Omni, Atlanta, Georgia.

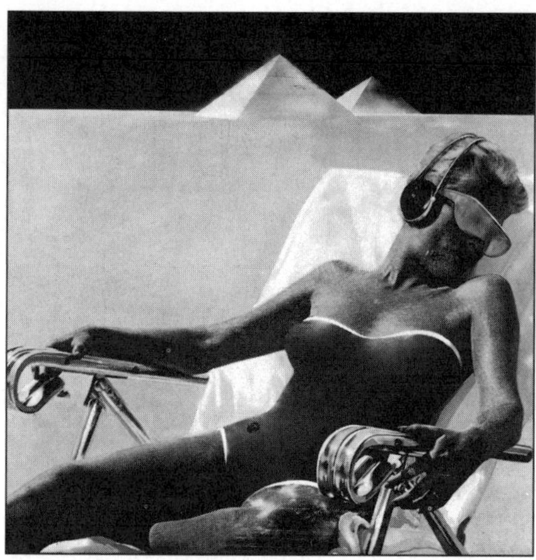

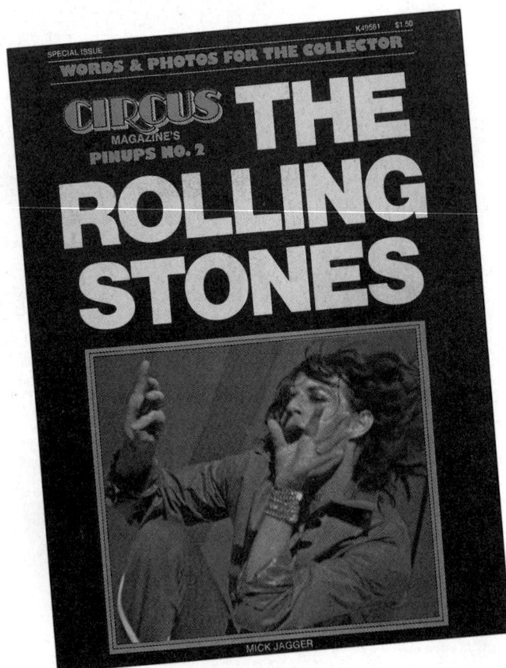

JULY 31
Concert at the Auditorium, Greenboro, North Carolina.

AUGUST 2
Concert at the Gator Bowl, Jacksonville, Florida and an audience of 65,000.
Mick Jagger says: 'There is really no reason to have women on tour unless they've got a job to do. The only other reason is to screw. Otherwise they get bored... and they just sit around and moan.'

AUGUST 4
Concert at the Freedom Hall, Louisville, Kentucky. Meanwhile in New York radio stations alert fans to forged tickets, selling at $10 each, for a fictional Stones concert supposedly in New Jersey.

AUGUST 5
The Stones have recorded ten of their North American shows for a possible live album.

AUGUST 6
Concert at the Coliseum, Hampton Roads, Virginia.

AUGUST 8
The final concert of the tour at the Rich Stadium, Buffalo, N.Y. In an audience of 80,000, 600 fans are injured and 170 arrested. They have played 45 gigs in 27 cities and grossed nearly $13 million.

AUGUST 10
The Stones go on holiday. Mick Jagger and Bill Wyman stay in the States while Charlie flies to Europe and Keith heads for Thailand. Ron Wood will start the Faces' American tour on 15 August.

AUGUST 11
In the USA, ABKCO Records release 'Out Of Time'/'Jiving Sister Fanny', taken from *Metamorphosis*.

AUGUST 24
In the States the Rolling Stones are accused by the Coalition Against Macho-Sexist Music of being 'perpetrators of sexist-rock'.

AUGUST 26
In Alamea County Superior Court, California, the Judge sets aside a previous $690,000 judgement against Mick Jagger imposed in July 1973 when local ranchers, who held Jagger responsible for the over-running of their property by 300,000 fans at the Altamont Speedway concert, were outraged when he failed to turn up in court. Judge Koniger accepted Mick Jagger's plea that he was not properly informed of the suit, and ordered a new trial. Six years after the event the case continues.

SEPTEMBER 3
At a party given by Peter Sellers in Hollywood, Bill Wyman on bass and Ron Wood on guitar jam with Bobby Keys on saxophone, Keith Moon on organ, David Bowie on alto sax and Joe Cocker on vocals.

SEPTEMBER 5
'Out Of Time'/'Jiving Sister Fanny' is released by Decca in the UK.

SEPTEMBER 13
Mick Jagger, on holiday with Bianca in Ireland as guests of the Guinness family at Leixlip Castle, announces that the Stones plan a three-week European tour before Christmas.

SEPTEMBER 15
Bill Wyman starts recording a solo album at the Record Plant with help from Van Morrison, Sly Stone, Joe Walsh, Leon Russell, Steven Stills and Joe Vitale.

SEPTEMBER 21
Mick Jagger attends Circasia 75, a charity show in Dublin, featuring Eric Clapton, Sean Connery, John Huston, Shirley MacLaine and Milo O'Shea.
Alexis Korner's LP, *Get Off Of My Cloud*, featuring Keith Richard on guitar and lead vocals on the title track, is released by CBS.

SEPTEMBER 26
Allen Klein hints he may soon release old and unissued Stones tracks including *Rock'n'Roll Circus* material and a jam session with other Chess label musicians.

SEPTEMBER 27
Ian Anderson of Jethro Tull says: 'Can you imagine how difficult it is to be one of the Rolling Stones? They've been going for over ten years. Can you imagine how difficult it is to be Mick Jagger or Keith Richard and thinking, "Christ, what are we going to do for the next album?". Mick looks so young, I saw him at Madison Square Garden when we were playing. He came backstage. I didn't recognise him. He's five years older than me and he really looked so young.'

OCTOBER 4
Ron Wood, on tour with the Faces in Honolulu says: 'I actually gained five or six pounds on the Rolling Stones tour, can you believe it?'
In Dublin, Mick Jagger is in the audience for a Johnny Cash concert.

OCTOBER 10
'If You Don't Want My Love'/'I Got A

Top left: Made In The Shade – *compilation album of 70s hits.* Centre: Circus *magazine featured pin-ups of the Stones on tour.* Bottom: Metamorphosis – *major compilation album of tracks from the Stones' first 12 years including both Brian Jones and Mick Taylor.*

Feeling' a new single from Ron Wood's solo album is released on Warner Brothers.

OCTOBER
Mick Jagger, in Paris looking at venues for a possible concert, goes to Carlos Santana's concert at the Pavillon.

OCTOBER 13
In New York Ron Wood says to Pete Townshend: 'You helped Eric get off drugs, can't you help me get off the road?' Townshend replies: 'Join the Rolling Stones, they don't tour that often.'

OCTOBER 19
The Stones and Ron Wood arrive at the Mountain Recording Studios in Montreux to work on their new album.

NOVEMBER 30
In Montreux the recording sessions come to an end.

DECEMBER 2
Rolled Gold enters the British Top 30 at Number 19. It will remain in the chart for thirteen weeks with a highest position of Number 7.

DECEMBER 3
The Rolling Stones and Ron Wood continue work on the new album at the Musicland Studios in Munich. In London Ron's wife Krissie is arrested for alleged possession of cannabis and cocaine after a raid on the Woods' home in Richmond. Krissie's friend Audrey Burgon is also arrested. Under headlines such as 'Sleeping Beauties', newspapers report that the two women were found 'sleeping together'.

DECEMBER 6
The Tallahassie *Sun* reports that Florida teenagers hurled Rolling Stones and Elton John records on a bonfire after a local preacher, Charles Boykin, declared them 'sinful' following a survey he conducted which showed that of 1,000 unmarried mothers, 984 had had sex while rock music was played.

DECEMBER 10
Although Krissie Wood and Audrey Burgon are cleared of possessing cannabis, the jury fail to reach a verdict on the charge of possessing 15 milligrams of cocaine. The date for the re-trial will be announced later.

DECEMBER 16
Recording sessions in Munich come to an end.

Above right: *The stuff that legends are made of: the giant phallus used on the 1975 tour epitomised the Stones' much vaunted decadence.*

DECEMBER 18
Keith Richard is 32. Rod Stewart quits the Faces. Spokesman Tony Toon says: 'Rod feels he can no longer work in a situation where the group's lead guitarist, Ron Wood, seems to be permanently on loan to the Rolling Stones.' Rumours increase that Ron is about to join the Stones.

DECEMBER 19
Mick Jagger in Paris just before flying to New York commenting on Rod Stewart's decision says: 'I don't think Ron even knows of this yet. All I can say at the moment is that no agreement has yet been signed between us... There's nothing finalised at all. But as I say, we've only just learned of the split.'

DECEMBER 20
Andy Warhol has recently completed a series of prints of Mick Jagger.

DECEMBER 23
Mick, Bianca and Jade fly to Rio de Janeiro for Christmas.

DECEMBER 26
The Rolling Stones top a list compiled by *Performance Magazine* on audience-drawing power based on figures provided by US concert promoters. US rock magazine *Creem* votes the Rolling Stones best group, best R&B group and best live band; Ron Wood most valuable player and *Made In The Shade* best re-issue album.

JANUARY 3
In the *New Musical Express*, Mick Jagger receives the best dressed musician award for 1975. Keith Richard is placed seventh.

JANUARY 9
David Bowie rehearses at Keith Richard's home in Jamaica for his forthcoming American tour.

JANUARY 10
The Rolling Stones hold a formal business meeting with Ron Wood in New York.

JANUARY 13
Mick Jagger and Andy Warhol autograph 250 portfolios of ten prints. Each set is offered at $7,200; individual prints at $875. Mick commissions Warhol to paint four portraits.

JANUARY 15
At Bonhams auction of musical memorabilia in Chelsea, Mick Taylor sells the gold disc of 'It's Only Rock'n'Roll' for £75; a signed acetate of *Goats Head Soup* goes for £5, various T-shirts go for between £5 and £8 each. A lace shawl belonging to Bianca raises £22.

JANUARY 18
The Rolling Stones mix their new album in New York at the Atlantic studios.

JANUARY 27
The Rollling Stones appear with Led Zeppelin, Yes and Emerson, Lake and Palmer on the double album released by Atlantic called *By Invitation Only (Pick Of The Pops)*, with 'Angie' and 'It's Only Rock'n'Roll'.

FEBRUARY 7
After a photo session in Florida with the Stones for the cover of the new album, Ron Wood flies to the Bahamas, to work on Eric Clapton's new album.

FEBRUARY 26
Bill Wyman's solo album, *Stone Alone* is released on Rolling Stones Records. Bill Wyman sings, plays bass, piano, guitar and percussion and wrote eight of the twelve tracks.

FEBRUARY 27
Reports suggesting that Mick Jagger is recovering in a New York hospital from a drugs overdose are denied. He is in hospital, but with severe influenza.

FEBRUARY 28
It is finally announced officially that Ron Wood has joined the Rolling Stones.

MARCH 12
The Rolling Stones announce their European tour.

MARCH 26
In Geneva, Switzerland, a second son, Tara, is born to Anita Pallenberg and Keith Richard.

MARCH 31
At 6.15pm Radio Station KHJ in Los Angeles gives the Stones' unreleased new album its premiere. The Stones stop the broadcast in order to prevent a bootleg being taped and released before the official album.

APRIL 1
Promoter Harvey Goldsmith confirms that over one million postal ticket applications have been received for the Stones' Earls Court concerts, the equivalent of 67 shows.

APRIL 6
The Stones add three dates to the Earls Court concerts. Ron Wood's wife Krissie, and her friend Audrey Burgon are cleared of possessing cocaine. Krissie, who is three months' pregnant says 'All I want to do now is to go home and wait for my baby.' She is, however, ordered to pay £12,000 costs.

APRIL 10
The Rolling Stones, minus Keith who will join them later, but with Billy Preston, meet near Mougins in the South of France to start rehearsing for the European tour.

APRIL 15
Decca Records release a single of 'Honky Tonk Woman'/'Sympathy For The Devil', produced by Jimmy Miller.

APRIL 20
Black And Blue is released on Rolling Stones

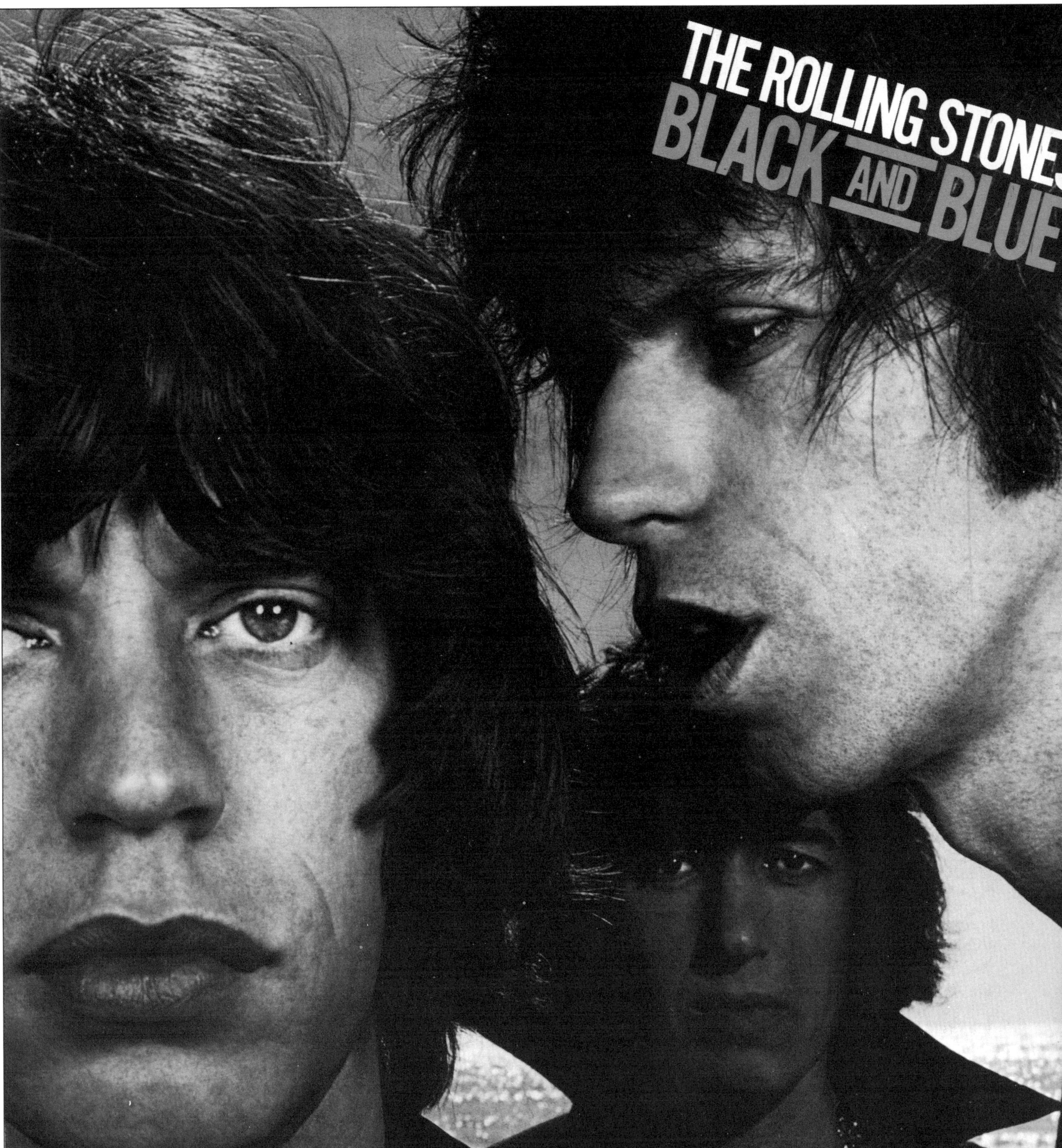
THE ROLLING STONES
BLACK AND BLUE

Records and features eight songs all by Jagger and Richard apart from 'Cherry Oh Baby' a reggae track by Eric Donaldson. The album was recorded in December 1974 and March/April 1975 in Rotterdam, Munich and Montreux. It is produced by the Glimmer Twins and Ron Wood appears on two numbers. A single 'Fool To Cry'/'Crazy Mama' is also released. In America the flipside is 'Hot Stuff'.

APRIL 25
The Stones finish rehearsals and split before meeting in Frankfurt for the first leg of the tour.

APRIL 27
Black And Blue enters the British Top 30 at Number 30. It will stay in the charts for fifteen weeks, reaching a highest position of Number 2.

APRIL 28/29
The Rolling Stones open their European tour in West Germany, with two concerts at the Festhalle in Frankfurt.

APRIL 30
Concert at the Munsterlandhalle, Munster, West Germany.

MAY 1
The *Daily Mirror* reports that Keith Richard and Anita Pallenberg plan to get married on stage. Keith Richard says: 'I've been asked so often by the press and by both our families when we are going to get married that I thought we might as well. There are so many papers we have to produce, especially when we travel with the children, that it might just simplify things to have the same name on our passports.'
However it is more likely that they will settle for a Register Office ceremony.

MAY 2
The municipal authorities in Hamburg refuse to allow the Stones to play the Congresscentrum, so the concert is switched to the Osteenhalle, Kiel.
The *Sunday Mirror* reports that Ron Wood is planning to quit Britain because of 'police persecution'. Referring to the raid on his home when police knocked down the door he said: 'I love Britain but I haven't lived there since last year mainly because I wouldn't feel safe in my own bed... That whole thing was really disgusting. It makes me feel sick to think about it.' But tax advantages are also behind the move. 'It's really sad. How would you feel if you were only allowed to keep about 2% of what you earn?'
Keith Richard comments: 'I think it was me and Anita the police were after. Before they went to Woody's home they broke into a little cottage at the end of his garden where I sometimes stay when I'm in Britain. I was out of the country at the time but it looks as though they were hoping to pin something on Woody and me in one go.'

MAY 3
Concert at the Deutschlandhalle, West Berlin.

MAY 4
Concert at the Stadthalle, Bremen.

MAY 6/7
Concerts at the Forêt Nationale, Brussels, Belgium.

MAY 8
The Rolling Stones return to London and Mick Jagger goes to David Bowie's concert at the Empire Pool, Wembley. *Black And Blue* enters the US Top 30 at Number 26. It will stay in the chart for a total of fourteen weeks, with a highest position of Number 1. 'Fool To Cry' enters the British singles chart also at Number 26. It will stay in the chart for nine weeks, reaching Number 4.

MAY 10/11
Concerts at the Apollo Theatre, Glasgow. On the second night, to cool down at the end of the show, Mick Jagger douses himself and the front two rows of the audience with buckets of water. He tells the *Daily Mirror* 'It's great to be back. I would love to live here again... People overestimate us, we are not as good as people think.'
In Munich West German police report that the Baader Meinhof Group are threatening to bomb the Munich Olympiahalle when the Stones play there in June.

MAY 15
Concert at Gramby Hall, Leicester. Eric Clapton joins them on stage. 'Fool To Cry' enters the US Top 30 at Number 20. It will remain in the charts for seven weeks, reaching a highest position of Number 9.

MAY 17/18
Concerts at New Bingley Hall, Stafford. Touts ask £40 for £3 tickets.

MAY 19
Keith Richard crashes his Bentley into the central barrier on the M1, near Newport Pagnell, Buckinghamshire, just after 5 am. Although the car is a write-off, Anita, Marlon and Keith are unhurt. When the police arrive, Keith is arrested and taken to Newport Pagnell police station and then released. A 'substance' has been found in his car and a police spokesman says: 'The substance has to be identified before any charges can be made.'

Above left: *Mick and Bianca on the island of Mustique. The ups and downs of their stormy marriage were reported almost daily in the press.* Top right: *The 1976 tour poster confirms Ron Wood as a full-time member of the group.* Centre: *'Fool To Cry'.* Bottom: *This image for* Black And Blue *incurred the wrath of Californian feminists.* Far right: *A coy Ron Wood.*

MAY 20
Garth Pearce of the *Daily Express* reports that an incident such as Keith's arrest has been the dread of tour manager Peter Rudge since the tour opened in Frankfurt, jeopardising remaining concerts. The capital outlay and expenses are so great that they need every penny of the £60,000 they gross every night. During the British leg, the Stones merely hope to break even due to the immense tax difficulties they face on income earned in the UK.

MAY 21
Mick Jagger becomes Godfather to five-month old Jean-Paul Menzies, son of the Stones' personal assistant Anna Menzies, at the Christening in Clapham, London.
The Stones play the first show at Earls Court, London in front of 17,000 fans. Princess Margaret goes backstage. Mick Jagger says: 'This is the worst toilet I've played in, and I've seen toilets. There just aren't any places to play in London. It really is a problem that we have nowhere else. Give me any Cow Arena and I'll kick the shit out of it anytime.'
After the show the Stones give a party at the Cockney Pride pub in Piccadilly. Among the guests are Caroline Kennedy, Liza Todd, Lulu, Susan Hampshire, Patrick Taylor and Mick Taylor.

MAY 22/23/24/25/26
Concerts at Earls Court.
Mick Jagger says: 'It's not the Rolling Stones that destroy people. They destroy themselves.'
Black And Blue is at Number 1 in America.
Ron Wood is involved in a dispute with a company called Deltapad who claim he's under contract with them which should prevent him from playing with the Stones. By agreement, part of his earnings from the Earls Court gigs are frozen as they are also claiming damages.

MAY 27
Last show at Earls Court. A Stones spokesman says fears of the tour being curtailed are unfounded as Keith's case will take time to come to court.

MAY 29/30
Concerts at the Football Stadium, The Hague, Netherlands.

JUNE 1
Concert in the Westfalenhalle, Dortmund, West Germany.

JUNE 2
Concert at the Sporthalle, Cologne.
Charlie Watts celebrates his 35th birthday.

JUNE 4/5/6
Concerts at the Abattoirs, Paris. Keith Richard and Anita Pallenberg's ten-week-old son Tara dies 'of a flu virus' in a Geneva hospital. The death is kept secret as Keith insists the tour must not be disrupted.

JUNE 9
'Substances' found in Keith Richard's Bentley are identified as cocaine. Keith claims their presence is a mystery to him. Newspapers suggest that the Stones are being used as drug carriers unwittingly.
Concert at the Palais des Sports, Lyon, France.

JUNE 11
The Stones play in Spain for the first time, in Barcelona.

JUNE 13
Concert at the Parc de Sports de l'Ouest, Nice.

JUNE 15
Concert at the Hallenstadium, Zurich.

JUNE 16/17
Concerts at the Olympiahalle, Munich.

JUNE 17
Militant feminists in Los Angeles protest against the *Black And Blue* poster which

features a girl tied up.

JUNE 18
News of baby Tara's death appears in the press.

JUNE 19
Concert at the Neckarstadion, Stuttgart with an audience of 60,000.

JUNE 21/22
The Stones play in Zagreb, their first time in Yugoslavia.

JUNE 23
Final date of the 1976 Tour of Europe at Vienna's Stadthalle, where 16,000 people attend.
During the tour several shows have been recorded for a live album.

JULY 26
Mick Jagger is 33. He celebrates his birthday with a party at home in Montauk. Guests include neighbour Andy Warhol.

AUGUST 2
Ron Wood announces that he and Krissie are planning to live in Los Angeles for at least six months, for tax reasons, and that Krissie will have her baby there in October. On their recent return from holiday in France, Krissie was stopped and searched. Ron says: 'They walked up to me and said. ''We've reason to believe your wife has a connection with the pop business''. They ignored me. They'd never do that to Keith Richard, now, would they?'
Keith Richard appears in Court charged with possessing cannabis and cocaine and three driving offences. He is bailed to appear in court next month in Newport Pagnell.

AUGUST 21
The Rolling Stones perform at the Knebworth Festival in front of an audience of around 200,000. A police spokesman says: 'The fans were as good as gold. They were a damn sight better than football crowds.' The Stones play till 1.40 am. It is rumoured to be their last gig.

AUGUST 23
The *Daily Mirror* reports a scuffle at Heathrow Airport as photographers pursue Bianca Jagger seen embracing a friend on their arrival from New York. A spokesman for Bianca says: 'She flew in from New York with Barry Cross, a friend in the record business. She was asked to pose for pictures

---

Left: *Keith and Mick during the 1976 tour. Mick was the obvious front man, but Keith's influence on the musical impetus of the band was crucial to their success.* Right: *Mick in full flight at Earl's Court, London; he often resorted to acrobatics.*

and refused, then she ran away. Mr Cross followed her and drove her to see Mick Jagger.' Later the Jaggers parted company again, Mick stayed at the hotel, while Bianca went to their home in Chelsea. The couple are denying rumours that their marriage is on the rocks.

SEPTEMBER 6
Keith Richard appears in court at Newport Pagnell on drug charges. He will appear in court again next month.

SEPTEMBER 20
Mick Jagger and Ron Wood are in Los Angeles sifting through 150 hours of concert material for their live album.

SEPTEMBER
Mick Jagger sees the Sex Pistols at London's 100 Club: 'I thought they were pretty good. Well, not good really but… they could be.'

SEPTEMBER
Rolling Stones' sound engineer Keith Harwood dies in a car crash. Bill Wyman sets up a trust fund for his family.

OCTOBER 2
Mick Jagger and Ron Wood are busy at the Atlantic Studios mixing the live tapes hoping to have the album ready by Christmas. While in New York they go to watch the TV studio show *Saturday Night Live* featuring Eric Idle and Joe Cocker.

OCTOBER 6
Keith Richard arrives two and a half hours late for his court appearance in Newport Pagnell, blaming the fact that his trousers had not been returned from the cleaners on time. Chairman of Magistrates, Mrs Mary Durbridge, says: 'It strikes me as extraordinary that any gentleman of his stature can only afford one pair of trousers.' She makes him forfeit his bail of £100. Keith elects to go on trial on separate charges of possessing cocaine and LSD and his bail is renewed at £5,000.

OCTOBER 22
Mick Jagger meets MCA Records' President Mike Maitland in Los Angeles to discuss the new Rolling Stones' record contract.

OCTOBER 25
Mick Jagger tells *Woman's Own*: 'I got married for something to do. I thought it was a good idea. I've never been madly, deeply in love. I wouldn't know what that feels like. I'm not an emotional person.'

OCTOBER 30
Krissie Wood gives birth to a baby boy, Jesse James, in Hollywood.

DECEMBER 18
Keith Richard is 33 today.

JANUARY 10/11
Keith Richard appears at Aylesbury Crown Court charged with possessing cocaine and LSD. Mick Jagger attends the hearing. The cocaine was found in a silver tube attached to an ornamental necklace found in the wrecked car while the LSD was in a piece of folded paper in the pocket of a jacket he was wearing. Keith's defence is that he didn't know the drugs were there and that because they share each others clothes and jewellery it could have belonged to any member of the group. Defence counsel, Sir Peter Rawlinson, QC, claims Richard was 'singled out, stripped and searched' by the police. There was no suggestion that he was under the influence of drink or drugs. Sir Peter challenges a police suggestion that the necklace was one Keith had been photographed wearing at a concert in Leicester. If the prosecution were right, he would have been 'flaunting his possession of a tube used for sniffing cocaine in front of thousands of fans, many policemen and photographers'. In his final speech, Sir Peter asks the jury to give the accused an impartial hearing and not to be prejudiced by any views they might have of the Rolling Stones.

JANUARY 12
Keith Richard is found guilty of possessing cocaine but cleared of possessing LSD. He is fined £750 and ordered to pay £250 costs. Celebrating with Mick Jagger in a pub afterwards, Keith describes the result as 'a good old British compromise'.

JANUARY 22
Mick Jagger, Keith Richard, Bill Wyman and Charlie Watts take out an injunction against the *News of the World* to prevent them running the screenplay and pictures from *Cocksucker Blues* directed by Robert Frank.
The *New Musical Express* reports that the Stones' new recording deal with Polydor will be announced at the Cannes MIDEM Festival.

JANUARY 23
Robert Frank, director of *Cocksucker Blues* tells the *News of the World*: 'I've been approached by lawyers, asking me to return my copy of the film. I have refused, I regard the copy I have as my property and do not intend to return it.'

JANUARY 27
Bill Wyman is amongst the guests at the after-gig party for Lynyrd Skynyrd at the Rainbow Theatre, London.

FEBRUARY 5
The Rolling Stones fly to Los Angeles via Paris and New York, to tie up the new recording deal and to look for studios where they can finish their live album. While in New York, Mick and Elton John's lyricist Bernie Taupin, go to the Queen concert at Madison Square Garden.

FEBRUARY 16
The Rolling Stones announce their new record deal with EMI who are to distribute the band's records worldwide, with the exception of the USA and Canada where the future of the Rolling Stones' label has still to be decided. EMI will get six albums, as well as publishing rights to an extensive part of the Jagger/Richard catalogue. The deal will take effect after the spring release of the band's forthcoming live double album, which will be their last under the distribution deal with WEA. The exact financial terms remain unclear. Widespread press reports that the deal carried a £1,000,000 guarantee were dismissed both by EMI managing director Leslie Hill and the Stones' publicist Les Perrin as 'purely speculative'. Mick Jagger commented: 'In this Jubilee year, I think it is only fitting that we sign with a British company.' Their last-minute rejection of the Polydor deal is rumoured to be because they were annoyed at the way the company leaked news of the signing at Cannes.

FEBRUARY 17
Bill Wyman talks to the *Daily Express* about his experience of groupies: 'There'd be a girl hiding behind your shower curtain when you checked into your room. It was very hard to resist when you were in Cleveland, Ohio on a cold winter's night, bored and fed-up, it was like manna from heaven.'

FEBRUARY 18
Keith Richard is fined £25 in London for driving without tax on the night of his drugs arrest in last May.

1

The Rolling Stones

LOVE YOU LIVE

IL Rock

FEBRUARY 24
On arrival in Toronto from London, Keith Richard and Anita Pallenberg are stopped at customs and when Anita's 28 pieces of luggage are searched, ten grams of cannabis and traces of heroin are found. Anita is arrested and then released on a promise-to-appear notice. Keith is not charged.

FEBRUARY 27
Royal Canadian Mounted Police raid the Harbour Castle Hotel where Keith and Anita are staying and both are arrested for possession of heroin for re-sale. Keith is released on $1,000 bail. Anita is released without bail to appear in court on 3 March.

MARCH 3
Anita's Toronto hearing is postponed until 14 March. A member of the Stones' entourage says: 'You can spot the Mounties in the lobby because they wear tiny receivers in their ears... We found a transmitter in Keith's room. We still don't know whether there was an informer in the hotel. The band, expecially Mick, are desperate and depressed. They think this is their last album.'

MARCH 4
The Stones play at the El Mocambo Club before an audience of 300. The whole concert is recorded for their new live album. The 300 are the winners of a radio contest 'Why I Would Like To Go To A Party With The Rolling Stones'. A Rolling Stones spokesman says before the gig: 'They're nervous. They've been rehearsing for the past week and are wondering what people will think of them when they hear them this close.' Margaret Trudeau, wife of Canada's Prime Minister, attends the concert and then gives a party for the band at the Harbour Castle where she has taken a suite. It is her sixth wedding anniversary. Mick Jagger says: 'I wish we could make money doing gigs like this.' Ronnie Wood says: 'It's strange playing in a club. I haven't played one in eight or nine years.'
In New York Robert Stigwood announces that he has withdrawn a seven million dollar bid for American recording rights to the Stones. He denies that it has anything to do with Keith Richard's drug bust, saying that the decision was made for 'commercial reasons' but rumours persist that the charges are affecting negotiations and that the reported $15 million recording deal, the biggest in history, is in jeopardy.

MARCH 5
The Rolling Stones play a second gig at the El Mocambo Club in Toronto, which is recorded for the live album. Chet Flippo of *Rolling Stone* magazine says it's the greatest show he's ever seen. Margaret Trudeau says: 'It's quite a buzz, I've always been a Rolling Stones fan.' Commenting on Mrs Trudeau, Charlie Watts says: 'I wouldn't want my wife

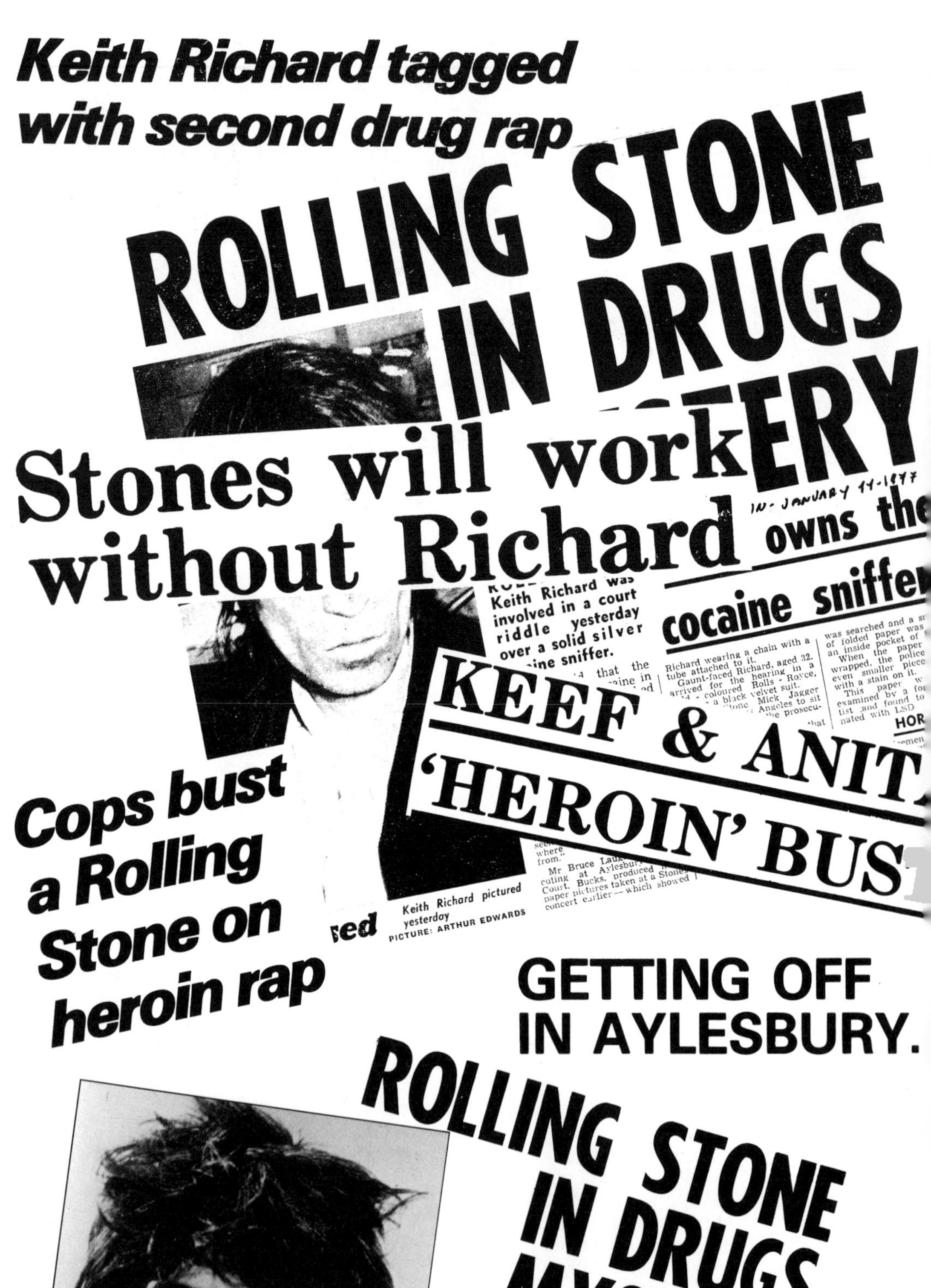

Above: *Throughout 1977 Keith's run of drugs busts continued. Media coverage ran wild. The cocaine trial in the UK was overshadowed by the threat of a life sentence for the Canadian drugs charges, casting the biggest ever doubt over the Stones' future.*

associating with us.' Bill Wyman says: 'She's helping to improve English-Canadian relations.' After the show the Stones and Margaret Trudeau leave for a private party.

MARCH 6
Mick Jagger says in Toronto: 'It was fun on stage last night but all these girls were grabbing my balls. Once they started they didn't stop. It was great up to a point, then it got very difficult to sing.' On Margaret Trudeau he says: 'She just dropped by. Someone said she wanted to come to the gig, so we took her. I had never met her before. But I guess she likes to go out to clubs and go rocking and rolling like everyone else.' On the Stones' future he comments: 'We can't really do a five year plan at the rate things are going. I did do a plan for two years, but it's going to be changed,' and adds that if Keith Richard is jailed the band will continue to tour. 'If the Rolling Stones wanted to tour badly or wanted to go on stage, I think they'd have to. Obviously we wouldn't if Keith were only in jail for a short period of time... but we can't wait five years.' Charlie Watts says: 'When my drums start to blow up, that's the last performance.'

MARCH 7
Keith Richard appears in court. The hearing for his heroin charge, which could carry a life sentence if he is found guilty, is set for 14 March, but he is also informed of a second charge. The Mounties claim that during the initial raid they seized a second substance and laboratory tests have proved it was a fifth of an ounce of cocaine. He will appear in court tomorrow in a private hearing, a decision made following rowdy scenes when he is grabbed by the hair by a man identified as a freelance photographer for a left-wing publication and called 'limey' and 'junkie bastard' by the man and three friends. No date for the trial is set.
The Rolling Stones/Margaret Trudeau affair is held by many to be a contributory factor in the drop in the value of the Canadian dollar which falls one and a half cents against the pound.

Above: *Margaret Trudeau provoked a political scandal by her involvement with the Stones.*

MARCH 9
The Stones fly to New York. Keith and Anita remain in Toronto.

MARCH 10
Gossip columnist Suzi of the *New York Daily News* reports that it is Ron Wood, not Mick Jagger, who is the object of Mrs Trudeau's affections. 'He can probably tell you more about where Margaret is staying than maybe even the Prime Minister.' Ron Wood is staying at the Plaza Hotel. Mick Jagger issues a press statement: 'Margaret Trudeau is a very attractive and nice person, but we are not having an affair. I never met her before and haven't seen her since I got to New York. In fact I haven't seen her since Sunday. What can I say? I'm in New York to be with my wife and my daughter.' Margaret Trudeau tells the *Toronto Sun*: 'I'm very fond of him. I'd like to think he is a friend. But after all, I'm a married lady.'

MARCH 11
Canadian Prime Minister Pierre Trudeau tells the *Toronto Sun* that his wife has cancelled all engagements indefinitely because 'she wants to take the pressure off and become a private person for a while... I think that if she goes to rock concerts she has to expect to be noticed and written about. I have no complaints about that but I believe that my wife's private life is her affair and mine.' On her association with the Stones when one of them is before the court on drug charges, Trudeau comments: 'I don't indulge in guilt by association.'

MARCH 12
More than 60 Andy Warhol prints of Mick Jagger are on show at the Pigeonhole Gallery, Kings Road, London, priced at £3,700 each. Margaret Trudeau flies back to Ottawa from New York. The Stones' tour promoter, Peter Rudge, says: 'I don't want her round us one minute longer. I'll be glad when she is as far away from us as possible.'

MARCH 14
At the Brampton Courtroom, Toronto, Anita Pallenberg is fined $400. She says: 'The judge was kind to me,' Keith Richard is remanded on bail until 27 June.

MARCH 18
Mick and Bianca Jagger, Bill Wyman and Astrid, and Ron and Krissie Wood attend the Eagles' concert at Madison Square Garden, New York. Ron Wood joins them on stage for an encore. Earlier the three Stones and their wives showed up backstage at the New York Palladium to watch Iggy Pop and David Bowie.

MARCH 26
It is widely rumoured that Bianca Jagger and film star Warren Beatty are having an affair. Bianca comments to Warren: 'So we had an affair? You must be pretty bad, I don't even remember!' Meanwhile in London the police raid Keith Richard's Chelsea house where he stayed until Christmas. Nothing is found.

APRIL 1
Keith and Anita leave Toronto for New York. The Rolling Stones re-sign with Atlantic Records for the North American distribution of Rolling Stones Records. Earl McGrath replaces Marshall Chess as president of Rolling Stones Records. According to the *Toronto Star* the Stones have become the highest-paid recording artists in the world. The Atlantic deal is said to be worth $21 million for six albums which, added to the EMI world-wide deal will give the Stones $10.5 million for each of their next six albums.

APRIL 26
While in New York, Mick Jagger, together

with Stevie Wonder, has been at Electric Lady contributing to Peter Frampton's new album.

APRIL 30
Muddy Waters says: 'Then all at once there was the Rolling Stones. When they did it, they created a whole wide open space for the music. They said who did it first and how they came by knowin' it. They told the truth about it and that really put a shot in my arm with the whites. I tip my hat to 'em. They took a lot of what I was doin', but who cares? It took the people from England to hip my people - my white people - to what they had in their own backyard.'

MAY 2
Fashion designer Halston organises a birthday party for Bianca at the newly opened Studio 54 club in New York. Mick's present is a white horse.
Ron Wood says: 'With or without Keith, the Rolling Stones must produce the goods. If he goes to jail we'll just have to work things out from there. But there is no way that we have played our last gig together.'

MAY 9
Columnist Bob Weiner of New York's *Soho News* writes of Bianca: 'If she weren't married to Mick Jagger, she'd be scrubbing kitchen floors.'

MAY 15
Nils Lofgren, on tour in Britain, sings a song dedicated to Keith Richard, called 'Keith Don't Go', continuing 'Don't Go To Toronto'.
Ron Wood goes to hear Muddy Waters play at the Roxy, Los Angeles.

MAY 25
The Rolling Stones meet in New York to edit the live album tapes.

JUNE 12
In England, Charlie Watts plays a jazz set at the Swindon Arts Centre. The concert is recorded for a possible live album. All profits go to local charities. Charlie says: 'I have always liked this type of music. I listen to a lot of jazz and blues records, especially Charlie Parker, when I'm at home. If we had about four gigs together, then the sound would have been a lot better.'

JUNE 20
Mick Jagger and Keith Richard mix the live album at Atlantic Studios on Broadway.

JUNE 25
The Japanese press reports their Government will refuse the Stones permission to tour (even though they aren't planning to) as a result of Keith Richard's drug convictions.

JUNE 27
Keith Richard fails to make a court appearance in Toronto to set a date for his trial because he is receiving treatment for drug addiction, says his lawyer Austin Cooper, who asks for an adjournment. The case is postponed till 19 July. Judge Gordon Tinker says: 'I intend to treat Mr Richard like everyone else.' The Judge asks for medical evidence to show what progress has been made.

JULY 1
Bianca is in Paris working on her movie *Flesh Coloured*. She spends time with David Bowie with whom gossips claim she is having an affair.

JULY 2
Mick Jagger attempts to prevent publication of *The Man Who Killed Mick Jagger*, a novel by David Littlejohn, Associate Dean of the University of California, on the grounds that someone might try to put the theory into practice. Apparently the author asked Jann Wenner, editor of *Rolling Stone*, whether he should clear the title with Jagger but was told not to bother: 'I know him. He is continually fantasising and in dread about being shot and killed by some nut at a rock concert.'

JULY 12
Mick Jagger says in New York: 'I think rock'n'roll has its limitations as a musical form. Even as a political, economical force, you know. But it's part of it. Then there's also tennis... I don't take anything seriously any more. I mean since the age of fourteen I haven't taken anything really seriously... whatever I do.'

JULY 18
Ron Wood sells his Richmond home, The Wick, for £300,000. Mick Jagger visits the Pathe Marconi Studios in Paris in his search for a possible recording venue for the next album.

JULY 19
Keith Richard again fails to appear in Court in Toronto. His lawyer says he is still undergoing treatment at the Stevens Clinic in New York. The hearing is postponed until 2 December. Keith tells the *Daily Mirror* later: 'Having treatment can be a very tough thing, but there are certain medical advances that have been made which make it a lot easier. There are ways of avoiding cold turkey with electro-therapy. You know, all that rolling around the room in agony is for the movies. You just go into hospital for two or three days. There are no needles involved. They just use a small electric battery and circulate it between your ears. The main problem is resisting the temptation to go back to the stuff.'

Above left: *Andy Warhol and Mick Jagger, twin darlings of the New York media, at the* Love You Live *launch party.*

JULY 20
The soundtrack of a Japanese movie called *Metamorphosis* features 'Criss Cross', an unreleased Stones track recorded in Jamaica in 1972.

JULY 24
Bill Wyman plays with the Clarence Brown Band at the International Jazz Festival in Montreux, Switzerland.

JULY 28
The Rolling Stones have been offered almost £1,000,000 by NBC-TV to play one concert in the Bahamas next May to be shown simultaneously in cinemas throughout the world by means of closed-circuit satellite hook-up.

AUGUST 8
Keith Richard says: 'We've been very very lucky in that we've got a band that can live together and work together and sometimes not see each other for months on end and still make it groove. I don't know if I could take it if I had to live all the bullshit that seems to go down when bands break up... There aren't many drummers like Charlie Watts who can play rock'n'roll and other things and still swing which is the basic thing. That goes for the rhythm section as a whole... I sometimes sway between being a prisoner and an outcast. I'm not sure whether they're keeping me in or pushing me out. You have to put so much effort and organisation into breaking any of those well-trodden paths... I'm not a junkie.'

AUGUST 10
The Rolling Stones Greatest Hits Vols 1 and 2 are released on ABKCO Records in New York. They are also known as the TV albums. In various European countries they are sold as a double album set at a lower price.

AUGUST 25
The *Daily Mirror* reports that Mick Jagger is trying unsuccessfully to patch up his failing marriage on the Greek island of Hydra. At a local disco the Jaggers are seen sitting at separate tables. A photographer friend, Nick Karantilion, says: 'They both seemed very unhappy. Mick was in a very distressed mood. After spending the evening with them I am convinced they are busting up.'

AUGUST 26
In Frankfurt, German fans collect money in aid of Keith Richard and plan to march to the Canadian Embassy to present a petition to the Ambassador.

SEPTEMBER 12
Mick Jagger gives a press conference at the

Right: *Mick in relaxed mood; however newspaper reports were predicting the break-up of his marriage.*

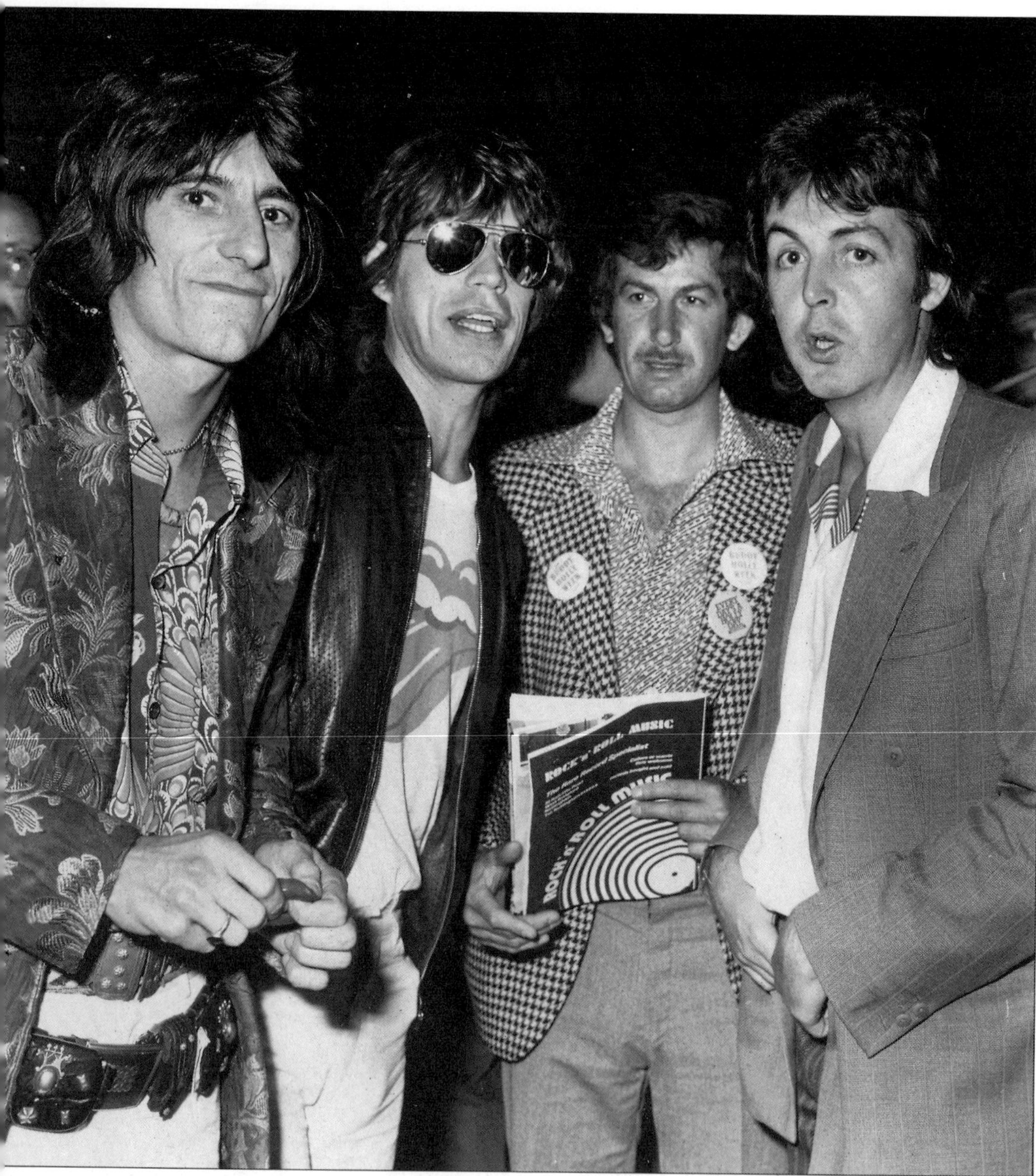

Savoy Hotel London to publicise the new album *Love You Live*, to be released next week.

SEPTEMBER 13
The Rolling Stones minus Keith Richard, attend the *Love You Live* launch party at the Marquee in London.

SEPTEMBER 14
Mick Jagger and Ron Wood are in the audience at the Crickets' concert at the Kilburn Gaumont, to mark the 41st anniversary of Buddy Holly's birth. Mick Jagger says in the *Evening Standard*: 'Rock'n'Roll music is for adolescents. It's adolescent music. It's a dead end. I think the whole history of rock'n'roll has proved that. There's nothing wrong with it, but it's just for kids. My whole life isn't rock'n'roll. It's an absurd idea that it should be. But it's no more than anybody's whole life might revolve around working in Woolworth's. Keith Richard is the original punk rocker. You can't really out-punk Keith - it's a useless gesture.' In the *Daily Express* he says of his relationship with Bianca: 'So many people have been nasty and tried to divorce or divide us. I am very thick-skinned but it affects me a bit and affects Bianca an awful lot. She gets very upset about it. We have no intention of splitting up.' He says of Keith Richard: 'He's been having treatment in a New York hospital and has now finished it. At present he is living in the country outside New York. We all know Keith could get nothing or life imprisonment. If he got life, I would carry on with the band but I don't know what I'd do. I'd be very upset. I'm sure Keith could write in prison, he'd have nothing else to do. I think the law's out to get us. Once you get any notoriety it seems to happen.'

SEPTEMBER 16
Love You Live is released. The album was recorded live in Paris last year and at the El Mocambo Club in Toronto in March and produced by the Glimmer Twins. The cover design is by Andy Warhol.

SEPTEMBER 17
Robert Frank, director of *Cocksucker Blues*, reveals in New York that he has been paid an undisclosed sum not to release the film until March 1979 as it is felt certain scenes could prejudice the outcome of Keith Richard's trial in Toronto.

SEPTEMBER 20
An hour-long film of the Stones in concert in Paris last year, is shown on BBC TV's *The Old Grey Whistle Test*.

SEPTEMBER 23
Ladies And Gentlemen, The Rolling Stones is given its European premiere at the Rainbow Theatre, London.

SEPTEMBER 27
The Stones give a party at the Trax Club, New York to launch *Love You Live*.

OCTOBER 1
Love You Live enters the British Top 30 at Number 18. It will stay in the Top 30 for seven weeks, reaching Number 3.

OCTOBER 3
Keith Richard says: 'Punks should take a few courses in swearing. They don't have the stamina to be real rock stars.'

OCTOBER 6
Mick Jagger says: 'I told EMI, if I go on the telly and do worse things and say worse swear words than the Sex Pistols, will you sack us? 'Cos there's no way you're going to get your money back. They just said: "No way, Mr Jagger...". I'm afraid most rock'n'roll stars are just interested in themselves. You go on stage... you get egotistical, of course you do. You think you are really important, and you are not. I don't think everyone in rock'n'roll is important. We're all full of shit. When I go on the road I just go crazy, I become a total monster. I don't recognise anybody, I don't even see them. I feel guilty about it afterwards, then I laugh, because the whole thing is a joke. But Keith is worse than I am. Is he a prima donna? Oh yeah!'
Keith Richard and Ron Wood fly from Washington to Paris by Concorde to join the other Stones for recording sessions. On arrival Keith takes a taxi to his flat but can't remember its address and has to phone the

office in New York as he's forgotten it.

OCTOBER 10
The Stones start cutting a new album at the Pathe Marconi Studios in Paris. They plan to record till early December. Keith Moon attends an early session.

OCTOBER 15
Love You Live enters the US Top 30 at Number 18. It will stay in the Top 30 for seven weeks, with a highest position of Number 5.

OCTOBER 19
The French press reports that Mick and Bianca Jagger will soon divorce as Mick is dating Texan model Jerry Hall.

OCTOBER 24
Russian spy ships listen in on a NATO exercise and a pilot jams the air-waves with a Rolling Stones tape.

OCTOBER 28
Mick Jagger goes to the Stiff Records Package show at the Lyceum Ballroom and sees Ian Dury, Elvis Costello, Nick Lowe and Wreckless Eric.

NOVEMBER
Arcade Records in the UK release a double Rolling Stones compilation album called *Get Stoned* featuring 28 tracks from 1963-71.

NOVEMBER 17
At Sotheby's London auction rooms, Bianca buys a photograph of Mick taken by Cecil Beaton on the set of *Performance*.

NOVEMBER 19
Get Stoned enters the British Top 30 at Number 29. It will stay in the Top 30 for ten weeks, with a highest position of Number 10.

NOVEMBER 26
The Rolling Stones break recording sessions for a week so that Keith can face trial in Toronto. Mick Jagger goes to Morocco with Jerry Hall, American model and former girlfriend of Bryan Ferry.

DECEMBER 2
Keith Richard appears in court in Toronto. He is remanded to a higher court next February. He tells the court that he has made repeated efforts to cure himself of drug addiction, but that every time a tour comes up, he begins taking the drug again.
Jimmy Page denies that Led Zeppelin are breaking up, and that he will replace Keith Richard within the Stones. He says: 'I've played with Ronnie Wood and Keith Richard and we have a good time, but it's only jamming. I was upset because it looks like it was a stab in the back of Keith, and I really like and respect him.'

DECEMBER 5
The Rolling Stones resume work on their new album in Paris.

DECEMBER 11
Bianca Jagger flies out of London amid reports of imminent divorce proceedings.

DECEMBER 21
The Rolling Stones break their recording sessions for Christmas.
The Rolling Stones are listed in the *1977 Guinness Book of Records*, as the loudest band of the year.

DECEMBER 25
Mick Jagger and Jerry Hall spend Christmas in London while Keith Richard and Anita are in New York.

DECEMBER 27
Mick Jagger and Jerry Hall fly to Barbados using the names 'Jagger Beaton' and 'J. Hall Beaton'. A British airways official comments: 'Well, it's a new name for Mr Jagger. He usually flies under the name of Phillips and Bianca used the name only two weeks ago when she flew on Concorde to New York.'

Left: *Middle-aged ravers Ron Wood, Mick Jagger and Paul McCartney, celebrate the 41st anniversary of Buddy Holly's birth seen here with Eddie Cochran fan-club president, Tony Garrett.* Right: *By the end of 1977 it was common knowledge that Mick was regularly seeing American model Jerry Hall.*

NINETEEN 78

JANUARY 6
Bianca is seen at Studio 54 in New York with tennis star Bjorn Borg. Mick returns to Paris via New York to continue work with the other Stones on the new album.

JANUARY 25
As Mick Jagger and Jerry Hall leave the Elysée Matignon Club in Paris, Mick punches a photographer who retaliates, knocking Mick down onto the pavement.

JANUARY 26
At MIDEM in Cannes, Ron Wood signs a solo recording contract with CBS records.

JANUARY 27
Charlie Watts plays in Swindon with Bob Hall's Skiffle Group. Ian Stewart records the gig with the Mighty Mobile. The resulting album, *Jamming The Boogie*, including material taped at last August's gig, will be released in August.

FEBRUARY 3
Bianca issues a statement about her relationship with Mick through her agent: 'There is no disagreement between us and we are tired of the harassment and falsely attributed statements.'

FEBRUARY 6
Keith Richard's legal representatives fly to Toronto and Keith's court appearance is postponed to 6 March.

FEBRUARY 11
Keith Richard is interviewed by *High Times* magazine in America.
Question: 'Can the Rolling Stones keep going for another fifteen years?'
Keith Richard: 'Oh yeah, I hope so. There's no way to tell. We know a lot of the old black boys have kept going forever. A lot of the old black boys, the old blues players, as far as we're concerned they're virtually playing the same thing. They kept going until the day they dropped... There's no denying there's a high fatality rate in rock'n'roll. Up until the middle sixties the most obvious method of rock'n'roll death was chartered planes. Since then drugs have taken their toll, but all the people that I've known that have died from so-called drug overdoses have all been people that have had some fairly serious physical weakness somewhere.'
Question: 'Have you ever been in a dangerous situation with drugs?'
Keith Richard: 'No. I don't know if I've been extremely lucky or if it's that subconscious careful, but I've never turned blue in somebody else's bathroom. I consider that the height of bad manners, I've had so many people do it to me and it's really not on, as far as drug etiquette goes, to turn blue in someone else's john... I feel very hopeful about the future. I find it all very enjoyable, with a few peak surprises thrown in. Even being busted... it's no pleasure, but it certainly isn't boring. And I think boring is the worst thing of all.

FEBRUARY 16
Krissie Wood is in a London hospital with minor injuries following a car crash.

FEBRUARY 20
Mick and Bianca deny they are splitting up.

MARCH 1
Mick Jagger offers a reward for the return of the bracelet and ear-rings he gave Jerry Hall last Christmas which she has lost in the Paris Metro.

MARCH 3
The Stones finish recording the new LP. Since early October, they have recorded 44 tracks for the new album at the Pathe Marconi studios in Paris and with the Mighty Mobile. Editing is completed by the end of March, when Mick and Keith will fly to New York to finish the final editing at the Atlantic Studios. Meanwhile, Ron goes to LA, Bill and Astrid to Barbados and Charlie to London.

MARCH 6
The date for Keith Richard's trial by the Canadian High Court is set down for 23 October.

MARCH 9
Krissie Wood files divorce proceedings against Ron Wood citing model Jo Howard in the petition. In Paris Ron says: 'It's being dealt with in a civilised manner.'

APRIL 1
For the first game of the North America Soccer League played by the Philadelphia Furies, the team owned jointly by Mick Jagger, Peter Frampton, Rick Wakeman and Paul Simon, a train is chartered from New York to take the team and rock stars Bruce Springsteen, Eric Clapton, Carly Simon, James Taylor and Andy Gibb to the match. Mick Jagger arrives by helicopter in time to watch his team lose by 3-0 to the Washington Diplomats.

APRIL 19
Ian Stewart jams with Alexis Korner at Alexis' 50th birthday gig in London.

APRIL 27
Mick and Keith go to Kingston, Jamaica for the One Love Peace Concert and to see reggae singer Peter Tosh who has signed with Rolling Stones Records.

MAY 2
Bianca celebrates her 34th birthday at Studio 54. Ryan O'Neal, Liza Minnelli, Truman Capote and David Frost are among the guests.

MAY 5
Mick Jagger attends a Muddy Waters gig at the Roxy, L.A. In the US magazine, *Hit Parader*, he says: 'If you are with a woman and the sexual relationship is working like a Rolls Royce or Mercedes Benz, everything smoothes out. The other things don't become important, they're trivia.' About the new album he says: 'I'm very pleased with what the band was playing in Paris, when we recorded. And I'm pleased with what I'm playing too. I played guitar on the album. I enjoyed playing guitar more than singing almost. I like to do both, the trouble is I can't do both very well yet.'

MAY 6
Bo Diddley says: 'Me and the Rolling Stones, we're pretty tight. They welcomed me here in London when I first came here and I'll never forget that. They came to the Cumberland Hotel and gave me a pair of gold cuff-links with my initials on them... they've used a helluva lot of my licks and I guess because we've struck up such a relationship, I never said anything about it.

MAY 13
The Rolling Stones announce their American tour, including six outdoor concerts, in will open in mid-June in Florida and close on 23 July in Los Angeles.

MAY 14
Bianca Jagger files for divorce in London. The Rolling Stones are in Woodstock, New York, rehearsing for their forthcoming tour.

MAY 19
'Miss You'/'Far Away Eyes' is released on Rolling Stones Records, the first Rolling Stones single to be distributed by EMI. Written and composed by Jagger/Richard and recorded in Paris, it is produced by the Glimmer Twins.

JUNE 9
Some Girls is released on Rolling Stones Records. Produced by the Glimmer Twins, it was recorded in Paris at the Pathe Marconi Studios, with the Mighty Mobile. All tracks are written by Jagger and Richard, except 'Just My Imagination', an old Temptations hit.

JUNE 10
The Rolling Stones open their 1978 North American tour at the Civic Center, Lakeland, Florida.
'Miss You' enters the British Top 30 at Number 17. It will stay in the charts for eight weeks, reaching Number 2 after three weeks.

JUNE 12
Concert at the Fox Theatre, Atlanta, Georgia.

JUNE 14
Concert at the Capitol Theater, Passaic, New Jersey.

JUNE 15
Concert at the Warner Theater, Washington, D.C.

JUNE 17
Concert at the John F. Kennedy Stadium, Philadelphia in front of more than 90,000 people. Mick has an attack of flu but goes on in spite of doctors' orders not to. After the concert he flies to New York for Bob Marley's concert at Madison Square Garden.
Some Girls enters the British Top 30 at Number 11, it will stay in the charts for twelve weeks, reaching Number 2. 'Miss You' enters the US Top 30 at Number 23. It will stay in the charts for fourteen weeks, reaching Number 1.

JUNE 19
Concert at the New York Palladium. Among the 3,000 audience are Paul and Linda McCartney, Carly Simon, Bob Marley, Diane Keaton and Warren Beatty.

JUNE 20
Mick Jagger says: '*Some Girls* is all combinations. "Beast of Burden" is a

Above: *Mick and Jerry Hall demonstrating their Rolls Royce relationship.*

combination. ''Miss You'' is an emotion. It's not really about a girl. To me, the feeling of longing is what the song is about. I don't like to interpret my own fucking songs, but that's what it is.' Asked if he trains before undertaking such a tour he says: 'Oh God, Yes! Nobody could do it without. I go horse riding, rowing and I've got a karate guy who trains me. Those karate exercises are really good. They're very similar to dance exercises and stretch you. You could start pulling muscles otherwise, especially at whatever age I am.' Ronnie Wood says: 'I'm a lot less musically frustrated than I was with the Faces although at the time I didn't know I was frustrated. With this album, I've definitely taken a stand with my playing. During the first Rolling Stones tour I couldn't get used to having the freedom to be able to do whatever I wanted because the Faces were limiting where the Rolling Stones let me rip. Those Paris sessions made me feel how much of a Rolling Stones member I have always been. It's really weird. I feel like I've been with them right from the start.'

JUNE 21
Concert at the Coliseum, Hampton Roads, Virginia.

JUNE 22
Concert at the Convention Center, Myrtle Beach, South Carolina.

JUNE 24
Some Girls enters the US Top 30 at Number 18. It will stay in the charts for 35 weeks, including two weeks at Number 1.

JUNE 28
Concert at the Midsouth Coliseum, Memphis. Asked why the new album is called *Some Girls*, Keith Richard replies: 'Because we couldn't remember their fucking names.'

JUNE 29
Concert at the Rupp Arena, Lexington, Kentucky. One fan is shot and seventeen are arrested.

JULY 1
Concert at the Municipal Stadium, Cleveland, Ohio.

JULY 4
Concert at the Rich Stadium, Buffalo.

JULY 5
Concert at Orchard Park, New York State. Fans riot when the Stones refuse to play an encore.
The *Daily Mirror* reports that Raquel Welch and Lucille Ball, having discovered themselves portrayed unflatteringly on the cover of *Some Girls*, their lips and eyes overpainted in fluorescent colours, are threatening legal action against the Stones and Atlantic Records. As one of America's richest women, the 'humiliated' Ms Ball's threat is taken seriously and in the States the sleeves are recalled and the offending photographs blacked out. In Britain new covers are being printed.

JULY 6
Concert at the Masonic Temple, Detroit.

JULY 8
Concert at Soldier Field, Chicago with an audience of 80,000. Afterwards Mick goes to a Lefty Dizz gig at the Kingston Mines in downtown Chicago.

JULY 9
While in Chicago, Mick, Keith, Ron and Charlie join Muddy Waters on stage at the 400-seater club, the Quiet Knight.

JULY 10
Concert at the Coliseum, St Paul, Minnesota. Bill Wyman is knocked unconscious when he falls off the stage after the show.
Several US black radio stations ban the *Some Girls* album because of the lyrics of the title track. Mick Jagger refuses to change them.
Records are broken as a second concert at Anaheim Stadium, Los Angeles sells out of 55,000 tickets in two hours.

Above: *The 1978 tour confirmed Keith and Mick as undeniably mature but still masterful showmen.* Right: *This album cover design for* Some Girls *was threatened with legal action for the unflattering portrayals of Lucille Ball and Raquel Welch.*

JULY 11
Concert at the Kiel Auditorium, St Louis, Missouri.

JULY 13
Concert at the Superdrome, New Orleans, the biggest ever indoor concert, with more than 80,000 in the audience. More than $1,000,000 is taken in ticket sales.
Asked if he feels a 'marked man' in the States, Keith Richard says: 'You mean, how come all these other people have busted the Stones and the American police, who are pretty sharp, haven't? I am a very lucky man that I've never encountered any real problems with the American police. I think it's because they are now starting to understand. They realise what happened to Brian Jones, which was nothing more than sheer persecution. Hollywood is the end of the line for so many people. It's a killer and if you're weak you can be sure it'll get you. It's like when we were rehearsing in New York, we tried to find John Lennon and get him back into the scene. I mean, what the fuck is Lennon doing farming cows in upstate New York? What's that all about?'
When asked why he's playing guitar on tour, Mick Jagger answers: 'Two guitars is enough in a band, most bands get by on just one. But by the same token, a lotta bands have used three guitars effectively, and as long as all three don't play together too much, it has interesting possibilities. When I'm singing I tend to stop playing at the beginning of a number, so it sounds normal. Then when I start playing on the chorus, it can give that extra lift. I don't know if Keith and Woody agree, but I think it enables them to solo together while knowing that I'm playing the bottom rhythm part and so nothing is lost.'
Some Girls reaches Number 1 in the US charts.

JULY 16
Concert at Folsom Field, Boulder, Colorado.
In the US the contentious cover of *Some Girls* now reads, 'Please accept our apologies. We are being reconstructed.'

JULY 18
Concert at the Will Rogers Memorial Center, Fort Worth, Texas. Peter Rudge says: 'If the Rolling Stones won't do the small dates, who will? We had to tour and this is part of it.
Fiddle player Doug Kershaw joins the band on stage to play 'Far Away Eyes'. After the show Bill Wyman says: 'I went to see Kershaw in New Orleans and had to get him on with us. What an incredible show tonight; reggae with Peter Tosh, Cajun, country and rock'n'roll with a little blues thrown in.' To the audience Mick Jagger says: 'If the band's slightly lacking in energy, it's because we spent all last night fucking. We do our best.'

JULY 19
Concert at the Sam Housten Coliseum, Houston, Texas.

JULY 21
Concert at the Community Center, Tucson, Arizona. Linda Ronstadt duets with Mick Jagger on 'Tumbling Dice'.

JULY 22
The Stones arrive in Los Angeles.
Mick Jagger, his daughter Jade, Jerry Hall and Diana Ross go to Bob Marley's concert at the Starlit Amphitheatre in Burbank.

JULY 23
Concert at the Anaheim Stadium, L.A. Richard Dreyfuss, Valerie Perrine, Sylvester Stallone and Steve McQueen are in the audience.

JULY 24
Second sell-out show at the Anaheim Stadium, L.A. Nicky Hopkins and Bobby Keys join the Stones on stage.

JULY 25
A Judge in Los Angeles blocks Mick Jagger's share of the L.A. concerts pending settlement of Marsha Hunt's suit to increase his weekly contribution to their daughter Karis from £8.50 to £300.

JULY 26
Mick Jagger is 35 and the Stones finish their US tour at the Oakland Coliseum in front of an audience of 55,000. Mick and Jerry spend a few days with tour promoter Bill Graham in Corte Madera, Marin County, where they are joined by Brian Jones' fourteen-year-old son, Julian.

JULY 29
Of the British Press in New York, Mick Jagger says: 'They were brought over to see us and all they wanted to do was get drunk. They're awful people. They're horrible. They are trash. I'd never live in England again, not when people like that are living there.'

AUGUST 1
In Los Angeles the Rolling Stones mix live material recorded during their tour. Work on new material continues through the month at the old RCA studios.

AUGUST 7
The Stones' publicist, Les Perrin, dies in London at the age of 57.

AUGUST 28
A single, 'Beast of Burden'/'When The Whip Comes Down' is released in the USA. Both tracks, taken from *Some Girls*, are written by Jagger/Richard and produced by the Glimmer Twins.

SEPTEMBER
Rehearsals continue at Wally Heider's Studio, Sunset Boulevard, L.A.

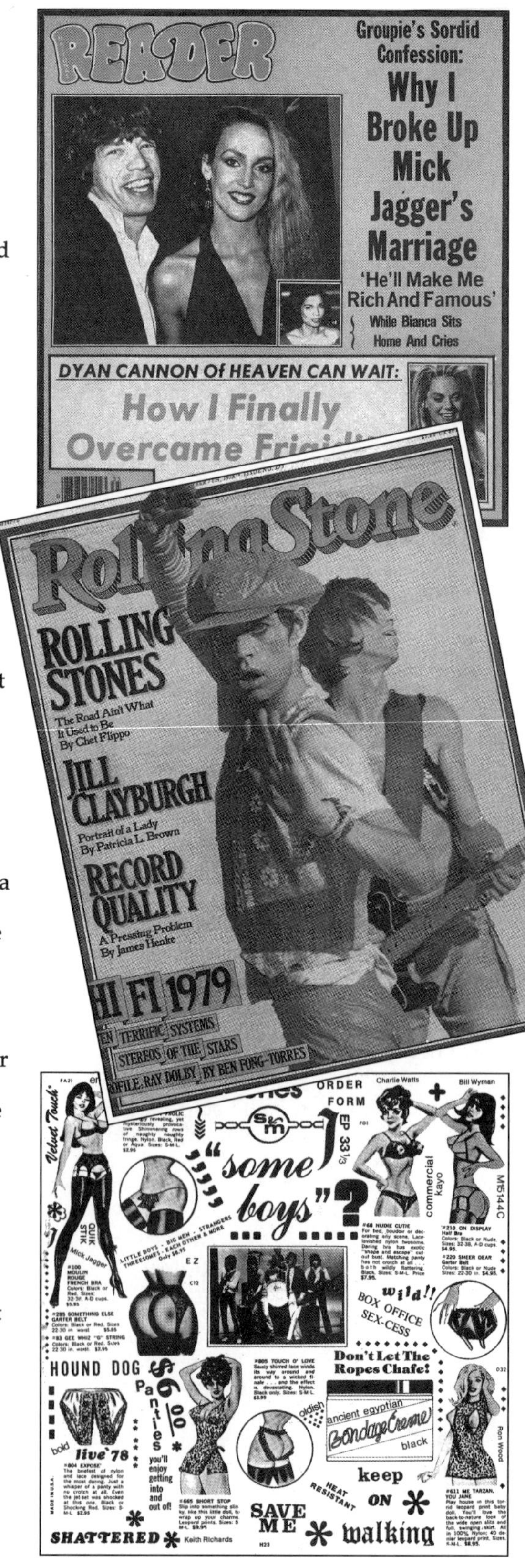

Top: Reader *magazine hits new depths of sleaze.*
Centre: Rolling Stone *still finds its namesakes important enough to make the lead cover story.*
Bottom: *Bootleg EP called 'Some Boys' featuring tracks recorded live during the US tour.*

SEPTEMBER 13
Bill Wyman and Charlie Watts attend the funeral of the Who's drummer, Keith Moon, who was found dead in his London flat on 7 September.

SEPTEMBER 15
'Respectable'/'When The Whip Comes Down' is released in the UK on Rolling Stones Records.

SEPTEMBER 16
Bill Wyman says: 'Before I did my solo albums I was getting so depressed, I was thinking about leaving the band because it was no more fun. Ron Wood came along and, especially in the last year, he's pulled both sides together, and I think he was the main reason for the band being so close and super friendly. Really being able to talk to one another. He's always laughing and joking and he can always make you laugh. There's such a great rapport going now between the band that people actually say to each other: "You played great tonight!" - which we've never said in twelve years... If you play badly or something goes wrong, you get put down, so you never get that uplift, but Ron started to get that happening, and now everybody congratulates everybody and it's "Thanks for a great show!" and I really get off on that. Now I've got a new lease of life, a second wind, and it doesn't cross my mind ever to leave, or that the band's going to break up. And touring, doing shows, getting on the road, Keith thinks that's the most important thing, and he's probably right. The more you work on the road, the better you play and the better the next session gets and the next tour.'

SEPTEMBER 29
Rolling Stones Records release ex-Wailer Peter Tosh's new single '(You Gotta Walk) Don't Look Back', with vocal support by Mick Jagger.

SEPTEMBER 30
'Beast of Burden' enters the US Top 30 at Number 27. It will stay in the charts for nine weeks, with a highest position of Number 7.

OCTOBER 3
It is reported in the press that Mick Jagger wrote 'Some Girls' after spending a night with two black girls.

OCTOBER 7
The Rolling Stones appear on *Saturday Night Live* and while in New York, do some recording.
The nationwide organisation PUSH campaigns against the lyrics of 'Some Girls'. The offending lyrics are: 'Black girls want to get fucked all night, but I don't have much jam...' PUSH President, the Reverend Jesse Jackson, claims: 'It is an insult to our race and degrading to our women.' He is pressing

Atlantic to stop further production and sale of the album. Mick Jagger repeats his assertion that the song is a parody. Hal Jackson, programme director of an influential black station in New York says: 'I know Mick very well - the guy's not a bigot, but it was a stupid thing for him to do.'
'Respectable' enters the British Top 30 at Number 26. It will stay in the charts for three weeks, with a highest position of Number 22.

OCTOBER 20
Mick Jagger arrives in London. Keith Richards spends two days quietly resting at his home in Westchester. During the past four months, Keith has let it be known that he has restored the final 's' to his surname.

OCTOBER 22
A daughter, Leah, is born to Ron Wood and Jo Howard in Los Angeles.

OCTOBER 23
Nearly two years after the original offence, Keith Richards' case comes to trial in Toronto. After plea bargaining between prosecution and defence lawyers, Keith Richards pleads guilty to possession of heroin. This is a lesser charge than the original one of 'trafficking with a narcotic'. The Judge elects to sentence the next day. His defence lawyer, Austin Cooper, pleading for probation, describes Keith's nine-year battle aginst addiction and his promise to donate $1,000,000 to a rehabilitation clinic. 'In 1969 he started with heroin and it got to the state where he was taking such quantities of the drug and getting no euphoria from it. He was taking such powerful amounts - as much as two and a half grams a day - just to feel normal.' He tells of three unsuccessful attempts to cure the addiction but the fourth is now working. 'He should not be dealt with as a special person, but I ask your Honour to understand him as a creative tortured person - as a major contributor to art form. He turned to heroin to prop up a sagging existence. I ask you to understand the whole man. He has fought a tremendous personal battle to rid himself of this terrible problem.'
During the trial Keith Richards explains: 'If you want to get off it you will, and this time I really wanted it to work. I've got to stay on the treatment if I want to stay off it for good, if I want to kick it for good.' When the Judge referred to the glorification of drugs in his songs and music, Keith replied: 'That is a misconception. I mean, about one per cent of our songs glorify the use of drugs, and Mick Jagger wrote them anyway, not me.'
Judge Lloyd Graburn gives Keith Richards a one-year suspended sentence and orders him to give a special concert at the Canadian National Institute for the Blind. This is to be done within the next six months; if not, Judge Graburn states: 'You may be taken before a provincial Judge and sentenced as a result.' He is also ordered to continue his

KEITH RICHARDS
RUN RUDOLPH RUN
STONE IS SENTENCED ..TO PLAY!
Drama as court hears of Stone's nightmare years
DAILY EXPRESS OCTOBER 26, 1978
DRUG TORTURE OF STONE KEITH
Now he fights to stay out of jail
MY DRUG SLAVERY!
Keith Richards... the "hell" of success

addiction treatment and to report to a Toronto probation officer within the next 24 hours and on 7 May and 24 September to give an account of the progress of his treatment. The packed court erupts as delighted fans cheer the sentence. The Judge is not amused.
Keith leaves Toronto and flies back to New York.

OCTOBER 25
A mad ticket scramble begins as tickets go on sale for the concert at the Canadian Institute for the Blind which has only 225 seats. In New York Keith Richards jams with Dave Edmunds, Nick Lowe and Rockpile at the Bottom Line. He says: 'I feel good about the sentence, it's very strange... we could change the venue for the concert, but I'll play where I'm told.'

OCTOBER 26
Mick Jagger leaves London before Bianca's legal representative can serve divorce papers on him. A spokesman says: 'I think Mick Jagger left as soon as he heard they were after him. He has a feeling about these sort of things.'

Above left: *The band show no sign of tailoring their act to approaching middle age.* Left: *Mick belts out a song at the Anaheim Stadium. Fans had begun queueing on the previous Thursday for the Sunday concert, at which the Stones played for less than 1½ hours.*

OCTOBER 28
In response to the campaign by the Reverend Jesse Jackson, Atlantic Records' Chairman Ahmet Ertegun recommends 'Some Girls' be re-edited. He says: 'Even though I know he didn't mean it... it is not our wish to demean, insult, or make less of a people without whom there would be no Atlantic Records!... Mick Jagger is certainly not a racist. He is consciously anti-racist. he owes his whole being to black people and black music.' The Stones also issue a statement: 'It never occurred to us that our parody of certain stereotypical attitudes would be taken seriously by anyone who has heard the entire lyrics of the song in question. No insult was intended and if any was taken, we sincerely apologise.' However later Mick is reported to comment: 'If you can't take a joke, it's too fucking bad.'

OCTOBER 29
Keith Richards flies from New York to Jamaica, while Mick Jagger leaves Jamaica for New York.
In Canada the lenience of Keith Richards' sentence continues to provoke angry comment. The *Toronto Sun* writes: 'Imagine the laughter among Rolling Stones' fans throughout the world... Their hero got busted and got off.' But Keith Richards' remark after the trial is what really drives Canadians mad. When reminded that he had once said 'They're out to make rock'n'roll illegal,' Keith replies: 'Well, they've missed another chance at it. Don't lock up the rock.' Former Prime Minister John Deifenbaker is outraged and urges an appeal. On the other hand, Canada's largest circulation paper the *Toronto Globe*, describes the verdict as a 'model of enlightened sentencing, one which should pave the way for a more equitable and civilised treatment of convicted drug addicts in Canadian courts.'

NOVEMBER 21
The *Toronto Star* reports that the Ontario administration wants Keith Richards to go to jail for heroin possession as a deterrent to his teenage fans. In a letter to Justice Minister Otto Lang, Attorney General Roy McMurtry says the Judge 'erred in principle' in failing to jail Keith Richards and asks Lang to appeal against the leniency of the one-year suspended sentence.

NOVEMBER 22
Federal Crown Prosecutor John Scollin wins an extension until 3 May 1979 to appeal against the sentence imposed by trial Judge Lloyd Graburn.

NOVEMBER 29
A single 'Shattered'/'Everything Is Turning To Gold', produced by the Glimmer Twins is released in America on Rolling Stones Records. 'Shattered' (Jagger/Richards) is taken from *Some Girls* while the flip side is an unreleased Jagger/Richards/Wood composition, recorded in Paris last year.

DECEMBER 3
Mick Jagger and Jerry Hall fly to Washington to attend the first annual Kennedy Center Awards Gala.
Keith Richards' first solo single 'Run Rudolph Run' (Chuck Berry)/'The Harder They Fall' (Jimmy Cliff) is released on Rolling Stones Records in America. The A-side was recorded in London late in 1976, the flip side in Los Angeles last August.

DECEMBER 10
Charlie Watts, Ian Stewart and Alexis Korner are among the members of a specially convened Big Band playing at Dingwall's in London's Camden Town, to celebrate 50 years of boogie woogie.

DECEMBER 15
After six years, Japan relaxes its ban on the Rolling Stones.

DECEMBER 18
Keith Richards celebrates his 35th birthday in New York before returning to London to spend Christmas with his family.

DECEMBER 25
Mick Jagger spends Christmas in Hong Kong.

DECEMBER 28
In *Rolling Stone*, the Rolling Stones are voted artists of the year, and *Some Girls* album of the year, in the 1979 Critics Awards.

JANUARY 13
Keith Richards says: 'We never did anything consciously to shock people. All we ever did was answer the call of nature.' When asked what he misses about England, he replies: 'The sarcastic coppers.'

JANUARY 18
The Rolling Stones fly to Nassau, Bahamas, to cut new material at the Compass Point Studios.

JANUARY 20
The *New Musical Express* votes *Some Girls* best dressed album of 1978.

JANUARY 23
A Los Angeles Court orders Mick Jagger to pay $1,500 a week to Marsha Hunt, when he is declared father of her daughter Karis.

JANUARY 25
Rolling Stones's poll for 1978 votes the Rolling Stones band of the year, *Some Girls* album of the year and 'Miss You' single of the year. The *Daily Mail* reports that Mick Jagger has been granted an eviction order against the caretakers of his Berkshire house, Stargrove, recently sold for £200,000. He agrees to waive it for 28 days to give the couple time to find somewhere else to live. Mr and Mrs White were not disputing that they should vacate Stargrove but felt that, after working for Mick Jagger for ten years, they should have been told earlier that he was selling. As it was, they only found out from an estate agent. Mick Jagger did not ask for costs and the Judge said: 'I am glad to hear that, in all the circumstances.'

JANUARY 27
'Shattered' enters the US Top 30 at Number 27 where it stays for just two weeks before dropping out.

FEBRUARY 5
Bianca's divorce suit includes a demand for half of Mick's estimated £10,000,000 fortune in settlement. Before their St Tropez marriage in 1971, Mick insisted that Bianca sign an agreement keeping their property separate. She has hired celebrated Hollywood lawyer Marvin Mitchelson to represent her. Michelson had also represented Marsha Hunt.

FEBRUARY 8
Mick Jagger and the other Rolling Stones charter a plane to search for their road manager Alan Dunn and his girlfriend Ramona Herman, who disappeared on a boating trip in the heart of the Bermuda Triangle. However, they are picked up safely by the crew of the yacht *Drummer*. Alan has been with the Stones since 1963.

FEBRUARY 16
Keith Richards' single 'Run Rudolph Run'/'The Harder They Come' is released in the UK on Rolling Stones Records.

FEBRUARY 17
The *New Musical Express* reports that Keith Richards is in a dilemma about returning to Canada to give the charity concert that was part of his sentence. As the Ministry of Justice would like his case re-opened because of the leniency of the sentence, he could be served with a subpoena and have his passport confiscated. But if he doesn't return he will be violating the terms of his suspended sentence.

MARCH 20
Keith Richards announces he will give two benefit concerts for the Canadian National Institute for the Blind in Toronto next month. The concerts will be held in the 5,000 seat Varsity Arena during the afternoon and evening of Sunday 22 April. Having been granted leave to appeal, the Justice Minister will now be able to serve the notice of appeal as Keith will be on Canadian territory.

APRIL 5
American lawyers acting for Bianca finally manage to serve divorce papers on Mick Jagger in New York.

APRIL 21
The Rolling Stones and the New Barbarians play two concerts at the Oshawa Civic Stadium, Toronto, the only concert the Stones give in 1979. The New Barbarians is a band formed for the occasion by Keith and Ron, also featuring Bobby Keys, Stanley

Clarke, Joseph Modelliste and Ian McLagan. Keith Richards is served with notice of appeal of his sentence and appears in court to discuss the progress of his probation with Judge Graburn.

APRIL 24
The New Barbarians play their first US date in Ann Arbor, Michigan.

APRIL 25
The New Barbarians play in Denver, Colorado.

APRIL 26
The New Barbarians play in St Louis, Missouri.

APRIL 28
The New Barbarians play at the Cobo Hall in Detroit, Michigan.
Cocksucker Blues is shown officially in Los Angeles.

APRIL 29
The New Barbarians play at the Sports Arena in Milwaukee.

APRIL 30
The New Barbarians play at the Amphitheater in Chicago.

MAY 2
The New Barbarians play in Pittsburgh, Pennsylvania.

MAY 3
The New Barbarians play in Cincinnati.

MAY 4
Mick Jagger appears at the High Court in London for a three-hour private hearing on his divorce. Although he refuses to comment, the discussion is believed to hinge on whether the divorce should be settled in US or British courts. British property laws would benefit Mick Jagger but Bianca would benefit from an American settlement.

MAY 5
The New Barbarians play at the Capital Center, Largo, Washington.

MAY 7
The New Barbarians play at Madison Square Garden, New York.

MAY 8
The New Barbarians play at the Richfield Coliseum, Cleveland, Ohio.

MAY 9
In Los Angeles Mick's lawyers make a statement that, although he made love to Bianca as recently as October 1977, their marriage 'was over in every true sense in 1973'. At issue is the size of Mick Jagger's fortune. Bianca claims half of the £13,000,000 she says he has earned since 1971, while Mick maintains he only has about £2,000,000 left.

MAY 10
The New Barbarians play in Birmingham, Alabama.

MAY 11
Ron Wood's solo album *Gimme Some Neck* is released on CBS. Recorded in Paris and mastered in Los Angeles, it is produced by Ray Thomas. All tracks are written by Ron Wood, except 'Seven Days' by Bob Dylan. The album features help from Keith Richards, Mick Jagger, Charlie Watts, Bobby Keys, Ian McLagan and Mick Fleetwood.

MAY 12
Charlie Watts and Rocket 88 (Ian Stewart, Alexis Korner and Dick Morrissey) play at the Venue in London while the New Barbarians are playing a concert at the Summit in Houston, Texas.

MAY 13
The New Barbarians play at the Tarrant County, in Dallas, Texas.
At the Cannes Film Festival, Mick and Bill Wyman attend a party for the Who's films *Quadrophenia* and *The Kids Are All Right*.

MAY 14
In court in L.A., Judge Harry Shafer hears from Bianca's lawyers that her allowance has been cut from £8,000 to £1,000 a month. The judge orders Mick to maintain his wife in the 'sumptuous style' to which she has become accustomed. 'She should not be starved into submission,' he says.

MAY 16
The New Barbarians play in Tucson, Arizona.

MAY 17
The New Barbarians play in Phoenix, Arizona.

MAY 20
The New Barbarians play at the Coliseum, in Oakland, California.

MAY 21
The New Barbarians finish their sell-out US tour at the L.A. Forum.

MAY 26
Mick Jagger and Charlie Watts are guests at Eric Clapton's wedding to Patti Boyd, George Harrison's former wife, held at Clapton's house near London.

Above left: *Mick and Jerry Hall are seen increasingly together, especially in New York.*

JUNE 1
A new compilation album is released in Europe on Rolling Stones Records. Called *Time Waits For No One* it is the last album under their distribution contract with WEA Records. The tracks included are produced by Jimmy Miller and the Glimmer Twins.

JUNE 2
In Los Angeles, Judge Shafer orders Mick Jagger to pay Bianca £1,500 a week maintenance until the final settlement is decided.

JUNE 18
The Rolling Stones meet in Paris to cut a new album at the Pathe Marconi Studios.

JUNE 27
Keith Richards' appeal opens before five Court of Appeal judges in Toronto. Keith's lawyer submits that Keith is now free of drugs, but that a jail term would be very likely to cause a relapse. In an affidavit filed with the Court, Keith Richards declares that 'I have grimly determined to change my life and abstain from any drug use. I can truthfully say that the prospect of ever using drugs again in the future is totally alien to my thinking. My experience has also had an important effect not only on my happiness, but on my happiness at home in which my young son is brought up.' Crown prosecutor John Scollin argues that he deserves to be jailed and that Canadian justice will be called into disrepute if he is not. The Court reserves its decision.

JUNE 30
Bianca flies to Nicaragua to try to rescue relatives and children caught up in the civil war there.

JULY 1
The Rolling Stones continue to work on their album in Paris.

JULY 6
Mick Jagger returns to London for four days of private hearings on his divorce. He is growing a beard.

JULY 9
Bianca returns to London to raise aid for victims of the Nicaraguan civil war. Her family are safe but she says: 'I can do nothing to help them financially at present because I have no money. Although Mick was told by a judge in the United States to pay me money, he hasn't done so. After the divorce hearing, I intend to fly back to Nicaragua to work for

WILD HORSES COULDN'T DRAG ME AWAY!
APRIL 22, 1979
rock&folk
interview: KEITH RICHARDS
QUEEN
BERNARD LAVILLIERS
FRANK ZAPPA
Toronto Star
Monday April 23, 1979
15 cents
MORE PICTURES FROM THE STONES CONCERT/ A2
Bared to the waist, a pouting Jagger drives Richards along in last night's concert at the Oshawa auditorium
Stones peaked as time ran out
Rock's greats were rolling when suddenly -- the end
Deafening and delightful

Right: *Keith pays his dues: The Stones played a benefit concert for the Canadian National Institute for the Blind in Oshawa, Ontario on the instructions of Keith's trial judge after he was found guilty of possessing heroin.*

the Red Cross, although it will be a very stiff task to raise my fare.'

JULY 10
Asked by reporters outside the High Court in London how Bianca is, Mick replies: 'Terrible!'

JULY 16
Mr Justice Eastham rules that Mick's divorce should be heard in England but he makes no order preventing Bianca proceeding with her petition in America, as such an order would be 'discourteous' to the American judiciary, so it is still undecided where the divorce will finally be heard. The seven-day private hearing has cost an estimated £20,000.

JULY 20
At Keith Richards' Westchester home in New York State, 17-year-old Scott Cantrell of Norwalk, Connecticut, shoots himself in the presence of Anita Pallenberg, with a .38 calibre Smith and Wesson revolver. He and Anita were watching TV in bed and, when Anita got up to tidy the room, Cantrell shot himself in the head. The police arrive and he is rushed to Northern Westchester hospital where he dies just after midnight, Anita is taken into custody and questioned for twelve hours.

JULY 21
Anita Pallenberg is released on $500 and her passport is confiscated. She is charged with possession of stolen property as the revolver is found to have been stolen in Fort Lauderdale, Florida. She tells detectives that Scott had been playing with the gun all evening and talking of Russian roulette.

JULY 23
Scott Cantrell's brother Jim says: 'I think the circumstances of his death should be gone over with a fine comb. Nothing I have heard makes any sense. What was this woman doing tidying the bedroom at 10.30 at night? There is something very, very fishy about this. Police are saying it was a self-inflicted wound, but I just don't believe my brother would do such a thing.' A long-time friend, Jeffery Sessler, 25, who was in a downstairs room with Keith and Anita's son Marlon at the time of the shooting, and who called the police, says Anita was not having an affair with Cantrell. He says: 'The two were watching a programme to commemorate the tenth anniversary of man setting foot on the moon. She felt very sorry for him. He didn't seem to have a friend in the world. He told us his mother committed suicide on Christmas Day and that no one loved or cared for him. Anita invited him to come and live at the place about a month ago. She wanted to let him work for the family as an odd job man, but quite honestly I don't think he could adapt to the warmth and love he was being shown here. Although Anita cared for him, it was not a sex-type relationship.'

JULY
In a flurry of Stones sixties covers, Kiss cut a version of '2000 Man'; the Records issue a new version of 'Have You Seen Your Mother Baby, Standing In The Shadow' while Jay Ferguson releases 'Let's Spend The Night Together', with a little of 'Have You Seen Your Mother...' mixed in. 'Out Of Time' is cut by Carillo, 'Stupid Girl' by Ellen Foley, and the Pointer Sisters record 'Happy'. In Paris the Stones continue to cut new material.

JULY 26
The *New York Post* reports that the first detectives to arrive at the Richards' house in South Salem, Westchester after the shooting were surprised at the filth and untidiness. The crumpled sheets had not been washed for weeks. A chair was propping up a broken corner of the heavy oak bed. An air freshener couldn't cover the stench. 'There was a powerful, unpleasant smell in the room, as if there was a dead cat somewhere,' said one detective.

JULY 28
Recording commitments in Paris cause Ron and Keith to postpone the New Barbarians' appearance at the Knebworth Festival from 4 to 11 August.

AUGUST 4
While recording in Paris the band deny rumours that they are planning any concerts in the Autumn.

AUGUST 11
The New Barbarians play at the Knebworth Festival.

AUGUST 16
According to the *New York Post* Anita Pallenberg and Scott Cantrell are linked with a witches' coven in South Salem (a part of New England long associated with witchcraft). A policeman talks of being attacked by 'a flock of black-hooded, caped people' a mile from Keith Richards' house. A fifteen-year-old neighbour, Steve Levoie, is quoted as saying he had been invited by Anita 'to pot and sex orgies. She's a sick person, she should be put away,' he says. 'The house was filthy, really dirty, and Anita was dirty herself. She even asked my sister if she wanted some coke... She had a lot of young boys who would come to the house all the time. She would ask for sex and talk of sex quite often. She never asked me, but who'd want a dirty old woman like that.' Friends of both Anita and Keith say that Keith rarely visits the house in Westchester and that his relationship with Anita has deteriorated.

AUGUST 17
In a continuation of the coverage of the witchcraft story, the *New York Post* reports that local boys talked of finding 'ritualistic stakes' and that Anita's neighbours had apparently found small animals, dogs and

---

Above left: *Bianca shepherded by famed divorce lawyer Marvin Mitchelson, hired to help her pursue her $25 million suit against Mick.*

cats 'sacrificed' near the house. Nuns at a local convent have told police of hearing 'strange chants, gun shots and loud music'.

AUGUST
Late in the month the Stones break recording sessions in Paris. Bill Wyman leaves for the States, Mick Jagger and Charlie Watts fly to London while Ron Wood and Keith Richards stay in Paris.

SEPTEMBER 2
Bill Wyman appears on the *Jerry Lewis Muscular Dystrophy Telethon* broadcast from Las Vegas, playing live on stage with Ringo Starr, Dave Mason, Todd Rundgren and Kiki Dee.

SEPTEMBER 12
The Stones resume recording sessions in Paris.

SEPTEMBER
Ron Wood and Keith Richards join Leonard Bernstein on stage at the Elysée Matignon in Paris.

SEPTEMBER 17
Five judges of the Ontario Court of Appeal reject Prosecutor John Scollin's appeal to jail Keith Richards, as they recognise that Keith has been cured of his addiction.

OCTOBER 15
The *London Evening News* reports that the Stones are to tour China next year, playing concerts in five or six major cities. The tour was apparently decided after Mick Jagger was invited by the Chinese to meet their Ambassador in Washington. Mick Jagger says: 'It's a great opportunity. We're all looking forward to playing to people who haven't to any large degree been exposed to rock music.'

OCTOBER 19
The Rolling Stones finish their recording sessions in Paris. The album, tentatively called *Saturday Where The Boys Meet* will be mastered in New York and released early in the New Year. Thermographic photographs of the band, taken in a Paris Studio, are to be used for the cover.

OCTOBER 20
WNEW in New York broadcasts a Rolling Stones special lasting 24 hours.

OCTOBER 21
NBC-TV pays CBS $250,000 for a clip of the Rolling Stones playing 'Satisfaction' on the *Ed Sullivan Show* for use in their history of TV specials. The clip lasts less than a minute.

Above right: *Anita Pallenberg leaving court at Lewisboro, New York State, with her lawyer Jacob Lefkowitz.*

Mick Jagger is featured on Neon Leon's new EP, sharing vocals on a version of 'Heart of Stone'.
Mick Jagger flies to London for Jade's eighth birthday.

OCTOBER 22
Back in Paris, the Stones are at baby Leah Wood's first birthday party.

OCTOBER 26
Mick and Keith fly to New York, Ronnie goes to Los Angeles while Bill and Charlie stay in Europe, Charlie to play several gigs in Germany and Holland with Rocket 88.

NOVEMBER
Mick and Keith mix the new album at Electric Lady in New York.

NOVEMBER 2
After eight years of marriage, Bianca is granted a Decree Nisi and given custody of Jade.

NOVEMBER 10
Charlie Watts, Ian Stewart and original Rolling Stones lead guitarist Jeff Bradford, have been recording with sixties blues singer Brian Knight and an album will be released early next year.

NOVEMBER 15
Ron Wood's paintings appear in a book, *Starart*, devoted to paintings by musicians such as Joni Mitchell, John Mayall and Klaus Voorman.

NOVEMBER 19
Anita Pallenberg is cleared by a Westchester Grand Jury of any involvement in the death of Scott Cantrell. However she is indicted on two charges of illegal possession of a weapon, a misdemeanour. Scott's father says: 'I think they were lovers and she had supplied him with drugs. A 37-year-old woman should have known better than to associate with a seventeen-year-old boy in her bedroom. I feel she is fully responsible for the death of my son no matter how they wrap it up.'

NOVEMBER 25
Keith Richards appears on the new Steve Cropper album. He also contributes to a new Screamin' Jay Hawkins album and, together with Ron Wood also appears on Ian McLagan's solo album, *Trouble Shooter*, which will be released early in the new year.

DECEMBER 15
A Rolling Stones spokesman denies rumours that Bill Wyman is leaving the group.

DECEMBER 18
Keith Richards celebrates his birthday at a party at the Roxy Roller Disco in new York, where he meets top model Patti Hansen.
Charlie Watts and Rocket 88 play at the Venue, London.

DECEMBER 30
Charlie Watts, Alexis Korner and Jack Bruce play at Dingwalls, in Camden Town, London.

DECEMBER 31
Anita Pallenberg pleads guilty to the illegal possession of a .38 calibre pistol at Lewisboro Town Court. The charge of possession of a second gun is dropped.
In New York, Ron Wood and David Bowie are in the audience at the Trax to see Sam and Dave, and it is rumoured that Mick and Jerry bump into Bianca at Woody Allen's New Year's Eve party.

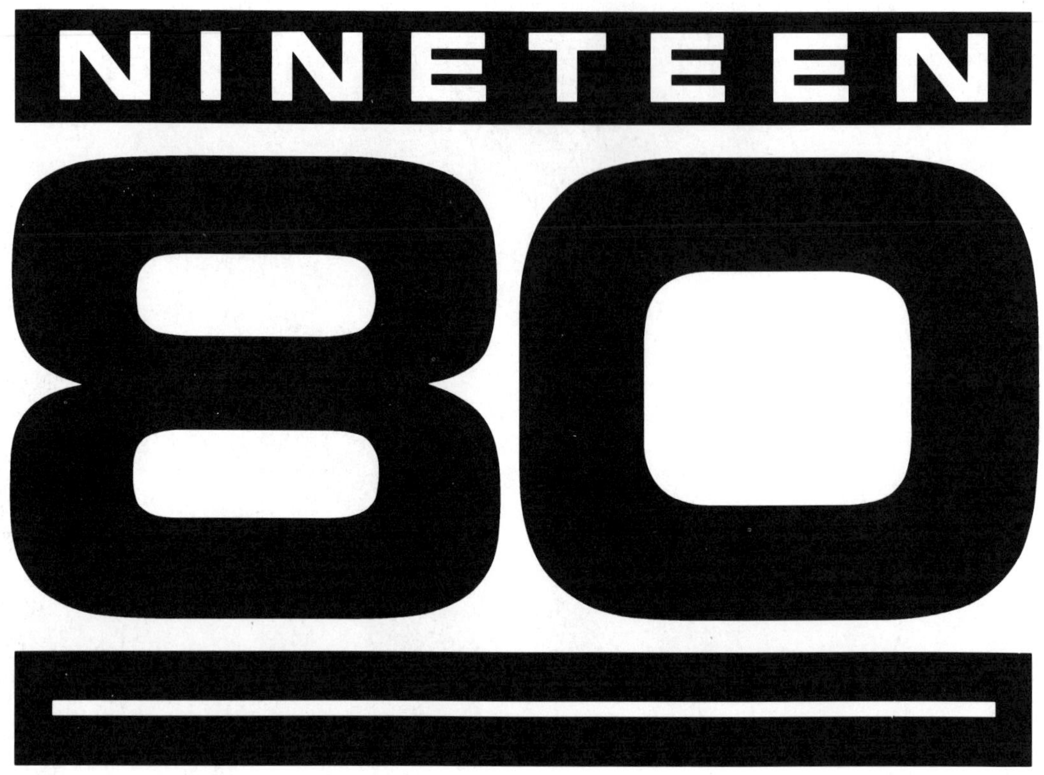

JANUARY 13
In Milwaukee fans riot as the New Barbarians, minus Keith Richards and Ian McLagan, give a concert in settlement of a lawsuit against them and their promoter, following their concert at the same Milwaukee venue last spring.

FEBRUARY
Mick Jagger attends a Presidential campaign soirée for Edward Kennedy in New York.

FEBRUARY 18
Bill Wyman tells David Wigg of the *Daily Express* that he has decided to quit the Rolling Stones in 1982, on the group's twentieth anniversary. Wyman says: 'That's it for me, mate. I want to do other things. I only got into rock'n'roll for a bit of fun and to see the world for a couple of years. It ended up becoming such a part of me. But I refuse to let it dominate my life.' He has not apparently told the rest of the group. 'I don't think it's any of their business. They wouldn't tell me. Twenty years, that's a nice time to stop. I'd rather pack it in while we're up there at the top. Another few years and we might be pushing it... I know I don't want to be a middle-aged rock'n'roller. Probably some people think I am already.'

FEBRUARY 22
Ron Wood and Jo Howard are arrested on St Marteen in the Dutch Antilles and charged with possession of cocaine.

FEBRUARY 26
The charges against Ron and Jo are dropped and the couple are released when it is revealed that 200 grams of cocaine was in fact planted on them. They return home to Los Angeles.

MARCH 3
In New York, Judge George Hunter Roberts imposes a fine of $1,000 on Anita Pallenberg who pleaded guilty to possession of a firearm. He also gives her a one-year conditional discharge.

MARCH 13/14
Bill Wyman is at the Pye Studios in London mixing live tapes of Buddy Guy and Junior Wells recorded at the Montreux Jazz Festival in 1974.

APRIL
In late April the Rolling Stones meet in New York to shoot promo segments for the new album, and remix some tracks. Afterwards Bill Wyman and Charlie Watts fly back to Europe, Ron Wood flies to Los Angeles, Mick Jagger and Keith Richards stay in New York.

JUNE 18
In Paris, South American millionaire Nelson Seabra gives a party at the Pré Catelan, at which all the guests are dressed in red. Mick Jagger goes with Jerry Hall and Bianca arrives with Andy Warhol.

JUNE
In an interview in *Hit Parader*, Ron Wood says: 'You can't believe your freedom within the Rolling Stones' structure. It's a bit binding elsewhere; people expect a little bit much from you, or they treat you like you're on show all the time, but being a member of the Stones is something very special and when the Rolling Stones go on stage it's the best feeling in the world. There's a very mature attitude in this group.'
When asked why he had never made a solo album, Mick Jagger says: 'Well, I think about it, but doing it is another thing, and I'm just so lazy.' When asked if he thinks his music is for teenagers he says: 'I don't even know if I'm making music at all. It sounds like a racket to me... The thing is, I'm not really working enough. It seems to come and go. Sometimes you're working very hard, and then there are other times I just don't bother and I get kind of impatient with myself, but that's just how it seems to go.'

JUNE 20
A new single 'Emotional Rescue'/'Down In The Hole' is released on Rolling Stones Records. Both tracks are Jagger/Richards compositions, recorded at the Pathe Marconi Studios in Paris last year and produced by the Glimmer Twins.

JUNE 23
The Rolling Stones, minus Keith Richards who is in New York, host a party at the Duke

THE ROLLING STONES
ON ROLLING STONES RECORDS AND TAPES

of York's Barracks in Chelsea to launch their new album in the UK. *Emotional Rescue* is released on Rolling Stones Records, and was recorded in Paris and the Bahamas over the past year. All the tracks are by Mick Jagger and Keith Richards plus one co-written by Ron Wood. Release of the album has been delayed until now because it was to have included a track called 'Claudine' written about Claudine Longet, who was convicted of shooting her lover to death in 1976. The Rolling Stones have apparently been forced by Atlantic Records' lawyers to drop the track. It is reported that first pressings of the record which include the song are already fetching £500 on the black market.

JUNE 25
Charlie Watts says in the *Daily Mail*: 'I can't keep up being a Rolling Stone all the time. Plus the fact that I hate rock'n'roll. Rock'n'roll is a load of old rubbish isn't it? I like the people involved, but not the whole showbiz thing.'

JUNE 26
The Rolling Stones (minus Charlie Watts who missed the plane from France) give a party at the Danceteria in New York to promote *Emotional Rescue*. Later Keith Richards joins Jim Carroll on stage at the Trax, where Mick Jagger, Ron Wood, Jerry Hall and Carly Simon are in the audience.
Keith Richards says: 'Rock'n'roll has lasted because nothing else has come along.'

JUNE 28
Mick Jagger tells the *New Musical Express*: 'No one has security for life. Security doesn't lie in money, it lies in a lot of other things. Money doesn't hurt but sometimes it can be a terrible burden to some people. It isn't to me.'

JULY 5
Emotional Rescue enters the British Top 30 at Number 23. It will stay in the charts for eleven weeks, including four weeks at Number 1. The single 'Emotional Rescue' enters the British Top 30 at Number 13. It will stay in the charts for six weeks, reaching Number 8.
In America the album enters the Top 30 at Number 5 and stays in the charts for nineteen weeks, including seven weeks at Number 1. The single enters at Number 22 and remains in the charts for twelve weeks, including four weeks at Number 3.

JULY 26
Mick Jagger spends his 37th birthday in Morocco with Jerry Hall and Jade. In America the new album reaches Number 1.

AUGUST 2
Asked about Bill Wyman's reported wish to leave the group, Mick Jagger tells *Melody Maker*: 'He seems to be quite serious about it, which is all right with me. I don't mind... I don't think Charlie Watts is going to leave but if Bill wants to leave, I mean, what can I do? If people want to leave a band they just do. You don't prevent them...' On harassment by the *paparazzi*; 'We only hit photographers when they're really rude or if we're really bored. I don't mind punching up photographers on the street. It's quite fun sometimes, as long as you win.'
Question: How long do you want to be in rock'n'roll?
Jagger: 'I don't know. Maybe forever?'

AUGUST 21
Mick Jagger says in *Rolling Stone*: 'I'm afraid rock'n'roll has no future. There is no future in rock'n'roll. It's only recycled past.
Keith Richards: 'Rock'n'roll is as healthy as ever. We all tend to forget that it's 90 per cent crap anyway. But the 10 per cent is good. The younger kids have sort of got the right idea on how to play it, you know; they have the right attitude. And that's what rock'n'roll is; an attitude.'
Bill Wyman: 'I am going to retire from the Rolling Stones... I don't want to wait until I'm sixty; that'd be too late... You do get frustrated in a band like the Stones because it can be so restrictive. There are five people with five different tastes; Keith might be mad about reggae and Jerry Lee Lewis; Mick's listening to the New York radio stations and funk; Charlie Watts is back in England listening to Bix Beiderbecke; and I'm here in the South of France listening to Hank Williams. There are factors that hold the band together, apart from the music, but we don't see each other so much. But we tend to come together only when there's work. It really is like Christmas with the family; you get on all right, but you know you wouldn't be able to stand it if they were living with you for a month.'

AUGUST 30
Decca releases a special series of double A-side Stones' singles packed in a special collector's box. The box also features a full colour poster and a silver/blue enamel badge. The whole package is on sale only through special mail order.

SEPTEMBER 16-21
Cocksucker Blues is shown to the public at the Whitney Museum, New York, 'for educational purposes'. Filmmaker Robert Frank has to accompany the film to each screening.
Mick and Keith are in a London studio to edit leftovers for a future LP.

SEPTEMBER 18
Mick Jagger pays over two million francs for a château in the small town of Poce-sur-Cisse, near Amboise in the Loire Valley.

SEPTEMBER 19
Another single from the *Emotional Rescue* album, 'She's So Cold'/'Send It To Me', is released on Rolling Stones Records.

OCTOBER 1
Earl McGrath resigns from his position as President of Rolling Stones Records and is replaced by Vice-President Art Collins.

OCTOBER 3
Bill Wyman starts work on the soundtrack of *Green Ice* in his villa in the South of France. The film stars Ryan O'Neal and Omar Sharif.

OCTOBER 11
The Rolling Stones return to the Pathe Marconi Studios in Paris to cut new material and edit other tracks for a new album. 'She's So Cold' enters the British Top 30 at Number 29. It will stay in the charts for three weeks, only making it to Number 27.

NOVEMBER 1
'She's So Cold' enters the US Top 30 at

Above: *After Keith overcame his heroin habit, he was generally seen in the company of a bottle.* Far right: *Mick and Jerry in the more respectable company of Bjorn Borg.* Right: *Promotional material for* Emotional Rescue.

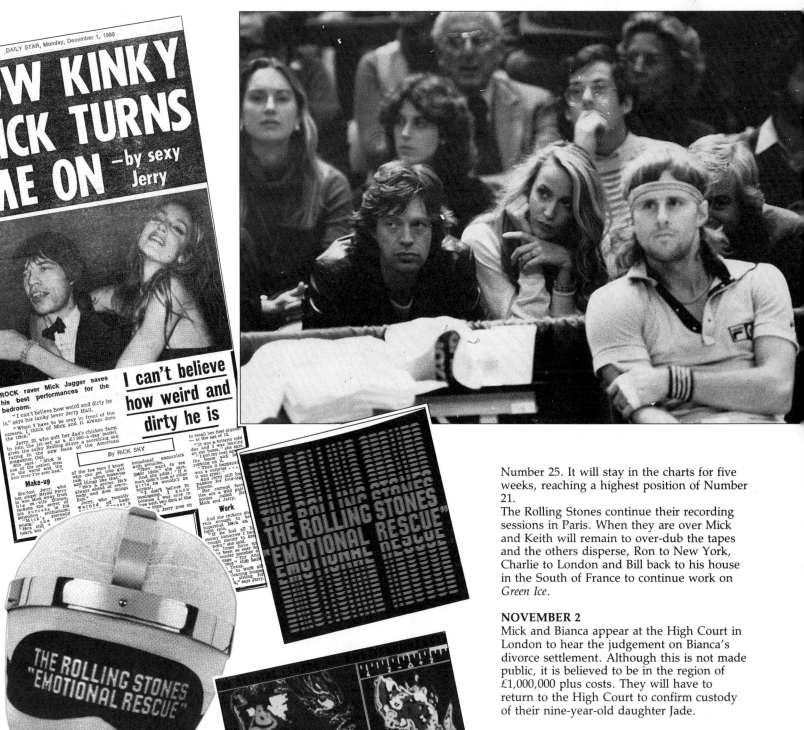

DAILY STAR, Monday, December 1, 1980

HOW KINKY MICK TURNS ME ON —by sexy Jerry

I can't believe how weird and dirty he is

By RICK SKY

ROCK raver Mick Jagger saves his best performances for the bedroom.

"I can't believe how weird and dirty he is," says his lanky lover Jerry Hall.

"When I have to be sexy in front of the camera, I think of Mick and it always does the trick."

Jerry, 23, who quit her dad's chicken farm to join the jet-set as a £1,000-a-day model, gives the sulky Rolling Stone a scorching sex rating in the new issue of the American magazine, Oui.

She says: "Mick is one of the sexiest men in the world and the best lover I've ever had."

Make-up

Six-foot Jerry, who left singer Bryan Ferry to woo Mick away from his ex-wife Bianca, reckons the secret of his success is his schoolboy enthusiasm.

"Mick's eternally young," she reve...

"He's still a ... heart, but ...

of the few men I know who can get into girl talk . . . about make-up and things like that."

"He's a genius. He's always ahead of everybody and does things first."

Jerry, who recently warned off Lady ...

occasional encounters with groupies.

"They want to see their idols," she says. And she adds: "If a man didn't look at other girls he wouldn't be normal.

"I don't believe in monogamy. I know because I was once in love with two men at the ... time."

... Jerry goes on to recall her first orgasm — at the age of 12.

"It was a bitterly cold day and I was leaning on my horse," she says. "I put my coat ... the horse and ... rubbing on it.

"Then it happened ... was a surprise . . . it was great."

And Jerry still ha... passion for four-leg... friends.

Her current favo... ites are a wild pair ... ponies called ... Mick and Jerry.

Work

And she reckons she... rich enough to kee... superstud Mick on ... tight rein.

"If he lost all h... money tomorrow I hav... enough money to kee... both," she said.

...ut times have no... ...s been so easy fo... ...ounder member o... ...uage "Try Any... Once" club back ... Texas. ...d to work all ... cleaning houses ... sitting for ...k," says Jerry.

Number 25. It will stay in the charts for five weeks, reaching a highest position of Number 21.

The Rolling Stones continue their recording sessions in Paris. When they are over Mick and Keith will remain to over-dub the tapes and the others disperse, Ron to New York, Charlie to London and Bill back to his house in the South of France to continue work on *Green Ice*.

NOVEMBER 2

Mick and Bianca appear at the High Court in London to hear the judgement on Bianca's divorce settlement. Although this is not made public, it is believed to be in the region of £1,000,000 plus costs. They will have to return to the High Court to confirm custody of their nine-year-old daughter Jade.

DECEMBER 1

Jerry Hall tells the *Daily Star*: 'I can't believe how weird and dirty Mick Jagger is. When I have to be sexy in front of the camera, I think of Mick Jagger and it always does the trick. Mick is one of the sexiest men in the world and the best lover I've ever had... He's a genius. He's always ahead of everybody and does things first.'

DECEMBER 8

John Lennon is shot dead in New York.

Bill Wyman phones SNEW-FM from France to express his feelings live on the air.

JANUARY
Mick Jagger and Jerry Hall fly to Peru where Mick will star in his first film for nearly twelve years. The film, called *Fitzcarraldo* and directed by Werner Herzog, will be shot in a small town in the jungle called Iquito. Shooting will take at least four months.

JANUARY
Neighbours demand that Keith Richards vacate his Manhattan apartment as they are disturbed by the loud rock music he plays all day.
At MIDEM in Cannes, a launch party is held for Bill Wyman's *Green Ice* soundtrack.

JANUARY 27
Keith Richards is in the audience for a Jerry Lee Lewis concert at the Ritz, New York.
Atlantic Records release *Rocket 88*, a live album of the band of the same name, featuring Charlie Watts, Ian Stewart and others. Charlie Watts has designed the cover. Produced by Ian Stewart, it was recorded live at the Rotation Club in Hanover in November 1979.

FEBRUARY 8
Keith Richards joins Etta James on stage at the Lone Star Cafe in New York for a version of 'Miss You'.

FEBRUARY 21
Bill Wyman tells *Melody Maker*: 'Mick Jagger is a fantastic performer and no other band has a Mick Jagger. He's no good without the band and the band would be a little dull without him; however, we could go on stage without him, while he could not go on stage without us. Altogether we're a powerful line-up. We simply have to decide whether next year is the deadline.'

FEBRUARY
In Peru work on *Fitzcarraldo* stops due to severe problems on location, not the least being attacks by Amazonian Indians. Most of the crew return to Munich, actress Claudia Cardinale leaves the set. Shooting will resume next May. Mick and Jerry return to New York, and he decides to drop out of the project altogether.
Keith Richards cuts material with Bobby Keys at the Eldorado Recording Studio in Hollywood.

MARCH 4
An athology album called *Sucking In The Seventies* is released in America on Rolling Stones Records, produced by the Glimmer Twins. The album contains a live version of 'When The Whip Comes Down' recorded at the Midsouth Coliseum, Memphis, on 28 June 1978 plus an unreleased version of 'Dance' called 'If I Was A Dancer (Dance Part 2)'.

MARCH
Mick Jagger, Jerry Hall, Keith Richards and Patti Hansen fly to Barbados for a short holiday.

APRIL 3
Several stores in America refuse to sell the *Sucking In The Seventies* album, because of the title. As a result the Stones lose more than $250,000 in revenue.

APRIL 4
Sucking In The Seventies enters the US Top 30 at Number 29. It will stay in the charts for six weeks, reaching a highest position of Number 17.

APRIL 13
Sucking In The Seventies is released in the UK.

APRIL
After a break for Easter with Jerry in Mustique, Mick joins Keith in New York to put the final touches to the new album at the Atlantic Studios. Ronnie Wood cuts material for a solo album in Los Angeles.

JUNE
Polydor release the soundtrack of *Green Ice*, produced, written and arranged by Bill Wyman. A single is taken from the album called 'Tenderness'/'Noche De Amor'.
Charlie Watts and Ian Stewart appear on Brian Knight's new album, *A Dark Horse*, on PVK Records, as does former Stones guitarist Jeff Bradford. Mick Jagger, Keith Richards, Charlie Watts, Bobby Keys, Patti Hansen and Shirley Watts are at the Ritz to see Jimmy Cliff.

JUNE
Keith Richards and Patti Hansen go to see Chuck Berry at the Ritz. Keith goes backstage after the show but Berry does not recognise him and Keith gets a punch in the eye.

JUNE
The Stones all meet up to shoot promo footage for the new album.

JUNE
Bill Wyman sues the *Daily Star* after their claim that he is quitting the Rolling Stones. Bill says: 'The Rolling Stones are the biggest project in my life, and always will be.'

JULY 2
The Stones shoot a video for a track from the new album at the St Marks Bar in Greenwich Village. They also run through two old blues numbers during the set.

JULY
Bill Wyman releases a solo single, 'Je Suis Un Rock Star'/'Rio De Janeiro' which he both wrote and produced. It is also released in a disco version.

JULY 26
Mick Jagger spends his 38th birthday in New York.

AUGUST 8
'Je Suis Un Rock Star' enters the British Top 30 at Number 26. It will stay in the charts for five weeks, reaching a highest position of Number 11.

AUGUST 14
The Rolling Stones start five weeks of rehearsals at Long View Farm in Brookfield, Massachusetts.

AUGUST 16
Radio Station WMMR-FM in Philadelphia jumps the gun to become the first in the world to play The Rolling Stones' new album, *Tattoo You*. Rolling Stones Records were planning to start airplay in a week's time.

AUGUST 17
A new single 'Start Me Up'/'No Use In Crying', taken from the forthcoming album, is released on Rolling Stones Records and produced by the Glimmer Twins. The A-side is a Jagger/Richards composition and the flip side is credited to Jagger/Richards/Wood.

AUGUST 20
In the *Daily Express*, Bill Wyman asks readers to send him Rolling Stones memorabilia, particularly relating to the early sixties, to help him maintain his collection of fourteen trunks-full of material.

AUGUST 26
At the JFK Stadium in Philadelphia, Mick Jagger officially announces a massive US tour, opening there on 25 September and ending at the Jefferson Coliseum in Birmingham, Alabama on 6 December. Mick Jagger denies that this tour will be their last.

AUGUST 29
'Start Me Up' enters the British charts at Number 30. It will stay in the charts for seven weeks, reaching a highest position of Number 4.

AUGUST 31
Tattoo You is released on Rolling Stones Records. Produced by the Glimmer Twins, it was recorded at the EMI/Pathe Marconi Studios in Paris and at the Compass Point Studio, Nassau, Bahamas in 1979 and 1980. 'Worried About You' and 'Slave' were originally recorded in Rotterdam, early in 1975. 'Tops' and 'Waiting For A Friend' were originally recorded at the Dynamic Sound Studios, Kingston, Jamaica in 1972. All tracks are written by Mick Jagger and Keith Richards, except 'Black Limousine' and 'No use In Crying', written by Jagger/Richards/Wood. It was mixed at the Atlantic Studios, New York.

SEPTEMBER 1
It is announced that the forthcoming US tour will be sponsored by Jovan Inc, a perfume company based in Chicago. It is the first time in the history of rock'n'roll that a tour has been sponsored in this way.

SEPTEMBER 7
Tattoo You sells over a million copies in the US in the first week of release.

SEPTEMBER 14
The Rolling Stones play a warm-up show at a little-known club called Sir Morgan's Cave (capacity 350) in Worcester, Massachusetts. The gig is supposed to be secret as they are billed under the pseudonym of Blue Monday and the Cockroaches. However, because a local radio station is given the responsibility of distributing 300 forgery-proof tickets, a rival station broadcasts the truth out of spite and the club is besieged by over 4,000 fans trying to get in. Seventy riot-control police with helicopters are drafted in to control the crowd, and eleven fans are arrested, but calm is restored when a policeman suggests that the club doors be opened so that the fans can hear the Stones playing from outside. After the show Keith Richards says: 'It was great. Probably better than we thought, because it was our first gig, and technically it was really rough. It was as if we were playing the Station Hotel in Richmond in 1963. You don't forget those things. It was sort of like, "Well, we did it then, we can do it now".' Mick Jagger says: 'Within three or four years I won't be able to do what I do now on stage any more.' He admits that many rock stars are reluctant to tour after John Lennon's death: 'But you can't spend your life being paranoid. There'll always be nutters and you have to watch out for them.'

SEPTEMBER 18/19
Mayor Kevin White of Boston bans the Rolling Stones from playing at the Orpheum for another two warm-up gigs, since he fears a repeat of the riots in Worcester.

SEPTEMBER 19
The Rolling Stones cancel two pre-tour gigs, one at the Ocean State Performing Arts Center, in Providence and another planned for 20 September.

SEPTEMBER 25
The Rolling Stones open their tenth American tour at the JFK Stadium in Philadelphia, with an audience of 90,000.

SEPTEMBER 26
Second sell-out concert at the JFK Stadium, Philadelphia. The band are using three different stages for this tour. The biggest is 200 feet wide and 50 feet high and is the largest ever built for a concert. The stage is draped with large canvases by Japanese designer Kazuhikde Yamazaki, and features abstracts of a car, a US flag and a guitar. A similar but smaller stage is used for smaller stadia. For medium-sized indoor shows, the Rolling Stones use a different stage; the drums are on a platform surrounded by a miniature building which houses the amplifiers. Steps allow access to the top of the 'house'. The platform rotates at times, so that everyone in the audience can see all the Stones whatever their position in the auditorium, including those sitting at the back of the stage. All three stages have a hydraulic lift which can carry a band member within feet of the audience and another spectacular platform to lift Mick Jagger up over the audience. The Rolling Stones travel from city to city on a Boeing 707, while the equipment is transported in a fleet of trucks. The tour organiser is Bill Graham.
Tattoo You is Number 1 in both Britain and the States.

SEPTEMBER 27
Concert at the Rich Stadium, Buffalo, with an audience of 80,000.

SEPTEMBER 28
Mick Jagger says: 'It's weird. Last time we toured people came to the shows but there was a kind of ''so what'' about the whole thing. This time they are going crazy. We are at our best on stage relating to an audience and it's great to be back, feeling that electricity.'
The *Daily Mail* reports that Keith is planning to marry 23-year-old American model Patti Hansen in December at the end of the Stones' marathon tour.

OCTOBER 1
Concert at the Metro, Rockford, Illinois. This date was not included in the original itinerary but fans in Rockford, headed by Dallas Cole and Dennis Logan of radio station WZOK, mounted a petition and when they had amassed 36,000 signatures wrote to tour promoter Bill Graham. The Stones agreed on 15 September. The 9,000 fans attending the show were selected from among those who signed the petition.

OCTOBER 3/4
Two concerts at Folsom Field, Boulder, Colorado, with audiences of 62,000 for each show.

Above: *Mick and Keith walking freely in Greenwich Village only a year after John Lennon was shot dead in midtown New York.*

OCTOBER 7
Concert at the San Diego Stadium with an audience of 60,000.

OCTOBER 9-11
Two concerts at the Los Angeles Coliseum. Bob Dylan, Jack Nicholson, Peter O'Toole are among the 90,000-strong audience. 95 fans are arrested.

OCTOBER 14
Concert at the Kingdome, Seattle, with an audience of 72,000. In New York, 40 postal workers are put on special assignment to handle the huge number of ticket applications for Stones concerts in the New York area.

OCTOBER 15
Second sell-out concert in Seattle. Before the second show a woman is arrested outside the Kingdome and charged with menacing behaviour. She had been boasting that she was going to kill Mick on stage. Later a sixteen-year-old girl, Pamela Lynn Melville, falls 50 feet to her death after leaning too far over a rail that an usher had already told her not to sit on.

OCTOBER 17/18
Open air concert in Candlestick Park, San Francisco, with an audience of 146,000. It is the biggest-ever crowd for an open air show in San Francisco.

OCTOBER 20
Mick Jagger joins Mayor Dianne Feinstein in a public service TV 'Save the Cable Cars' appeal. Later Mick dines with Jackie Onassis.

OCTOBER 21
Jade Jagger celebrates her tenth birthday at the Roller Disco in New York.

OCTOBER 24/25
Two concerts at the Tangerine Bowl, Orlando, Florida. 60,000 attend each show. Bill Wyman's 45th birthday party is held at Disneyland.

OCTOBER 26
Concert at the Fox Theatre, Atlanta. This is the smallest hall of the tour - the capacity crowd is only 4,000.

OCTOBER 28
Concert at the Astrodome, Houston. This time the audience is back to 50,000. 22-year-old Wesley Shelton is shot dead outside the Astrodome by a 16-year-old boy.

OCTOBER 29
Second concert in Houston.

OCTOBER 31
Concert at the Cotton Bowl, Dallas, with an audience of 80,000. The Stones, minus Charlie, talk about the tour on radio CFOX-FM.

NOVEMBER 1
Second Dallas concert.

NOVEMBER 3
Concert in the Freedom Hall, Louisville with an audience of 50,000. After the show the Stones fly back to New York.

NOVEMBER 4
All 100,000 seats for both concerts at Madison Square Garden, New York, and the three Meadowlands concerts in New Jersey, are sold in a matter of hours. There were over four million postal applications. In London Mick Jagger is interviewed live by Richard Skinner on BBC Radio 1's *Rock On*.

NOVEMBER 5
First concert at the Byrne Arena, Meadowlands, New Jersey. BBC TV broadcasts an interview with Mick Jagger by Rona Barrett.

NOVEMBER 6
Second Meadowlands concert. Tina Turner, who opens all three shows, joins the Rolling Stones on stage for a version of 'Honky Tonk Woman'.
Decca Records release a Stones anthology album called *Slow Rollers*.

NOVEMBER 7
Final Meadowlands concert.

NOVEMBER 9
Concert at the Civic Center, Hartford, Connecticut. 56 fans are arrested and twelve injured when gatecrashers cause a riot.

NOVEMBER 10
Second concert in Hartford.

NOVEMBER 11
Asked about the huge number of postal ticket applications for the Madison Square Garden concerts, Mick says: 'It may be three grandmothers in Queens sending in tons of ticket requests for all I know.'

NOVEMBER 12
First sell-out concert at Madison Square Garden. Screamin' Jay Hawkins opens the show.

NOVEMBER 13
Second Madison Square Garden concert. The *New York Post* reports: 'Police put together the largest security force since Pope John Paul II's New York visit.'

NOVEMBER 15
The Madison Square Garden concerts have been a big draw for star names. The *Sun* reports Peter O'Toole dancing on stage, while Jack Nicholson, Anjelica Huston and Shelley Duval are all seen backstage. Other stars in the audience, all paying full price for their tickets, include Bob Dylan, Tina Turner, Robert Redford, Robert de Niro, Tony Curtis, Morgan Fairchild, Paul McCartney, Carly Simon, Ryan O'Neal, Ali McGraw and John McEnroe. Bianca is also in the audience. She says: 'It was superb. They seem to get better as the years go on.' John McEnroe is subjected to a 90-minute guitar lesson from Bill Wyman in his hotel suite. McEnroe says: 'I loved every minute of it.' Morgan Fairchild wonders.: 'How in the world does Mick Jagger keep going at his age? He's a bundle of energy.' (Mick is now 38.) The *Sun* also reports that Mick keeps fit by weight-lifting and seven-mile daily runs. Mick says: 'A tour is great fun for a while, but it's like sex, you don't want to do it all the time.' Keith comments: 'Why is everyone making such a big deal about a bunch of middle-aged madmen going on tour?... There's no good reason why the Rolling Stones can't grow old gracefully. I'll be playing rock in a wheelchair. It's what I do for a living.'

NOVEMBER 16/17
Concerts at the Richfield Coliseum, Cleveland. Etta James opens both shows.

NOVEMBER 19
Concert at the Checkerdrome, St Louis.

NOVEMBER 20
Concert at the Unidome, Cedar Falls. The Stray Cats open the concert.
Another single from *Tattoo You* is released in America by Rolling Stones Records, called 'Waiting On A Friend'/'Little T&A'.

NOVEMBER 21
Concert at the Civic Center, St. Paul, Minnesota. The Stray Cats open the show again.

NOVEMBER 22
Keith Richards, Ron Wood and Mick Jagger jam with Muddy Waters, Buddy Guy and Junior Wells on stage at the Checkerboard Lounge, Chicago.

NOVEMBER 23/24/25
Concerts at the Rosemont Horizon, Chicago. The Neville Brothers open all the Chicago shows.

NOVEMBER 27/28
Concerts at the Carrierdrome, Syracuse, with an audience of 42,000. Molly Hatchet opens both shows.

NOVEMBER 30
Concert at the Silverdome, Pontiac, Michigan. The audience is 70,000 strong.

DECEMBER 1
Second concert in Pontiac, taped by Radio KBFH for future broadcast. Iggy Pop and Santana open both shows.

DECEMBER 4
En route for New Orleans, the Stones give a riverboat party on the Mississippi.

DECEMBER 5
Concert at the Superdrome, New Orleans. The audience is 90,000.

DECEMBER 7/8/9
Concerts at the Capital Center, Washington, D.C. Radio KBFH tape the show for future broadcast.

DECEMBER 11
Concert at Rupp Arena, Lexington, Kentucky.

DECEMBER 13
Concert at the Sun Devil Stadium, Phoenix, Arizona, with an audience of 77,000.

DECEMBER 14
Concert at the Kemper Arena, Kansas City. Mick Taylor joins the Rolling Stones on stage.

DECEMBER 15
Second Kansas City concert.

DECEMBER 18
Concert at the Hampton Coliseum, Hampton Roads, Virginia. The concert is broadcast on TV simultaneously in most major US cities. It is Keith Richards' 38th birthday and after the show a birthday party for him and Bobby Keys, whose birthday is the same day, is held backstage. Keith's children, Marlon and Dandelion and his mother, Doris, have flown in for the celebrations.

DECEMBER 19
Second Hampton Roads concert, the final show of the tour. Audiences for the concerts total more than 2,000,000 people. After the show the band fly to New York.

DECEMBER 20
It is estimated that the Stones have grossed over $50 million during their 50-date US tour, the longest they have ever undertaken. They have also earned about $10 million in merchandising concessions, about $1.5 million from record sales, as well as $4 million in sponsorship from Jovan. A film of the tour has also been shot, directed by Hal Ashby, for probable release during 1982.
After the tour, Charlie returns to London, Bill to the South of France, while Mick rests a few days in his apartment in Manhattan, before also going to France. Ron Wood stays in his apartment in Greenwich Village and, within a few days, Keith returns to England.

DECEMBER 26
Ron Wood and family fly to London.

Top: *The Stones open their tenth American tour in Philadelphia, 1981.* Above: *Grim rather than grinning Keith features on the cover of* Rolling Stone *during the 1981 US tour.* Right: *Mick duetting with Tina Turner on stage during the sell-out American tour.*

JANUARY
The newly re-formed Mamas and Papas have cut seven demo tracks, four of which are produced by Mick Jagger and Keith Richards. Backing musicians include Keith and Mick Taylor on guitars and Ron Wood on bass.

JANUARY 11
A single taken from *Tattoo You*. 'Hang Fire'/'Neighbours', is released in America on Rolling Stones Records.

FEBRUARY 3
Mick Jagger and Keith Richards fly to Los Angeles to work with Hal Ashby on the film of the tour.

FEBRUARY 18
Ron Wood joins Bobby Womack on stage at the Ritz in New York. Later they jam with Steve Marriott and Wilson Pickett.

FEBRUARY
Despite help from Alec Guinness and Hal Ashby, Mick Jagger cancels plans to produce and act in the film version of Gore Vidal's book, *Kalki*.

FEBRUARY 24
One Plus One is re-released in France.

MARCH 4
In the *Rolling Stone* Readers' Awards, the Rolling Stones are voted best band of the year; Mick Jagger is voted best male vocalist; *Tattoo You* is album of the year and 'Start Me Up' best single of the year. Jagger and Richards are voted best songwriters and Keith best instrumentalist. The *Rolling Stone* Critics' Awards name the Rolling Stones Artist of the Year; *Tattoo You* best album and 'Start Me Up' best single.

MARCH 5
Bill Wyman's new single 'Fashion'/'Girls' which he both wrote and produced is released by A&M.

MARCH
Mick and Keith start editing tapes of the US tour at the Power Station Studio, New York.

MARCH 18
Keith Richards and Ron Wood jam with Jimmy Cliff at the Hit Factory, New York, where Jimmy Cliff is recording a new album.

MARCH 26
Bill Wyman's new solo album, *Bill Wyman*, is released on A&M. A picture disc version is also available in a limited edition. All tracks are written by him and it was recorded in London early last year. It reaches Number 25 in the British album charts.

APRIL
Decca re-release the Stones' first three EPs as a 12-inch single.
The band put the finishing touches to the new live album. Bill is the only one not involved as he is busy promoting his own recent releases.

APRIL 17
Ron Wood joins Toots and the Maytals on stage at the Ritz in New York and he plays six numbers with the band.

APRIL 19
Mick Jagger talks to *Woman's World* about his five-year liaison with Jerry Hall: 'I won't marry anyone again. If you're not successful at it, it isn't a case of try, try again. In our society there is no reason to get married... It's a near miracle that we have even survived in this business. It's because I know where to draw the line when the others are going over the edge. This, I think, is primarily due to my background. It takes a conventional upbringing in the English style to produce a normal human being. It gives you equilibrium, a balanced view.'

APRIL 28
At a press conference at Le Beat Route discotheque in London, Mick Jagger officially announces the European tour which will open in June in Rotterdam, where tickets are already sold out. The itinerary will take them to Holland, Germany, Denmark, Sweden, Britain, France, Ireland, Austria, Belgium, Switzerland and Italy. Tour Manager Bill Graham reveals that they have also been asked to play in Portugal, Yugoslavia and Hungary. The Stones will be supported by

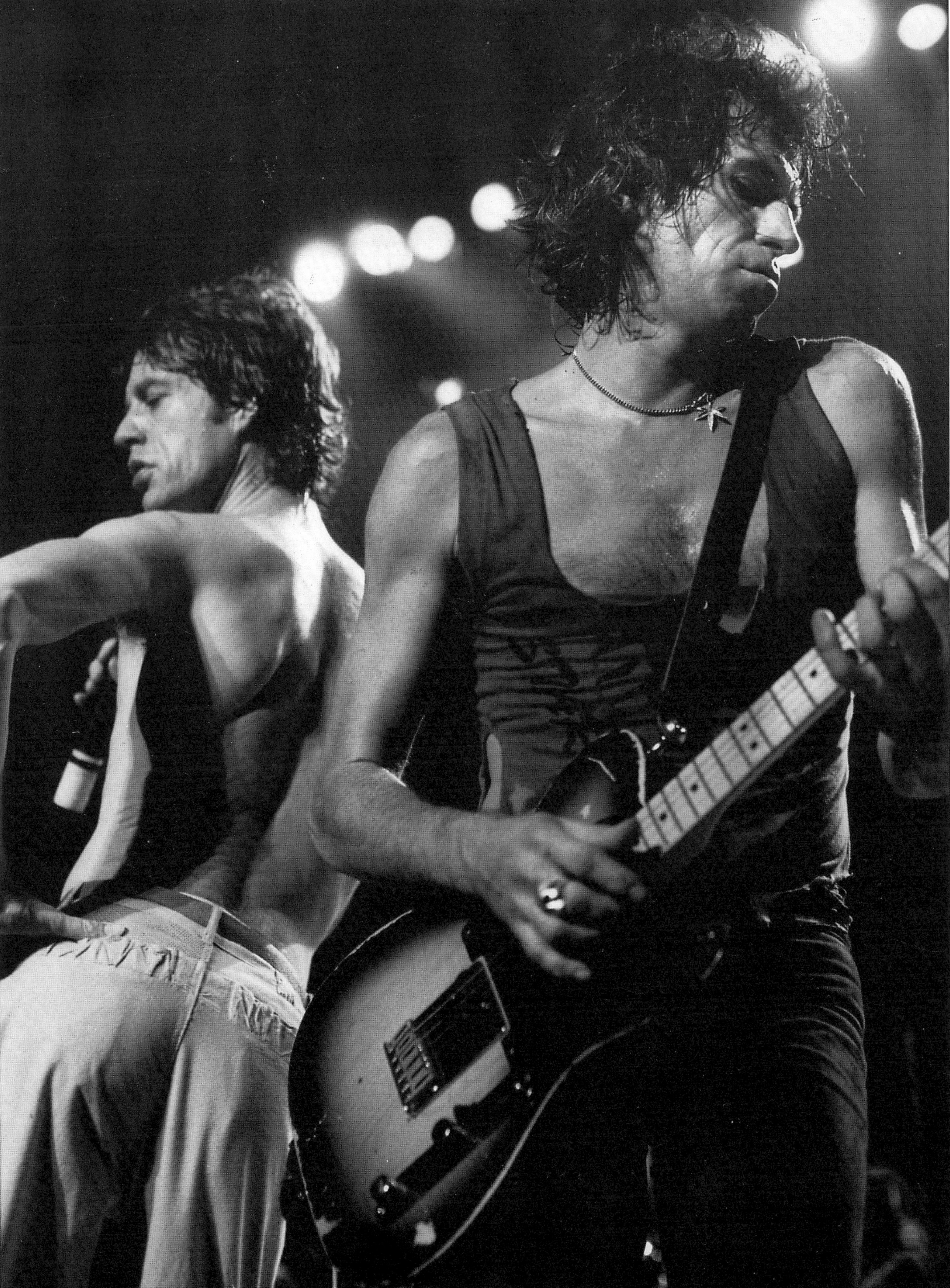

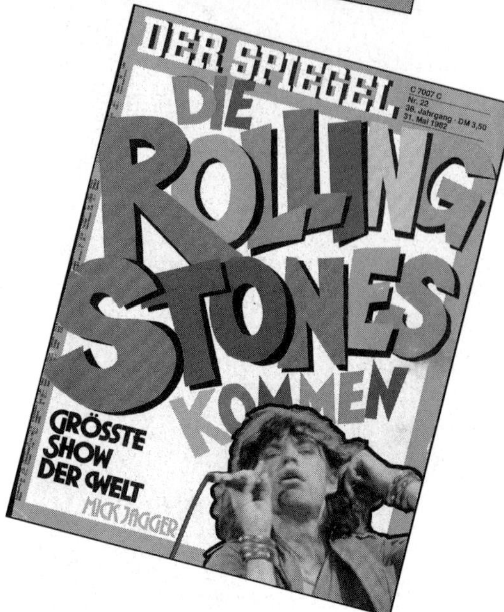

the J. Geils Band and local bands. The line-up will be augmented on the tour by Ian Stewart and Chuck Leavell on keyboards and Bobby Keys and Gene Barge on horns.
Keith Richards says: 'I need this to keep me young. When we started this band, we thought we had about two or three years. Now it's a habit, and it's absolutely vital that it works on the road. We need constant contact with a living audience. We're so excited at the prospect of doing Britain again after so long. Wherever we might make our home now, Britain is where our roots are.'
Charlie Watts says: 'I often think we ought to call it a day. But I keep telling myself I'd be selfish to put my own ambitions before the needs of everyone else. I'm a Rolling Stone and stuck with it for the present.'

MAY 26
The Rolling Stones open their sell-out European Tour in Scotland at the Capitol Theatre, Aberdeen. Advance copies of the new album *Still Life* are on sale at the concert.
In the *Daily Mirror* John Millar writes: 'They're back. And it's as if Mick Jagger and the Rolling Stones had never been away. Their first British concert for six years was a rocking, roaring success, an unforgettable night of nostalgia. From the first electric moment the Stones stepped on stage until the final sounds of "Satisfaction" died away, fans in the Capitol Theatre in Aberdeen were gripped by that old Mick Jagger magic.'

MAY 27
Concert at the Apollo Theatre, Glasgow.

MAY 28
Concert at the Playhouse, Edinburgh.
An interview with Mick in Glasgow is broadcast on the BBC's *Round Table*.
In the London *Evening News* John Blake writes: 'The wild-eyed little girls who fight their way to the stage have the faces of angels and the voices of banshees. But there is something else which is disconcertingly odd about the fans which at first it's hard to analyse. But then the realisation dawns -none of these adoring girls was born last time the Rolling Stones played this theatre in the early sixties. Then it was their mothers who stood in front of the stage with hands pleadingly outstretched and tears in their eyes.'

MAY 29
B. B. King, who sat in on a Rolling Stones' rehearsal says: 'I just went to listen, not to sing at all. But you know how Mick Jagger is, I couldn't leave without singing something.'

MAY 30
Paula Yates reports in the *News of the World* that Keith has recently met his father for the first time for 20 years. His parents split up not long after Keith left home in the early sixties.

MAY 31
The Stones play a surprise gig at the 100 Club in Oxford Street, London before an audience of 400. A spokesman says: 'They were keen to return to their roots.'

JUNE 1
A con-man organises a completely fake Stones concert at the Empire Theatre, Liverpool. He prints posters advertising the concert, sells 2000 tickets, then disappears.
The live album, *Still Life*, is released on Rolling Stones Records, recorded in the US at various venues. A single from the album 'Going To A Go Go' (Robinson/Johnson/Moore/Rogers)/'Beast Of Burden' (Jagger/Richards) is also released. The flip side is not included in the album. In Europe the single is also available as a picture disc, the Stones' first.
Ron Wood is 35.

JUNE 2
Concert at the Fejenoord Stadium, Rotterdam, 50,000 attend.
Charlie Watts is 42.

JUNE 3
Mick Jagger joins George Thorogood on stage at a club in the Hague.

JUNE 4
Second concert at the Fejenoord Stadium, Rotterdam.

JUNE 5
Third Rotterdam concert.

JUNE 6/7
Two concerts at the Niedersachsen Stadium, Hanover.

JUNE 8
Concert at the Waldbuhne, Berlin.
Two fires are started at the Paris racetrack where the Stones are due to play as fans protest against the 75 franc ($12) ticket price.
Florence's Anti Drug League accuse the Stones of using their European tour as an excuse to promote drug trafficking. Despite the controversy Stones' fans mass in one of the city squares to watch Rolling Stones' videos on a giant screen.

JUNE 10
Concert at the Olympic Stadium, Munich.
Patti Hansen, Anita Pallenberg and Andrew Oldham see Marianne Faithfull in concert at the Ritz, New York.

JUNE 11
Second concert in Munich. 50,000 fans turn up in spite of pouring rain.
Patti Hansen flies to Paris to meet Keith.

Left: *Magazines all over Europe headlined the Stones during the 1982 European tour.*

JUNE 12
In an interview with the Paris newspaper *Liberation*, Mick Jagger reveals that the Stones have sent a video of one of last year's American concerts to the British troops involved in the Falklands. He says it was done to give 'moral support' but refuses to comment on the war itself, stating that it's not his business.

JUNE 13
Concert at the Hippodrome d'Auteuil, Paris. *Still Life* enters the British charts at Number 20. It will stay in the charts for thirteen weeks, with a highest position of Number 2.

JUNE 14
Second Paris concert.

JUNE 15
The national Spanish football organisation withdraws its permission for the Stones to play in Barcelona at the Espanol Stadium on 7 July for security reasons. More than 20,000 tickets have already been sold.

JUNE 16
Concert at the Stade de Gerland, Lyon: 400 fans faint from the heat.
The Stones have to cancel their Madrid concert on 29 July for the same reasons as in Barcelona.

JUNE 18
On arrival at Goteborg airport in Sweden the Stones are extensively searched by customs men.

JUNE 19
Concert at the Nya Ullevi Stadium, Goteborg. 'Going To A Go Go' enters the British Top 30 at Number 23. It will stay in the charts for two weeks, its highest position being Number 19.

JUNE 20
Second concert in Goteburg.

JUNE 23
Concert at Newcastle United's football ground. It rains throughout the eight-hour show.

JUNE 24
On behalf of the Rolling Stones, Bill Wyman receives the British Music Industry's Silver Clef Award for outstanding achievement in the world of British music in London.
Keith Richards talks to Robin Denselow on BBC 2's *Newsnight* on the eve of the London concerts.

Top right: *It's back to basics with a surprise gig at the 100 Club in London's Oxford Street in front of an invited audience of 400 during the Stones' 1982 European tour.* Right: *Mick chooses a Free French look to liberate the audience at Wembley Stadium.*

JUNE 25
First concert at Wembley Stadium. Among the 75,000-strong audience are John McEnroe, David Essex, Michael Caine, Ringo Starr, Britt Ekland, Lulu, Billy Connolly, Princess Margaret's son Viscount Linley, Rowan Atkinson and all the Stones' parents. Black Uhuru and the J. Geils Band open the show.
Keith Richards tells the *Evening Standard*: 'I don't like to regret heroin because I learned a lot from it. It was a large part of my life. It is something I went through and dealt with. I'd regret it if I hadn't dealt with it, or if I had OD'd. I would definitely regret it then. A lot of my friends, who should by rights be around, aren't because of it. I don't think it makes a damned bit of difference to anybody going to get into it being told "don't". In fact it sometimes reinforces the desire to take it. Having been on it I know. If there is anything I do regret, it's its accessibility to very young kids.'
A&M release Bill Wyman's single 'Visions'/'Nuclear Reactions' taken from his solo album.

JUNE 26
Second sell-out Wembley concert.

JUNE 27
Concert at Bristol City football ground. Mick Jagger gives a press conference for seven European TV companies. About the London concerts he says: 'These shows mean a lot to us and they better be good as well. We'll get our share of attention unless she [Princess Diana] has another baby or something.'

JUNE 29
Concert at the Festhalle, Frankfurt.

JUNE 30
Second Frankfurt concert at the Festhalle.

JULY 1
Third Frankfurt concert.

JULY 3
Concert at the Prater Stadium, Vienna.
Still Life enters the US Top 20 at Number 7. It will stay in the charts for ten weeks, with a highest position of Number 2.

JULY 4
Concert at the Mungersdorfer Stadium, Cologne.

JULY 5
Second concert at Cologne.

JULY 7
In Los Angeles, Senator Robert K. Dornan says bands like the Rolling Stones, Led Zeppelin, the Beatles and Kiss have lyrics on the albums that are 'blasphemous, occult and Satan-worshipping in content'. He says: 'The trick is, you see, that they're only audible when played backwards!'

JULY 8
Concert at the Vicente Calderon Stadium, Madrid.

JULY 9
Second concert in Madrid. Afterwards the Stones fly to Nice.

JULY 11
Concert at the Comunal Stadium, Turin. Mick, wearing an Italian football jersey, predicts to the audience that Italy will beat West Germany in the World Cup Final 3-1. He is proved right.

JULY 12
Second concert in Turin.

JULY 13
The Rolling Stones arrive in Nice. In the evening Mick visits Roman Polanski at his villa in Ramatuelle.

JULY 15
The Stones fly from Nice to Basle, Switzerland for a concert at the St Jakob Stadium. After the show they fly straight back to Nice.

JULY 17
The Rolling Stones fly to Naples where they play at the San Paolo Stadium in front of an audience of over 83,000. Film director Michelangelo Antonioni goes backstage.

JULY 20
Concert at the Parc des Sports de l'Ouest, Nice. Afterwards Mick goes on to Regine's in Monte Carlo.

JULY 24
Concert at Slane Castle, near Dublin in Ireland.

JULY 25
Final concert of the tour at Roundhay Park, Leeds. Joe Jackson, George Thorogood and the J. Geils band open.

JULY 26
Mick Jagger celebrates his 39th birthday at Langan's Brasserie in London.

JULY 30
After the tour Mick goes to Paris on business; Keith flies to Jamaica to rest; Ron, Jo and children stay in England, as does Charlie Watts.

JULY 31
'Going To A Go Go' reaches Number 20 in the US charts, its highest position. It only has two weeks in the Top 30.

AUGUST 8
Bill Graham offers a £1,000 reward for the return of a map which disappeared on the last date of the tour in Leeds. The map marks all the tour venues and is covered with messages from the Stones to him.

AUGUST 31
It is announced that Hal Ashby's film of the 1981 US tour, known variously as *Rock's Off* and *Time Is On Our Side* will be shown on a large screen in St Mark's Square as part of the Venice Biennale, this year celebrating its fiftieth anniversary.

SEPTEMBER 1
The municipal authorities in Venice prohibit the outdoor premiere of the Stones' film for security reasons.
Redlands, Keith Richards' house in Sussex is once more damaged by fire. 65 firemen are needed to extinguish the blaze. No one is hurt and only the roof suffers serious damage.

SEPTEMBER
A documentary on the making of *Fitzcarraldo* called *Burden of Dreams*, which includes footage of Mick Jagger on the set, is showing in America.
Another single taken from *Still Life* is released in America, called 'Time Is On My Side'/'Twenty Flight Rock'. In England a 12-inch single of 'Time is On My Side'/'Twenty Flight Rock'/'Under My Thumb' is also released. Both are on the Rolling Stones Records label and are produced by the Glimmer Twins.

SEPTEMBER
Lord Weidenfeld of the UK publishing company Weidenfeld & Nicolson has signed Mick Jagger to write his autobiography. In America a 12-hour radio special called *The Rolling Stones, Past and Present* is broadcast on 275 stations in the States and Canada. Produced by David Pritchard and Alan Lysaght, it features interviews with the Stones, Alexis Korner, Dick Taylor and many others.

SEPTEMBER 25
Mick Jagger and daughter Jade see the Who and the Clash in concert in the JFK Stadium, Philadelphia, arriving from New York by helicopter.
Gossip columnists on both sides of the Atlantic report that Jerry Hall and millionaire racehorse owner Robert Sangster, now both in Los Angeles, are planning to marry. They met in June at Royal Ascot and were seen together at the Keenland Yearling horse sales in Kentucky. According to Jerry, 'Sangster could buy Mick ten times over'.

OCTOBER 4
Mick Jagger is accompanied to a party at Regine's in New York by socialite Cornelia Guest. They go on to Xenon where Mick meets Valerie Perrine with whom he is immediately rumoured to be having an affair.

NOVEMBER 7
Keith, Ron and Mick start work at the Pathe Marconi Studios, running through unused material from previous sessions and working on new material for the next album.

NOVEMBER 11
Bill and Charlie arrive from London to join the others in the studios.

NOVEMBER 12
John Blake reports in the *Sun*: 'Tearaway Rolling Stone Keith Richards is to get married at last. His bride-to-be is his beautiful model girlfriend Patti Hansen. They are planning a huge white wedding in New York within a month... with Mick Jagger as best man. ''Yes, it's true,'' a spokesman for the 38-year-old Stones' guitarist said yesterday. ''Keith was trying to keep it secret, but if the *Sun* knows about it there is no point in denying it.
Jerry Hall flies from New York to Paris.

NOVEMBER 13
Venezuelan model Victoria Vicuna also flies to Paris to join Mick Jagger.

NOVEMBER 17
Nigel Dempster reports in the *Daily Mail* on an abortive reconciliation between Mick and Jerry Hall. He claims a 'close friend' has told him 'far from the meeting being joyful, as described by ill-informed newspapers, Mick started at Jerry as soon as he met her at the airport. She really can't take his abuse any longer and has split. She does not want to see him again.'

NOVEMBER
A double anthology album is released by the discount label K-Tel called *The Best Of The Stones*.
The Rolling Stones are fined £200 for playing too loud; they exceeded by 20 decibels the permitted volume during their concert in Bristol.

DECEMBER
Jerry re-joins Mick in Paris.

DECEMBER 17
The Rolling Stones stop work temporarily on the new album. Bill, Ron and Charlie go back to London.

DECEMBER 20
Apparently reconciled, Mick and Jerry fly to the Caribbean island of Mustique where Mick is having a house built.

DECEMBER
Vandals spray obscene graffiti about Jerry Hall on the outer walls of Mick's new house in New York.

Right: *Mick on guitar at the second sell-out concert at Wembley.* Inset: *Ticket for the Munich concert.*

JANUARY 9
Mick, Keith and Jerry Hall fly to Los Angeles.

JANUARY 14
In Los Angeles, Mick plays the role of the Chinese Emperor in Hans Christian Andersen's *The Nightingale* for Showtime Cable TV's *Faerie Tale Theatre* series.

JANUARY 18
All the Stones except Bill are at a private screening in New York of *Let's Spend The Night Together*.

JANUARY
The *Sunday Express* reports that Charlie Watts has recently bought a 17th century house, set in 20 acres, near Barnstable, North Devon. 'His new home is a Grade 2 listed building with three reception rooms, six bedrooms and stabling, useful for Watts' ten horses.'

JANUARY 25
In an exclusive interview with John Blake in the *Sun* Mick Jagger talks for the first time about the possibility of the Stones splitting: 'It will disintegrate very slowly. Bill has been saying for years that he will retire from the group and one of these years he's finally going to do it. The band has done what it set out to do. I don't know what goals are left...' He claims his mother will be delighted to see the Stones end. He says: 'She has always been unhappy with what I do.'

FEBRUARY 11
Premiere of *Let's Spend The Night Together* at the Loew Theater in New York.

FEBRUARY
In *Playgirl* magazine Mick Jagger says: 'I go out everywhere, I mean there's no city that I get hassled in. I only get hassled on the road. I travel a lot. But I'm always working in a way.

FEBRUARY 25
John Ryles, Literary Editor of the *Sunday Times*, is hired as 'technical writer' for Mick Jagger's autobiography. Ryles will get £50,000 while Mick will receive more than £1 million, the highest price ever paid in England for an autobiography.

MARCH 24
Let's Spend The Night Together is released in Britain through the Classic Cinema chain.

APRIL 10
Mick and Jerry holiday on Mustique where Mick starts work on his autobiography and oversees the building of his house.

APRIL 15
Decca re-releases *Their Satanic Majesties Request*, with the original 3-D cover.

APRIL 28/29
Bill Wyman and Charlie Watts join Alexis Korner on stage at the Marquee in London for the club's 25th anniversary.

MAY 4
Keith flies off to San Francisco, where Patti Hansen starts work on the film *Hard To Hold*. Meanwhile Mick and Ron start work at the Hit Factory in New York editing and mixing tracks recorded in Paris for their new album. Keith joins them later in the month.

JUNE
Keith flies off to Jamaica leaving Mick to carry on with the new album with the Sugarhill Records rhythm section and horns. Speculation in both New York and London suggests Keith is becoming disillusioned with Mick.

JULY 4
Mick says in the *Daily Star*: 'When you get to my age you really have to work at staying young. You've got to be fit, because rock requires a tremendous amount of energy and I find that if your body is alive, your mind becomes alive. That's vital in a business that is as fast as this. Once I led the typical dissipated life of a rock star, full of drugs, booze and chaos. But these days my health is my most treasured possession. When I'm on tour I never touch hard liquor and I try to get as much sleep as I possibly can. I like to get as much as ten hours a night. I don't go to clubs or discos except to pick up girls.

JULY 16
Keith jams with Jerry Lee Lewis in L.A. The show is taped and will be shown on *Salute*'s debut broadcast on 25 September.

TIME IS ON OUR SIDE
the Rolling Stones
PTAH
STUDIO PTAH/P.CAPONI-I.CECCHETTI

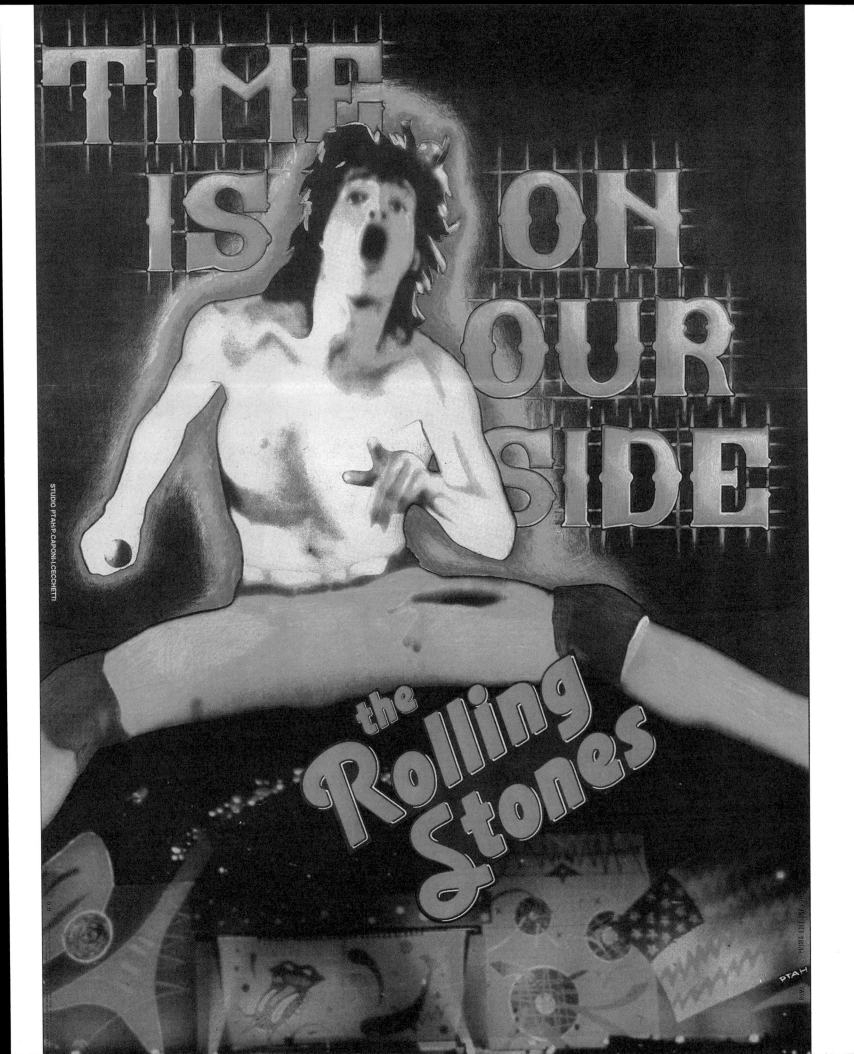

JULY 25
Pete Townshend writes an article for the *Times* to celebrate Mick's 40th birthday headlined 'Jagger: A Butterfly Reaches 40'.

JULY 26
Mick Jagger is 40 and spends the day in Vermont with Jerry Hall. He says: 'If anyone else asks me about my birthday I shall punch them in the mouth.'

JULY
Prince Rupert Lowenstein, the Stones' business manager, has various meetings on both sides of the Atlantic with representatives of Atlantic, CBS, EMI, MCA and other major record companies, to negotiate a new distribution deal for the band.

AUGUST 10
Keith goes to Marlon's 14th birthday party held at Anita Pallenberg's house in Long Island.

AUGUST 20
A baby boy, Tyrone, is born to Jo Howard and Ron Wood at the Mount Sinai Hospital in New York.

AUGUST 25
The Rolling Stones sign with CBS in a deal that is said to be worth nearly $28 million, by far the richest in the history of the music business. The contract is signed in Paris because of France's helpful tax laws. The group will be paid $6 million per album for a total of four albums over the next few years, plus additional promotional expenditure which could amount to another $1 million per album. The band's recordings will be distributed on CBS' Columbia label (but under the Rolling Stones' own logo) and will start on completion of their current contract with Atlantic Records. Sheldon Vogue of Atlantic says: 'We certainly hate losing them, but the numbers they were asking just didn't make sense to us.' The Stones' first recording for CBS will probably not be released until the spring of 1985. Given their past rate of output, the last album of the contract could be released in 1990, when Mick will be 47 years old.

AUGUST 27
Jerry and Mick are expecting a baby in five months' time.

AUGUST
Bill Wyman separates on amicable terms with his partner of fourteen years' standing, Astrid Lundstrom.

SEPTEMBER 20
Bill Wyman and Charlie Watts take part in a charity concert at the Royal Albert Hall in aid of ARMS (Action for Research into Multiple Sclerosis). Eric Clapton, Stevie Winwood, Jimmy Page, Jeff Beck and Ronnie Lane, who suffers from the disease and has to be helped on stage, also take part.

SEPTEMBER 21
Second concert at the Royal Albert Hall in the presence of the Prince and Princess of Wales, this time in aid of Prince Charles's charity, the Prince's Trust.

SEPTEMBER 24
Keith and Mick tape promo sequences for the new album in New York.

OCTOBER 17
The Stones meet in Paris.

OCTOBER 18
The band shoot footage for the video for the new single 'Undercover Of The Night', directed by Julien Temple, on stage at the Bain Douches Club.

OCTOBER 24
Mick, Keith and Julien Temple fly to Mexico City to shoot sequences for the 'Undercover Of The Night' video. They are accompanied by Jerry and Patti.

OCTOBER 28
Mick appears on the first edition of Channel 4's *The Tube*.

OCTOBER 30
Mick and Keith finish shooting 'Undercover Of The Night'. Mick and Jerry fly to Europe and Keith and Patti take a long holiday in Cabo San Lucas, Mexico.

OCTOBER 31
The single, 'Undercover Of The Night'/'All The Way Down' is released on Rolling Stones Records. Written by Jagger and Richards and produced by the Glimmer Twins and Chris Kimsey, it is taken from the forthcoming new album. A disco-mix version of the single is also available with the instrumental version of 'Feel On Baby' as flip-side.

NOVEMBER 7
The new album, *Undercover*, is released simultaneously in the US and UK on Rolling Stones Records. It features ten new tracks written by Mick Jagger and Keith Richards, one of which, 'Pretty Beat Up' is co-written by Jagger, Richards and Wood. Produced by the Glimmer Twins and Chris Kimsey, it was recorded last autumn and early this year at EMI Pathe Marconi Studios in Paris. For the first time in a record, the album features a brochure advertising the new Rolling Stones official fan club and the *Beggars Banquet* newsletter.

NOVEMBER 9
At a press conference in Madison Square Garden, Stones tour Manager Bill Graham announces a mini tour of the US for the multiple sclerosis charity ARMS which will feature the same musicians who played the two benefit concerts at the Royal Albert Hall in London in September, including Bill, Charlie and Ian Stewart.

NOVEMBER 10
BBC TV's *Top Of The Pops* bans the Stones' 'Undercover Of The Night' video. A BBC spokesman says: 'It is exceedingly violent all the way through and we couldn't consider it for *Top Of The Pops* which goes out in the early evening.' John Blake in the *Sun* previews the video in which Mick is seen relaxing at the Holiday Inn in Mexico City when three wild-eyed gunmen burst into his suite. The leader of the terrorists, who shoots Jagger, is played by Keith Richards. Mick says: 'A lot of "Undercover Of The Night" was inspired by the things I read about all the people who've disappeared in Argentina.

NOVEMBER 11
Mick appears on Channel 4's youth-orientated programme, *The Tube* to defend the video. It has been broadcast during the programme, at 5.30 pm, minus the scene in which Jagger is shot through the head, which is banned by the Independent Broadcasting Authority. Mick says: 'It follows the song. The song is about repression, it's about violence. We're not trying to dress it up and sell the record with advertising clichés. There's no gratuitous violence in it at all. We're not trying to glamorise violence. We're

Above: *The album is* Under Cover, *but Mick still makes the front page at 40.*

trying to make something interesting that has a valid point.

NOVEMBER 12
'Undercover Of The Night' enters the British Top 30 at Number 27. It will stay there for five weeks, rising to Number 8, its highest position.

NOVEMBER 18
Old Rolling Stones videos are shown on *The Tube*. The Stones' London office is preparing a sanitised version of the 'Undercover Of The Night' video, suitable for *Top Of The Pops*. Decca release a two-album set featuring 23 artists including the Stones, titled *Formula 30*.

NOVEMBER 19
Undercover enters the British charts at Number 18. It will stay in the Top 30 for eight weeks, reaching Number 1.

NOVEMBER 25
Decca release the first three Stones' EPs -'The Rolling Stones', 'Five By Five' and 'Got Live If You Want It' - in mono and 12-inch versions.

NOVEMBER 28/29
ARMS, featuring Charlie Watts and Bill Wyman, play the Reunion Arena, Dallas. The US benefit tour also takes in San Francisco, Los Angeles and New York.

DECEMBER 3
Undercover makes Number 1 in the British charts. It also enters the US Top 30 at Number 13, peaking at Number 4, with eight weeks in the Top 30. The single, 'Undercover Of The Night' enters the US Top 30 at Number 15. It will stay in the chart for seven weeks, with a highest position of Number 9.

DECEMBER 9
Final concert of the ARMS tour at Madison Square Garden.

DECEMBER 16
Undercover is banned in Singapore because of the sleeve.
Mick flies to Cabo San Lucas in Mexico.

DECEMBER 18
Keith Richards, 40 today, secretly marries Patti Hansen in Cabo San Lucas, Mexico. Mick is the only Stone to attend the wedding at the Finisterra Hotel but Julien Temple videos the ceremony.

DECEMBER 23
Mick and Bette Midler videotape a promo version of her new single, 'Beast Of Burden'.

Right: *Mick and Jerry discuss marriage plans en route for Barbados. Their baby will be born in February 1984, but the wedding is indefinitely postponed.*

JANUARY 1
Alexis Korner dies, aged 55, at the Westminster Hospital.

JANUARY 18
The Rolling Stones start shooting a new video in Mexico City for the next single, 'She Was Hot' again directed by Julien Temple.

JANUARY 20
The press report Mick is sponsoring Britain's gymnastic team for the Los Angeles Olympic Games to the tune of £32,000. His donation is intended partly as a 'backing Britain' gesture and partly as a tribute to his own father Joe, a Physical Education instructor.

JANUARY 23
'She Was Hot'/'Think I'm Going Mad' is released on Rolling Stones Records. The A-side is taken from *Undercover* while the flip side was recorded in Paris during sessions for *Emotional Rescue*. Both tracks are written and produced by Mick and Keith. A limited edition picture disc is available only in the UK.

JANUARY 25
The Stones finish shooting the new video in Mexico; they have also shot sequences for a possible video for 'Too Much Blood'. Producer Michael Hamlyn says the new video is not as controversial as the one for 'Undercover': 'It's really tame by comparison, more a comedy than a controversy.

FEBRUARY 3
The first part of Mick's interview on *Friday Night Videos* is transmitted in New York.

FEBRUARY 4
'She Was Hot' enters the US Top 100 at Number 83, peaking at Number 44, with nine weeks in the charts.

FEBRUARY 10
The second part of Mick's interview is shown with a sanitised version of the video for 'She Was Hot', its first airing. This new edit is eventually distributed to MTV who had banned the original version, which featured the Stones' trouser flies popping open at the prospect of Anita Morris, a sexy dancer notorious for her part in the Broadway musical *Nine*. In the video she plays a temptress first seen in Mick and Keith's bedrooms. Her next appearance, on stage with the entire band, is when their trouser buttons begin to pop. The violent *Undercover* video has been regularly shown on MTV but a spokesman said: 'We have had some raunchy videos before, but this was too much.'

FEBRUARY 11
'She Was Hot' only reaches Number 40 in the UK charts, with a mere two weeks in the charts altogether.

FEBRUARY 25
Keith flies to Paris to check out a studio where the Stones plan to record their next album.

MARCH 2
Jerry Hall gives birth to a daughter, Elizabeth Scarlett, at the Lennox Hill Hospital, New York. The baby weighs 8lb 2oz and Mick is present at the birth.

MARCH 5
Bodyguards flank Jerry and the baby as they leave the hospital following police warnings of death threats made against the Jagger family.

MARCH 27
In the *Sun*, Bill Wyman tells John Blake: 'I've lost touch with whoever Mick is now. I'm sure he has as well. Seven or eight years ago I could talk with Mick about books, films and intelligent things, but now I just talk to him in asides. Mick is a very difficult person to know now. I'm not worried about saying what I think about Mick. He's not my boss. We are a band, you know, and Keith Richards runs the Rolling Stones really. Mick is a brilliant man but in the final count he just has his share of the five votes, no more. He has been like a business associate for twenty years of working. Charlie is great. He knows what he wants to be and that's what he is; Woody is difficult because he is very shallow. Great for a good laugh, but you can't talk to him. I think Keith didn't understand where I was coming from for a long time because I

didn't get drunk or take drugs like him. But he has become perfectly straight over the past five years and he and I are now the best of mates.

MARCH 30
Mick, Jerry, Elizabeth and Jade travel to Nassau in the Bahamas.

APRIL 4
An upset Bill Wyman appears on New York TV via satellite from London on *News Nightwatch* categorically denying the *Sun* interview published a week ago.

APRIL 16
Mick returns to New York to appear in court as a witness in the Stones' suit against former manager Allen Klein. Later he talks business with Michael Jackson. The *Daily Express* reports on the court hearing, describing how Klein was once chased by Mick around the Savoy Hotel in London screaming, 'Where's my money?', whereupon Klein, terrified by Mick's furious demands for alleged debts of £500,000, fled into the street. The newspaper continues: 'The two men have been personal enemies for years and have not spoken since Klein accused Jagger of insulting his daughter by pulling a face at her. Their amazing row ten years ago was over a contract giving Klein the rights to pre-1970 Rolling Stones material. The confrontation was described yesterday by Jagger at a Manhattan court, where he is fighting to have the contract nullified... Jagger said: "I wanted to be reasonable and cool but the moment he walked in I blew my top and screamed at him 'Where is my $800,000?' [sic]." Jagger explained that the rights Klein held were mainly to uncompleted recordings of practice sessions and how, throughout the seventies, he feared Klein would damage the Stones' reputation by releasing the material. Mick says: "The group are upset as this stuff is rubbish... I do not want him in my life. It's like dealing with the Russians".'

APRIL 23
The Stones drop their suit against Allen Klein on condition he pays them royalties regularly twice a year.

MAY 6
Mick starts wòrk with Michael Jackson at A&R's New York studios on a song called 'State Of Shock'.

MAY 10
The *Daily Express* reports difficulties over the preparation of Mick's autobiography which is reported to be 'dull'. Publishers Weidenfeld & Nicolson, who are believed to have paid £2,000,000 for the rights are thought to be disappointed and a spokesman for the British paperback company, Futura, who have mass market rights says: 'No sex. No rock'n'roll. It's just boring stuff about his ordinary parents, and his ordinary upbringing. I was surprised at the poor quality.' Jagger suffers from a poor memory and ghost writer John Ryle has a hard task to bring the manuscript up to scratch. In New York Mick finishes working on 'State Of Shock'.

MAY 12
Mick flies to Mustique to spend a week with his family before continuing recording his solo album at the Compass Point Studios in the Bahamas.

JUNE 1
Ron Wood makes a guest appearance on the New York set of the film *9½ Weeks* in a sequence featuring a reggae band.

JUNE 5
Charlie Watts and Ian Stewart are among the many musicians saluting the memory of Alexis Korner at a benefit concert in Nottingham. The money raised goes to cancer research.

JUNE 8
The *Daily Mirror* reports that Mick has approached Bill Wyman for help in recalling events for his autobiography as Bill has everything recorded on computer. But according to the *Mirror* Bill's reaction was ' "Get Stuffed." He added that Jagger would have to be very patient and read it all later. In *his* book.'

JUNE 11
'State Of Shock' by the Jacksons, featuring Mick Jagger on vocals, is released on Epic.

JUNE 14
The Rolling Stones are the first band ever to earn the Madison Square Garden's coveted Platinum Ticket Award. They won it for appearances in 1981 and today are the first group to be included in the Madison Square Garden Hall of Fame.

JUNE 24
Mick, Jerry, Jade, Karis, Mick's parents and brother Chris, together with Jerry's mother and Charlie and Shirley Watts, attend the Christening of Elizabeth Scarlett at St Mary Abbot's Church in Kensington. Shirley Watts is godmother.

JUNE 26
The Stones, apart from Ron Wood, meet to discuss future plans in their office in Munroe Terrace, Chelsea.

JUNE 29
Rewind, an anthology album, is released in Europe on Rolling Stones Records, distributed by EMI. The British version includes 'It's Only Rock'n'Roll' and 'She's So Cold', two tracks not on the American release. The cassette version also includes 'Emotional Rescue' and 'Hang Fire'. Mick and Bill have

Top left: *Bill and Charlie attempt to go acoustic during the shooting of the 'She Was Hot' video.* Above left: *The picture disc drips with Freudian innuendo.*

made a promo video for the album in which Bill portrays the curator of a rock'n'roll museum and Mick a visitor. In Britain, Rolling Stones Records release a single as well, 'Brown Sugar'/'Bitch', which is also produced as a limited edition picture disc, in the form of the cover of the *Sticky Fingers* album.

JUNE 30
'State Of Shock' by Mick and Michael Jackson, enters the US Top 30 at Number 30. It stays in the charts for fifteen weeks, with a highest position of Number 3.

JULY 2
Rewind is released in America on Rolling Stones Records, distributed by Atlantic. The American release includes 'Hang Fire' and 'Emotional Rescue' not included on the British LP. The cassette also includes 'It's Only Rock'n'Roll' and 'Heartbreaker'. Rolling Stones Records also release the single 'Miss You'/'Too Tough'.

JULY 7
Rewind enters the UK Top 30 album chart at Number 28. It stays in the charts for seven weeks, with a highest position of Number 12.

JULY 14
'State Of Shock' enters the UK Top 30 at Number 20. It will peak at Number 14 and remain in the charts for six weeks.

JULY 23
Mick's forthcoming solo album fuels speculation about splits within the group. One source says: 'He wants the new album to be totally different from anything he's done with the Stones. He's going to take his career in a whole new direction.' The album is produced by Trevor Horn, well known for his technical wizardry. Another Stones' source believes that Mick is bugged by the feeling that he hasn't received due acknowledgement for the Stones' success: 'He wants to show everyone just what he's capable of without the support of the rest of the group. He wants the ego trip.' Mick issues a vehement denial that the Stones are to split. He says: 'Rumours like this come up regularly and have done since the sixties. The truth is we're very much together as a band. In fact, we all met up three weeks ago in London to discuss future Stones projects. They include recording a new album in December and the possibility of touring next year... I am doing a solo album, but that was part of a record deal we signed a year ago. But the deal with CBS also involves making at least five albums together, so we'll be around for some time. Besides, the Stones have all done solo projects before. Bill Wyman has recorded three albums.' Mick also denies that he and Bill are at odds over the autobiography; 'I haven't asked Bill or anyone for information for the book. We're still the best of mates. In fact we were working on a video together last week.'

JULY 27
The *Evening Standard* reports a typical Mick Jagger joke which backfired when Jagger and guitarist Jeff Beck were working together in the Bahamas: 'Jeff insisted that Mick left the studio so he could concentrate on a guitar solo. Mick was later to describe it as one of the best he had ever heard. However, Jagger returned, listened to the tape and, stone-faced, ordered the recording engineer to erase it. Beck was furious and, after telling Mick where he could put his album, stormed towards the door. The engineer protested but Jagger was emphatic, "Wipe it," he repeated. Beck stormed out, whereupon Jagger, a schoolboy grin on his face, turned to the engineer and said he had simply been testing the guitarist's well-known short temper. "Too late," wailed the hapless flunkey, "you told me to wipe it so I have".

JULY
A 60-minute video of the ARMS concert shot at the Royal Albert Hall last year is released, called *The Ronnie Lane Appeal For Arms*.

AUGUST
Decca re-release a re-mastered version of *Beggars Banquet*, with the original and once banned cover.

SEPTEMBER
Bill is producing an album, provisionally called *Up In Arms*, by a band known as Willie and the Poor Boys. The line up includes several well known musicians, including Charlie Watts.
The Stones have to postpone recording their first album for CBS because Mick is continuing work on his solo album at the Power Station Studios in New York. Herbie Hancock, Nile Rodgers and Bill Laswell play in the sessions, while members of Duran Duran visit the studio. Bill goes to Vienna to discuss a film project with Austrian director Robert Dornhelm. Bill is to finance and to write the soundtrack for a film called *Echo Park*.

OCTOBER
In Los Angeles, producers of the US soap opera *Dallas* attempt to lure Mick into the cast with an alleged fee of £1,000,000. He turns it down.

OCTOBER 26
Ron is interviewed at the Hard Rock Cafe in New York for a live broadcast on WNEW-FM. Julien Temple, interviewed on UK TV Channel Four's *The Tube* tells how Keith Richards tests the nerves of people who are going to work closely with him. On their first meeting, Keith was armed with a sword stick which he held at Temple's throat. Later he took him on a hair-raising drive through the streets of Paris at speeds of over 100 miles an hour.

NOVEMBER
At the beginning of the month, the four original Stones meet in Amsterdam to discuss the band's future plans.

NOVEMBER
A boxed set of eleven original master recording albums is released under the title *The Rolling Stones*, by Mobile Fidelity Sound Lab. They are directly transferred from original tapes from 1964 to 1970. The boxed set is only available as a limited edition.

NOVEMBER 14
Under the title *Video Rewind*, Vestron release a collection of promo video classics, including the never shown 'Too Much Blood', the censored 'Undercover Of The Night' and 'She Was Hot', all three directed by Julien Temple.

NOVEMBER
Mick, Jerry and Julien Temple fly to Rio de Janeiro to start shooting the promo video for Mick's new album.

NOVEMBER 28
Ron and Jo fly to Dallas for the opening of an exhibition of Ron's paintings called 'Portraits of Friends', at the Foster Goldstrum Gallery. Among the 30 or so pictures are portraits of Sid Vicious, Elvis, Jimi Henrix, Count Basie and the Stones. It runs until January 1985.

DECEMBER 1
Video Rewind enters the Top 20 music video chart at Number 2, reaching Number 1 next week, where it stays for two weeks.

DECEMBER 9
Charlie Watts and Ian Stewart play a charity gig for Ethiopia in Edinburgh.

DECEMBER
Rolling Stones Records release the 12-inch version of 'Too Much Blood'; the single includes three different versions of the song. Produced by the Glimmer Twins, it is the last Stones record put out by Atlantic.
The German division of Decca releases a 4-album set called *The Rest Of The Best*. Previously unreleased tracks include 'Memphis Tennessee', 'Bright Lights Big City' plus a bonus single of the censored 'Cocksucker Blues'.

DECEMBER
Ron and Jo leave New York to spend Christmas in England.

DECEMBER 25
Keith and Patti spend Christmas in New York as do Mick and Jerry, having completed shooting of the video in Brazil. They fly to Mustique for New Year's Eve.

JANUARY 3
Ron Wood and Jo Howard are married at St Mary's Church in Denham, Buckinghamshire. All the Stones, except Mick, are there.

JANUARY
In London, Decca withdraws *The Rest Of the Best* released in Germany because of the inclusion of 'Cocksucker Blues'. The album set will be re-released without the single.

JANUARY 11
Ron and Jo are among the guests at the Roof Garden in Kensington, London, at a party given by the *Daily Mirror* to celebrate their signing of columnist John Blake, formerly with the *Sun*.

JANUARY
Mick and Keith start work in the Pathe Marconi Studios in Paris on ideas for the Stones' next album.

FEBRUARY 4
Mick Jagger's first solo single, 'Just Another Night'/'Turn The Girl Loose' is released by CBS simultaneously in the UK and US. Both tracks are written by Mick and co-produced by Mick, Bill Laswell and Nile Rodgers. The single is also released in a 12-inch version, remixed by Francois Kevorkian. The US 12-inch features the album version of the song plus one other version, while in England it features four versions. The single is taken from the forthcoming album, *She's The Boss*.

FEBRUARY 5
Mick tells the *Daily Mirror*: 'The other Stones might think it's possible that if the album did really well it might be the end of the Stones. But I know it won't be. But it was still strange working without the others. It is rather like having a wife and a mistress. The Stones thing is like a long marriage. I know them very well. I know their strengths and weaknesses. I almost have telepathy with them after all these years.

FEBRUARY 16
Mick tells *Melody Maker*: 'It wasn't just a pose in the first place. In that period we were very angry and violent. But a lot of that soon disappeared when we achieved success. By 1965 the Stones were part of Show Business in a way. A successful band, internationally known. And if it hadn't been for all the drug busts... that changed things an awful lot... it changed our attitude to everything... we were just a good-time band having a very good time on the road making the music we wanted and making records that I think were pretty good. Then we got into this whole thing of being busted and went to jail and everything and that put us back to where we started so we had to spend our energy and time fighting that, rather than making music which was really boring. Boring and time-consuming.

FEBRUARY 17
'Just Another Night' enters the British charts at Number 30. It will stay in the charts for four weeks, reaching Number 27 as its highest position.

FEBRUARY 23
'Just Another Night' enters the US Top 30 at Number 28. It stays in the charts for eight weeks, peaking at Number 10.

MARCH 4
Mick Jagger's first solo album, *She's The Boss*, is released by CBS. All the tracks are written by Mick, one co-written with Keith Richards and two with Carlos Alomar. It is co-produced by Jagger, Bill Laswell and Nile Rodgers and recorded at the Compass Point Studios, Nassau, Bahamas and the Power Station Studios in New York. Musicians include Nile Rodgers, Jeff Beck, Herbie Hancock, Sly Dunbar, Robbie Shakespeare, Bill Laswell, Bernard Edwards, Ian Hammer and Pete Townshend.

MARCH 11/12
Bill, Charlie and Ron tape a six-song video at Fulham Town Hall in London for the Willie and the Poor Boys project. Bill says:
'We have three goals in mind when we put together the Willie and the Poor Boys project. We want to raise money for ARMS, of course, and keep the public aware that money is always needed for multiple sclerosis research. We also want to make a new generation aware of some of the music that inspired all of us when we were growing up.

The music has its origin in the 1940s and 1950s. It's a combination of blues, swing, boogie and early rock-styles. As a side benefit, this project will provide exposure for a number of excellent musicians who are not as well known as they should be.'

MARCH 16
She's The Boss enters the British charts at Number 16. It will stay in the charts for six weeks, with a highest position of Number 6. In the USA it enters at Number 22, peaking at Number 8, with nine weeks in the Top 30. It is reported that Charlie Watts' sixteen-year-old daughter Seraphina and another sixth-former have been expelled from Millfield School, a £6,000-a-year mixed progressive boarding school in Somerset. An incident involving cannabis is said to be involved.

MARCH 18
Patti Richards gives birth to a daughter, Theodora Dupree, at the New York Hospital. Keith is present at the birth.

APRIL 1
Mick starts work on the video for his next single 'Lucky In Love', directed by Julien Temple.

APRIL 8
Mick appears on *The Old Grey Whistle Test* on BBC TV in London.

APRIL 11
The Stones resume work on the new album in Paris; the release date has been put back from June to September.

APRIL
It is rumoured that Mick has been asked to return the advance he received for his autobiography, since he seems unable to produce a manuscript.

APRIL 19
Another Mick Jagger single, 'Lucky In Love'/'Running Out Of Luck', taken from *She's The Boss*, is released on CBS. The A-side is co-written by Mick and Bill Laswell. A 12-inch version is also available.

APRIL 27
'Lucky In Love' enters the US chart at Number 65. It only makes Number 38, but is in the Top 100 for eleven weeks.

MAY
Jerry Hall attends a party for the launch of the new James Bond movie *A View To A Kill* and confirms that she's expecting a baby this August.

MAY 24
The album, *Willie And The Poor Boys*, is released on Bill's own label, Ripple, distributed by Decca. Produced by Bill Wyman, it features rock'n'roll classics including 'Baby Please Don't Go', 'You Never Can Tell', and 'Let's Talk It Over'. Bill and Andy Fairweather Low have written a track called 'Poor Boy Boogie'. Musicians on the album include Kenny Jones, Henry Spinetti, Chris Rea, Steve Gregory, Ray Cooper, Paul Rodgers, Jimmy Page, Geraint Watkins, Andy Fairweather Low, Micky Gee, Charlie Watts and Bill himself.
A single taken from the album is also released consisting of 'Baby Please Don't Go'/'Let's Talk It Over'.

MAY
It is announced that Mick will take part in the major rock event of the year, Live Aid, to be staged on 13 July both in London at Wembley Stadium and in Philadelphia at the JFK Stadium, to raise money for Ethiopian famine victims.

JUNE
The Stones finish work at the Pathe Marconi Studios in mid-June. Thirty tracks have been recorded.

JUNE 29
The planned transatlantic duet between Mick and David Bowie for Live Aid is scrapped for technical reasons so they record a version of 'Dancing In The Street' in a London studio in just twelve hours, and after the session shoot a video in the East End of London to be shown worldwide during the concert on 13 July.

JULY 13
The Live Aid concert is staged simultaneously in London at Wembley Stadium and at the JFK Stadium, Philadelphia and broadcast via satellite all over the world, including the USSR, to an audience of 1.6 billion people, making the event the biggest ever in show business. In Philadelphia Mick performs backed by Hall and Oates, then Tina Turner joins him for a medley of 'State Of Shock' and 'It's Only Rock'n'Roll', and he rips her skirt off during the set, his first-ever live solo. Later Ron and Keith join Bob Dylan on stage, for the final act of the concert. Mick and David Bowie's video of 'Dancing In The Street' is broadcast as one of the highlights of the event.

JULY 15
Mick shoots a video for 'Hard Woman' in Los Angeles. It is another track from *She's The Boss*.

JULY 16/17
Mick, Keith and Ron mix tapes at the RPM Studio in New York. Jimmy Page visits them in the studio and adds some guitar work to a couple of tracks.

JULY 26
Mick celebrates his 43rd birthday at a party held for him at the Palladium in New York.

AUGUST 4
Keith and Patti visit Anita Pallenberg, Marlon and Keith's dad, on Long Island.

AUGUST 9
The Stones have a photo session at Annie Liebowitz' studio and in Battery Park, New York, for the cover of their next album.

AUGUST 16
Legendary guitarist Les Paul visits Keith and Ron as they continue mixing in New York.

AUGUST 17
The Stones take a break from the album for three weeks. Mick's solo album *She's The Boss* has now sold two million copies in America.

AUGUST 19
Charlie Watts breaks his leg in three places after a fall in the cellar of his house in Devon. He is told to rest until November.

AUGUST 23
The single of 'Dancing In The Street', sung by Mick Jagger and David Bowie is released worldwide on EMI America. Recorded at four different studios in New York, it is produced by Clive Langer and Alan Winstanley with further production from Nile Rodgers and Mick Jagger. The single also comes in a 12-inch version.
In America 5,000 theatres all over the country show the 'Dancing In The Street' video, making it the largest ever exposure for a promotional video. EMI America have also printed more than 20,000 posters.
Rumours circulating in Hollywood suggest that Mick and David Bowie are planning to film a re-make of *Some Like It Hot*.

AUGUST 28
James Leroy Augustine is born to Jerry Hall and Mick Jagger at the Lennox Hill Hospital, New York.

SEPTEMBER 7
'Dancing In The Street' goes straight into the UK Top 30 at Number 1, staying in the Top 30 for nine weeks.

SEPTEMBER 9
'Dancing In The Street' goes gold in the UK, making it the fastest selling single of the year so far.

SEPTEMBER 14
'Dancing In The Street' enters the US Top 30 at Number 25, peaking at Number 7, with eight weeks in the Top 30.

SEPTEMBER 30
Jerry Hall appears on BBC TV's prime time *Terry Wogan Show*. She claims that Mick jumps up and down singing 'Jumping Jack Flash' to get their new baby James Leroy to sleep.

OCTOBER 12
The *Daily Mirror* reports that Mick has publicly torn a strip off Sting at a New York disco in response to remarks made by Sting about his fellow rock stars in an interview. Among other things Mick is supposed to have shouted: 'Keep your mouth shut. We don't go slagging each other off.'
Ron and Keith contribute guitar back-up to 'Silver And Gold', a track recorded by Bono of U2 with drummers Steve Jordan and Keith LeBlanc, recorded at the Right Track Studio in New York. The track will be included in *Sun City*, the anti-apartheid album which features many top rock stars.

OCTOBER 15
Keith, Mick and Ron take a break from mixing the new album and go on holiday. Within a couple of days Keith, Patti, Theodora and Patti's mother, fly to Barbardos. It is revealed that Patti is expecting another baby in late July.
Ron has a small recording studio installed in the basement of his house in New York.

OCTOBER 21
Mick and Chris Jagger fly to India. It is rumoured that Mick is looking for a suitably romantic venue for marrying Jerry Hall.

NOVEMBER 8
James Leroy is christened at St Mary Abbot's Church in Kensington, London. Godparents are Anjelica Huston, the Stones' business manager Prince Rupert Lowenstein and Mick's personal assistant Alan Dunn.

NOVEMBER 18
Charlie Watts and his 29-piece Big Band open at Ronnie Scott's Jazz Club in London for a week of performances. The Big Band includes Jack Bruce (cello), Stan Tracey (piano), Jimmy Deuchar (trumpet), Peter King (alto sax), Bobby Wellins (tenor sax), plus two drummers besides Charlie. Keith, Mick and Ian Stewart go to the opening night. Bill visits later in the week.

NOVEMBER 25-27
Keith, Ron and Mick resume work on the album at the Right Track in New York.

NOVEMBER 30
Mick joins Tina Turner on stage for a version of 'Honky Tonk Woman' at the Charlotte Coliseum in North Carolina.

DECEMBER 12
While waiting to see a specialist doctor for a check-up in a West London clinic, Ian Stewart dies from a heart attack, at the age of 47. He had been suffering from intense respiratory trouble for a few days.
Ronnie Lane will say in an interview in *Musician* magazine: 'You will not find any more of a purist than Stu [Ian Stewart]. He was what we call a one-off. Once they made him, they didn't make any more.

DECEMBER 18
Keith celebrates his 42nd birthday quietly with a small party at the San Lorenzo restaurant. Charlie and Bill are among the guests.

DECEMBER 20
Ian Stewart's funeral is held at Randall's Park Crematorium, Leatherhead, Surrey. All the Stones are there. Mick has flown in from the Caribbean, Ron and Jo from New York, Bill's former wife Diane also attends, as does Ian Stewart's ex-wife and 14-year-old son Giles. Jeff Beck, Eric Clapton and Kenny Jones are also there. The Stones themselves sing the 23rd Psalm.
Shirley Arnold, who worked for the band for many years, says of Ian: 'You could never pay him a compliment. But they all absolutely adored him, without ever saying it... He was so totally unaffected by it all, the razzmatazz backstage and all the chicks - he found it quite boring. He'd much rather read a comic in the corner. When we were into all the drugs years ago, Stu would put on a face or say, "Oh, you silly". Over the years there have been so many people around the Stones who have died one way or another. But you never thought it would happen to Stu. He was such a private guy. That funeral, and Mick with tears in his eyes. I'm sure if Stu had seen it he would have found it all quite amusing.'

DECEMBER 23
Keith and Ron return to New York to spend Christmas with their families, while Mick flies to Mustique to join Jerry and the children. Bill and Charlie stay in England.

Divisions at work. Top right: *Ron and Keith rehearsing with Bobby Womack.* Above right: *Mick with Nile Rogers, who produced his solo album,* She's The Boss.

JANUARY 2
Jamaican singer Patrick Alley sues Mick Jagger over 'Just Another Night', claiming Mick has plagiarised the song which Alley says he wrote and recorded back in 1982 for his album *A Touch Of Patrick Alley*.

JANUARY 23
Keith Richards presents Chuck Berry with the first award of the first Rock'n'Roll Hall of Fame ceremony, conceived by Atlantic Records' President Ahmet Ertegun. Keith says of Chuck: 'I lifted every lick he ever played.'

FEBRUARY 7
All the Stones gather in New York to work on the video for their new single, 'Harlem Shuffle', in a studio on 54th Street and 10th Avenue. It features the band performing, cut with animated footage of cats dancing in a Harlem ballroom.

FEBRUARY 23
The Stones play an invitation gig at the 100 Club in London's Oxford Street, in memory of Ian Stewart. The band billed to play is Stewart's blues band, Rocket '88, but rumours that the Stones would play prove true. A Stones' spokesman says after the show: 'The chances of the Stones getting together are 100 per cent better than they were before the gig at the 100 Club. It looks as though all the trouble seems to be sorted out. Mick and Keith both left the club with their arms around each other. The band are keen to lay bets that they'll be gigging within 18 months. A week or so ago, I would have said there was no chance at all.'

FEBRUARY 25
Jeff Baker of the *Daily Star* reports on the concert: 'The Stones [played] with the guts and energy of a teenage garage band. There was none of the super-slick, high tech sound of their recent albums. This was the Stones going back to their roots, playing muddy and dirty, ripping through old classics.
In Los Angeles, the Stones win a Lifetime Achievement Award at the American Grammy music awards. At 3.00 am London time, Eric Clapton presents the award to the Stones at the Roof Garden Club, linked via satellite with L. A. The 'Harlem Shuffle' video is shown for the first time at the awards.

MARCH 3
'Harlem Shuffle'/'Had It With You' is released on Rolling Stones Records, the first record to be distributed by CBS. 'Harlem Shuffle' is a cover of the early sixties hit credited to the songwriting team of Relf/Nelson. The B-side is by Jagger, Richards and Wood and both were recorded at the Pathe Marconi Studios in Paris. It is the first single produced jointly by Steve Lillywhite and the Glimmer Twins. The single also comes in a 12-inch version, the first side mixed in New York, the second in London.

MARCH
Copies of *Dirty Work* are stolen from a truck in New York and within hours, radio stations both in America and Europe are playing it. This forces CBS to bring the album's release forward by a day to 24 March.

MARCH 15
'Harlem Shuffle' enters the British charts at Number 30. It will stay in the charts for six weeks, its highest position being Number 7. It enters the US charts at Number 47, and will stay in the charts for fifteen weeks, peaking at Number 5.

MARCH 23
The Charlie Watts Orchestra plays at Fulham Town Hall in London. The show is recorded for a live album to be released later in the year.

MARCH 24
Dirty Work is released on Rolling Stones Records, the first album distributed by CBS. Recorded in February and June 1985 at the Pathe Marconi Studios in Paris and mixed at the RPM and Right Track Studios in New York. It is also the first album co-produced by the Glimmer Twins and Steve Lillywhite. Jagger and Richards have written three tracks; Jagger, Richards and Wood four tracks and Richards and Chuck Leavell one track. The reggae number 'Too Rude' is credited to Roberts and 'Harlem Shuffle' to Relf/Nelson.

APRIL 4
Mick returns to London from the Caribbean, to start work on the title track of Walt Disney's *Ruthless People*.

APRIL 5
Dirty Work enters the British charts at Number 12. It will stay in the charts for eleven weeks, with a highest position of Number 3.

APRIL 11
Dirty Work enters the US charts at Number 21. It stays in the charts for the 25 weeks, with a highest position of Number 4.

APRIL 15
USA Today magazine begins a three-day special on the Stones written by John Milward, headlined 'Rolling Stones Hit Rocky Times' detailing the growing rift between Mick and Keith. According to Milward, Keith has received a telegram from Mick saying he would not be touring to promote *Dirty Work* because he will be recording a solo album.

APRIL 19
The Charlie Watts Orchestra play at Ronnie Scott's Jazz Club in London, where they will be appearing for a week.

MAY 1
The Stones gather at Elstree Studios to shoot the video for their new single 'One Hit To The Body', directed by Russell Mulcahy. Mick and Keith stage an on-screen scuffle to parody the press speculation about their relationship.

MAY 19
The new single 'One Hit To The Body'/'Fight', taken from the *Dirty Work* album, is released on Rolling Stones Records. Both tracks are written by Jagger, Richards and Wood and co-produced by Steve Lillywhite and the Glimmer Twins. The single also comes in a 12-inch version.
A copy of the long-lost promo film for 'We Love You', shot in 1967, directed by Patrick Whitehead, is discovered in a barn near London.

MAY 24
The feud between Mick and Keith continues. Keith is quoted as saying: 'If Mick tours without the band I'll slit his throat.'

JUNE 2
Ron flies to New Orleans to take part in a TV special on Fats Domino. He spends the next couple of days rehearsing with Paul Shaffer and drummer Steve Jordan.

JUNE 6
No sooner does he arrive in New York from Southampton on the liner *Queen Elizabeth II*, than Keith flies on to Chicago to join Chuck Berry on stage at the blues festival in Grant Park in front of an audience of 70,000.

JUNE 7
Keith and Chuck Berry see Dr John at Billy Mulligan's in Chicago. Later they jam with Junior Wells at the Checkerboard Lounge.

JUNE 8
Keith flies from Chicago to Los Angeles and joins Etta James on stage at the Vine Street Bar for a version of 'Miss You'.

JUNE 11
A few hours after his arrival in New York from Los Angeles, Keith shoots a sequence for NBC's *Friday Night Videos*, in which he plays some Stones' classics including 'Around And Around', 'Wild Horses', 'Tumbling Dice', 'Jumpin Jack Flash' and 'Honky Tonk Woman', with Marcus Miller on bass and Paul Shaffer on guitar.

JUNE 20
Mick takes part in a concert for the Prince's Trust at the Empire Pool, Wembley, to raise funds for the young unemployed. He performs 'Dancing In The Streets' with David Bowie. Also taking part are Paul McCartney, Elton John, Phil Collins, Tina Turner, Eric Clapton. The Prince and the Princess of Wales are in the audience.

JULY 5
In London Ron joins Rod Stewart on stage at Wembley Stadium for a Faces reunion at the end of the show. Bill joins them for the grand finale. There is an audience of 60,000.

JULY 7
Ron joins Keith in Detroit at Tamla Motown's United Sound Studio to produce, and also back, Aretha Franklin's own version of 'Jumpin' Jack Flash' which will be included in her new album *Aretha*, released as a single and will be the title track of a film of the same name starring Whoopi Goldberg.

JULY 9
A promo video for 'Jumpin' Jack Flash' is shot at the United Sound Studio. Aretha, Keith, Ron, sound engineer Steve Lillywhite, Whoopi Goldberg and backing musicians are all included in the video.

JULY 12
Keith is in St Louis with Chuck Berry to discuss a film project based on Chuck's life.

JULY 15/16/17
For three consecutive nights, Ron joins Bob Dylan on stage for ten numbers at Madison Square Garden, New York.

JULY 21
Mick Jagger's single entitled 'Ruthless People'/'I'm Ringing' is released by Epic in America. The A-side was written for the Disney movie of the same name and credited to Hall, Jagger and Stewart, recorded in New York and London. The flip side is by Jagger and was recorded in London.

JULY 26
Mick Jagger celebrates his 43rd birthday with a party at home in London. Guests include Eric Clapton, Tina Turner, Sting and Nick Rhodes.

JULY 28
Patti Richards gives birth to a daughter, Alexandra Nicole, at the Lennox Hill Hospital, New York.

JULY 30
Ron and Jo Wood sell their New York house and move to London to live permanently in their new house in Wimbledon.

AUGUST 2
'Ruthless People' enters the US charts at Number 83. It only makes a highest position of Number 51, with eight weeks in the charts.

AUGUST 3
The *News of the World* runs an exclusive interview with sixteen-year-old Mandy Smith whose affair with Bill Wyman started two-and-a-half years ago when she was only thirteen. Mandy apparently feels able to tell all since she has left Bill for a man more her own age, described by the journalist Hugh Dehn as a 'penniless beach boy' named Keith. Among other 'kiss-and-tell' revelations, Mandy says: 'My mother approved of my relationship with Bill. It was an unusual one.' They apparently met at the Mayfair Disco in Tottenham (history does not relate how Bill Wyman came to be there) and later he came to dinner at the family home in Muswell Hill where Mandy and her sister thought they might set him up for their mother. Though Bill was well aware of her age he took her out anyway on a first date to Tramp for dinner with Keith and Patti Richards. She moved in with Bill 'gradually' and he paid for her to go to a private school in Kensington. As Mandy was below the legal age of consent Wyman took considerable pains to keep their affair private. 'Bill knew the risk he was taking but it didn't occur to me,' Mandy is quoted as saying.
Ingenuously admitting that she wasn't leading a normal life, she eventually gave Bill the push after finding she was being left at home on her own, excluded from his work: 'Bill is just an ordinary bloke really, but he is very conscious of his public image. In the end I just felt so lonely and it didn't seem right.'

AUGUST 9
Mick, Jerry and family arrive in Paris to spend a few weeks' holiday in Amboise.

AUGUST 20
Bill Wyman's affair with Mandy Smith is not to be pursued by the police as neither Mandy nor her 38-year-old mother have any intention of testifying against him. Scotland

Yard have questioned both several times, but Mrs Smith said that she allowed the affair to develop: she knew about it all.

AUGUST 21
The *Sun* claims Bill is sitting out the Mandy Smith scandal behind the locked gates of his French home.

AUGUST 29
Aretha Franklin's 'Jumpin' Jack Flash' is released, produced by Keith Richards and Ron Wood on Arista. The track is also included on her new album, *Aretha.* The single is also available as a 12-inch, featuring five different versions and a picture disc of Aretha and Keith.

SEPTEMBER 14
Charlie arrives in New York for a couple of days of talks to discuss a short East Coast tour for his orchestra and the release of their live album.

SEPTEMBER 15
Mick arrives in L.A. to discuss plans for his next album with Dave Stewart of the Eurythmics.

SEPTEMBER 16
While dining in a restaurant with Dave Stewart, Mick punches a photographer who tries to take a picture.

SEPTEMBER 26
A commercial videocassette of Mick, entitled *Running Out Of Luck,* is released a year late by CBS-Fox Video.

SEPTEMBER 27
Aretha Franklin's 'Jumpin' Jack Flash' enters the US charts at Number 61. It stays in the charts for eleven weeks, with a highest position of Number 21.

OCTOBER 6
Bill finally returns to London from the South of France.

OCTOBER 8
Keith arrives in St Louis for a further week of rehearsals with Chuck Berry at his house in Wentzville on the outskirts of St Louis. Other members of the band include Chuck Leavell on keyboards, Bobby Keys on sax, Steve Jordan on drums, Johnny Johnson on piano and Joey Spampinato on bass.

OCTOBER 16
Chuck Berry celebrates his 60th birthday with two concerts at the Fox Theater in St Louis. Footage of both shows will be included in a film tribute to Chuck Berry called *Hail! Hail! Rock'n'Roll,* directed by Taylor Hackford, with Keith Richards as musical director. Anita Pallenberg and Marlon Richards are in the audience.

NOVEMBER
ABKCO Records re-releases the first fifteen Stones' albums originally released on London Records. They have been digitally remastered and are also available on CD. *Beggars Banquet* now appears with its original 'toilet' sleeve. CBS are distributing a promo CD for radio stations, featuring tracks previously released in the Stones' Atlantic Records period.

NOVEMBER 15
Mick starts recording his new solo album at the Wisseloord Studio in Hilversum, Holland, with Jeff Beck and Omar Hakim.

NOVEMBER 23
Keith joins Eric Clapton on stage at the Ritz, New York, for 'Cocaine' and 'Layla'.

NOVEMEBER 27
As Keith flies back to Jamaica, Charlie and his 33-member orchestra arrive in New York to play eight dates on the East Coast.

NOVEMBER 29
The Charlie Watts Orchestra plays its first American date at the West Hartford Music Hall, Connecticut.

DECEMBER 1
The Charlie Watts Orchestra's first album *Live At Fulham Town Hall,* is released on Columbia in the UK and US. The Orchestra plays in Philadelphia.

DECEMBER 2
Stomping at the Ritz in New York with the Charlie Watts Orchestra.

DECEMBER 3
The Charlie Watts Orchestra play a second night at the Ritz. Keith arrives from Jamaica.

DECEMBER 4
Keith goes to the Charlie Watts Orchestra's final show at the Ritz.

DECEMBER 13
Mick finishes working at the Wisseloord Studio for the time being; he has recorded about seven tracks for his solo album.

DECEMBER 18
Keith spends his 43rd birthday in Jamaica with Patti and the children, after which the family flies to New York.

DECEMBER 21
Mick and Jerry fly to Mustique. David Bowie will join them after Christmas.

The Stones in unusually relaxed mood during the shooting of a video for 'One Hit To The Body'. Tension between Mick and Keith was said to be at its height at this time.

JANUARY 6
Mick and Jerry leave Mustique and fly to Barbardos so that Mick can continue working on the album.

JANUARY 21
Jerry Hall is arrested at the Grantley Adams Airport in Barbados and charged with importing 20 pounds of marijuana. She had gone to the airport to collect clothes and make-up forwarded from Mustique. An employee of Mustique Airways said another small packet had arrived at their desk for her but it was not labelled. When she suggested that it was opened to make sure it was hers, it was found to contain marijuana.
Local police and customs officials hold her in a cell overnight and Mick is not told of her arrest until six hours later. Jerry is eventually released on bail of $5,000, paid by Mick. She categorically denies that the marijuana belongs to her or that she knows anything about it. A trial is set for 13 February and she is ordered to surrender her passport and report to Holetown police station twice a week until then. Mick engages a top Barbadian lawyer, Elliott Mottley, and Jerry's New York lawyer, Peter Partcher, is summoned and is expected to arrive in a matter of hours to advise on the case.

FEBRUARY 13
Jerry Hall appears in court. Witnesses back up her claim to innocence. The trial is adjourned to 16 February.

FEBRUARY 16
Jerry's trial is resumed in front of Barbados Magistrate Frank King. During a seven-hour hearing the prosecution's flimsy case against her is torn apart when Customs Supervisor Casper Walcott admits that he previously lied to the court. After close questioning from the defence, during which he changes crucial items of evidence several times, he admits that he had been asked specifically by detectives to look out for the package containing marijuana and it seems clear that Jerry was being 'ambushed' by the police and customs officers. Mr Walcott denies that when charged with importing the drug Jerry said to him 'Is this some kind of sick joke?' The case seems certain to be thrown out, but Jerry Hall bursts into tears when the Magistrate decides to adjourn for another two days to consider the 'complicated legal arguments' before delivering his verdict.

FEBRUARY 20
Jerry Hall is in court again to hear Magistrate Frank King's verdict. She has to endure an eight-minute summing up before he finally pronounces her 'Not Guilty'. She states that her enforced 31-day stay in Barbados has cost her £130,000 in modelling assignments. Immediately after the hearing she and Mick fly back to New York.

FEBRUARY 23
Jerry tells a New York TV chat show that she and Mick will soon marry. Rumours suggest it will happen in Texas within the next three weeks with either Keith Richards or Chris Jagger as best man. Meanwhile Mick continues to work on his solo album at the Right Track Studio in New York, while Keith enters Studio 900 to work on what will eventually be his first solo album. Meanwhile, in London Ron Wood is also working on his solo album in the basement of his house in Wimbledon.

MARCH 3
According to an interview in the *Sun* Keith and Mick are at each other's throats again, because Mick has decided on a solo tour. He Keith, who is apparently determined to keep the Stones going, says: 'I'm not sure when it all started to go wrong. Up until the beginning of the eighties you could have called me up at the North Pole and Mick at the South Pole and we would have said the same thing. We were that close. I didn't change but he did. He became obsessed with age – his own and others. I don't see the point of pretending that you are 25 when you're not.

MARCH 20
Bill Wyman has his say about Mick and the Stones' possible split in an interview on the satellite TV service, *Music Box*: 'Mick is the guilty one. He has decided to do his own thing and be famous in his own right... It's a pity we didn't go out with a big bang. Instead we went out with a whimper... I don't know if we will ever go back on the road. That depends on the glamour twins,

Mick and Keith Richards, becoming friendly again. They're the problem.'

APRIL 1
Bill, and Mandy Smith in a separate party, Jerry Hall and Bianca Jagger, also in separate parties, are all in the audience at the International AIDS Day concert at Wembley Arena in London.

APRIL 8
On the last night of recording his solo album in Studio 900, Keith, along with Ian Neville and drummers Steve Jordan and Charley Drayton, has to vacate the recording studio on 19th Street with some of their equipment, due to heavy smoke and fire in the building. They jam in the street until the fire service arrives.

APRIL 12
Keith and his family, including his mother Doris and his daughter Angela, who has changed her name from Dandelion, fly to Jamaica for a two-month holiday.

APRIL 13
At a press conference at the Champagne Exchange in London, Bill announces his AIMS project (Ambition, Ideas, Motivation, Success). He plans to take the Stones' mobile studio around Britain to give unknown local bands the opportunity to record their music and break into show-biz. Bill will produce the bands for free, and will forego any percentage from subsequent record sales.

MAY
Ron Wood has issued a writ for libel against the *Sun* newspaper, over an article alleging that he spent the night with a girl he picked up in a London nightclub. Ron says: 'Usually I just laugh about things that are written about me, but this time things have gone too far. I have never even met this girl, let alone gone to bed with her. Anyway my writ number is 13/13, which I think will prove to be doubly unlucky for them.'

MAY 26
Ron and Jo leave London to spend nine days in Italy where Ron will interview several rock stars, including Prince, David Bowie, Peter Gabriel and Genesis, for Italian RAI-TV.

MAY 27
Keith arrives in Los Angeles from Jamaica for a conference with Virgin in relation to both his solo deal and the *Hail! Hail! Rock'n'Roll* soundtrack.

JUNE 13
The Charlie Watts Orchestra plays at the Hollywood Bowl during the Playboy Jazz Festival.

JUNE 14
The Charlie Watts Orchestra plays another

Going it alone. Left: *Mick's 1987 solo singles.* Above: *Keith tells all (again) to* Rolling Stone. Top: *Charlie doing what he likes best – on stage with the Charlie Watts Orchestra.*

date at the Hollywood Bowl. In New York Keith finishes mixing *Hail! Hail! Rock'n'Roll* at the Electric Lady Studios. The album will be released in the autumn.

JUNE 23
The Charlie Watts Orchestra plays at the Avery Fisher Hall in New York. Keith, Patti and Mick Taylor are in the audience.

JULY 4
The Charlie Watts Orchestra plays at the Pistoia Blues Festival in Italy.

JULY 13
Keith meets Richard Branson at the Westbury Hotel in New York, to talk about the Virgin deal.

JULY 15
All the Stones, apart from Keith, attend a fund-raising banquet for AIMS, organised by Bill at the Hilton Hotel in London.

JULY 17
Keith Richards signs his first ever solo deal, with Virgin Records in New York. His album will be released next year.

JULY 20/23
Mick shoots the video for his next single 'Let's Work' in a Manhattan studio, directed by Zbigniew Rybczynski.

JULY 27/28
Mick shoots another video, in London this time for 'Say You Will', directed by Mary Lambert.

AUGUST 22
The *Sun* reports that Mick's projected tour, due to start in October, is to be shelved due to a row with Jeff Beck. A spokeman for Mick says: 'He had been rehearsing for the tour for a month. Jeff is well known for being difficult to work with and tempers finally snapped. But the tour has been postponed because Jeff is a brilliant guitarist and will be very hard to replace. It now looks like the tour will go ahead in the New Year.'

AUGUST 29
After a couple of weeks at Le Studio, Keith and Patti leave Montreal, driving back to New York.

AUGUST 31
Mick Jagger's new single, 'Let's Work'/'Catch As Catch Can' is released on CBS. Side One is written and produced by Mick Jagger and Dave Stewart. The flip side is written and produced by Mick alone.
Mick and Jerry are at Dave Stewart's marriage to Siobhan of Bananarama at the Chateau of Dangu.

SEPTEMBER 7
Mick and Dave Stewart work on new material at Stewart's house in London.

SEPTEMBER 9
Mick records 'Let's Work' for future transmission on BBC 1's *Top of the Pops* in London.

SEPTEMBER 12
'Let's Work' enters the US charts at Number 75. It will stay in the charts for nine weeks with a highest position of Number 39.

SEPTEMBER 14
Mick's new solo album, *Primitive Cool*, is released on CBS. Recorded at Wisseloord Studios, Holland, and at the Blue Wave Studios in Barbados, Mick has written seven tracks and three are jointly written with Dave Stewart. Mixed at the Right Track Studios in New York, production credits are variously Jagger, Jagger and Keith Diamond, Jagger and David Stewart.

SEPTEMBER 19
'Let's Work' enters the UK charts at Number 35, its highest position.

SEPTEMBER 25
Bill attends the opening of La Brasserie nightclub in Atlanta, Georgia, in which he has invested – as has Ringo Starr. Later he and Ringo jam with Jerry Lee Lewis.

SEPTEMBER 26
Primitive Cool enters the UK charts at Number 23. It will stay in the charts for five weeks, with a highest position of Number 18.

SEPTEMBER 27
The News of the World in London claims that tracks on Mick's album, such as 'Kow Tow' and 'Shoot Off Your Mouth', are aimed at Keith as part of their long-running feud. A spokesman is quoted as saying: 'Mick is very bitter about the row with Keith. He's had a real go at Keith and hopes he listens to the album and realises the significance.'

OCTOBER 3
Hail! Hail! Rock'n'Roll is premiered at the New York Film Festival in the Lincoln Center. Keith and Chuck Berry are there.
Primitive Cool enters the US charts at Number 81. It will stay in the charts for 20 weeks, but only makes Number 41.

OCTOBER 7
Keith and Patti are in Hollywood for the West Coast premiere of *Hail! Hail! Rock'n'Roll* at the AMC Century.

OCTOBER 20
At the County Club in Los Angeles, in front of an audience of fans who won tickets through a radio competition, Mick Jagger is videotaped live on stage for his next single, 'Throwaway', directed by Mary Lambert. Backing him are Jeff Beck on guitar, Terry Bozie on drums, Doug Wimbish on bass, Phil Ashley on keyboards and three women backing singers.

OCTOBER 29
Ronnie opens a three-week exhibition of his paintings called 'Decades', at the Katherine Hamnett Gallery in association with Christie's Contemporary Art. For each decade he has produced signed, limited edition lithographs of legendary musicians of the last 30 years.

OCTOBER 31
Ron flies to Miami for the opening of his entertainment complex, Woody's On The Beach, which includes a restaurant, art gallery and nightclub.

NOVEMBER 4
Ron and Bo Diddley open a North American tour in Columbus, Ohio, at the Newport Music Hall. Known as the Gunslingers' tour, the itinerary takes in Detroit, Toronto, Cleveland, Boston, Monroeville, Providence, Washington, Raleigh, Chicago and New York. In Memphis and Dallas Charlie Sexton replaces Diddley. All are small venues, the largest capacity is Chicago's Riviera with a capacity of 2,500.
The *Sun* follows up the Jagger/Beck row with Jeff's side of the story: 'I quit the tour because Mick only offered me peanuts to play with him. It was laughable, an insult. I wanted to teach him a lesson because I believe if you want the best you have to pay for it. The kind of money he offered is what you pay an ordinary session musician. Mick's problem is that he's a meanie. He is no better than a glorified accountant. He counts every single penny. For someone with his money, I can't believe how tight he is... I'd still love to go on tour with the old geezer. He's just got to make me a proper offer. To show there's no hard feelings, I went to Los Angeles with him to film the video for his next single ''Throwaway''.'

NOVEMBER 9
Another Jagger single 'Throwaway'/'Peace Of The Wicked' is released on CBS in America and Britain. Elsewhere in Europe, 'Say You Will'/'Shut Up Your Mouth' is released instead.

NOVEMBER 14
CBS Records re-release the whole Stones back catalogue.

NOVEMBER 25
Ron and Bo Diddley play the final date of their American tour at the Ritz in New York, where they are joined on stage by former Temptations, Eddie Kendricks and David Ruffin.

DECEMBER 19
Ron and Bo Diddley play at the official opening of Woody's On The Beach, in Miami.

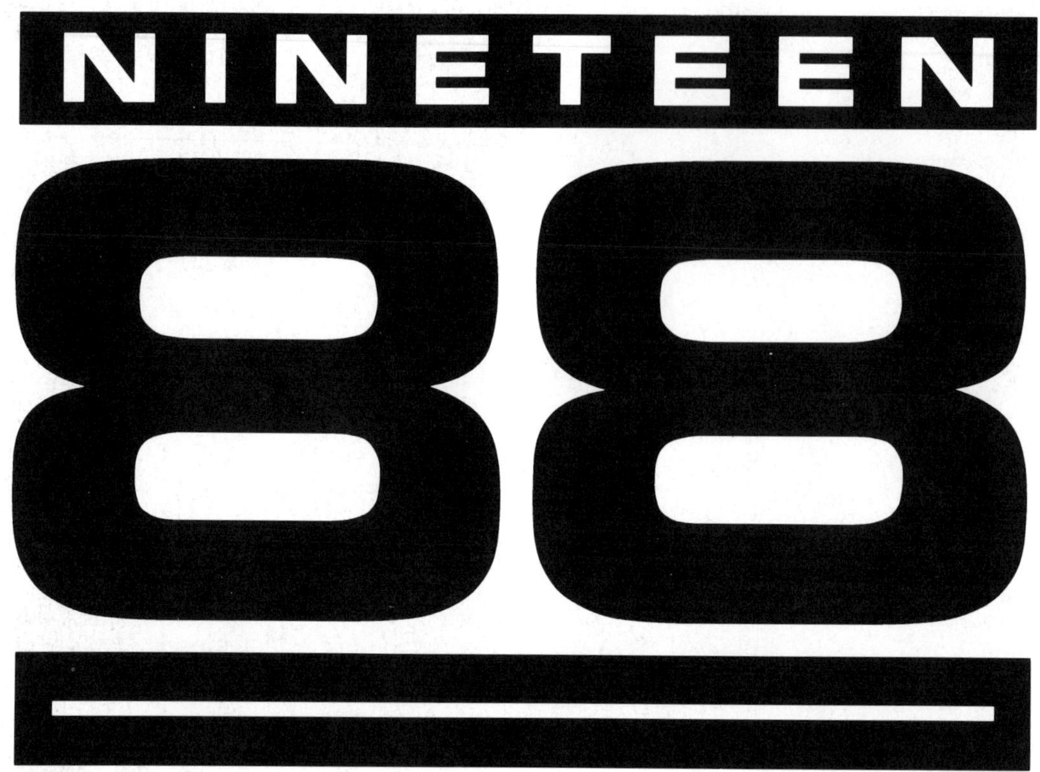

JANUARY 7/8
Mick Taylor plays at Woody's On The Beach, and Ron joins him on stage.

JANUARY 20
Mick is at the annual Rock'n'Roll Hall of Fame held at the Waldorf Astoria in New York where he introduces the section on the Beatles (he calls them the 'four-headed monster'), and joins George Harrison and Bruce Springsteen on stage for 'I Saw Her Standing There'. Ringo, George and John's sons Julian and Sean are also there. Mick then joins Bob Dylan and Bruce Springsteen for 'Like A Rolling Stone' and, backed by Jeff Beck on guitar, takes the stage solo for 'Satisfaction'.

FEBRUARY
Mick and his band, featuring Phil Ashley and Richard Cottle on keyboards, Simon Phillips on drums, Joe Satriani and Jimmy Ripp on guitar, Doug Wimbish on bass, plus backing singers, start rehearsals at the SIR studios in New York.

FEBRUARY 14
In the *People* Bill says: 'I gave up watching *Top Of The Pops* when I discovered the noise of traffic in the King's Road was a lot more entertaining. I'd rather sit outside a pub and listen to that. You know most of the groups aren't really singing or playing. They're miming and there's every chance they didn't even play on their own record. These days that's done by somebody else. The last thing you need worry about is how well you can play. All you have to do well is act at being a pop star. Songwriters, session musicians, synthesisers and pre-recorded tapes take care of all the real work. Our record companies have actually gone backwards in the last ten years. They used to promote original groups who became world-famous. Now they churn out stuff which is either extremely monotonous or indistinguishable from the dross you hear in American supermarkets.'

FEBRUARY 20
At the Royal Albert Hall, Bill, Ron, Phil Collins, Kenny Jones, Eddy Grant, Ian Dury, Chris Rea and Elvis Costello take part in a benefit show organised by Bill Wyman for the Great Ormond Street Hospital for Sick Children's Wishing Well Appeal. Terence Trent d'Arby sings 'Honky Tonk Women' and 'It's All Over Now', sparking rumours that he will replace Mick in the Stones.

MARCH 1
It is reported that Mick will earn £1 million per night during his short solo tour of Japan. All tickets for the Tokyo Dome were sold the day the tour was announced.

MARCH 2
Ron Wood and Bo Diddley – the Gunslingers – start a two-week Japanese tour.

MARCH 12
At the same time as Ron is playing in Osaka, Mick is there rehearsing. The two meet up in Mick's hotel bedroom.

MARCH 15
As Ron and Bo Diddley play their last Japanese date in Tokyo, Mick plays his first ever concert in Japan at the Osaka Castle Hall in front of 11,000 fans.

MARCH 16
Mick's second concert at the Osaka Castle Hall.

MARCH 18
Back in the USA, the Gunslingers play at the Los Angeles Palace. Meanwhile Mick again plays at the Osaka Castle Hall.

MARCH 19
Mick has another concert in Osaka.

MARCH 22
Mick plays at the Tokyo Kerakuen Dome in front of an audience of 55,000.

MARCH 23
Mick has another concert at the Kerakuen Dome. Tina Turner joins him on stage for a duet of 'Brown Sugar' and 'It's Only Rock'n'Roll'.

MARCH 25
Mick completes his Japanese tour at the Nagoya International Exhibition. Over a quarter of a million Japanese fans have seen

him and offers from Australian and America promotors are rumoured to be the highest ever.

MARCH 26
The Gunslingers' final concert is held at the Magic Mountain Amusement Park, L.A.

MARCH 27
Now it is Mick's turn to guest for Tina Turner during her show at the Osaka Castle Hall for a duet this time of 'Honky Tonk Women'.
Ron visits an exhibition of his paintings in Sherman Oaks. In the UK, the *New Musical Express* reports that Australian entrepreneur Gunter Roth has offered $20 million for Mick Jagger's ashes when he dies, to make egg-timers for his millionaire fans.

APRIL 6
An extremely rare three-track Rolling Stones single, recorded in October 1962, of Muddy Waters' 'Soon Forgotten', Jimmy Reed's 'Close Together' and Bo Diddley's 'You Can't Judge A Book' sells for £6,000 at Phillips Auction Rooms in London. The tracks, which are contained in an EMI disc acetate, were recorded at Curly Clayton's studio in London with Tony Chapman as drummer. During the past few weeks Bill has taken legal action to try to prevent the sale.

APRIL
Jamaican reggae musician Patrick Alley pursues his action against Mick Jagger, accusing him of copyright infringement with the song 'Just Another Night', which Alley claims he wrote in 1979 and which featured on his album *Just A Touch of Patrick Alley*, released in 1982. He claims Jagger has copied both words and music and is suing Mick and CBS for an estimated $7 million in profits from the 1985 album, *She's The Boss*. Jagger strongly denies the charges. Court proceedings will begin at White Plains Federal Court, New York State in a couple of weeks.

APRIL 18
Mick is in court as proceedings open at White Plains Federal Court, New York.

APRIL 20
Drummer Sly Dunbar, who played on *She's the Boss*, brings his drums to the court as testimony. Patrick Alley says Dunbar also played on *his* record. Dunbar says: 'It's possible I played on the record, or it could be someone copying me.' He plays the drums in court, to the recordings, adding that the beat is not the same on each.

APRIL 22
Mick sings various songs in court and plays tapes to show the development of his song, 'Just Another Night'.

APRIL 26
Mick Jagger is cleared of copyright infringement with 'Just Another Night'. He says: 'My reputation is really cleared. If you're well known, people stand up and take shots at you. But the trial was a bit of a waste of time for everyone.'

MAY 13
Mick prevents Jade from appearing in a film in the role of a young prostitute.

MAY 18
For the first time since May 1986, all five Rolling Stones meet at the Savoy Hotel, London, to discuss future plans and agree to start working again next year, recording an album and possibly undertaking a major world tour.

JUNE 10
The *Sun* reports that Bill Wyman is abandoning his AIMS scheme after Pernod pulled out from sponsorship and no other sponsors have stepped in. He says: 'All the firms are really mean. I just wanted to give some youngsters a break.'

JUNE 28
The Gunslingers play a concert at the Hammersmith Odeon in London before embarking on a string of concert dates in Italy, Germany and Spain.

JULY 22
The British book trade weekly reports: 'Viking Penguin and Viking/NAL in the US have secured world English Language rights in the autobiography of Rolling Stone Bill Wyman... Penguin are not prepared to reveal the size of the advance, but concede that it is substantial; the total figure could well be close to £3 million.'

JULY 26
Mick attends Jerry's first night as Cherie in *Bus Stop*, the role made famous on screen by Marilyn Monroe, at the Montclair Stage College Theater in New Jersey. Later they celebrate her success and his 45th birthday at the Ten Park Restaurant.

JULY 29
Ron and Bo Diddley finish their European tour.

AUGUST 19
Mick flies to London and continues work with Ron on new material.

AUGUST 22
As he leaves Heathrow en route for New York, Mick tells the press the Stones will get together next year for a new album and a tour. Meanwhile in a *Rolling Stone* magazine survey, 25 top American critics vote 'Satisfaction' the best single of the last 25 years.

AUGUST 23
Mick and Keith meet in New York to discuss future plans. Ron and Jo and family arrive in Antigua for a two-week holiday.

AUGUST 24
Mick flies to San Francisco to rehearse with his band for the forthcoming Australian tour.

SEPTEMBER 9
Mick and his band arrive in Sydney from San Francisco.

SEPTEMBER 14
At a press conference in Sydney, Mick says he will retire from touring when he is 50. He says: 'You can't be nineteen for ever. I'll just want to sit back in a chair.'

SEPTEMBER 17
Mick plays a surprise gig at the Kardomah Cafe in Sydney, before an audience of 400.

SEPTEMBER 22
More interviews for Keith in Paris, while Mick opens his Australasian tour in Brisbane at the Boondall Entertainment Centre.

SEPTEMBER 23
Keith's solo single 'Take It So Hard'/'I Could Have Stood You Up', written and produced by Keith and Steve Jordan, is released on Virgin. It is taken from his forthcoming album, *Talk Is Cheap*.
Mick gives another concert in Brisbane.

SEPTEMBER 26
Mick plays at the Sydney Entertainment Centre.

SEPTEMBER 27
Mick plays a second concert at the Sydney Entertainment Centre.

SEPTEMBER 29
Anita Pallenberg, Marlon and Chris Jagger attend a party thrown by Ron Wood at the Hamilton Gallery in London, for the British publication of his book *The Works*. He also shows six new paintings of the Stones.
In Australia, Mick has a third show at the Sydney Entertainment Centre.

OCTOBER 1/2
Mick plays two more dates at the Sydney Entertainment Centre.

OCTOBER 4
Keith Richards' first solo album *Talk Is Cheap* is released on Virgin. All tracks are written and produced by Keith Richards and Steve Jordan. Recorded at the Air Studios, Montserrat, Le Studio in Montreal, Studio 900 and Hit Factory in New York; it was mastered at Atlantic Studios and the Hit Factory in New York.

OCTOBER 5/6
Keith and his band, known as the X-Pensive Winos, (Steve Jordan on drums, Charley

Drayton on bass, Ivan Neville on keyboards and Waddy Wachtel on guitar), rehearse at the American Sound Studio in New York.

OCTOBER 6
In *Rolling Stone* Keith says: 'Mick's and my battles are not exactly as perceived through the press or other people. They're far more convoluted, because we've known each other for most of our lives – I mean, since we were four or five. So they involve a lot more subtleties and ins and outs than can possibly be explained. But I think there is on Mick's part a bit of a Peter Pan complex. It's a hard job, being the frontman. In order to do it, you've got to think in a way that you're semi-divine… Last month or so I've been in touch with the other Stones. Mick suddenly called up, and the rest of them: "Let's put the Stones back together." I'm thinking, I'm just in the middle of an album. Now what are you trying to do? Screw me up? Just now you want to talk about putting it back together? But we talked about it. I went to London and we had a meeting… I love Mick. Most of my efforts with Mick go to trying to open his eyes: "You don't need to do this, You have no problem, all you need to do is just grow up with it."… I tip my hat to Mick a lot. I admire the guy enormously. In the seventies, when I was on dope and I would do nothing but put the songs together and turn up and not deal with any of the business of the Stones, Mick took all of that work on his shoulders and did it all and covered my ass. And I've always admired him very much for that. I mean, he did exactly what a friend should do. When I cleaned up and *Emotional Rescue* time came around – "Hey I'm back, I'm clean, I'm ready; I'm back to help and take some of the weight off your shoulders" – immediately I got a sense of resentment. Whereas I felt that he would be happy to unburden himself of some of that shit, he felt that I was homing in and trying to take control. And that's when I first sensed the feeling of discontent, shall we say. It wasn't intended like that from my point of view, but that's when I first got a feeling that he got so used to running the show that there was no way he was going to give it up.'

OCTOBER 6/7
Mick plays two shows at the International Tennis Centre in Melbourne.

OCTOBER 10/11
Mick gives two concerts at the Burswood Superdome in Perth, Western Australia.

OCTOBER 14/15
Mick gives two concerts at the International Tennis Centre in Melbourne again.

OCTOBER 16
While in London to promote his album, Keith, whose own home in Jamaica was damaged by the recent hurricane, plays at the Smile Jamaica concert in aid of Hurricane victims.

OCTOBER 17
Mick plays another date at the International Tennis Centre, Melbourne.

OCTOBER 19
Jerry Hall says in *Today*: 'The Stones don't take drugs any more. They can't. They're too old.'

OCTOBER 21
Mick plays at the Sydney Entertainment Centre.

OCTOBER 22
Talk Is Cheap enters the US charts at Number 75. It will stay in the charts for nineteen weeks, with a highest position of Number 24.

OCTOBER 28
At the Hard Rock Cafe, Keith announces his own US tour with the X-Pensive Winos, to start next month. All 4,000 seats at the Beacon Theater in New York sell out in a matter of hours.

OCTOBER 30
Mick gives a concert at the Stadion Utama Senayan in Jakarta, Indonesia.

NOVEMBER 3
Keith goes to a party at U.S. Blues club in New York to help celebrate the tenth anniversary of *Beggars Banquet*, the Rolling Stones' official fanzine.

NOVEMBER 5
Mick finishes his Australasian tour at the Western Spring Stadium in Auckland, New Zealand, and flies to London.
In L.A., Vivid Productions are putting together a video of tracks from *Primitive Cool.* In addition to recent footage of the Australian concerts and other live performances at Marin County, California, the video includes shots of the young Jagger, former US President Richard Nixon and the Vietnam War.

NOVEMBER 9
Ron plays with Jerry Lee Lewis at Woody's On The Beach, David Bowie is in the audience.

NOVEMBER 10
Keith and Patti spend a week in Antigua.

NOVEMBER
In *Options* magazine Keith says: 'I can't forget that I am English. But it still pisses me off that they kicked us out of our own country. We didn't have the sort of money they were asking for, so we left. What really fascinated me was that they really thought three Herberts with guitars were a threat to the social structure of the country…

NOVEMBER 16
At the High Court in London, Ron Wood receives undisclosed libel damages and a public apology from the publishers of newspaper reports that he cheated on his wife with a model half his age.

NOVEMBER 24
Keith and the X-Pensive Winos open their US tour at the Fox Theater in Atlanta, with an audience of 4,000. The line-up apart from Keith is Steve Jordan, Charley Drayton (bass and drums), Waddy Wachtel (guitar), Ivan Neville (keyboards), Bobby Keys (saxophone) and Sarah Dash (back-up vocals).

NOVEMBER 25
Keith's band play at the New Display Club, Memphis, the smallest venue with an audience of less than 1,000.

NOVEMBER 27
X-Pensive Winos concert at Constitution Hall, Washington, D.C.

NOVEMBER 29
X-Pensive Winos concert at Beacon Theater, New York.

DECEMBER 1/2
X-Pensive Winos concert at the Tower Theater, Philadelphia.

DECEMBER 3
X-Pensive Winos concerts at the Orpheum Theater, Boston.

DECEMBER 4
Second X-Pensive Winos concert at the Orpheum Theater, Boston. Mick, Jerry and the children leave London to spend Christmas in Mustique.

DECEMBER 7
X-Pensive Winos concert at the Music Hall, Cleveland.

DECEMBER 8
X-Pensive Winos concert at the Fox Theater, Detroit.

DECEMBER 10
X-Pensive Winos concert at the Aragon Ballroom, Chicago.

DECEMBER 13
X-Pensive Winos concert at the Kaiser Auditorium, San Francisco.

DECEMBER 14
X-Pensive Winos concert at the Universal Auditorium, L.A.

DECEMBER 15
X-Pensive Winos concert at the Hollywood Palladium, L.A.

DECEMBER 17
The X-Pensive Winos finish their American tour at the Brendan Byrne Arena in New Jersey, in front of 22,000 fans.

JANUARY 13
Mick and Keith meet in Barbados to plan the new Stones' album. The *Daily Mirror* reports that bass players Adam Clayton of U2, John Entwistle of the Who and Mark King of Level 42 are secretly being head-hunted to join the Rolling Stones. The band are being honoured at the Hall of Fame ceremony at the Waldorf Astoria on 18 January but are prevented from playing as Bill is refusing to go. He says that the Award is 'too little, too late', so Ron is delegated to recruit a substitute bassist for the occasion.

JANUARY 16
Ron opens an exhibition of his paintings which will run for two weeks at the Hamilton Gallery in London.

JANUARY 17
Mick and Keith arrive in New York from Barbados while Ron flies in from London.

JANUARY 18
The Rolling Stones are inducted into the Rock'n'Roll Hall of Fame at the Waldorf Astoria in New York. Mick, Keith, Ron and Mick Taylor are there on behalf of the band. The names of Brian Jones and Ian Stewart are also included in the citation. Mick says: 'It's slightly ironic that tonight you see us on our best behaviour, but we've been awarded for 25 years of bad behaviour... we're not quite ready to hang up the number yet.' Paying tribute to Brian Jones he says: 'His individuality and musicianship often took us off the bluesy course, but with some marvellous results.' And of Ian Stewart: 'He was a friend, a great blues pianist, whose invaluable musical advice kept us on a steady and bluesy course most of the time.' In his induction speech, Pete Townshend of the Who says: 'Guys, whatever you do, don't grow old gracefully.' The evening continues with Mick joining Stevie Wonder for a medley of 'Uptight'/'Satisfaction', followed by a duet with Tina Turner of 'Honky Tonk Women' with Keith, Ron and Mick Taylor on guitar. The set continues with 'Can't Turn You Loose' and 'Bony Maronie', both with Little Richard, and the four Stones finish with 'Start Me Up'. The absence of Bill Wyman and the presence of Mick Taylor fuels the usual rumours that the former Stone will soon rejoin the band, with Ron replacing Bill on bass.

JANUARY 19
Charlie Watts joins Mick, Keith and Ron for talks in New York.

JANUARY 21
Ron plays at one of the Presidential Inauguration parties for President-Elect George Bush, in the Convention Center in Washington, D.C. Ron joins Percy Sledge, Bo Diddley, Willie Dixon and Koko Taylor. Later George Bush puts in an appearance faking guitar on stage, for a jam session featuring Ron, Billy Preston, Albert Collins and Steve Cropper.

FEBRUARY 9
Keith shoots a video at the North River Bar in New York with members of the Memphis Horns, Charley Drayton, Sarah Dash and Steve Jordan, for his new single, 'Make No Mistake'/'Struggle', about to be released on Virgin, taken from his solo album.

FEBRUARY 18
Bill plays at the Kampuchea Appeal concert at Ringwood Recreation Centre near Southampton. Promoters Bill Graham and Michael Cohl fly to Barbados to discuss the forthcoming American tour with Mick, Keith, the Stones' financial advisor Prince Rupert Lowenstein, their US business manager Joseph Rascoff and American attorney John Branca.

FEBRUARY 20
Charlie joins Mick and Keith in Barbados.

MARCH 9
Bill and Ron join the others in Barbados.
The *Daily Express* reports that Jade Jagger is in court as a witness in connection with a cocaine pushing case. It is claimed in court that she took cocaine with Lord Kagan's son, Josh Astor. They were apparently supplied by Thompson Twins' drummer, Julian Subero, who is described as the 'ringleader of the conspiracy'.

MARCH 15
In Barbados, the Rolling Stones sign the most lucrative rock contract in history, with Toronto promoter Michael Cohl, chief of Concert Productions International (CPI). He will promote the tour and handle the merchandising through his company Brockum. He will also oversee a multi-million dollar sponsorship deal, plus a pay-per-view television special. Cohl has guaranteed the Stones a staggering $65-$70 million and the band will play an estimated 50 to 60 dates across the US and Canada, starting next September.

MARCH 19
According to the *News of the World* Mick and Bill have fallen out because Bill has been dating one of Jade Jagger's seventeen-year-old girlfriends. However this time Keith acts as go-between and patches up the quarrel to save the forthcoming tour. Later Bill will say: 'Complete fabrication! I only vaguely know Jade. Me and Mick both wrote very strong legal letters to that paper.'

MARCH 28
The *International Herald Tribune* reports that Mick and Jerry are to receive damages from the *People* which published photographs of them nude in the bathroom. The paper has apologised, admitting it breached the couple's copyright, but has not disclosed the amount of damages it will pay.

MARCH 29
The Stones move from Barbados to Montserrat to start recording the new album at Air Studios.

MARCH 31
In the *Daily Express,* Mandy Smith announces that Bill has asked her to marry him. She is now 19, he is 52. She gushes: 'Bill asked me to marry him on Easter Sunday and I accepted immediately. It was really romantic. I'm delighted and so is he.' The proposal came in a phone call from Barbados, where Bill is recording with the Stones.
Bill's former long-time partner Astrid Lundstrom refuses to believe it. She says: 'I know he has no plans to get married and certainly not to that girl.' Astrid and Bill split up in 1983 after she had a total of six miscarriages.

APRIL 1
At a press conference in Antigua, Bill Wyman officially announces that he and Mandy will definitely be getting married.

APRIL 2
Bill returns to Montserrat to continue working on the new album.

APRIL 3
The *Daily Express* reveals more 'heart-rending' complications about Bill's forthcoming marriage. He says: 'Mandy is a Catholic and I am Church of England and she desperately wants the ceremony in June in a Catholic church: a white wedding with all the trimmings. But everywhere she has gone they have said "No," because I am divorced. Surely there is a Catholic church somewhere in Britain who will make Mandy's dream come true.' The Stones appear delighted at the news. Mick says: 'Love has no boundaries and I wish them every happiness for their future together.' Best man at the wedding will be Bill's 28-year-old son Stephen, from his first marriage.

APRIL 29
The Stones finish recording the new album at Air Studios in Montserrat, where they have cut sixteen new tracks. They plan to mix the new material in London next month. The Montserrat sessions have been documented on film for inclusion in a TV special, directed by Lorne Michael, called *The Return Of The Rolling Stones,* to be broadcast during the tour.

MAY 6
It is reported that Bill has bought Mandy a £30,000 engagement ring at Asprey's of Bond Street.

MAY 9
A party is held for the opening of Bill Wyman's restaurant, Sticky Fingers, in Kensington, London. In addition to Bill and his bride-to-be, other guests include Ron and Jo Wood, Chris Jagger, James Hunt, Barbara Bach, and Emma Samms. The restaurant, which is decorated with Stones memorabilia, including gold discs and Brian Jones' Gretsch guitar, will open to the public on 17 May. Speaking to the press, Bill says he will definitely marry in June and that the church is already booked. He says: 'It's not a matter of age, it's how you feel and we are very much in love. History is full of older men who have had successful marriages with younger women. When Picasso got married he was 94 and his wife was 37, and that marriage lasted. There is no reason why ours shouldn't be the same.
Meanwhile sceptics say the engagement ring cost nearer £2,000 than £30,000.

MAY 13
It is revealed that Bill and Mandy will get

Above: *Mick and Keith, now the best of friends, at the 1989 Hall of Fame induction ceremony at the Waldorf Hotel in New York.*

married on 5 June at St John the Evangelist Church in Hyde Park Crescent, followed by a reception at the Grosvenor House Hotel.

MAY
In mid-May the Stones, and co-producer/sound engineer Chris Kimsey, start mixing the new album at the Olympic Studios in Barnes, London. Meanwhile in America, dates are being scheduled across both the US and Canada for the massive tour which will open in September and last until Christmas or even later, if there is sufficient demand. They will play a special pay-per-view cable TV concert at the end of the tour which will be broadcast from a smallish venue. It seems the Stones plan to play smaller club dates as well as big stadiums. To market and promote the new album, the Stones have hired leaders in the field Cliff Burnstein and Peter Mensch who will also work as consultants for the tour. Rumours circulating in Canada suggest the Labatt Company may offer another $45 million to sponsor the Canadian dates.

MAY 17
The *Sun* reports a 5am drunken brawl in Amsterdam during which Charlie Watts knocks Mick out with a single punch. It happened after Mick woke Charlie up by shouting: 'Is that my drummer boy? Why don't you get your arse down here!'
A few minutes later furious Charlie walked up to Mick and yelled: 'Don't ever call me your drummer again – you're my fucking singer.' Then he hit Mick on the head. Keith says: 'We were having a group meeting in Amsterdam and I figured Mick and I would go out for a drink. We had a great time and at five in the morning Mick came back to my room. Mick was drunk — and Mick drunk is a sight to behold. Charlie was fast asleep and Mick shouted those words at him. Charlie shaved, put on a suit and tie, came down, grabbed him and went BOOM! Charlie dished him a walloping right hook. He landed in a plateful of smoked salmon and slid along the table towards the window. I just pulled his leg and saved him from going out into the canal below.'

MAY 18
Bill attends a London exhibition by photographer David Bailey and causes a sensation when he sticks a finger down model Denice Lewis' cleavage.

MAY 28
Bill captains a showbiz cricket team, Bill Wyman's XI, in a match at Stocks Country Club, Aldbury, Hertfordshire, against Eric Clapton's XI. The charity match raises more than £25,000 for the Starlight Foundation for terminally ill children. The charity was founded by actress Emma Samms, who flew in from the US for the match. Other stars include David Essex, Ron Wood, Gary Brooker, Andy Fairweather Low, Ken Follet and Mike Rutherford. Rival team captain Eric Clapton fails to turn up as he missed his flight from New York.

MAY 31
Keith Richards attends the first annual International Rock Awards at the Armory in New York. Introducd by Eric Clapton, Keith is saluted as a 'Living Legend' and awarded a twelve inch statuette of Elvis Presley. He and the X-Pensive Winos then play 'Whip it Up' and 'You Keep A-Knockin'', featuring Eric Clapton, David Edmunds, Tina Turner, Clarence Clemons and Jeff Healy. The show, on ABC TV, is broadcast live in 50 countries. After the show Keith flies back to England to resume mixing the new Stones' album.

JUNE 2
Bill Wyman secretly marries Mandy Smith in a Register Office ceremony in Bury St Edmunds, Suffolk. The only guests are the witnesses: Bill's son Stephen and Mandy's sister Nicole. The same evening Bill and Mandy appear on Terry Wogan's TV chat show, before an audience of seven million viewers. Bill says: 'We fooled everyone. We've got the Blessing on Monday and we let everyone think that was the actual wedding. We did it to confuse people so that we wouldn't be besieged by photographers... It was all over in fifteen minutes. If I'd have known it was that easy I'd have done it years ago.' Bill's mother, 76-year-old Kathleen Perks, didn't know about the wedding until Bill phoned to tell her it was over. She says: 'The first I knew of it was when he phoned me after the ceremony and invited me to a celebration lunch. I'm very disappointed they didn't invite me. I suppose it's typical of Bill, he's always been a bit of a rebel.'

JUNE 5
Bill and Mandy Wyman have their marriage blessed at the Anglican Church of St John the Evangelist in Hyde Park Crescent, London. 170 guests attend the ceremony. The Reverend Thaddeus Birchard from Louisiana says: 'I don't suppose there is much point pretending that this is an ordinary marriage blessing in an ordinary church full of stars. There are only two stars here today, Mandy Smith and Bill Wyman, because they have taken their situation, with all its perfections

Above: *Mick in Morocco with the Master Musicians of Joujouka. Twenty years after Brian Jones first recorded them their hypnotic pipe playing is featured on a track from* Steel Wheels *called 'Continental Drift'.*

and imperfections and put that before Almighty God.' After the ceremony Bill, Mandy and their relatives join 400 guests at a reception at the Grosvenor House Hotel. All the Stones and their wives are there. Other guests include Elton John, Eric Clapton, Kim Wilde, Paul Young, Kenny Jones, Andy Fairweather Low, and Mike Rutherford. Keith says: 'She's made an honest man of him.'

JUNE 10
Bill and Mandy arrive at Bill's house in Vence where they spend their honeymoon.

JUNE 12
The *Daily Mirror* reports: 'Generous Mick Jagger lavished £200,000 on a genuine Picasso etching as a wedding gift for his old chum Bill Wyman. But, as he handed over the present, Charlie Watts quipped: "You should have kept the original and given Bill a copy – he'd never know the difference." '

JUNE 16/17
Mick, Keith and Ron spend two days in Tangier, Morocco, recording a track called 'Continental Drift' to be added to the new album, backed by the Master Musicians of Joujouka, the same musicians recorded by Brian Jones in 1968. The session, recorded in the open courtyard of the Palace Ben Abbou, is filmed by a BBC TV crew and will be broadcast in the autumn.

JUNE 20
Jagger and Richards continue to mix the new album at the Olympic Studios in London. Ron's leisure complex, Woody's On The Beach, closes down, in part because neighbours have complained about the noise.

JULY 1
Mick wins £5,000 on the Irish Derby by correctly predicting the first three horses past the post.

JULY 11
In front of 500 reporters and hundreds of screaming fans lined up behind police barricades, the Rolling Stones announce the *Steel Wheels* tour, named after their forthcoming album, at a press conference from an open flatcar on a train in New York's Grand Central Station. The *Daily Mirror* reports that Jagger ripped off his shirt in the steaming heat and told reporters that he would be preparing for the tour with 'a little slow walking' and said: 'I don't see it as a farewell concert. It's the Rolling Stones in 1989. I've been asked this since 1966. It won't be our last tour.' When asked to describe their energy level Bill replied: 'Ask my wife.' The Stones are taking over an entire hotel, a junior school and three houses in Washington, Connecticut, as a base for the tour. The school is to be used for rehearsals and the hotel is to house their staff. Security guards have fitted steel gates, and closed circuit TV to keep fans at bay. The Stones will live in the houses while there, though Mick has taken a large house in the more remote township of New Preston.

JULY 15
Ticket sales break all previous records in the first four cities of the tour. In Toronto 120,000 are sold in under six hours; in Cincinatti 54,000 in two and a half hours; in East Troy, Wisconsin 40,000 in three hours and in Raleigh, North Carolina 55,000 in four and a half hours. Meanwhile the concert scheduled for 21 September in Philadelphia is cancelled as the 70-year-old JFK Stadium is deemed unsafe.

JULY 16
The Stones are rehearsing in Washington, Connecticut. Bill causes a scare when he collapses complaining of heart pains. However a doctor diagnoses food poisoning.

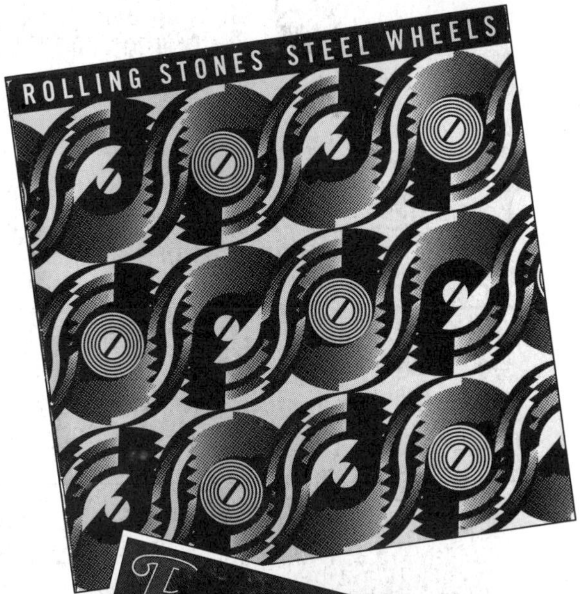

JULY 19
Residents of Washington, Connecticut form a 'Roll the Stones Out of Town' action group as they say the band have 'ruined their tranquillity'. Many properties appear to have been bought up to house the entourage and security guards patrol the grounds 24 hours a day. Irate resident Michelle Coulette says: 'It's like an army has moved into town and taken over. You're afraid to take a walk because Stones security goons will stop and question who you are and what you're doing there.'

JULY 26
Mick is 46 and the Stones have a barbecue to celebrate. Meanwhile ticket sales continue to break records throughout the States.

Above left: *Mandy Smith finally makes it as a legitimate member of the Stones' entourage.* Above: *Facing the future with confidence: a publicity shot promoting the Steel Wheels tour and album.* Top right: *The* Steel Wheels *album cover.* Far right: Rolling Stone *and* Time *magazines salute the Stones' amazing staying power.* Right: *The programme for the Rolling Stones North American tour.*

AUGUST
Early in the month the Stones shoot the video for their forthcoming single, 'Mixed Emotions', at the girls' school in Washington, Conn., where they are rehearsing. They also tape a video for the track 'Rock And A Hard Place', a track from the upcoming album.

AUGUST 8
Today reports that businessman Malcolm Potier outbid Mick for the purchase of the remote Scottish island of Ghia. Potier, who paid £6 million, says: 'I was a bit worried about Mick Jagger because he has a lot more money than I have. But the owner wanted to sell it to someone who knew the island.'

AUGUST 12
The Stones play an impromptu show at Toad's Place, a small club in New Haven, Connecticut, in front of an audience of 500 people.

AUGUST 13
The Stones leave Washington and continue rehearsals at the Nassau Coliseum, Long Island.
In London the *Sunday Mirror* reports that Mandy Wyman is unable to join Bill as she is suffering from a severe allergy to yeast.

AUGUST 15
In America ABKCO Records release a four-album set *The Rolling Stones Singles Collection: The London Years.* The set features all the Stones' singles from 1963-1971, digitally remastered, produced variously by Andrew Oldham, Jimmy Miller and the Rolling Stones and a 72-page illustrated booklet is included.

AUGUST 17
The new single 'Mixed Emotions'/'Fancyman Blues' is released on Rolling Stones Records simultaneously in the UK and US. The A-side only is taken from the forthcoming album, *Steel Wheels,* and both tracks are written by Jagger and Richards and produced by the Glimmer Twins and Chris Kimsey. It also comes in a 12-inch version.

AUGUST 19
230,000 tickets are sold for the concert at the Shea Stadium, New York – a sell out. Tickets for two previously announced concerts on 26 and 28 October go in one and a half hours, and the third concert, on 29 October, sells out in one hour and three minutes! And an additional concert slotted in on 25 October sells out in less than four hours.

AUGUST 24
Thirteen love letters written by Bill Wyman in 1964 to a mystery girl, Babs, and a gold

---

Left: *Mick on stage during the Steel Wheels tour. His drive and energy unabated, he can still inspire a stadium full of excited fifteen-year-olds.*

bracelet inscribed 'To Barbara, in gratitude, Bill Wyman, 1967' are sold for £1,430 at another rock auction at Christie's in London.

AUGUST 26
'Mixed Emotions' enters the US Top 100 at Number 47. It reaches a highest position of Number 5.

AUGUST 27
The Stones arrive in Philadelphia. The press build-up to the tour gathers momentum. In the *Sunday Mirror* magazine, Mick says: 'It was really easy working with the guys again...Though Keith is more sensitive than I, we didn't have any major rows. We're not an old married couple who can't live together and can't live apart; we're two men who've been friends for 30 years. Occasionally you want to strangle even the closest of friends.' About Brian Jones and the damage caused by drugs, Mick says: 'If we'd all been a little more mature it could all have been avoided. It was a malaise of the time. Let everyone do what they want, don't worry about people killing themselves. I was too smart to go that far with drugs. But what happened to Brian seems such a tragic waste now. It was almost the same with Keith as well.'

AUGUST 28
Police mount a 24-hour watch on Mick after Hell's Angels threaten to kill him on stage, twenty years after Altamont, the cause of the vendetta.

AUGUST 29
Steel Wheels is released on Rolling Stones Records in the US. All tracks are written by Mick and Keith except one which is co-written with Steve Jordan. Produced by the Glimmer Twins and Chris Kimsey, it was recorded in Montserrat last Spring and mixed at the Olympic Studios in London.
In America, ABC Radio Network has acquired broadcasting rights to the *Steel Wheels* tour, including a three-hour concert to be broadcast in December, with a band interview and phone-in. Sponsors are queueing up to support the tour – so far, MTV are media sponsors, the Labatt Brewery sponsor the Canadian dates, and Budweiser Beer the US dates.

AUGUST 31
The *Sun* reports extortionate black market rates for *Steel Wheels* tour tickets as desperate fans pay up to £1,000 for £25 tickets.
The Rolling Stones open the *Steel Wheels* tour, their first in seven years, at the Veteran Stadium, Philadelphia, in front of a crowd of 55,000 people. There are 28 arrests outside the stadium and 52 are hurt when drunken fans clash with police. Tom Moon, rock critic for the *Philadelphia Inquirer* writes: 'Five middle-aged English dudes led 64,000 yanks to a fantastic two and a half hour party sing-song. The fireworks were superfluous. This concert was hotter than any Roman candle.' Jonathan Takiff, of the *Philadelphia Daily News* writes: 'They cheered Mick Jagger's contemptuous trademark strut. He looked incredibly fit and still moves with agility – communicating his sassy, sneering body language to ecstatic fans.'

Jerry Hall with daughter Elizabeth Scarlett and son James on the Steel Wheels tour. For the first time the Stones' wives and children accompanied them on tour.

SEPTEMBER 1
Second concert at the Veteran Stadium, Philadelphia. More than two million fans tried to get tickets for the two Philadelphia concerts. 23-year-old Tom Costello says: 'They just blow today's bands away.'
In *USA Today* Edna Gundersen writes: 'In a year swarming with 60s legends from the Who to Bob Dylan to Paul McCartney and Ringo Starr, the Stones threaten to storm the 90s still unchallenged as the World's greatest rock'n'roll band, a mantle bestowed on them in 1969 and disputed by almost no one.'

SEPTEMBER 3
Concert at the Exhibition Stadium, Toronto – their first visit to Canada since 1977. The audience is 60,000.

SEPTEMBER 4
Second sell-out concert at the Exhibition Stadium, Toronto. They gross $1.5 milion in associated souvenir sales.

SEPTEMBER 6
The Stones, linked by satellite from the Three Rivers Stadium in Pittsburgh to the MTV studios in New York, play 'Mixed Emotions' in the Video Awards ceremony transmitted all over America.

SEPTEMBER 7
Rolling Stone documents the shaky path leading to *Steel Wheels* and the tour: 'Last January Jagger and Richards set up camp at Eddy Grant's studio in Barbados to test their writing mettle and the limit of their patience with each other. Before leaving New York, Richards told his wife, Patti, he'd be back in either two weeks or 48 hours. "Because I'll know in 48 hours whether this thing was going to work or if we were just going to start cattin' and doggin'."
Ron Wood says: 'I never lost any sleep over it, because I know how these guys work. They operate on a whim, a feel." He admits that Charlie Watts and Bill Wyman weren't quite as confident: "They wanted to make sure that Mick and Keith were serious about it. Not just going through the motions. But with Charlie and Bill, once they were convinced, it made all the difference. Because it wasn't going to work if they weren't behind it."
Keith says: "I can never think of starting something up again in order to make it the last time. This is the beginning of the second half."

SEPTEMBER 8
Concert at the Alpine Valley Stadium, East

Troy. It is announced that an NBC-TV documentary, *It's Only Rock'n'Roll*, produced by the Stones and Lorne Michael, will be networked all over America. The two-hour special features scenes from the early days, including drug busts, up to recording sessions for the new LP, the press conference in New York and the tour rehearsals in Connecticut.

SEPTEMBER 9
Second concert at the Alpine Valley Stadium, East Troy. *The Rolling Stones Singles Collection: The London Years* enters the US charts at Number 108, and reaches a highest position of Number 88.
'Mixed Emotions' enters the British charts at Number 41. It will stay in the charts for five weeks, reaching a highest position of 33.

SEPTEMBER 11
Third and final concert at the Alpine Valley Stadium, East Troy.
Steel Wheels is released on Rolling Stones Records in the UK.

SEPTEMBER 14
Concert at the Riverfront Stadium, Cincinatti, with an audience of 54,000.

SEPTEMBER 16
Concert at the Carter-Finley Stadium, Raleigh, North Carolina in front of an audience of 55,000. Local police expect 15,000 ticketless fans and 150 uniformed police, 32 plainclothes officers and a temporary jail are in readiness, though not in fact needed. *Steel Wheels* enters the US Charts at Number 44. It reaches a highest position of Number 1.
The Rolling Stones Story, a three-hour radio special covering their whole career, is broadcast all over America by United Station Programming Network.

SEPTEMBER 17
Concert at Busch Stadium, St Louis.

SEPTEMBER 19
Concert at the Cardinal Stadium, Louisville, Kentucky.

SEPTEMBER 21/22
Two concerts at the Carrier Dome, Syracuse, New York.

SEPTEMBER 23
Steel Wheels enters the British charts at Number 12 and reaches Number 2.
Meanwhile in America *Hot Rocks Volume 1* re-enters the Top 200 at Number 186, making its 234th week in the charts. The Stones now have three albums in the US charts.

SEPTEMBER 24
Concert at the R.F.K. Stadium, Washington, D.C.

SEPTEMBER 25
Second concert at the R.F.K. Stadium, Washington.

SEPTEMBER 27
Concert at the Municipal Stadium, Cleveland, Ohio.

SEPTEMBER 29
Concert at the Sullivan Stadium, Boston.

OCTOBER 1
Second concert at the Sullivan Stadium.

OCTOBER 3
Third concert at the Sullivan Stadium.

OCTOBER 5
Concert at the Legion Field, Birmingham, Alabama.

OCTOBER 7
Concert at the Cyclone Field, Ames, Iowa.

OCTOBER 8
Concert at the Arrowhead Stadium, Kansas City.

OCTOBER 10/11
Two concerts at the Shea Stadium, New York.

OCTOBER 18
First concert at the Los Angeles Coliseum.

OCTOBER 19
Second Concert at the Los Angeles Coliseum.

OCTOBER 21/22
Two more concerts at the Los Angeles Coliseum.

OCTOBER 25
Concert at Shea Stadium, New York.

OCTOBER 26
Concert at Shea Stadium.

OCTOBER 28/29
Two more concerts at Shea Stadium.

NOVEMBER 1/2
Concerts at the B.C. Place, Vancouver.

The Stones on stage in Oakland, California, during the sell-out Steel Wheels tour.

NOVEMBER 4
Two concerts at the Alameda Stadium, Oakland.
'Rock And A Hard Place' enters the US charts at Number 79.

NOVEMBER 5
Second concert at the Alameda Stadium, Oakland.

NOVEMBER 8
Concert at the Astrodome, Houston.

NOVEMBER 10/11
Concert at the Texas Stadium, Dallas.

NOVEMBER 13
Concert at the Superdome, New Orleans.

NOVEMBER 15/16
Concerts at the Orange Bowl, Miami.

NOVEMBER 18
Concert at the Tampa Stadium.

NOVEMBER 20
'Rock And A Hard Place'/'Cook Cook Blues' is released in the UK.

NOVEMBER 21
Concert at Grant Field, Atlanta.

NOVEMBER 25
Concert at the Gator Bowl, Jacksonville.

NOVEMBER 26
Concert at the Death Valley Stadium, Clenson, South Carolina.

NOVEMBER 29/30
Concerts at the Metrodome, Minneapolis.

DECEMBER 3/4
Concerts at the Skydome, Toronto.

DECEMBER 6/7
Concerts at the Hoosier Dome, Indianapolis.

DECEMBER 9/10
Concerts at the Silverdome, Detroit.

DECEMBER 14
Concert at the Olympic Stadium, Montreal.

DECEMBER 16/17
Concerts at the Convention Center, Atlantic City.

DECEMBER 18
Keith Richards is 46 today.

DECEMBER 19
Concert at the Convention Center, Atlantic City.

DECEMBER 31
The beat goes on...

An Owl Book

THE FIRST THIRTY YEA

"When I first saw them I didn't know whether to say hello or bark. But then I got to know them. They are something, really something."

—GENE PITNEY, REPORTED IN *The Daily Mirror* (NOVEMBER 28, 1963)

The world would have to get used to the Rolling Stones. For once they hit the scene, rock 'n' roll would never be the same. From the earliest gigs at the Ealing Jazz Club in West London to the phenomenal Steel Wheels tour almost thirty years later, they continue to be the most watched, the most quoted, the most photographed, the most reviled, and the most loved band in modern history.

The Rolling Stones Chronicle is a book to match its subject, the most complete account ever compiled on the lives and careers of its members from 1960 to the present. Set in an illustrated diary format with close to 350 black-and-white photographs and featuring rare Stones memorabilia, it covers every stage of the band's history with insider details on recording sessions, performances, chart positions, press remarks, and much more. You'll also get the bottom line on three decades' worth of rumors, busts, romances, tragedies, glamour, and gossip that continue to swirl around these bad boys of rock 'n' roll.

As energetic and mesmerizing as the Stones themselves, this book is a must for every serious fan.

Massimo Bonanno is a drumer in a British rock band and has written for numerous music magazines in Europe. He owns one of the most extensive collections of Rolling Stones photographs and memorabilia in existence.

lusic/Biography
:t:0790:001445:50

ISBN 0-8050-130
90
9 780805 013016